Resolving International Conflicts
Liber Amicorum Tibor Várady

Resolving International Conflicts

Liber Amicorum Tibor Várady

Edited by:

Peter Hay

Lajos Vékás

Yehuda Elkana

Nenad Dimitrijevic

CEU PRESS

Central European University Press
Budapest–New York

Published in 2009 by
Central European University Press

An imprint of the
Central European University Share Company
Nádor utca 11, H-1051 Budapest, Hungary
Tel: +36-1-327-3138 or 327-3000
Fax: +36-1-327-3183
E-mail: ceupress@ceu.hu
Website: www.ceupress.com

400 West 59th Street, New York NY 10019, USA
Tel: +1-212-547-6932
Fax: +1-646-557-2416
E-mail: mgreenwald@sorosny.org

ISBN 978-963-9776-46-3 cloth

Library of Congress Cataloging-in-Publication Data

Resolving international conflicts : liber amicorum Tibor Várady / edited by Peter Hay ... [et al.].
p. cm.
Includes bibliographical references.
ISBN 978-9639776463 (cloth : alk. paper)
1. Conflict of laws I. Hay, Peter, 1935- II. Varady, Tibor, 1939- III. Title.

K7041.R448 2009
340.9–dc22

2009008784

Printed in Hungary
by Akadémiai Nyomda

Contents

Greeting from the Rector

The Festschrift, edited by three dedicated and knowledgeable colleagues of Tibor Várady, namely Peter Hay (Emory University and CEU), Lajos Vékás (ELTE), and Nenad Dimitrijevic (CEU), is an impressive and beautiful tribute to the many-faceted and influential scholarly, academic–administrative, and legal public work and life of Tibor Várady, presented to him on his seventieth birthday.

I came to Central European University ten years ago as President and Rector and had the task to make it a real research university. In this Tibor was a staunch supporter. Always alert, gently critical, and ready with wise advice, he was one of the most important faculty members to help me during those years.

Tibor excelled and continues to excel in many areas: he was Minister of Justice of Serbia at a crucial point of its recent stormy past. His role in the Hague tribunal in the last few years is being considered by experts as a masterpiece of professional acuity and humane wisdom.

One of the important streams in CEU's Department of Legal Studies is International Business Law—conceived, founded and continuously ably led by Tibor Várady. Tibor's role in the Senate of CEU, and in the search committee for my successor last year, was of great weight.

Tibor's academic contributions—which I cannot appreciate in professional terms—, have rewarded him with the widespread international recognition, lending him a standing of which we, his colleagues, and the University, which he helped to build, can be and are proud.

And so it goes. One could add further dimensions of his achievements at great length. I would rather end on a personal note: Tibor is a wonderful, warm, wise human being, and it makes me proud to be able to call him my friend.

Yehuda Elkana

Acknowledgments

The editors would like to express their gratitude to those who contributed to bring this project to completion. Mária Balla and Viktor Yevpak worked together on compiling Tibor Várady's bibliography; they provided invaluable help in collecting background information and in dealing with administrative issues. Viktor did an excellent job in checking for the internal consistency of references in each contribution.

István Bart, the director of CEU Press, offered his unwavering support, securing the conditions for our efficient work on the project. Linda Kunos and Bálint Bethlenfalvy, CEU Press editors, were prompt, reliable, and friendly in carrying their part of labor.

Peter Hay, Lajos Vékás, and Nenad Dimitrijevic gratefully acknowledge the special contribution of their co-editor, Yehuda Elkana, who, in his capacity of the CEU President and Rector, generously supported this endeavor from its inception.

Tibor Várady–Introduction

Tibor Várady, the Internationalist

PETER HAY

On May 25, 2009, friends, colleagues, and former and present students celebrate the seventieth birthday of Tibor Várady, a true—and great—internationalist. Many criss-cross the world today, young scholars once again master a foreign language and immerse themselves in a foreign legal culture and its methodology. Earlier, European émigrés of the World War II era brought with them an immense wealth of knowledge of legal history and, of course, mastery of their laws of origin. A number of them—but far too few—also achieved scholarly renown in their new homes. There were linguistic barriers, also the lack of "proper" academic qualification by new-country standards, and, at times, a decidedly insular orientation on the part of the larger host community.

By any of these measures, Tibor Várady is nearly unique. In the course of his life, he has been part of three academic communities and contributed to them—not by moving from one to the next, *seriatim*, but simultaneously. Fluently multilingual, his academic life and contribution are at once Serbian, Hungarian, and American. His early academic life and career in Yugoslavia and Serbia are most sensitively recounted by his former student and now Budapest colleague, Prof. Dimitrijevic, in the essay immediately following. His scholarly achievements were many, and they are continuing. His text on Yugoslav, now Serbian, Private International Law is of continued importance—especially since the Yugoslav statute of the time bore his imprint.

In Budapest, Tibor Várady not only built the International Business Law program of Central European University's Legal Studies Department to be the leader in Central and Eastern Europe, but also contributed significantly—as counselor and adviser to the administration—to the growth and success of Central European University as a whole.

In the United States, he moved from visiting professor at Cornell and then Emory to a tenured position as professor of law at Emory. His course book on *International Arbitration*, with Prof. John Barceló of Cornell and the late Arthur von Mehren of Harvard, appeared in its fourth edition in 2009 and is now a standard text in American law schools.

Today, Professor Várady divides his time among his principal academic and personal "home and abode" in Budapest, his annual spring-semester full-time teaching at Emory, continued contact with Novi Sad, international arbitration assignments (wherever they might take him), and occasional "special assignments," such as his appearance before the International Court of Justice.

His friends and colleagues salute him, extend their warmest best wishes, and offer this *Festschrift* as a small measure of their esteem and appreciation.

Tibor Várady in Yugoslavia and Serbia

NENAD DIMITRIJEVIC

Back in times of Yugoslav socialism, Tibor was teaching at Novi Sad Law School. Corridors there were gray, the atmosphere was ideology-laden, and courses were mostly boring. A typical lecture strategy consisted of reciting paragraphs, reading from one's own textbook, and adding obligatory ritual references to Marx, Lenin and the Party.

But Tibor acted differently. For one, he never thought that arrogance had been a measure of one's academic importance—from the very first class, students would find themselves in a company of a decent, kind man, who obviously did not even consider the idea of establishing anything resembling an authoritative relationship in the classroom. Tibor would never preach about some special importance of private international law in the universe of legal disciplines. He preferred to begin his encounters with students by telling a story. For instance, he would say about a car accident (a light one, with nobody being injured, Tibor would hasten to add) that involved a German and a French citizen: the accident happened in the Yugoslav (today Croatian) seaside town of Split; everyone involved—the French and the German guys, and the local police—was nice, considerate and eager to settle things amicably; there was a problem, however: a precious vase that the French man had bought at a local antique dealer, broke in the accident; the circumstances of the accident were not clear, and the exact value of the vase was not known either; thus, in order to establish whether the German driver was obliged to pay the compensation—and, if yes, how much—it was necessary to go the court.

At this point Tibor would turn to his students to ask them which court and which rules, in their opinion, should settle the matter between two citizens from different countries, in a case that happened in a third country. Students would at first be silent. It was very unusual for a professor to ask for their opinion during a lecture. Did this man try to fool them, to show them how ignorant they were? What if their response turned out wrong or even stupid? But, Tibor was fast to dispel such uneasiness: he convincingly demonstrated that in-class dialogue is an important technique of mastering the art of legal reasoning. Indeed, the "Socratic method" was Tibor's gentle way of teaching students to engage in active reflection instead of passive accumulation of facts that was so dominant in other classes.

And, sooner than students would realize, there they were: in the province of law. The insights they would gain in Tibor's class were pointing beyond the narrow disciplinary knowledge. They learnt that—'out there'—there may be contexts in which law really mattered for human lives, as a general, transparent and neutral guideline, the ultimate task of which was to protect equality of free individuals. In short, without ever taking an ideological stance, Tibor would demonstrate the worth of a political and legal order based on the principle of the rule of law.

Still, nobody was free from the ruling ideology of the time. Not being its promoter, Tibor was exposed to increased scrutiny by its self-styled guardians among those colleagues, who found strong reasons to be watchful: he was an internationally renowned scholar and arbitration expert; he held a professorship in the Unites States; his classes in Novi Sad were too different; finally, he was a member of an ethnic minority. However, they could have been less than happy with the fact that they could not possibly accuse Tibor of 'bourgeois revisionism'. His political inclinations were genuinely leftist: while he was not interested to serve the ruling ideology, he always strongly believed that social justice is a value worth of human efforts. And, much before cosmopolitanism became fashionable, he was a genuine man of the world—nationalism was far removed from a man who deeply cared for Hungarian culture, but who equally enjoyed academic writing and teaching in English or writing beautiful essays about jazz in Serbian.

We all know about the atrocities that happened in then-Yugoslavia in the nineties. Soon after Tito's death, the communist masks started to drop, revealing the ugly faces of the Balkans nationalists. In Serbia, nationalist hysteria, inspired by and starting from the top, rapidly engulfed the whole society. Those who were not ready to hate 'others' were, with frightening ease, made enemies and traitors. Tibor found himself once again in the minority. In the late eighties, he was among the founders of the Association for the Yugoslav Democratic Initiative, a group of intellectuals from all the Yugoslav nations that went public with a simple message: stop hate speech before the spiral of animosities produces bloodshed. In consequence, Tibor's position in Novi Sad became increasingly difficult.

Then, in 1992, the Serbian dictator Slobodan Milosevic made a strange error, by agreeing to accept American-Serbian businessman Milan Panic as the Prime Minister of the rump-Yugoslavia. Panic proved to have liberal views, and Tibor was appointed Minister of Justice in his government. This government lasted only a number of months before Milosevic crushed it. In this short time Tibor courageously fought for the adoption of laws he deemed necessary for the establishment of a democratic legal system. In Parliament he had to defend the bills in front of a nationalist majority, whose members were persistently insulting and threatening him. While his friends were genuinely worried for his safety, Tibor never stepped back. A true gentleman, his only response to intimidations consisted of sound arguments.

Upon the fall of the Panic government, nationalists at Novi Sad Law School intensified their efforts to expel Tibor, and he was forced out in May 1993. Upon such an experience, most people would probably be overwhelmed by bitterness and would cut all ties with the old institution and society. But not Tibor. This strangely non-aggressive man sticks to his principles, and to his love for Serbia. This was most obvious in his selfless agreement and engagement to represent Serbia in the 2007/2008 proceedings before the International Court of Justice.[1] The new Serbia finally came to appreciate and to pay public tribute to his contribution when, in 2007, it decorated him as one of only three new "Knights of Profession".

[1] These proceedings are addressed in the contribution by Professor Bederman at pp. 21–45 below.

Expanded Judicial Review of Awards After *Hall Street* and in Comparative Perspective

JOHN J. BARCELÓ III

Preface

Professor Tibor Várady and I have known each other for more than forty years, going back to when we first met during two years of graduate law study in Cambridge, Massachusetts in the late 1960's. I think of us as "Doktor Brüder," because we shared a "Doktor Vater," the late Harold Berman, who was our mentor and dissertation supervisor, simultaneously, at Harvard Law School, where we both received doctorates in law, Tibor in international arbitration and I in international trade. We both held a common respect and warm affection for Hal that continued over many years after Tibor and I joined Hal in the ranks of the professoriate. While at Harvard, we also studied under the late Arthur von Mehren, Harvard's renowned scholar in comparative law, conflict of laws, and arbitration. Years later, in collaboration with Arthur, we began a project that we have worked on together for more than fifteen years, the coursebook: T. Várady, J. Barceló, and A. von Mehren, INTERNATIONAL COMMERCIAL ARBITRATION—A TRANSNATIONAL PERSPECTIVE, appearing in a 4th edition in 2009. It was Tibor who introduced me to the subject and who proposed that I join the project. Collaboration on the book and the exchange of ideas, analyses and perspectives concerning other papers, books, and lectures—not limited to arbitration law—and even concerning a World Court case that Tibor was lead counsel on, has been a source of intellectual stimulation, challenge and satisfaction for me over many years. Our early intellectual friendship also grew into warm personal friendship—or was it the other way around. I am happy to express in this public way my great respect for Tibor and his work—blessed as he is with extraordinary intellectual and personal gifts—and my gratitude to him for sharing with me both kinds of friendship.

I. Introduction

The New York Convention's lasting achievement has been to require courts worldwide[1] to enforce arbitration agreements and the awards resulting from them, subject, in the case of awards, to very limited grounds for rejection. The Convention makes arbitration agreements truly binding by protecting the resulting awards from excessive court interference at the enforcement stage. Without that protection, it would have been easy to undermine arbitration agreements. What a court gave with one hand (sending the parties to arbitration) it could have taken back with the other (rejecting the resulting award). Sometimes, however, parties would actually **prefer** a more thorough and intrusive court review of an award's merits. This essay addresses the question whether such a preference—if clearly expressed contractually—will (or should) be respected in national arbitration law.

The issue does not arise under the New York Convention per se, but rather under the national arbitration law of the seat of arbitration, the lex arbitri. In international arbitration parties tend to choose a "neutral" jurisdiction as the seat of the arbitration, and look to the arbitration law (lex arbitri) of the seat to provide the curial law or framework procedural law to facilitate and supervise the arbitration. The courts of the seat, applying their national arbitration law, exercise a more important role in reviewing a resulting award than do the courts of other jurisdictions where the award may be brought for enforcement. The former are sometimes said to have primary jurisdiction, and the latter, secondary jurisdiction.[2] Under the New York Convention, if the award is annulled at the seat, other countries may refuse to enforce it.[3] The Convention does not accord the same consequence to court rejection of an award in other (secondary) jurisdictions. Thus, judicial review of an award at the seat is especially important. At the same time, review of the award at the seat is governed entirely by national arbitration law, unconstrained by the New York Convention. For that reason a party wanting serious judicial scrutiny of an award—including review of fact finding and application of law—would want that

---

[1] There are now 144 parties to the U.N. Convention on the Recognition and Enforcement of Foreign Arbitral Awards. See http://www.uncitral.org/uncitral/en/uncitral_texts/arbitration/NYConvention_status.html

[2] See Karaha Bodas Co., L.L.C. v. Perusahaan Pertambangan Minyak Dan Gas Bumi Negara, et al, 335 F. 3d 357, at 368 (2003).

[3] New York Convention Article V(1)(e).

review to occur at the seat. Can that be accomplished by express language in the arbitration agreement calling for such an intrusive level of court review in the primary jurisdiction?

This question has been extensively litigated in the United States and partly—but not completely—put to rest by a recent U.S. Supreme Court decision, Hall Street Associates v. Mattel,[4] holding expanded review provisions unenforceable under the Federal Arbitration Act.[5] Before *Hall Street* was decided, Professor Várady wrote an important and insightful analysis[6] of the expanded judicial review issue when it first gained prominence in the United States through back and forth litigation in the 9th Circuit *Kyocera* case.[7] He returned to the issue in lectures he delivered in the Xiamen Summer School in China in 2007. In the published version of the Xiamen lectures Professor Várady included a discussion of *Hall Street,*[8] which was decided after he had delivered his original lectures. I have chosen the expanded review topic as a tribute to his work—taking it as the starting point for further inquiry. Section II below summarizes Professor Várady's analysis and conclusions. Section III asks what motivates parties to opt for expanded judicial review. Section IV discusses the possibilities within the United States for expanded judicial review after the *Hall Street* decision—which did not completely close the door on expanded review. Section V explores briefly how other countries are likely to treat expanded

---

4 __U.S. __; 128 S.Ct. 1396 (2008).

5 The American Review of International Arbitration has recently published a series of articles commenting on the *Hall Street* decision: Alan Scott Rau, *Fear of Freedom*, 17 Amer. Rev. Int'l Arb. 469 (2006); Hans Smit, *Hall Street Associates v. Mattel: A Critical Comment*, id. at 513; Mark Beckett, *Beyond Agnosticism: The Policy Justification for the Supreme Court's Decision in* Hall Street Associates, id at 525; David W. Rivkin & Erik P. Tuchmann, *Protecting Both the FAA and Party Autonomy: The* Hall Street *Decision*, id. at 537.

6 Tibor Várady, *On the Option of a Contractual Extension of Judicial Review of Arbitral Awards—What Is Actually Pro-Arbitration?* (56 Zbornik Pravnog fakulteta u Zagrebu, 2006, 455–478).

7 The original 9th Circuit three-judge opinion was decided in 1997: Lapine Technology Corp. v. Kyocera Corp., 130 F. 3d 884 (9th Cir. 1997) (enforcing an expanded judicial review clause under the FAA). The latest and final decision was rendered by the 9th Circuit sitting en banc: Kyocera Corp. v. Prudential-Bache Trade Services, Inc., 341 F.3d 987 (9th Cir. 2003) (reversing the 1997 decision and refusing to enforce an expanded judicial review clause).

8 Tibor Várady, THE ELUSIVE PRO-ARBITRATION PRIORITY IN CONTEMPORARY COURT SCRUTINY OF ARBITRAL AWARDS (to be published in the Hague by Nijhoff in 2009) (see Section II. The Impact of Party Autonomy on the Scope of Court Scrutiny of Arbitral Awards).

review clauses. Throughout the discussion the underlying inquiry is the one originally formulated by Professor Várady: which result, for or against expanded review, is the more pro-arbitration.

II. Professor Várady's "Pro-Arbitration" Inquiry[9]

The main thrust of Professor Várady's analysis is to stress the dilemmas that arise no matter which way a court chooses to react to expanded review clauses. Because there are difficulties and dilemmas associated with either enforcing or rejecting such clauses, Professor Várady notes the relative indeterminacy of the broader inquiry concerning which solution is the more favorable to arbitration. First, he notes that if the expanded review provision is struck down, the continued viability of the arbitration agreement itself is cast into doubt. Would the offending clause be severable, or, on the other hand, would it be so central to the basic agreement that without it the parties could not be said to have entered a binding agreement to arbitrate? That question has been answered in different ways by different courts.[10]

Of course if the parties are made aware of the problem at the drafting stage, they can easily provide a solution by expressly approving or rejecting severability. If they do not do so, however, the outcome is uncertain. The *Hall Street* Court did not address severability, because it was not an issue the Court had agreed to review. The Ninth Circuit in its final *Kyocera* opinion opted for severability, but its analysis was at least partly influenced by unique features of the case, namely, that it had endured for years, that the award against Kyocera had been repeatedly upheld—even applying expanded review—and that to reject the award at the end of the day based on rejection of the review clause would have given Kyocera an undeserved windfall benefit.[11] Even without these equitable considerations, it seems likely that U.S. courts, given their generally pro-arbitration

[9] The discussion in this section summarizes Professor Várady's analysis in his forthcoming book. See supra fn 8.

[10] The final en banc decision of the 9th Circuit in *Kyocera* held the clause to be severable. Kyocera Corp. v. Prudential-Bache Trade Services, Inc., 341 F.3d 987 (9th Cir. 2003). On the other hand the Court of Appeal of Paris has held the arbitration clause itself to be invalid when the parties have included a clause (found invalid) calling for court review of an award's merits in international arbitration. De Diseno v. Mendes, CA Paris (Oct. 27, 1994), 1995 Rev. Arb. 863, 2d decision, and P. Level's note.

[11] 341 F.3d 987, at 1002.

stance, will opt for severability, unless something unique in the parties' agreement stresses the importance of a particular expanded review provision. But in any given case, if the parties fail to include an express provision on severability, the outcome will be hard to predict.

Professor Várady takes the analysis to a broader level, however, by focusing on consequences for the award within the New York Convention system. From this perspective more uncertainty is introduced. Even if a U.S. court opts for severability, that would not necessarily bind a foreign court asked to enforce the resulting award under the New York Convention. A foreign court could decide for itself under New York Convention Article V(1)(a) (concerning invalidity of the arbitration agreement as a ground for rejecting the award) whether failure of the expanded review clause invalidates the entire arbitration agreement and thus defeats the award's enforceability.[12] Indeed, even Article V(1)(d) of the Convention (concerning failure to follow the parties' agreed arbitral procedure as a ground for rejecting the award) could block enforcement, unless—as Professor Várady notes—the procedure of judicial review is characterized as "post arbitral procedure" rather than an element of the party-agreed "arbitral procedure."[13]

A second difficulty arises if the expanded review provision is honored and the reviewing court finds errors of fact or law. What follows next? Does the court issue a judgment correcting the award? If so, do we now have a court judgment for enforcement, but no longer a viable award? Or does the court remand the case to the arbitral tribunal for further consideration—in which case would any subsequent award introduce the famous two-awards problem, under which courts in some countries (notably France) might enforce the first award,[14] and courts in other countries, the

---

[12] New York Convention Article V(1)(a) provides as a ground for non-enforcement that: "* * * the [arbitration] agreement is not valid under the law to which the parties have subjected it or, failing any indication thereon, under the law of the country where the award was made * * *." For arbitration within the United States good arguments could be advanced that U.S. law should control the validity of the arbitration agreement, but other solutions are also possible.

[13] New York Convention Article V(1)(d) provides as a ground for non-enforcement that: "* * * the arbitral procedure was not in accordance with the agreement of the parties, * * *."

[14] See Société PT Putrabali Adyamulia v. Rena Holding, 2008 Revue critique de droit international privé 109–112 and Note by Sylvain Bollée (French Cour de cassation ordered enforcement in France of a first award that had been set aside in England for error of law, even after a second award had been rendered by the arbitral tribunal as a substitute for the first award).

second? The two-awards problem can arise, of course, whenever the home jurisdiction annuls an award—for whatever reason—and a second arbitration (or at least a second award) ensues. Unique difficulty related to expanded review arises primarily whenever the reviewing court simply renders a judgment correcting the award, rather than returning the case to the arbitrators for their further consideration. Thus, this source of risk could be reduced if the parties were to include a provision authorizing the arbitral tribunal's continued jurisdiction whenever a reviewing court sets aside an award, either partly or completely.

After surveying these difficulties and dilemmas Professor Várady comes down in the end on the side of the *Hall Street* majority. He concludes:

> And finally, the basic problem is with the contractual provision itself. Party agreements on expanded judicial review of arbitral awards are ill-advised. Pro-arbitration is the avoidance of this clause.

Yet even if this conclusion is sound for the vast majority of arbitrations—and I am inclined to believe that it is—one may still be troubled by the rigidity of an arbitration regime that says to sophisticated commercial parties that if they want arbitration they may have it, but only according to one particular formula. Adding to one's sense of unease is the way this outcome clashes with the acknowledged rationale for pro-arbitration policy: allowing sophisticated commercial parties to agree by contract on how to resolve disputes.[15] The Supreme Court in *Hall Street* left this tension unresolved by grounding its result in the text of the Federal Arbitration Act itself, without discussing how this result could be aligned with the act's purpose, which essentially was to ensure that courts enforced arbitration agreements according to the way the parties drafted them.[16]

---

[15] In Volt Information Sciences, Inc. v. Board of Trustees of Stanford, 489 U.S. 468 (1989), the Supreme Court itself explained: "There is no federal policy favoring arbitration under a certain set of procedural rules; the federal policy is simply to ensure the enforceability, according to their terms, of private agreements to arbitrate." Id. at 476.

[16] See Alan Scott Rau, supra note 5, for criticism of the *Hall Street* decision because of its inconsistency with party autonomy. The *Hall Street* dissent by Justices Stevens and Kennedy is based primarily on this point. See 128 S.Ct. 1396, at 1408.

III. Why Do Parties Opt for Expanded Judicial Review? (Is Arbitration Flawed?)

To this sense of unease at the rigid legal paternalism underlying the *Hall Street* result, one might add another perspective. Traditional arbitration may have a certain ingrained tendency or institutional characteristic, which some parties might consider a flaw. In particular, some observers have suggested that arbitral awards—at least by comparison to the results in litigation—are driven less by strict application of legal rules to objectively determined facts and more by a tendency of arbitrators to search for compromise solutions. Empirical support for this view can be found in studies showing that parties with considerable arbitration experience find the results in arbitration highly unpredictable.[17]

Structural features of arbitration also seem to support the compromise-award thesis. Once arbitrators have plenary (unreviewable) power over the merits, they certainly have the ability to render compromise awards. Two features of the system suggest that they may have strong incentives to do so. First, important arbitrations involving large sums usually are heard by panels of three arbitrators, one appointed by each party and the third chosen by the other two. In international arbitration all three arbitrators must be independent,[18] but human nature is human nature. Even legal scholars who insist on arbitrator impartiality and independence also express a nuanced understanding of a human tendency of a party-appointed arbitrator to be at least somewhat disposed toward the party who appointed him or her.[19] The Chair of the tribunal, of

---

[17] See Christian Bühring-Uhle, Lars Kirchhoff & Gabriele Scherer, ARBITRATION AND MEDIATION IN INTERNATIONAL BUSINESS at 106–108 (2d ed. 2006). See also Jens Dammann & Henry Hansmann, *Globalizing Commercial Litigation*, 94 Cornell L. Rev. 1, 32–39 for a critique of commercial arbitration based on their assessment that arbitrators tend to reach compromise awards and hence fail to apply legal rules and a contract's terms with analytical rigor. Dammann and Hansmann are skeptical that this "defect" of arbitration can be remedied and favor instead choice of court clauses where a court in a neutral, third country is chosen.

[18] See, for example, ICC Arbitration Rules Article 7(1): "Every arbitrator must be and remain independent of the parties involved in the arbitration."

[19] See Giorgio Bernini, *Report on Neutrality, Impartiality, and Independence* in THE ARBITRATION PROCESS AND THE INDEPENDENCE OF ARBITRATORS 31–37 (ICC ed., 1991) ("* * * I readily concede, also in the light of existing practices, a margin of discretion in allowing departure from the basic canon of neutrality. As regards impartiality, however, the acceptance of possible deviations must be reduced to the barest minimum." Id. at 32–33).

course, will prefer unanimity. The path of least resistance for a Chair deliberating with co-arbitrators inclined in opposite directions could well be—at least in more instances than would occur in judicial decision making—to search for some form of compromise award.

A second structural feature of arbitration may be even more important. All arbitrators hope to be reappointed in future cases—not necessarily by the same parties or arbitrators, of course. But their chances of being reappointed are improved if they do not "ruffle feathers" by deciding too decisively for one party and humiliating the other. In this way they gain a reputation for judiciousness and fairness. Once parties and their attorneys get into the heat of legal battle, it is hard to imagine a litigator who does not believe that she or he deserves to win on at least some points. Arbitrators who decide completely in favor of one party are thus likely to be viewed by the losing party as inadequate or incompetent arbitrators—an opinion the losing party and counsel are not likely to keep to themselves. A savvy arbitrator thus may perceive a self-interest in rendering a compromise award so that no litigator goes away with a motive to run down the reputation of members of the tribunal.

Parties negotiating a complicated international transaction with elaborate terms and a specific choice of law clause will understandably want these contract terms and legal rules applied strictly to resolve any disputes. At the same time they may also prefer the traditional advantages of arbitration, namely avoidance of the other party's judicial system and an award that can be enforced worldwide. In this circumstance parties might want to opt for arbitration, but subject to expanded judicial review at the seat as a partial safeguard against the structural features of arbitration that encourage compromise awards. Arbitrators who know the merits of their award will be scrutinized more closely by a reviewing court can be expected to take more seriously their adjudicatory responsibility to find facts objectively and interpret and apply law.[20] Of course this perceived benefit would come at a cost, in reduced finality of the award and increased delays, opportunities for obstruction, and litigation expense. But might it not be "pro-arbitration" to leave the trade-off decision to the parties, rather than narrowing their options to just two: either full-fledged litigation or traditional arbitration?

---

[20] See Mark Beckett, supra note 5, at 532–533 (arguing that expanded review would force arbitrators to write longer, more detailed awards to withstand judicial scrutiny).

The *Hall Street* Court professed not to know whether its ruling would encourage or discourage arbitration,[21] and based its holding instead on what it asserted to be the constraints inherent in the statutory language of the Federal Arbitration Act.[22] At the same time, by including the following language the Court did not completely close the door to expanded review:

> In holding that §§ 10 and 11 provide exclusive regimes for the review provided by the statute [the FAA], we do not purport to say that they exclude more searching review based on authority outside the statute as well. The FAA is not the only way into court for parties wanting review of arbitration awards: they may contemplate enforcement under state statutory or common law, for example, where judicial review of different scope is arguable.

Professor Várady concludes in his published Xiamen lectures that this language leaves the door to expanded review in the United States only slightly ajar and that it will not have much practical significance—especially in international arbitration—because such arbitration "normally takes place within the framework of the FAA." But of course the extent to which this is true will depend on a least two factors: first, the degree to which there are consumers of international arbitral services who—at least in some settings—would prefer expanded judicial review (perhaps to counteract a perceived tendency toward compromise awards in arbitration) despite the added costs; and second, the degree to which there is a legal alternative to the FAA regime announced in *Hall Street*. Only future experience will tell us about the first factor. The next section takes up the second issue—what legal options for expanded review are still available in the United States after *Hall Street*.

IV. Expanded Judicial Review in the United States After *Hall Street*

IV. 1. State Law Authority for Expanded Judicial Review

In the wake of *Hall Street*, parties searching for expanded judicial review when arbitrating in the U.S. will presumably turn to state arbitration law. For this purpose the New Jersey and California arbitration statutes should

[21] 128 S.Ct. at 1406. ("We do not know who, if anyone, is right, and so cannot say whether the exclusivity reading of the statute is more of a threat to the popularity of arbitrators or to that of courts.")

[22] Id.

attract considerable attention. In the case of New Jersey the state arbitration law is quite explicit. It was one of the early state arbitration statutes and contains provisions almost identical to FAA Chapter 1 § 10.[23] However the New Jersey arbitration act also contains the following provision:

> c. * * * [N]othing in this act shall preclude the parties form expanding the scope of judicial review of an award by expressly providing for such expansion in a record.[24]

Thus, the plain language of the New Jersey statute authorizes expanded judicial review.

The California arbitration statute is not as explicit. Nevertheless, the California Supreme Court has recently construed the statute as allowing expanded review where the parties expressly opt for it. In Cable Connection, Inc. v. DIRECTV, Inc.,[25] the California Supreme Court refused to follow *Hall Street*, even though the state statute contained language almost identical to that of the FAA. The California Court held that parties could validly agree to expand judicial review of an award in California state courts where the California arbitration statute applied. The case involved a claim for withheld commissions and wrongful charges brought by a group of satellite TV retail dealers located in four different states of the U.S. against DIRECTV, a company that broadcasts TV programming throughout the country. Because the dealer agreements involved interstate commerce and called for arbitration (in Los Angeles), the FAA technically applied. But because the arbitration clause provided that "[t]he decision of the arbitrators may be entered and enforced as a final judgment in any court of competent jurisdiction * * *,"[26] DIRECTV, the losing party in the arbitration, filed in a California state court to vacate the award.

The group of retail dealers, apparently without attempting to remove the dispute to federal court, litigated the case in state court on the theory that the California arbitration act was controlling. Holding in part that the group of retail dealers had thus waived any claim that they were proceeding under the FAA, the California Court decided that the case was governed by the California arbitration act.

The arbitration clause in *DIRECTV* provided that the arbitrators were to apply California substantive law and were to include factual findings

[23] 9 U.S.C. §10.
[24] New Jersey Statutes Annotated 2A:23B-4.
[25] 44 Cal. 4th 1334; 190 P. 3d 586 (2008).
[26] 44 Cal. 4th 1334, 1341 fn 3.

and reasons in a written award. The clause allowed for expanded judicial review in the following language:

> The arbitrators shall not have the power to commit errors of law or legal reasoning, and the award may be vacated or corrected on appeal to a court of competent jurisdiction for any such error.[27]

The Court held that this language was enforceable under the provision of the California arbitration act that allowed a court to vacate an award "(4) where the arbitrators exceeded their powers * * *."[28]

The *DIRECTV* court concluded that *Hall Street* specifically allowed state arbitration law to apply in a case like this. It held that although the FAA is superior federal law, the FAA does not pre-empt state arbitration law where, as here, the state law is fundamentally consistent with the FAA goal of ensuring the enforceability of agreements to arbitrate. The *DIRECTV* court vacated the award and returned the case to the arbitrators because it found that the arbitrators had misapplied both California state law and the applicable AAA arbitration rules by allowing the arbitration to go forward as a class action.

IV. 2. State Law and International Arbitration

Although *DIRECTV* itself involved domestic—not international—arbitration, nothing in California or New Jersey law would prevent parties to an international transaction from placing the seat in either state[29] and

---

[27] 44 Cal. 4th at 1341.

[28] California Code of Civil Procedure, § 1286.2, subd (a)(4).

[29] For a U.S. court to exercise set-aside jurisdiction, the seat must be in the U.S. Whether it would also have to be in the state whose arbitration law the parties choose is not clear. The California statute, for example, provides for enforcement or vacation of an award, even if rendered in another state. See California Code of Civil Procedure, § 1286 ("If a petition or response under this chapter is duly served and filed, the court shall confirm the award as made, whether rendered in this state or another state, unless in accordance with this chapter it corrects the award and confirms it as corrected, or vacates the award or dismisses the proceedings.") To avoid potential issues, of course, international parties would be well advised to place the seat in the state whose arbitration law they want to have applied.

The California arbitration law contains special provisions for international arbitration that apply only if the arbitration is in California. See California Code of Civil Procedure, Title 9.3 ("Arbitration and Conciliation of International Commercial Disputes) and § 1297.12 ("This title, except [certain cited provisions] applies only if the place of arbitration or conciliation is in the State of California.") These special provisions,

explicitly choosing that state's arbitration act as the lex arbitri. If the parties also expressly opt for expanded judicial review and litigate the set-aside action in state court, presumably the expanded review clause would be honored. *DIRECTV* so holds. Though the *DIRECTV* parties were domestic, they were engaged in interstate commerce; thus, the FAA, by its terms, applied (as it would in an international case). Still, when litigating in state court, the parties were allowed to substitute the state arbitration act and its grounds for court review. The remaining question is whether the same result would follow were the case removed to federal court.

In analyzing this issue, it helps to consider two scenarios that would likely arise where international arbitration is involved: first, one in which a U.S. party transacts with a non-U.S. party and second, one in which both transacting parties are non-American. Assume under either scenario that the parties agree to arbitrate in California and that they include an expanded judicial review clause identical to that in *DIRECTV*. Assume, further, that they expressly provide that the arbitration is to be governed by the California Arbitration Act and that the award may be enforced in California state courts. Will this form of arbitration agreement yield expanded judicial review in federal court despite the *Hall Street* ruling?

To answer this question we must consider how a set-aside petition might reach the federal court. After the award is rendered, the losing party will seek to have it set aside under the expanded judicial review provisions of the agreement. For that purpose the losing party, seeking to rely on *DIRECTV*, would presumably file for set aside in a California state court.[30] But in an effort to avoid *DIRECTV*, the respondent (the winning

---

however, apply to such issues as enforcing an arbitration agreement, selecting arbitrators, and to the arbitral proceedings. They do not appear to affect the general provisions in Title 9, Chapter 4 on "Enforcement of the Award" (containing the set aside provisions interpreted in *DIRECTV*).

[30] The winning party could of course race to the court house and file in federal court for recognition and enforcement of the award under FAA Chapter 2, because (as explained later in the text) the award falls under the New York Convention, and a Chapter 2 action (in contrast to a Chapter 1 proceeding) provides a federal substantive law basis for federal jurisdiction. But in that action the losing party could move to set aside the award, and the set aside action would go forward first—at least this is the law of 2d Circuit. See Yusuf Ahmed Alghanim & Sons v. Toys "R" Us, 126 F.3d 15 (2d Cir. 1997). Because the set aside action would arise under Chapter 1 and hence would not be based on federal substantive law, the question becomes whether the federal court must apply the state or the federal standard of review where federal substantive law does not apply to the merits. The same issue arises if the case reaches the federal court by removal from the state court, which is the pattern analyzed in the text.

party in the arbitration) would presumably petition to remove the case to federal court and would argue that the limited review grounds of the Federal Arbitration Act Chapter 1 must be applied. Thus, the two crucial questions become: (i) can the case be removed and if so, (ii) would federal or state arbitration law apply to the removed case in federal court?

On the removal issue, the respondent will probably succeed. If one party is American and the other, non-American, the case could clearly be removed on the basis of diverse citizenship. Even if both parties are non-American (or diversity is incomplete), however, the case still seems removable. Precisely this pattern arose in Banco De Santander Central Hispano, S.A. v. Consalvi Intern. Inc.,[31] a recent federal district court case in the Southern District of New York. There two non-American parties arbitrated in New York, and the losing party brought a set-side claim in New York state court. The respondent nevertheless successfully removed the case to federal court. Under the generally applicable U.S. removal statute, the petition for removal would not have succeeded. [32] But the respondent also based its petition on § 205 of the FAA, which contains special provisions for removal of "an action * * * [that] ***relates*** to an arbitration agreement or award **falling under the Convention** * * *."[33]

The *Banco de Santander* award fell under the Convention by the Convention's own terms and specific provisions of U.S. law. Most commonly an award falls under the Convention because it was rendered outside the country where enforcement is sought. But the Convention also applies to an award rendered within the enforcing country—our case—if the enforcing country considers the award "non-domestic." [34] Under U.S. law an award involving two non-Americans—even if rendered in the U.S.—would be considered non-domestic.[35] The *Banco de Santander* award thus

[31] 425 F. Supp. 2d 421 (S.D.N.Y. 2006).

[32] The general removal statute is found at 28 U.S.C. § 1441(b). Under § 1441(b) removal is allowed only if the case, as filed by the plaintiff, could have been brought originally in federal court. In the *Banco De Santander* case, however, the losing party's set aside action arose under Chapter 1 of the FAA, which does not provide an independent basis for federal jurisdiction. And since the parties were two non-Americans (thus not satisfying diversity of citizenship), the claim could not have been brought originally in federal court.

[33] 9 U.S.C. § 205 (emphasis added).

[34] U.N. Convention on the Recognition and Enforcement of Foreign Arbitral Awards Article I(1).

[35] See 9 U.S.C. § 202. (By implication from the § 202 provisions, an award falls under the Convention if it involves two non-American parties.)

fell under the Convention,[36] and the court found that the set aside action—though not itself arising under the New York Convention—nevertheless **related to an award falling under the Convention**. Thus, under this precedent any set aside action filed in a state court but involving two non-Americans would seem to be removable to federal court. The basic point can be stated even more broadly; if the arbitration takes place within the United States but involves an international transaction, then the award will fall under the Convention and a set-aside action originally filed in state court will be removable to federal court under the terms of FAA §205.

The second issue—concerning which arbitration law the federal court must apply to the removed action—involves complex analysis. A full discussion of what law federal courts must apply in an action not based on federal substantive law—as is the case for a set aside action, which (even when the FAA Chapter 1 applies) does not arise under federal substantive law—is beyond this essay's scope. In general, however, the applicable *Erie* doctrine[37] provides that in such cases federal courts must apply federal procedural law and state substantive law. But is the standard (or ground) for court review of an award "procedural" or "substantive" under the *Erie* doctrine? Though the answer is not clear cut, existing case law supports the conclusion that the issue is substantive and, thus, that the federal court must apply the standards in the state arbitration statute for reviewing awards.

Gasparini v. Center for Humanities, Inc.,[38] a leading U.S. Supreme Court case on the *Erie* doctrine, is particularly instructive. In *Gasparini*, New York state enacted a statute designed to control excessive jury awards in tort actions by allowing trial judges expanded discretion in reviewing jury awards for excessiveness and appellate courts expanded discretion (for the same purpose) in reviewing lower court decisions. In a tort action brought in federal court because of diversity of citizenship, the Supreme Court held that the federal trial court must apply the expanded state standard—not the more restrictive federal standard—for review of jury damage awards. The Court noted that the state's purpose was substantive and also that requiring the state standard to apply would prevent forum shopping (as between state and federal court). The analogy to fed-

---

[36] The parties did not even dispute this point. See 425 F.Supp.2d at 428.

[37] The doctrine—which derives from the U.S. Supreme Court decision in Erie R. Co. v. Tompkins, 304 U.S. 64 (1938)—concerns what law a federal court must apply when the substance of the dispute is not governed by federal law.

[38] 518 U.S. 415 (1996).

eral court review of arbitral awards seems straightforward. In our scenario California's purpose is clearly substantive (to reject awards founded on errors of law), and requiring a federal district court to apply the state review standard would, as in *Gasparini*, avoid forum shopping.

In summary, even after *Hall Street*, parties to an international transaction should still be able to obtain expanded judicial review in the U.S. if they draft the arbitration clause with considerable care. They should begin by choosing a seat in California or New Jersey—or in any other state allowing expanded judicial review—and by expressly providing that the chosen state's arbitration statute governs the arbitration. To avoid potential issues, they should probably also provide that the award can be enforced in the courts of the chosen state (or in any court having jurisdiction), that the arbitrators retain jurisdiction to adjust any award that has been vacated by a reviewing court, and that the arbitration agreement either is or is not intended to survive if the expanded review clause is not enforced.

V. Expanded Judicial Review in Other Countries

Turning briefly to other countries, we can see that some definitely allow expanded judicial review in set aside actions, but again generally only if the parties draft the arbitration clause carefully. One common pattern—analogous to the U.S. pattern just discussed—allows parties, even in an international transaction, expressly to opt for the seat's domestic arbitration regime (allowing expanded judicial review) in place of the normally applicable international regime (requiring limited review)

Switzerland is a country in point. The Swiss Private International Law Act [PILA] allows parties to an international arbitration agreement with seat in Switzerland to waive the provisions of the PILA and to opt instead for the Intercantonal Arbitration Convention (known as the Concordat).[39] Article 176(2) of the PILA provides:

> The provisions of this chapter [applying to international arbitration] shall not apply where the parties have agreed in writing that the provisions of this chapter are ex-

---

[39] Redfern and Hunter assert that parties to international arbitration are unlikely to choose this option and that it is known locally in Switzerland as the "nostalgia" clause [presumably because the Concordat law applied in Switzerland prior to January 1, 1989, when the Private International Law Act of 1987 came into force]. See Alan Redfern & Martin Hunter, LAW AND PRACTICE OF INTERNATIONAL COMMERCIAL ARBITRATION at 437 fn 21 (Student Ed. 2003).

> cluded and that the cantonal provisions on arbitration [normally applying to domestic arbitration] should apply exclusively.[40]

In a recent decision the Swiss Federal Tribunal explained that to come under this provision parties must meet three requirements: (i) their agreement must be in writing; (ii) the parties must explicitly opt out of the provisions of the PILA; and (iii) they must explicitly agree to be bound by the provisions of the Concordat.[41] Under Article 36 of the Concordat, an award can be annulled if:

> f. * * * the award is arbitrary in that it was based on findings which were manifestly contrary to the facts appearing in the file, or in that it constitutes a clear violation of law or equity.[42]

In some countries, where statutory provisions allow expanded review for domestic but not for international arbitration, court decisions have rejected the Swiss flexibility and have disallowed party attempts to choose domestic arbitration standards for international arbitration. France and Belgium follow this pattern.[43] In other countries with differential standards for domestic and international arbitration, such as Peru and Tunisia, the issue seems not yet to have arisen, or at least prominent commentators make no mention of it.[44]

---

40 International Council for Commercial Arbitration (J. Paulsson, ed.), IV INTERNATIONAL HANDBOOK ON COMMERCIAL ARBITRATION, Switzerland: Annex II—1 (March, 2008).

41 See Introduction to the Case Law Section, para. 9, 25 ASA Bull. (Issue #3) p. 519 (2007), citing a Swiss Federal Tribunal decision of 27 February 2007 (4P.304/2006); 25 ASA Bull. (Issue #3) p. 582.

42 International Council for Commercial Arbitration (J. Paulsson, ed.), IV INTERNATIONAL HANDBOOK ON COMMERCIAL ARBITRATION, Switzerland: Annex I—7 (March, 2008).

43 On French law, see Emmanuel Gaillard and John Savage, eds., Fouchard, Gaillard, Goldman, ON INTERNATIONAL COMMERCIAL ARBITRATION 917 (1999) (citing decisions of the Cour de cassation and the Court of Appeal of Paris). On Belgian law, see Guy Keutgen and Georges Albert Dal, "Belgium" in I International Council for Commercial Arbitration, (J. Paulsson, ed.), INTERNATIONAL HANDBOOK ON COMMERCIAL ARBITRATION at Belgium-37 (Supplm 49, April 2007) ("A contractual clause which provides for a right to appeal an arbitral award to the courts would be null and void.").

44 On Peruvian law, see Ulises Montoya Alberti, "Peru" in III International Council for Commercial Arbitration, (J. Paulsson, ed.) INTERNATIONAL HANDBOOK ON COMMERCIAL ARBITRATION at Peru 21–23 (Supplm. 27, December, 1998) (noting that appeal on the merits is available for domestic arbitration but not for international

In Italy, whether domestic or international arbitration is involved, parties may expressly provide for expanded judicial review.[45] The Italian Code of Civil Procedure, as amended through 2006, expressly provides for court review of an award, including an international award, for violation of the rules of law. Art. 829 para 2 provides: "The recourse [for nullity] for violation of the rules of law relating to the merits of the dispute shall be admitted if so expressly provided by the parties * * *." In Sweden, although the 1999 Swedish Arbitration Act contains no express provisions on the point, at least one commentator believes that expanded judicial review would be available if the parties expressly provide for it.[46]

Finally, English law has long provided for judicial review of awards for errors of law. The English pattern may well have originated, or been allowed to continue, because of the importance of providing a developed case law in commercial fields to guide merchants relying on English law to govern their transactions. Court review assured consistency in commer-

---

arbitration and omitting any discussion of whether parties to international arbitration are free to choose the domestic regime by express provision. On Tunisian law, see Habib Malouche, "Tunisia" in IV International Council for Commercial Arbitration, (J. Paulsson, ed.) INTERNATIONAL HANDBOOK ON COMMERCIAL ARBITRATION at Tunisia 12–13 (Supplem. 18, September, 1994) (noting that appeal on the merits is "regulated" in domestic arbitration but not available for international arbitration and omitting any discussion of whether parties to an international arbitration are free to choose the domestic regime). In Germany, whose arbitration law closely follows the UNCITRAL Model Law, no distinction is drawn between domestic and international arbitration, and the German statute is explicit in limiting court review of awards to the statutory grounds. Section 1059(1) of the ZPO (Code of Civil Procedure) provides: "Recourse to a court against an arbitral award may be made only by an application for setting aside in accordance with subsections 2 and 3 of this section." These subsections do not allow review on the merits.

[45] See Piero Bernardini, "Italy" in III International Council for Commercial Arbitration, (J. Paulsson ed.), INTERNATIONAL HANDBOOK ON COMMERCIAL ARBITRATION at Italy-47 (Supplm 49, April, 2007). See also, Jean-François Poudret & Sebastien Besson, COMPARATIVE LAW OF INTERNATIONAL ARBITRATION at 772 (2d ed. 2007).

[46] See Ulf Franke, "Sweden" in Vol. IV International Council for Commercial Arbitration, (eds. P. Sanders & A. van den Berg), INTERNATIONAL HANDBOOK ON COMMERCIAL ARBITRATION at Sweden-20 (Supplement 32, December, 2000) (commenting on Swedish Arbitration Act of 1999). Franke asserts: "The Act does not provide for any appeal on the merits to the courts. However, there [are] no restrictions for parties to make an arrangement to such effect, although this happens very rarely, if, indeed ever." Id.

cial fields where the same issues arose repeatedly.[47] Also arbitrations in England in some trades were frequently conducted by non-lawyer arbitrators,[48] who could not always be expected to understand or apply fine points of commercial law correctly. In the current 1996 English Arbitration Act judicial review of awards for errors of law is no longer automatically available, but is nevertheless authorized if, among other sufficient conditions, the parties expressly provide for it in their agreement.[49] Review for fact finding errors is not authorized,[50] and review for errors of law applies only where English law is the governing law of the contract.[51]

VI. Conclusion

Returning to Professor Várady's arresting inquiry concerning which approach—allowing of disallowing party choice of expanded judicial review—is more "pro-arbitration," this essay seeks to build upon Professor Várady's original analysis. We have seen that even for international arbitration in the United States after *Hall Street*, expanded judicial review still seems available—but only if parties draft their agreement carefully. Certain other countries also allow expanded review, but again often only if the parties' will is expressed with definiteness and precision. Thus, one might say that in most countries—and certainly this is so for the United States—the default position disfavors expanded review in international arbitration. On the other hand for parties who have a serious interest in expanded review (possibly to counteract a perceived tendency of arbitrators to render compromise awards), it is available if they place the seat in one of the accommodating jurisdictions and draft the agreement expertly. Serious consequences attach to such provisions, including the sacrifice of some of arbitration's efficiency and the introduction of the potential for further wasteful litigation. Thus, conditioning the availability of expanded review on the presence in the arbitration agreement of express and rather uncommon provisions seems to function in the way the writing require-

---

[47] Cf. Alan Redfern & Martin Hunter, LAW AND PRACTICE OF INTERNATIONAL COMMERCIAL ARBITRATION at 434 (Student Ed. 2003).

[48] See Redfern and Hunter, id. at 436 fn 13.

[49] See Jean-François Poudret & Sebastien Besson, COMPARATIVE LAW OF INTERNATIONAL ARBITRATION at 759 and cases cited at fn 332 (2d ed. 2007).

[50] Id.

[51] Id. The 1996 English Arbitration Act at Section 82(1) defines "question of law" as used in the act to refer to English law.

ment once functioned for arbitration in general—as a gatekeeper to ensure that those who enter are informed and conscious of what lies on the other side of the gate. Whereas the writing requirement was intended to guard against parties unwittingly giving up their rights to judicial justice, the drafting requirements incident to expanded review guard against parties unthinkingly re-introducing the potential burdens of judicial justice. Still, if this is the well-informed will of sophisticated commercial parties, would it not be pro-arbitration to endorse this form of party autonomy.

Tibor Várady's Advocacy Before the International Court of Justice

DAVID J. BEDERMAN

Can academics be great advocates? More particularly, can legal academics—trained in the dispassionate ways of scholarly discourse—be effective advocates in court? Are the skills and temperaments that may well be unique for great law teachers and scholars transferable to the realm of advocacy before domestic or international tribunals?

This contribution hopes to make some in-roads in explaining both the discordances and the synergies of legal professionalism by examining one aspect of the extraordinary advocacy and juristic career of Professor Tibor Várady. This is not an easy exercise since Várady's practice has largely been confined to the realm of international commercial arbitration (both as counsel and as an arbitrator), where the proceedings are private and confidential, and the awards only rarely published. Examining Várady's contributions—as an advocate—to the processes and institutions of international commercial arbitration is thus beyond the scope of this essay, even while other contributors to this *festchrift* will undoubtedly weigh-in on Várady's scholarship in these fields.

Instead, my focus here will be on Professor Tibor Várady's advocacy before a very visible international tribunal—the International Court of Justice ("ICJ," or "World Court") in The Hague—in a very public (some might say notorious) controversy concerning suits brought against Yugoslavia (and later Serbia and Montenegro, and (later still) against just Serbia) arising from the Balkans conflicts of the 1990s. Beginning in 2001, Várady served as Agent for Yugoslavia and its successors in phases of three cases before the ICJ: *Application for Revision of the Judgment of 11 July 1996 in the Case Concerning the Application of the Convention on the Prevention and Punishment of the Crime of Genocide (Bosnia & Herzegovina v. Yugoslavia)* (Yugoslavia v. Bosnia & Herzegovina (Preliminary Objections) [hereinafter "Bosnia Revision"]; *Case Concerning the Application of the Convention on the Prevention and Punishment of the*

Crime of Genocide (Bosnia & Herzegovina v. Yugoslavia) (Merits) ["Bosnia Merits"]; and *Case Concerning the Application of the Convention on the Prevention and Punishment of the Crime of Genocide* (Croatia v. Serbia) (Preliminary Objections) ["Croatia Preliminary Objections"].[1]

These three contentious cases before the World Court are obviously intertwined in a number of ways, and these will be explored in this essay. In an opening section, the background to the cases will be introduced—including the ICJ's judgment of July 11, 1996, accepting jurisdiction over the suit brought by Bosnia and Herzegovina against Yugoslavia based on the 1948 Genocide Convention.[2] The following three sections will examine, in turn, Professor Várady's advocacy on behalf of Yugoslavia in the Bosnia Revision, Bosnia Merits, and Croatia Preliminary Objections phases of the respective cases. The written and oral presentations and submissions made by Várady will be carefully reviewed in each of these three matters. A final section will offer an assessment and appreciation of Professor Várady's advocacy before the World Court.

I

Bosnia and Herzegovina (henceforth shortened to "Bosnia") was the first country to file a proceeding before the World Court implicating the 1948 Genocide Convention. Based on events arising from the Balkans conflicts of the late 1980s and early 1990s, Bosnia's application for a contentious

---

[1] The World Court also had on its docket other cases involving the former Yugoslavia, including the cases initiated by Yugoslavia against the members of the North Atlantic Treaty Organization (NATO) arising from the Kosovo intervention. See Cases Concerning the Legality of the Use of Force, 2002 I.C.J. 192 (Belgium), 195 (Canada), 198 (France), 201 (Germany), 204 (Italy), 207 (Netherlands), 210 (Portugal), 213 (United Kingdom); 2001 I.C.J. 13 (Belgium), 16 (Canada), 19 (France), 22 (Germany), 25 (Italy), 28 (Netherlands), 31 (Portugal) 34, (United Kingdom); 2000 I.C.J. 149 (Belgium), 152 (Canada), 155 (France), 158 (Germany), 161 (Italy), 164 (Netherlands), 167 (Portugal), 170 (United Kingdom); 1999 I.C.J. 988 (Belgium), 991 (Canada), 994 (France), 997 (Germany), 1000 (Italy), 1003 (Netherlands), 1006 (Portugal), 1009 (United Kingdom); 1999 I.C.J. 124 (Belgium), 259 (Canada), 363 (France), 422 (Germany), 481 (Italy), 542 (Netherlands), 656 (Portugal), 761 (Spain), 826 (United Kingdom), 916 (United States).

Because Professor Várady never formally entered an appearance as Agent or advocate in these cases, they will not be further considered in this contribution, except as required by context or circumstances.

[2] Convention on the Prevention and Punishment of the Crime of Genocide, Dec. 9, 1948, 78 UNTS 277.

case (filed on March 20, 1993) alleged that the Yugoslavia (and particularly the government of Serbia) materially aided and supported Bosnian Serb rebel forces within the territory of Bosnia against Bosnian Muslim and Bosnian Croat contingents, and that the conduct of Bosnian Serb forces rose to the level of genocide (as directed against Muslim and Croat populations within Bosnia), in violation of the 1948 Convention.[3]

In its application, Bosnia introduced a number of bases for jurisdiction of its case against Yugoslavia. Bosnia "principally relied," in the Court's characterization,[4] on Article IX of the Genocide Convention as the basis of jurisdiction. That article provides:

> Disputes between the Contracting Parties relating to the interpretation, application or fulfilment of the present Convention, including those relating to the responsibility of a State for genocide or for any of the other acts enumerated in article III, shall be submitted to the International Court of Justice at the request of any of the parties to the dispute.[5]

A "Contracting Part[y]" was defined in the Convention as one being signed and ratified "on behalf of any Member of the United Nations and of any nonmember State to which an invitation to sign has been addressed by the General Assembly."[6] Bosnia's reliance on the jurisdiction conveyed by the 1948 Convention was decisive for the World Court in rendering its judgment on Yugoslavia's preliminary objections to Bosnia's suit. The Court rejected all other alternative grounds raised by Bosnia as bases of jurisdiction.[7]

In its July 11, 1996 Judgment on Yugoslavia's preliminary objections to Bosnia's application, the Court made some key findings and holdings

---

[3] Case Concerning Application of Convention on Prevention and Punishment of Crime of Genocide (Bosnia & Herzeg. v. Yugo.), 1996 I.C.J. 595, 600–02 (July 11, 1996).

[4] Id. at 609 (¶ 16).

[5] *Genocide Convention*, supra note 2, art. IX. Article III, cross-referenced in article IX, provides that "The following acts shall be punishable: (a) Genocide; (b) Conspiracy to commit genocide; (c) Direct and public incitement to commit genocide; (d) Attempt to commit genocide; (e) Complicity in genocide." Id. art. IV.

[6] Id. art. XI.

[7] See 1996 I.C.J. at 617–21 (rejecting Bosnia's arguments based, *inter alia*, on an exchange of diplomatic correspondence in June 1992, the *Treaty of Saint-Germain-en-Laye* of September 10, 1919 (as part of the Paris Peace Conference ending World War One), and *forum prorogatum*). The Court concluded: "It follows from the foregoing that the Court is unable to uphold any of the additional bases of jurisdiction invoked by the Applicant and that its only jurisdiction to entertain the case is on the basis of Article IX of the Genocide Convention." Id. at 621 (¶ 41).

that would have a decisive impact on future proceedings. One of these was that:

> [t]he proceedings instituted before the Court are between two States whose territories are located within the former Socialist Federal Republic of Yugoslavia. That Republic signed the Genocide Convention on 11 December 1948 and deposited its instrument of ratification, without reservation, on 29 August 1950. At the time of the proclamation of the Federal Republic of Yugoslavia, on 27 April 1992, a formal declaration was adopted on its behalf to the effect that:
>
> > "The Federal Republic of Yugoslavia, continuing the State, international legal and political personality of the Socialist Federal Republic of Yugoslavia, shall strictly abide by all the commitments that the Socialist Federal Republic of Yugoslavia assumed internationally."
>
> This intention thus expressed by Yugoslavia to remain bound by the international treaties to which the former Yugoslavia was party was confirmed in an official Note of 27 April 1992 from the Permanent Mission of Yugoslavia to the United Nations, addressed to the Secretary-General. The Court observes, furthermore, that it has not been contested that Yugoslavia was party to the Genocide Convention. Thus, Yugoslavia was bound by the provisions of the Convention on the date of the filing of the Application in the present case, namely, on 20 March 1993.[8]

In response to Yugoslavia's objection to whether Bosnia had properly adhered to the Genocide Convention, the Court held that

> It is clear from the foregoing that Bosnia and Herzegovina could become a party to the Convention through the mechanism of State succession. . . .
>
> The Parties to the dispute differed as to the legal consequences to be drawn from the occurrence of a State succession in the present case. . . .
>
> Without prejudice as to whether or not the principle of "automatic succession" applies in the case of certain types of international treaties or conventions, the Court does not consider it necessary, in order to decide on its jurisdiction in this case, to make a determination on the legal issues concerning State succession in respect to treaties which have been raised by the Parties. Whether Bosnia and Herzegovina automatically became party to the Genocide Convention on the date of its accession to independence on 6 March 1992, or whether it became a party as a result - retroactive or not - of its Notice of Succession of 29 December 1992, at all events it was a party to it on the date of the filing of its Application on 20 March 1993.
>
> Since the Court has concluded that Bosnia and Herzegovina could become a party to the Genocide Convention as a result of a succession, the question of the application of Articles XI and XIII of the Convention does not arise.[9]

---

[8] 1996 I.C.J. at 610 (¶ 17).

[9] Id. at 611–12 (¶¶ 20, 21, 23, 24).

Having made these conclusions as to the Court's jurisdiction *ratione personae*—the identity of the disputing parties based on the 1948 Genocide Convention's provisions—the Court was then able to easily hold that it had jurisdiction *ratione materiae* (based on the subject-matter of Bosnia's substantive claims against Yugoslavia under the Genocide Convention).[10] That left one other jurisdictional matter:

> Having reached the conclusion that it has jurisdiction in the present case, both *ratione personae* and *ratione materiae* on the basis of Article IX of the Genocide Convention, it remains for the Court to specify the scope of that jurisdiction *ratione temporis*. In its sixth and seventh preliminary objections, Yugoslavia, basing its contention on the principle of the non-retroactivity of legal acts, has indeed asserted as a subsidiary argument that, even though the Court might have jurisdiction on the basis of the Convention, it could only deal with events subsequent to the different dates on which the Convention might have become applicable as between the Parties. In this regard, the Court will confine itself to the observation that the Genocide Convention—and in particular Article IX—does not contain any clause the object or effect of which is to limit in such manner the scope of its jurisdiction *ratione temporis*, and nor did the Parties themselves make any reservation to that end, either to the Convention or on the occasion of the signature of the Dayton-Paris Agreement. The Court thus finds that it has jurisdiction in this case to give effect to the Genocide Convention with regard to the relevant facts which have occurred since the beginning of the conflict which took place in Bosnia and Herzegovina. This finding is, moreover, in accordance with the object and purpose of the Convention as defined by the Court in 1951 and referred to above (see paragraph 31). As a result, the Court considers that it must reject Yugoslavia's sixth and seventh preliminary objections.[11]

The Court, therefore, concluded both that it had jurisdiction over Bosnia's application and that it was admissible.[12] In response to Bosnia's final submission[13] that Yugoslavia's preliminary objections were frivolous and an abuse of right,

> the Court emphasizes that ... it does not consider that Yugoslavia has, in presenting those objections, abused its rights to do so under Article 36, paragraph 6, of the Statute of the Court and Article 79 of the Rules of Court. The Court rejects the request made to that end by Bosnia and Herzegovina in its final submissions. The Court must, in each case submitted to it, verify whether it has jurisdiction to deal with the case, and, if

---

[10] See id. at 614–17 (¶¶ 27–33).

[11] Id. at 617 (¶ 34).

[12] See id. at 621–622 (¶¶ 42–45). See also Christine Gray, Case Note, 46 I.C.L.Q. 688 (1997); Peter H.F. Bekker & Paul C. Szasz, International Decision, 91 AJIL 121 (1997).

[13] See 1996 I.C.J. at 609 (¶ 15) ("to adjudge and declare that the Federal Republic of Yugoslavia has abused its right to raise preliminary objections as foreseen in Article 36, paragraph 6, of the Statute of the Court and to Article 79 of the Rules of Court....").

> necessary, whether the Application is admissible, and such objections as are raised by the Respondent may be useful to clarify the legal situation. As matters now stand, the preliminary objections presented by Yugoslavia have served that purpose. Having established its jurisdiction under Article IX of the Genocide Convention, and having concluded that the Application is admissible, the Court may now proceed to consider the merits of the case on that basis.[14]

The key holdings of the World Court in its July 11, 1996, judgment on preliminary objections—especially as to jurisdiction *ratione personae* and *ratione materiae*—were barely disputed in the dissents, separate opinions, and declarations appended to the ruling. In their separate opinions, Judges Shahabuddeen,[15] Weeramantry,[16] and Parra-Araguren,[17] all wrote in favor of some notion of automatic succession for obligations arising under the Genocide Convention (or similar human rights instruments) in cases such as the break-up of a federal entity such as the former Yugoslavia. Judge *ad hoc* Kreća (having been appointed by Yugoslavia) dissented,[18] and did take exception to the "automatic succession" theory as announced in the Court's judgment as to Bosnia's party-status under the Genocide Convention, and also openly questioned the Court's premises in assuming that Yugoslavia was also a party to that treaty.[19]

II

The stage was thus set for Professor Tibor Várady's first entry as an advocate before the Court, when Yugoslavia made an application, on April 24, 2001, of its intent to seek revision of the Court's Judgment of July 11, 1996.[20] Yugoslavia's application for revision[21] was based on article 61 of the ICJ Statute, which provides, in pertinent part, that

---

[14] Id. at 622 (¶ 46).
[15] See id. at 634.
[16] See id. at 640.
[17] See id. at 656.
[18] See id. at 658.
[19] See id. at 755–64 (¶¶ 91–98).
[20] In a letter dated April 20, 2001, Professor Várady—making his first appearance as the Agent of Yugoslavia—withdrew all counterclaims that Yugoslavia had filed against Bosnia in its Counter-Memorial of July 23, 1997. This was later acknowledged in the Court's Order of September 10, 2001. See 2001 I.C.J. 572. This was a necessarily bold move in order for Yugoslavia to have consistent positions before the Court when it sought revision of the earlier July 11, 1996 judgment on preliminary objections. Yugo-

> An application for revision of a judgment may be made only when it is based upon the discovery of some fact of such a nature as to be a decisive factor, which fact was, when the judgment was given, unknown to the Court and also to the party claiming revision, always provided that such ignorance was not due to negligence.
>
> The proceedings for revision shall be opened by a judgment of the Court expressly recording the existence of the new fact, recognizing that it has such a character as to lay the case open to revision, and declaring the application admissible on this ground.[22]

The "fact" that was the premise of Yugoslavia's application for revision was that, at the time the July 11, 1996, judgment on Yugoslavia's preliminary objections to jurisdiction was rendered, Yugoslavia was not a member of the United Nations, and thus not a party to the 1948 Genocide Convention.[23] Indeed, according to Yugoslavia's revision application, the Federal Republic of Yugoslavia (FRY)—as distinct from the former Socialist Federal Republic of Yugoslavia (SFRY)—was not a member of the United Nations until November 1, 2000, well after Bosnia had filed its case.

According to the revision application, the April 27, 1992, Declaration that had been adopted by the SFRY Assembly purported to have the new entity, FRY, "continu[e] the State, international legal and political personality of the Socialist Federal Republic of Yugoslavia, [and] shall strictly abide by all commitments that the SFR of Yugoslavia assumed internationally."[24] But other successor entities—most notably Bosnia—objected to FRY's assertion of continuity with SFRY, especially with respect to membership in the United Nations.[25] Based on these objections, the United Nations Security Council and General Assembly respectively issued resolutions indicating that "the Federal Republic of Yugoslavia (Serbia and Montenegro) cannot continue automatically the membership of the former Socialist Republic of Yugoslavia in the United Nations; and

---

slavia could not very well be seen as raising an objection to the Court's jurisdiction over it, even while it maintained counter-claims against Bosnia.

[21] Application Instituting Proceedings, Apr. 24, 2001, Application for Revision of the Judgment of 11 July 1996 in the Case Concerning the Application of the Convention on the Prevention and Punishment of the Crime of Genocide (Bosnia & Herzegovina v. Yugoslavia) (Yugoslavia v. Bosnia & Herzegovina (Preliminary Objections) (2000 General List No. 122) [hereinafter "Revision Application"].

[22] Statute of the International Court of Justice, June 26, 1945, arts. 61(1) & (2),156 U.N.T.S. 77.

[23] Revision Application, supra note 21, at 8.

[24] Id. at 10; see also Annex 1 (U.N. Doc. A/46/915 (Annex II)).

[25] See id. at 12.

therefore decides that [FRY] should apply for membership in the United Nations and that it shall not participate in the work of the General Assembly."[26] But FRY's legal status at the United Nations was complicated by other developments, including an opinion by the UN Under-Secretary-General and Legal Counsel which indicated that Yugoslavia remained a UN Member, receipt of dues payments by FRY to the United Nations, and the practice of the organization as a treaty depositary.[27] Nevertheless, FRY was consistently barred as a participant in various treaty meetings as a party.[28]

In an order issued April 8, 1993, the World Court took notice of these developments and concluded that "while the solution adopted is not free from legal difficulties, the question whether or not Yugoslavia is a Member of the United Nations and as such a party to the Statute of the Court is one which the Court does not need to determine definitively at the present stage of the proceedings."[29] The Court in its July 11, 1996, judgment recited all of these developments—and especially focusing on the FRY Declaration of April 1992—in order to hold that "it has not been contested that Yugoslavia was a party to the Genocide Convention."[30]

Yugoslavia's request for revision before the World Court emphasized this progression of confusing and ambiguous developments, and Várady's submission culminated in the key fact that gave rise to the application: that FRY was compelled, on October 27, 2000, to seek admission to the United Nations as a new member, which occurred on November 1 of that year.[31] As a consequence of this action, FRY was requested by the United Nations to take the necessary treaty actions with respect to those international instruments to which Yugoslavia had been a party. In a note addressed to the UN Secretary General, addressed March 8, 2001, FRY indicated that because it had not succeeded to treaty-party-status to the 1948 Genocide Convention, as FRY had not been a member of the United Nations (a necessary requisite for that party-status), therefore, FRY's accession would be effective as of the date of deposit on June 10, 2001.[32]

---

[26] See id. at 14 (quoting U.N. Doc. S/RES/777 (1992); and U.N. Doc. A/RES/47/1 (1992)).

[27] See id. at 16–20.

[28] See id. at 20–22.

[29] 1993 I.C.J. 3, 14 (Order of April 8) (¶ 18).

[30] 1996 I.C.J. at 610 (¶ 17).

[31] See Revision Application, supra note 21, at 30–32 (citing U.N. Doc. A/RES/55/12 (2000)).

[32] See id. at 34–36.

The balance of FRY's revision request was thus focused on the question of whether, taken together, all of this constituted new "facts," within the meaning of Statute article 61(1), so as to justify the Court's granting of an application for revision of judgment. The revision request took the position that these facts were of "such a nature to be a decisive factor," or motive, for the Court's July 11, 1996, judgment on preliminary objections.[33] If FRY was not a member of the United Nations as of the date of Bosnia's application, FRY could not have been a party to the Genocide Convention, and the premise for the only basis for the Court's jurisdiction in the case (as acknowledged by the Court in its opinion) was thus invalid. The revision request goes into quite a lot of detail as to why FRY could not possibly have become a party to the Genocide Convention by any means other than acceding as a UN member.[34] The revision request also made the point that these facts were "unknown to the Court and the party claiming revision as the time of the judgment," also within the meaning of Statute article 61(1). Concisely argued, the revision request suggested[35] that it had not been FRY's fault that its assumption of continuity with Yugoslavia had been refuted by the subsequent practice and decisions of the United Nations.[36] In any event, the revision request concluded,[37] the key jurisdictional premise of the Court's July 11, 1996, judgment—that FRY was the legal successor to Yugoslavia and that, therefore, FRY had been a party (at all relevant times) to the Genocide Convention—had been brought into question.

As Professor Várady acknowledged in his concluding oral remarks before the Court, "[r]evision is an exceptional remedy."[38] In the Court's

[33] See id. at 38; see also I.C.J. Verbatim Record, Nov. 4, 2002, I.C.J. Doc. CR 2002/40, at 36–41.

[34] See id. at 38–52. The revision request contains an excellent discussion of Statute article 35(2) and its "special provisions contained in treaties in force" language, and the relevant jurisprudence and doctrine for that provision. See id. (citing 2 Shabtai Rosenne, Law and Practice of the International Court, 1920–1966, at 628–30; Revisions of the Rules of the PCIJ, PCIJ ser. D (Acts and Documents Concerning the Organization of the Court), no. 2, at 104–06)). See also I.C.J. Verbatim Record, Nov. 4, 2002, I.C.J. Doc. CR 2002/40, at 18–24.

[35] See id. at 52–54.

[36] See I.C.J. Verbatim Record, Nov. 4, 2002, I.C.J. Doc. CR 2002/40, at 55–61 (discussing the relevant jurisprudence of Statute article 61, and the Application for Revision and Interpretation of the Judgment of 24 February 1982 in the Case Concerning the Continental Shelf (Tunisia/Libyan Arab Jamahiriya) Judgment, 1985 I.C.J. 207 (¶ 28)).

[37] See id. at 54–56.

[38] See I.C.J. Verbatim Record, Nov. 6, 2002, I.C.J. Doc. CR 2002/42, at 45.

history, applications for revisions of judgment, under Statute article 61, are rarely granted, and FRY's in this case was no exception. The Court handed down its judgment denying the application for revision on February 3, 2003.[39] After setting forth the elements of an article 61 revision, and indicating that the first-stage of the proceedings was devoted to whether the application would even be deemed admissible,[40] the Court framed the relevant question for analysis as to whether "there is here a 'fact' which, although in existence at the date of its Judgment of 11 July 1996, was at the time unknown both to the FRY and to the Court."[41]

Much of the Court's decision on admissibility for FRY's revision request thus turned on the epistemology of "facts." Bosnia, in its pleadings,[42] emphasized that there was a distinction to be drawn between "facts" and "the consequences of a fact." But the Court took an even simpler approach to cut the Gordian knot of FRY's revision request:

> under the terms of Article 61, paragraph 1, of the Statute, an application for revision of a judgment may be made only when it is "based upon the discovery" of some fact which, "when the judgment was given", was unknown. These are the characteristics which the "new" fact referred to in paragraph 2 of that Article must possess. Thus both paragraphs refer to a fact existing at the time when the judgment was given and discovered subsequently. A fact which occurs several years after a judgment has been given is not a "new" fact within the meaning of Article 61; this remains the case irrespective of the legal consequences that such a fact may have.
>
> In the present case, the admission of the FRY to the United Nations occurred on 1 November 2000, well after the 1996 Judgment. The Court concludes accordingly, that that admission cannot be regarded as a new fact within the meaning of Article 61 capable of founding a request for revision of that Judgment.[43]

The Court likewise rejected[44] FRY's contention that the November 2000 admission to the United Nations simply "revealed" a factual condition (or, rather, an infirmity) that had existed at the time of the Court's 1996 judgment. But this still left the tricky question of what, exactly, was FRY's status as a putative party to the Genocide Convention:

> Resolution 47/1 [of 1992, which indicated that FRY had not succeeded to Yugoslavia's UN seat] did not inter alia affect the FRY's right to appear before the Court or to

[39] See 2003 I.C.J. 3.
[40] See id. at 11–13 (¶¶ 14–16).
[41] Id. at 13 (¶ 17).
[42] See id. at 13 (¶ 22).
[43] Id. at 30 (¶¶ 67 & 68).
[44] Id. at 30–31 (¶ 69).

be a party to a dispute before the Court under the conditions laid down by the Statute. Nor did it affect the position of the FRY in relation to the Genocide Convention. To "terminate the situation created by resolution 47/1", the FRY had to submit a request for admission to the United Nations as had been done by the other Republics composing the SFRY. All these elements were known to the Court and to the FRY at the time when the Judgment was given. Nevertheless, what remained unknown in July 1996 was if and when the FRY would apply for membership in the United Nations and if and when that application would be accepted, thus terminating the situation created by General Assembly resolution 47/1.

The Court wishes to emphasize that General Assembly resolution 55/12 of 1 November 2000 cannot have changed retroactively the *sui generis* position which the FRY found itself in vis-à-vis the United Nations over the period 1992 to 2000, or its position in relation to the Statute of the Court and the Genocide Convention. Furthermore, the letter of the Legal Counsel of the United Nations dated 8 December 2000, cannot have affected the FRY's position in relation to treaties.[45]

In short, the Court, by a vote of ten-to-three,[46] rejected FRY's revision request on technical grounds that seemed to exacerbate, and not resolve, the problems raised by Yugoslavia in its application. Ruling that Yugoslavia's party-status under the Genocide Convention was a "*sui generis* position,"[47] was no real holding at all, and was not left unremarked in the separate, concurring and dissenting opinions.[48] These omissions and *lacunae* in the Court's February 3, 2003, rejection of the admissibility of FRY's revision request would have profound effects on later proceedings.

III

These became evident when Professor Várady appeared before the Court, in March and May 2006, in the oral proceedings on the merits of Bosnia's genocide claims against FRY (now denominated as "Serbia and Montenegro").[49] Professor Várady's role, in these proceedings, was confined to the explication of "the procedural side of this complex case," even while recognizing that "in this case fundamental humanitarian issues are at stake."[50] Nevertheless, Várady indicated, the Court was obliged to revisit the as-

---

45 Id. at 31 (¶¶ 70 & 71).

46 See id. at 32 (¶ 75). See also Nicholas Tsagourias, Case Note, 53 I.C.L.Q. 731 (2004); Ricky J. Lee, Case Note, 2003 Austl. Int'l L. J. 205.

47 Id. at 31 (¶ 71).

48 See id. at 36–37 (¶ 9) (Koroma, J., sep. op.); 39–48 (Vereschetin, J., diss. op.); 53–69 (Dimitrijević, *ad hoc* J., diss.).

49 See I.C.J. Verbatim Record, March 8, 2006, I.C.J. Doc. CR 2006/12, at 1.

50 Id. at 45 (¶ 1.2), 46 (¶ 1.5).

sumptions that had motivated it to accept—and confirm—jurisdiction in its July 1996 preliminary objections and February 2003 revision request rulings.[51] In a skillful bit of pleading, Várady indicated before the Court that *res judicata* principles should not preclude it from re-examining jurisdictional holdings, if such was required in light of new situations.[52]

And, perhaps not unsurprisingly, the Court itself offered just such a new situation to exploit in terms of the jurisdictional muddle surrounding Yugoslavia's status as a member of the United Nations (and a party to the Statute of the ICJ). This arose in the Court's decisions denying jurisdiction in the *Legality of the Use of Force* cases, where the Court returned to its *sui generis* characterization of Yugoslavia's status:

> To sum up, all these events testify to the rather confused and complex state of affairs that obtained within the United Nations surrounding the issue of the legal status of the Federal Republic of Yugoslavia in the Organization during this period. It is against this background that the Court, in its Judgment of 3 February 2003, referred to the "*sui generis* position which the FRY found itself in" during the period between 1992 and 2000.
>
> It must be stated that this qualification of the position of the Federal Republic of Yugoslavia as *"sui generis"*, which the Court employed to describe the situation during this period of 1992 to 2000, is not a prescriptive term from which certain defined legal consequences accrue; it is merely descriptive of the amorphous state of affairs in which the Federal Republic of Yugoslavia found itself during this period. No final and definitive conclusion was drawn by the Court from this descriptive term on the amorphous status of the Federal Republic of Yugoslavia vis-à-visor within the United Nations during this period. The Court did not commit itself to a definitive position on the issue of the legal status of the Federal Republic of Yugoslavia in relation to the Charter and the Statute in its pronouncements in incidental proceedings, in the cases involving this issue which came before the Court during this anomalous period.[53]

Far from resolving Yugoslavia's situation (as a member of the United Nations[54]), this statement further confused the picture as to whether FRY had ever been bound by Article IX of the Genocide Convention, within

---

[51] See id. at 47 (¶ 1.11), 52–54.

[52] See id. at 54–56 (¶¶ 1.39–1.44) (discussing 1949 Corfu Channel and 1999 Cameroon v. Nigeria decisions); I.C.J. Verbatim Record, March 9, 2006, I.C.J. Doc. CR 2006/13, at 60 (¶ 5.1) (discussing ICAO Council Case, 1972 I.C.J. at 52).

[53] See, e.g., 2004 I.C.J. ___ (Serbia v. Belgium) (Judgment of Dec. 15) (Prelim. Objections) (¶¶ 73 & 74). This same language was reflected in paragraph 73 of the judgments in regard to France, Canada, Italy, Netherlands, and Portugal, and in paragraph 72 of the Germany and United Kingdom judgments.

[54] This was the subject of in-depth review in Professor Várady's remarks before the Court on May 8, 2006. See I.C.J. Verbatim Record, May 8, 2006, I.C.J. Doc. CR 2006/44, at 10–30.

any relevant time-period, for purposes of the Court's jurisdiction, a confusion that Professor Várady detailed in his remarks to the Court.[55]

Perhaps Professor Várady's most spirited piece of advocacy before the Court (in this phase of the disputes, at least) may have occurred on May 8, 2006, when he returned to the question of the *res judicata* effects of the Court's earlier rulings on jurisdiction.[56] Not content with relying on his earlier submissions in this regard, Várady devoted substantial thought and reflection to the broader implications of international tribunals revisiting their jurisdictional rulings. Quite apart from its careful parsing of doctrinal literature,[57] the Court's own Rules of Procedure,[58] and the practices of a variety of international tribunals,[59] Várady's discussion was intended to defuse a powerful argument offered by his counterpart on the Bosnian advocacy team, Professor Alain Pellet, that a court's previous jurisdictional holdings should never be disturbed.[60]

Professor Várady also had to confront, in his final submissions before the Court in this phase of the proceedings,[61] the question of whether FRY should be estopped from challenging the earlier jurisdictional rulings, based on its previous litigation positions before the Court. Obviously, both sides had zig-zagged in their submissions over the years, and Várady made the powerful point that it was Bosnia which was primarily responsible for the ambiguous position that FRY found itself in. Simple consistency—and common sense—required that the Court reconcile its decision on FRY's United Nations membership (as reflected in the *Legality of the Use of Force* cases) with the jurisdictional problem raised in the current case. Várady noted that Professor Pellet's plea that inconsistent decisions before the Court were "a fact of life, if regrettable,"[62] was not a sensible ground for rejecting FRY's position.

Nevertheless, that was the upshot of the Court's February 26, 2007, judgment on the merits in the case between Bosnia and Serbia,[63] at least as

---

[55] See I.C.J. Verbatim Record, March 9, 2006, I.C.J. Doc. CR 2006/13, at 19–35.

[56] See I.C.J. Verbatim Record, May 8, 2006, I.C.J. Doc. CR 2006/44, at 50–69.

[57] See id. at 54–55 (¶¶ 3.17–3.20) (discussing work of Rosenne, Bos and Schwarzenberger).

[58] See id. at 56–57 (¶¶ 3.24–3.27).

[59] See id. at 65–69 (¶¶ 3.58–3.69) (reviewing cases from the inter-War Mixed Arbitral Tribunals, the European Court of Human Rights, and the ICJ).

[60] See id. at 59 (¶ 3.36), 61 (¶ 3.43).

[61] See I.C.J. Verbatim Record, May 9, 2006, I.C.J. Doc. CR 2006/45, at 56–63.

[62] See id. at 62 (¶ 6.32) (quoting CR 2006/36, at 22 (¶ 57) (Pellet)).

[63] See Bosnia Merits, 2007 I.C.J. ___ (Merits) (Judgment of Feb. 26) (¶¶ 67–79) (identification of the respondent party as "Serbia and Montenegro").

concerns the court's jurisdiction.[64] After reviewing the positions of the parties, and generally assessing the history of FRY's UN membership and treaty status under the Genocide Convention,[65] the Court was obliged to rule on Serbia's general contention concerning the application of *res judicata* principles to previous jurisdictional holdings of the Court. The Court, after distinguishing its prior language in the *Appeal Relating to the Jurisdiction of the ICAO Council (India v. Pakistan)* and *Corfu Channel (United Kingdom v. Albania)* cases,[66] rejected Serbia's argument that jurisdictional holdings could be revisited:

> It has however been suggested by the Respondent [Serbia] that a distinction may be drawn between the application of the principle of *res judicata* to judgments given on the merits of a case, and judgments determining the Court's jurisdiction, in response to preliminary objections; specifically, the Respondent contends that "decisions on preliminary objections do not and cannot have the same consequences as decisions on the merits". The Court will however observe that the decision on questions of jurisdiction, pursuant to Article 36, paragraph 6, of the Statute, is given by a judgment, and Article 60 of the Statute provides that "[t]he judgment is final and without appeal", without distinguishing between judgments on jurisdiction and admissibility, and judgments on the merits.... Furthermore, the contention put forward by the Respondent would signify that the principle of *res judicata* would not prevent a judgment dismissing a preliminary objection from remaining open to further challenge indefinitely, while a judgment upholding such an objection, and putting an end to the case, would in the nature of things be final and determinative as regards that specific case.[67]

In this general discussion, the Court concluded that the "only one procedure" available for a "party [that] believe[s] that elements have come to light subsequent to the decision of the Court which tend to show that the Court's conclusions may have been based on incorrect or insufficient facts" is a Statute Article 61 request for revision.[68] Otherwise, "the decision must remain final, even if it is in apparent contradiction to reality."[69]

---

[64] See id. at ¶¶ 80–141, 471(1). As the jurisdictional issues were the only matters addressed in Professor Várady's advocacy before the Court, this essay will confine itself to those sections of the Court's judgment.

[65] See id. at ¶¶ 80–104.

[66] See id. at ¶ 118. The Court also rejected the analogies, cited by Professor Várady, relating to the jurisdictional practices of the European Court of Human Rights and Mixed Arbitral Tribunals, as being a *lex specialis* and inapplicable in "overrid[ing] the clear provisions of the Court Statute, and the principle of *res judicata*." Id. ¶ 119. See also Separate Opinion of Judge Owada, ¶ 6.

[67] Bosnia Merits, at ¶ 117 (discussing Land and Maritime Boundary between Cameroon and Nigeria, 1999 I.C.J. 39; and FRY's earlier Application for Revision).

[68] Id. at ¶ 120.

[69] Id.

In applying *res judicata* principles to the 1996 judgment, accepting jurisdiction over FRY, the Court first indicated that that holding of jurisdiction was embodied in the *dispositif*, and "thus [was] established with the full weight of the Court's judicial authority."[70] The Court, it indicated,[71] could have ended its analysis on that ground, but chose nonetheless to examine Serbia's arguments as to why the 1996 judgment "was not conclusive on the matter."[72] This analysis, the Court described,[73] necessitated a review of what were the actual jurisdictional holdings in earlier phases of a case:

> the fact that the Court has in these past cases dealt with jurisdictional issues after having delivered a judgment on jurisdiction does not support the contention that such a judgment can be reopened at any time, so as to permit reconsideration of issues already settled with the force of *res judicata*.... the jurisdictional issues examined at a late stage in those cases were such that the decision on them would not contradict the finding of jurisdiction made in the earlier judgment. By contrast, the contentions of the Respondent in the present case would, if upheld, effectively reverse the 1996 Judgment; that indeed is their purpose.[74]

As for Serbia's contention that the Court had never made a definitive ruling on whether FRY succeeded to Yugoslavia's UN membership, and adherence to the ICJ Statute,[75] the Court waffled and indicated that it was not "unaware of the fact" that FRY's UN membership was "[not] free from legal difficulties."[76] Nor did the Court's 2004 ruling, in the *Legality of Use of Force* cases,[77] that FRY was not a member of the United Nations (and the ICJ Statute) for purposes of a jurisdictional holding, seem to trouble it much. In short, the Court concluded, it was allowed to change its mind—even if it meant that FRY was jurisdictionally whip-sawed: denied

---

[70] Id. at ¶ 123 (citing ¶ 47(2)(a) of the 1996 judgment).

[71] See id. Indeed, in his dissenting opinion, Judge Vice-President Al-Khasawneh, takes the Court to task on precisely this point by rising to Serbia's invitation to "present additional jurisdictional arguments." See Al-Khasawneh diss. op. at ¶ 28. Indeed, he was sharply critical of Serbia's "initiative" for application for revision in the earlier phase of the case. See id. at ¶¶ 22–27. Judge Owada, in his separate opinion, was even more blunt in his assessment: Serbia blundered by not bringing an application for an interpretation of the 1996 Judgment, under Statute article 60, as opposed to an application for revision under article 61. Separate Opinion of Judge Owada, ¶ 22.

[72] Bosnia Merits, at ¶ 124.

[73] See id. at ¶¶ 125–28.

[74] Id. at ¶ 128.

[75] See id. at ¶ 129.

[76] Id. at ¶ 130 (quoting 1993 I.C.J. at 14).

[77] 2004 I.C.J. at 299 (¶ 47).

applicant status in one set of cases *(Legality of Use of Force)* because it was not a UN member, but nevertheless deemed a proper respondent in the present cases because "it was by no means so clear ... that the Respondent was not a member of the United Nations at the relevant time."[78]

To justify this result, the Court had to extol the virtues of *res judicata* principles beyond any sensible recognition by holding that the 1996 judgment, at least "by necessary implication"[79] or "logical construction,"[80] as including a holding that FRY was a UN member and a party to the Statute. Somewhat peevishly, the Court's opinion noted that it "does not need, for the purpose of the present proceedings, to go behind that finding and consider on what basis the Court was able to satisfy itself on the point."[81] In short, the Court seemed to attach *res judicata* significance to an unstated assumption in its 1996 judgment on Serbia's preliminary objections to jurisdiction as to the fundamental question of whether FRY even had proper access to the Court as a party to its Statute. In a somewhat surprising aside, the Court responded to this argument in an argot of its overweening judicial supremacy:

> It appears to the Court that these contentions are inconsistent with the nature of the principle of *res judicata*. That principle signifies that once the Court has made a determination, whether on a matter of the merits of a dispute brought before it, or on a question of its own jurisdiction, that determination is definitive both for the parties to the case, in respect of the case (Article 59 of the Statute), and for the Court itself in the context of that case. However fundamental the question of the capacity of States to be parties in cases before the Court may be, it remains a question to be determined by the Court, in accordance with Article 36, paragraph 6, of the Statute, and once a finding in favour of jurisdiction has been pronounced with the force of *res judicata*, it is not open to question or re-examination, except by way of revision under Article 61 of the Statute. There is thus, *as a matter of law*, no possibility that the Court might render "its fi-

[78] Bosnia Merits, at ¶ 131. See also Joint Dissenting Opinion of Judges Ranjeva, Shi & Koroma, ¶¶ 17, 18. Judge Tomka, in his separate opinion, would have made a *de novo* ruling that FRY had succeeded to Yugoslavia's obligations under the Genocide Convention. See Separate Opinion of Judge Tomka, ¶¶ 24–36.

[79] Bosnia Merits, at ¶ 132. It was this aspect of the Court's ruling that drew a joint dissenting opinion by Judges Ranjeva, Shi and Koroma. See Joint Dissenting Opinion of Judges Ranjeva, Shi & Koroma, ¶¶ 2, 3 ("A matter that the Court has not decided cannot be qualified as *res judicata*.... An issue is not precluded by the doctrine of *res judicata* just because the Court says it is."). See also Separate Opinion of Judge Tomka, ¶¶ 11–15 (distinguishing a decision based on jurisdiction *ratione personae* from the concept of access to the Court); Declaration of Judge Skotnikov, at 1–4; Dissenting Opinion of Judge Mahiou, at ¶¶ 11–36; Separate Opinion of Judge *ad hoc* Kreća, at ¶¶ 1–74.

[80] Bosnia Merits, at ¶ 135.

[81] Id. at ¶ 132.

> nal decision with respect to a party over which it cannot exercise its judicial function", because the question whether a State is or is not a party subject to the jurisdiction of the Court is one which is reserved for the sole and authoritative decision of the Court.
>
> Counsel for the Respondent contended further that, in the circumstances of the present case, reliance on the *res judicata* principle "would justify the Court's *ultra vires* exercise of its judicial functions contrary to the mandatory requirements of the Statute". However, the operation of the "mandatory requirements of the Statute" falls to be determined by the Court in each case before it; and once the Court has determined, with the force of *res judicata*, that it has jurisdiction, then for the purposes of that case no question of *ultra vires* action can arise, the Court having sole competence to determine such matters under the Statute. For the Court *res judicata pro veritate habetur*, and the judicial truth within the context of a case is as the Court has determined it, subject only to the provision in the Statute for revision of judgments. This result is required by the nature of the judicial function, and the universally recognized need for stability of legal relations.[82]

The Court's ruling on jurisdiction and *res judicata* issues in the merits phase of the Bosnia case thus appeared to be a bit of an *ipse dixit*. Using the language of repose and "stability of legal relations," the Court declined—even in the face of a persuasive argument made by Serbia—to reconcile the contradictory sets of decisions in the *Legality of Use of Force* cases and the Bosnian genocide case. The Court not only expanded the ambit of its *res judicata* jurisprudence to cover jurisdictional holdings (which is hardly surprising), but also to positions that were, in the Court's own words, merely "by necessary implication" or compelled by "logical construction" to be included in the Court's holding. With these legal premises, it is hardly surprising that the Court would brush-aside Serbia's assertions of lack of jurisdiction.

IV

That leaves Professor Várady's involvement as Serbia's agent in the preliminary objections phase of the Croatia case. Croatia's application against FRY (later denominated as "Serbia") was filed July 2, 1999,[83] and

---

[82] Id. at ¶¶ 138 & 139. See also Separate Opinion of Judge Owada, ¶ 37 ("In a nutshell, my view on this question is that *the Court itself*, and not the Respondent, *is precluded now from taking a different position at this stage* which would be diametrically opposed to the one that the Court itself is deemed in law to have so definitively determined in the present case. The principle of consistency as an essential prerequisite for the stability of legal relations should support such an approach.") (original emphasis).

[83] Croatia Preliminary Objections, 2008 I.C.J. ___, at ¶ 1 (Preliminary Objections) (Judgment of Nov. 18).

was (obviously enough) analytically distinct from the Bosnia proceedings. Notionally, then, *res judicata* principles would not be applicable as a basis for barring the Court from giving a *de novo* decision as to its jurisdiction. FRY's Preliminary Objections, filed in 2002,[84] thus briefed anew the question of whether Court had jurisdiction *ratione personae* over FRY by virtue of article IX of the Genocide Convention, as well as addressing Serbia's objections to the admissibility of Croatia's claims as a matter of *ratione temporis* and mootness.[85]

The main contribution made by Professor Várady's written memorial in the Croatia preliminary objections phase was its assemblage of doctrine and practice in relation to the automatic succession of States to treaty obligations, such as the 1948 Genocide Convention. This discussion turned on a searching review of the customary law character of rules of automatic succession contained in the 1978 Vienna Convention on Succession of States in Respect to Treaties.[86] Serbia's brief examined the relevant *travaux préparatoires* of the Vienna Convention, the practice of the legal counsel of the United Nations, and depositary usages.[87] It was essential that the memorial disprove a rule of automatic succession, especially in relation to human rights instruments, and the brief drew on the international community's reaction to the successor situations for the former Soviet Union and East Germany.[88] Serbia also asserted that neither FRY's April 1992 declaration, or subsequent acts, had the legal effect of making it a party to the Genocide Convention, particularly under the *lex specialis* of its Article IX.[89] Indeed, Croatia's assertion of automatic succession for Serbia to the Genocide Convention was contradicted by its contemporaneous practice in the early 1990s.[90]

In Serbia's oral submissions to the Court, Professor Várady had the opportunity to finally seek a substantive ruling on the Court's jurisdiction *ratione personae* (under the Genocide Convention) and lack of access to the Court (based on FRY not being a UN member, nor a party to the

---

[84] Case Concerning the Application of the Convention on the Prevention and Punishment of the Crime of Genocide (Croatia v. Yugoslavia), Preliminary Objection of the Federal Republic of Yugoslavia (Sept. 2002) ["FRY's 2002 Preliminary Objection"].

[85] See id. at 93–124. As these issues appeared subsidiary to Professor Várady's advocacy before the Court, they will not be further considered here.

[86] Aug. 23, 1978, 1946 U.N.T.S. 3.

[87] FRY's 2002 Preliminary Objection, at 53–74.

[88] See id. at 58–63.

[89] See id. at 75–81.

[90] See id. at 67–75.

Court's Statute).[91] He asserted that, despite Croatia's pleadings to the contrary, the Court was required to undertake a *de novo* review of this matter, unfettered by *res judicata* concerns.[92] Realizing that the key weakness in Serbia's case was FRY's April 1992 Declaration, purporting to be bound by SFRY's previous international obligations (including, presumably, the Genocide Convention), Várady resorted to, first, a technical argument based on the fact that the declaration was not (properly speaking) a depositary action, and, second, that, in any event, FRY's move was objected to by Croatia and other UN members.[93] Moreover, Professor Várady pleaded before the Court,[94] jurisdiction could not be saved under an expansive reading of Statute article 35(1), whether or not the Court had been earlier seized of the matter, under the principles enunciated in the *Mavrommatis Palestine Concessions* case. Finally, Várady took aim in his pleadings to a novel argument raised by one of Croatia's counsel, Professor James Crawford, asserting that the article 10 of the International Law Commission's Articles on State Responsibility—concerning the imputability of acts of successful insurrectionary movements or *in statu nascendi*—was dispositive as to the question of the Court's jurisdiction *ratione temporis*.[95] In his concluding submissions,[96] Professor Várady returned to his theme of a search for consistency in the Court's rulings, and made a vigorous plea for the Court to deny jurisdiction in the Croatia case, if for no other reason than to square-the-circle with its prior holdings in the *Legality of Use of Force* cases.[97]

In introducing some "preliminary observations"[98] for its holdings, the Court emphasized that while jurisdiction *ratione personae* and lack of access to the Court were discrete and separate inquiries, the Court was free to decide the order in which to take up such matters,[99] which were to

---

[91] See I.C.J. Verbatim Record, May 26, 2008, I.C.J. Doc. CR 2008/8, at 15–21, 42–53.

[92] See I.C.J. Verbatim Record, May 29, 2008, I.C.J. Doc. CR 2008/12, at 8–9.

[93] See I.C.J. Verbatim Record, May 26, 2008, I.C.J. Doc. CR 2008/9, at 34–38.

[94] See I.C.J. Verbatim Record, May 29, 2008, I.C.J. Doc. CR 2008/12, at 13–22 (discussing P.C.I.J. (ser. A) No. 2 (1924)).

[95] Id. at 53–58.

[96] Id. at 62–67.

[97] Id. at 65 (¶ 20) ("The *Legality of Use of Force* cases belong to the new period in which the Court had the benefit of conclusive clarifications. Our present case—and all decisions to be taken in this case—belong to this new period.").

[98] Croatia Preliminary Objections, 2008 I.C.J. ___, at ¶ 65 (Preliminary Objections) (Judgment of Nov. 18).

[99] See id. ¶¶ 66–68.

be reviewed *de novo*.[100] On the question of Serbia's access to the Court under Statute article 35(1), the Court finally grasped the nettle of whether, because Croatia's application was instituted on July 2, 1999, instead of on or after November 2, 2000 (when Serbia became a party to the Statute), it should be dismissed. In short, the Court had to confront its consistent jurisprudence[101] that jurisdictional facts are assessed on the date of the institution of the proceeding, and not later. But, the Court noted, it "like its predecessor, has also shown realism and flexibility in certain situations in which the conditions governing the Court's jurisdiction were not fully satisfied when proceedings were initiated but were subsequently satisfied, before the Court ruled on its jurisdiction."[102] Relying on the so-called "*Mavrommatis* doctrine" of constructive satisfaction and cure of jurisdictional defects,[103] the Court indicated that it could not

> accept Serbia's argument that when the defect is that one party does not have access to the Court, it is so fatal that it can in no case be cured by a subsequent event in the course of the proceedings, for example when that party acquires the status of party to the Statute of the Court which it initially lacked.... it is not apparent why the arguments based on the sound administration of justice which underpin the *Mavrommatis* case jurisprudence cannot also have a bearing in a case such as the present one. It would not be in the interests of justice to oblige the Applicant, if it wishes to pursue its claims, to initiate fresh proceedings. In this respect it is of no importance which condition was unmet at the date the proceedings were instituted, and thereby prevented the Court at that time from exercising its jurisdiction, once it has been fulfilled subsequently.[104]

The Court also found that this conclusion was justified "by particular considerations relevant to" the cases,[105] including the timing of the filings and submissions.[106]

---

[100] See id. ¶¶ 69.

[101] See id. ¶ 79 (collecting cases to that effect).

[102] See id. ¶ 81.

[103] See id. ¶ 84. See also id. ¶ 82 (discussing Mavrommatis, Certain German Interests in Polish Upper Silesia, Northern Cameroons, and Military and Paramilitary Activities in and Against Nicaragua cases).

[104] Id. at ¶ 87. For a critique of the application of the Mavrommatis doctrine, see Separate Opinion of Judge Vice-President al-Khasawneh, at 2; Joint Declaration of Judges Ranjeva, Shi, Koroma & Parra-Aranguren, at 3–4 (¶¶ 6–10); Dissenting Opinion of Judge Ranjeva, at 8–10 (¶¶ 27–35); Dissenting Opinion of Judge Owada, at 4–13 (¶¶ 8–27); Separate Opinion of Judge Abraham, at 14–15 (¶ 51); Dissenting Opinion of Judge *ad hoc* Kreća, at 23–26 (¶¶ 78–88).

[105] Croatia Preliminary Objections, at ¶ 89.

The Court then turned to issues of jurisdiction *ratione materiae* under article IX of the Genocide Convention. As to be expected, the Court approvingly cited[107] FRY's April 7, 1992 Declaration and a diplomatic note filed before the UN on April 27, 1992, evincing an intent to assert that it was the "sole continuing State" arising out of the former Socialist Federal Republic of Yugoslavia.[108] "There can be no doubt," the Court noted, "from the subsequent conduct of those charged with the affairs of the FRY, that the declaration was regarded by the State as made on its behalf, and the commitments contained in it were endorsed and accepted by the FRY."[109] Responding to Serbia's arguments that neither the 1992 Declaration nor the diplomatic note was sufficiently specific as a treaty action in relation to FRY's party-status under the Genocide Convention, the Court concluded that such "need not comply with all formal requirements,"[110] and the Vienna Convention on State Succession allows for a "notification of succession" to be any "notification, however framed or named, made by a successor State expressing its consent to be bound by the treaty."[111]

The Court also brushed aside Serbia's argument—that the 1992 Declaration and diplomatic note could not have been legally effective because FRY was not then a UN member, as required by article XI of the Genocide Convention—by observing that article XI does not speak to a "continuation of, or succession to, the treaty rights and obligations of a predecessor State, in the manner and on the conditions recognized in international law."[112] The Court thus concluded that it had jurisdiction over Serbia *ratione materiae* under the Genocide Convention, and that Serbia had proper access to the Court.[113] That was essentially the substance of the Court's judgment on Serbia's preliminary objections in the Croatia case.[114]

---

[106] See id. ¶¶ 89–90. For a critique of Croatia's position as to Serbia's status, see Joint Declaration of Judges Ranjeva, Shi, Koroma & Parra-Aranguren, at 5–6 (¶¶ 13–14).

[107] Croatia Preliminary Objections, at ¶¶ 98 & 99.

[108] Id. ¶ 100. For criticism of the Court's reliance on these sources, see Joint Declaration of Judges Ranjeva, Shi, Koroma & Parra-Aranguren, at 6–7 (¶¶ 17).

[109] Croatia Preliminary Objections, ¶ 107 (cross-referencing ¶¶ 114 & 115).

[110] Id. ¶ 110.

[111] Vienna Convention on State Succession, supra note 86, art. 2(g).

[112] Croatia Preliminary Objections, 2008 I.C.J. ___, at ¶ 113 (Preliminary Objections) (Judgment of Nov. 18). See also Separate Opinion of Judge Tomka, at 1–6 (¶¶ 1–15); Dissenting Opinion of Judge *ad hoc* Kreća, at 36–51 (¶¶ 120–166).

[113] Croatia Preliminary Objections, ¶¶ 118–19.

[114] Inasmuch as the Court addressed Serbia's arguments as to jurisdiction *ratione temporis*, see id. ¶¶ 120–26, it deferred a decision to the merits phase of the case. See id. ¶¶ 127–

The Court's judgment on preliminary objections in the Croatia case thus, in many respects, perpetuated the conflict in jurisprudence that the ICJ has generated regarding Yugoslavia's status as a UN member and as a party to the Genocide Convention. The Court's extensive reliance on the *Mavrommatis* doctrine has the potential to revolutionize the ICJ's jurisdictional practices by replacing the pre-existing focus on jurisdictional facts as of the date of application with a much more flexible approach allowing for subsequent cure or remedy of jurisdictional defects. Whether the Court will deploy this doctrine selectively, in situations where it simply desires to grant jurisdiction without respect to other considerations, remains to be seen.

V

Assessing an advocate's success has to be more than tallying a won-loss record before any particular court. Obviously, if that standard were applied to the matters that Professor Várady briefed and pled before the International Court of Justice, one might come away with the impression that his advocacy had little impact on that tribunal and on the wider course of international legal proceedings. That would be quite mistaken, for a number of reasons.

First, one must take into account the context of the advocate's role and position in a particular litigation—the "brief" as a British barrister would put it. To put it mildly, to represent FRY (and then Serbia) in the genocide cases brought by Bosnia and Croatia raised delicate issues of professional responsibility. Professor Várady was always careful to confine his role to dealing with the threshold procedural and jurisdictional questions raised in these cases. His brief was to advocate a significant position of principal in any international adjudication: that jurisdiction, in all its respects, was properly vested in the relevant tribunal. All proceedings before the ICJ still are premised on the notion of the mutual consent of the State contestants, somehow manifested. The very legitimacy and authority of the Court depends on that principle, and no one could possibly object to a State advancing whatever arguments are necessary and proper to test the limits of the Court's jurisdiction, and to definitively circumscribe them. To criticize an advocate for making submissions that demand an international tribunal

30. The Court also rejected Serbia's objections as to Croatia's pled relief in relation to submission of persons to trial, return of cultural property, and provision of information on missing Croatian citizens. See id. ¶¶ 131–45.

to justify its exercise of jurisdiction over a sovereign State would be to profoundly misunderstand the international legal system. Whether one may dislike or condemn the substantive positions or policies of the State concerned should be irrelevant to the important points of process implicated in any jurisdictional set of inquiries that an international tribunal be required to address.

Second, one should consider the role of an advocate as much to frame issues for a court's resolution than to expect a particular outcome. In this respect, Professor Várady's advocacy before the ICJ will have broad implications for the Court's future procedural and jurisdictional practices. One such area will be for requests for revision under Statute article 61. Given the way that the Court rejected FRY's request for revision—and the tantalizing suggestion (made by some members of the Court in their individual capacities) that FRY should have made an article 60 request to "construe" the July 11, 1996 judgments as to its "meaning or scope"—it may be unlikely that we shall see another revision request again. In short, if FRY could not persuade the Court that its status as a UN member was not a new "fact," within the meaning of article 61, it may be that no party will be able to make that showing for future revision requests.

Another area that Professor Várady's advocacy will surely influence is how the Court's jurisprudence of *res judicata* for jurisdictional holdings is construed in the future. The ICJ's holding, in the Bosnian merits judgment, may well be considered a high-water mark for the Court's judicial activism and its espousal of a robust theory of its own judicial supremacy. The idea that, in the Court's own language, an erroneous jurisdictional holding "must remain final, even if it is in apparent contradiction to reality,"[115] is not one calculated to inspire much faith in the Court, even among those who value finality and repose in international judicial actions.

The last area that Professor Várady's written and oral advocacy before the ICJ will be remembered as being influential was in structuring the substantive argument on jurisdiction in the Croatian preliminary objections phase. At long last, after being liberated from the procedural shackles of revision and *res judicata*, Várady was finally able to present the substance of Serbia's jurisdictional objections based on matters of *ratione personae*, *materiae* and *temporis* (under the Genocide Convention and principles of State succession). The Court's reliance on the *Mavrommatis* doctrine to cure ostensible jurisdictional defects will assuredly be re-

[115] Bosnian Merits, at ¶ 120.

garded as its boldest move in these cases, and the one most likely to affect the course of future proceedings. But, in addition, the Court's rulings as to the significance of FRY statements as to continuity of succession and the proper construction of Genocide Convention article XI may also have broad implications in other cases where jurisdiction is premised on compromissory clauses, especially those in significant human rights instruments.

For an advocate to have had a hand in influencing the Court's direction for any *one* of these procedural and jurisdictional questions would certainly be noteworthy. But for Professor Várady to have had a direct stake in *all three* of these baskets of issues was virtually unprecedented in the recent annals of advocacy before the ICJ. And that leads me to a final consideration for assessing his advocacy before the Court, the one mentioned in the opening words of this contribution. That is the particular style and technique conveyed by the scholar-advocate in international proceedings. While it is relatively common for professors of public international law to make appearances as "counsel and advocates" before the Court, such representations by those specialized in private international law and international commercial arbitration have been quite rare[116] and certainly never as the State-appointed "agent" who manages the litigation.[117] Várady's practical experience in the litigation of private international commercial disputes undoubtedly influenced the practical decisions he was obliged to make in directing the litigation strategy for FRY and Serbia in these cases.

In his advocacy before the ICJ, Professor Tibor Várady exhibited the highest professional standards and the greatest fidelity to the values of international justice. This modest contribution has sought to memorialize these efforts, and place them in a broader context of the World Court's repertory of practice.

[116] M. Johannes Offerhaus, Professor of Private International Law at the University of Amsterdam, was chosen as a Judge *ad hoc* in the Case Concerning the Application of the Convention of 1902 Governing the Guardianship of Infants (Netherlands v. Sweden), 1958 I.C.J. 55. It is not clear that any similarly-chaired professor has appeared as an advocate before the Court.

[117] See ICJ Statute, supra note 22, art. 42(1) ("The parties shall be represented by agents.").

From “Real Seat” to “Legal Seat”: Germany’s Private International Company Law Revolution

PETER BEHRENS

Private international law (conflicts of law) has always ranked high on Tibor Várady’s agenda, not only in his capacity as an internationally recognized scholar but also as a renowned arbitral practitioner. It may therefore not be improper to contribute to this *Festschrift* in his honor an overview of the remarkable development of German private international law of companies away from the traditional “real seat doctrine” (which subjects companies to the law of the place of central administration) towards the “incorporation doctrine” (which subjects companies to the law of the place determined as their registered office or “legal seat” in the memorandum or articles of association). This development was triggered by the recent jurisprudence of the European Court of Justice (ECJ) on the freedom of establishment of companies, but it goes far beyond what is required to make German private international law of companies compatible with Community law. A draft bill on the private international law of companies published on 7 January 2008 by the German Ministry of Justice[1] is about to turn the whole system upside down. It represents nothing less than a revolution. In order to appreciate the full significance of this development, we shall first describe the traditional approach followed especially by German courts in order to determine the “proper law” applicable to companies (I.). We shall then analyse the impact of ECJ jurisprudence on German private international law of companies (II.), and give an overview of the ministerial draft bill on private international law of companies which is based on a totally new approach (III.). We shall finally draw some conclusions from a European perspective (IV.).

---

[1] Available at http://www.bmj.bund.de/files/-/2751/RefE.

I. The Traditional Approach

The traditional approach in German private international law of companies was based on the "real seat doctrine" according to which the "proper law" of a company, that is, the national rules of company law applicable to a specific company, was determined by the place where the "real seat" of the company was located.[2] It was the company law of this state which determined the existence, the legal status, the governance structure, the membership, the liability regime as well as the dissolution and the winding-up of a company. So, in order to be recognized as a separate legal entity with legal capacity, a company had to be validly incorporated in the "real seat" state. In other words, the place of incorporation and the "real seat" had to coincide within one and the same state. In case of a divergence of the place of incorporation and the "real seat," the company would not have been considered incorporated under the "proper law."

The legal consequences thereof used to be quite drastic: The company was considered non-existent; it was not merely considered null and void, but iiterally a "nothing" (*nullum*). A company which had its "real seat" abroad but which had nevertheless been incorporated (registered) in Germany had to be liquidated and de-registered. A foreign company incorporated abroad which had its "real seat" in Germany was not "recognized." Therefore, irrespective of its legal status in the state of incorporation, it could not acquire rights and obligations, sue or be sued in court. Its assets were rather considered to be owned by the shareholders who were consequently held jointly and severally liable for the company's debts. Strictly speaking, German courts did not really apply German company law to foreign companies due to their domestic "real seat"; rather they applied no company law at all.

---

[2] The "real seat" doctrine had been adopted by the Reichsgericht [Imperial Court] from the very beginning of the 20th century already; see, e.g., the landmark decision of the Reichsgericht (RG) published in the official court reports in private law matters RGZ, Vol. 117, p. 215, 217. After World War II, the successor of the Reichsgericht, the Bundesgerichtshof [Federal Court] followed the same doctrine; see the leading case published in the official court reports in private law matters BGHZ, Vol. 97, p. 269, 272. The "real seat" doctrine was equally supported by a large majority of legal writers: see for a full account of this approach, including comprehensive references, Kindler, in *Münchener Kommentar zum Bürgerlichen Gesetzbuch* [Munich Commentary on the Civil Code], Vol. 11: *Internationales Wirtschaftsrecht* [International Economic Law], Article 50-245 EGBGB (Einführungsgesetz zum Bürgerlichen Gesetzbuch [Law introducing the Civil Code]), 4th ed. 2005, nos. 5 and 400–405; Kegel/Schurig, *Internationales Privatrecht* [Private International Law], 9th ed. 2004, § 17 II 1.

The definition of the "real seat" of a company has always met with some difficulties.[3] Various criteria have been suggested for its localization: the place of effective management, the place where the most important decisions are taken, the place where board meetings (or shareholders' meetings) are held, the principal place of business. The Federal Court (BGH), in a landmark decision, has not used any of these far from unequivocal criteria. Instead it has defined the "real seat" as the place where the fundamental decisions of the management are effectively transformed into day-to-day business transactions.[4] The major advantage of this definition appears, if it is applied to groups of companies (parent-subsidiary relationships). Whereas many of the other criteria mentioned may lead to subjecting subsidiaries to the law of their parent company (which, in light of the legal consequences for multinational groups of companies would be disastrous, because subsidiaries could not be incorporated outside the home state of the parent company), the Federal Court's (BGH) definition allows for the presumption that subsidiaries, even if controlled by their parent companies, do have a "real seat" of their own, because the fundamental decisions taken at the level of the parent company are always implemented at the level of the subsidiary companies.

The adoption of the "real seat" doctrine has always been justified by the protection of creditors', minority shareholders', employees' and even the state's interests.[5] All these interests have been said to gravitate around the place where the company's central management is located or, according to the Federal Court's (BGH) definition of the "real seat," where the fundamental management decisions are transformed into day-to-day business transactions. However, the more the business transactions of companies operating in a globalised environment grow into international dimensions, the less this assumption really holds. States' and employees' interests should not be taken into account in this context, because they are not normally protected by company laws in the first place. Their protection is a matter of public law and labor law rules respectively which are subject to conflicts of law rules of their own. But also shareholders' interests should not matter here, because minority shareholders may protect them-

---

[3] See Kindler (footnote 2), nos. 434 et seq.

[4] BGHZ, Vol. 97, p. 269, 272.

[5] See for a critical account of these justifications Behrens, "Internationales Gesellschaftsrecht" [Private international law of companies], in Ulmer/Habersack/Winter, *GmbHG – Großkommentar* [Commentary on the Limited Liability Companies Act], 2005, Einleitung B [Introduction B], nos. B 15–B 27.

selves by simply staying away from investing in a company that has its "real seat" in a state different from the state of incorporation. So what may matter at all, are creditors' interests which, however, in a globalized economic environment are no longer concentrated within the state of incorporation of the company.

II. The Impact of European Community Law on the Use of Connecting Factors

National law, including private international law, must be compatible with European Community law. Due to the principle of precedence of Community law over Member States' laws, national rules which are incompatible with Community law cannot be applied by national courts or governmental agencies. The "real seat" doctrine is nothing but a national rule of private international company law. However, for more then three decades after the entering into force of the Rome-Treaty, its compatibility with Community law had never been questioned. It was not before 1988 that it finally became a prominent issue whether the "real seat" doctrine might in fact be incompatible with the freedom of establishment of companies as granted in Article 58 EC-Treaty [today Article 48 EC].[6] That year, the ECJ in its *Daily Mail* judgment,[7] took the opportunity to address this question for the first time, even though there was no compelling reason for the Court to do so. At issue was a restriction imposed by British tax law upon a "real seat" transfer by the *Daily Mail and General Trust plc* from the UK to the Netherlands without giving up the registered office ("legal seat") of the company in England where it had been incorporated. Instead of limiting itself to the tax issue, the ECJ jumped on the question whether the freedom of establishment allowed a company to change its "real seat" in a way that would result in a divergence of the place of central management ("real seat") and the place of incorporation (determined by its registered office, i.e., its "legal seat"). The answer given by the ECJ was squarely negative:

---

[6] See for one of the very first analyses of this problem Behrens, "Niederlassungsfreiheit und internationales Gesellschaftsrecht" [Freedom of establishment and private international law of companies], *Rabels Zeitschrift 52* (1988) 498–525 [Contribution in honor of *Ulrich Drobnig's* 60th birthday], arguing that the "real seat" doctrine was in fact incompatible with Community law.

[7] ECJ Case 81/87 *Daily Mail* [1988] ECR 5483.

> Articles 52 and 58 of the Treaty [now Articles 43 and 48 EC] cannot be interpreted as conferring on companies incorporated under the law of a Member State a right to transfer their central management and control and their central administration to another Member state while retaining their status as companies incorporated under the legislation of the first Member State.

This holding implied that Member States were considered to be free to opt for the "real seat" doctrine as the relevant conflicts of law rule for companies without violating the EC-Treaty. The Court's position appeared, however, barely compatible with the wording of Article 58 [now Article 48] of the EC-Treaty. This provision reads as follows:

> Companies or firms formed in accordance with the law of a Member State and having their registered office, central administration or principal place of business within the Community shall, for the purposes of this Chapter, be treated in the same way as natural persons who are nationals of Member States.

This text makes it abundantly clear that for a company to be able to avail itself of the freedom of establishment, it must have been validly incorporated in one of the Member States (which presupposes that the company has its registered office or "legal seat" within the Member State of incorporation) *and* it must have its registered office, central administration *or* principal place of business *within the Community* (but not necessarily within the Member State of incorporation, except, of course, for the registered office). In other words: Article 48 EC allows for a localisation of the "real seat" and the "legal seat" in different Member States.

This reading is supported by Article 43 EC which defines the contents of the freedom of establishment for natural persons. The 2nd paragraph of this provision clearly provides as follows:

> Freedom of establishment shall include the right to take up and pursue activities as self employed persons and to set up and manage undertakings …

"Set up and manage undertakings" in this context clearly means that nationals of any Member State are entitled to establish their entrepreneurial headquarters (i.e., primary establishment) in any other Member State, since "the setting up of agencies, branches or subsidiaries" (i.e., secondary establishments) is already expressly covered by the 1st paragraph of Article 43 EC. If, according to Article 48 EC, companies validly incorporated in a Member State shall have the same rights as nationals of Member States, they are clearly also entitled to set up their headquarters (i.e., their "real seat") in any Member State other than the Member State of incorporation.

It took, however, more than ten years until the ECJ finally got a chance to clarify its position in the *Centros* case.[8] At issue was an application by an English private company for the registration of a branch in Denmark. The registration was made dependent upon the fulfilment of a minimum capital requirement contained in Danish company law on the grounds that the English company did exclusively business in Denmark. The ECJ held:

> (21) Where it is the practice of a Member State, in certain circumstances, to refuse to register a branch of a company having its registered office in another Member State, the result is that companies formed in accordance with the law of that other Members State are prevented from exercising the freedom of establishment conferred on them by Articles 52 and 58 of the Treaty.
>
> (22) Consequently, that practice constitutes an obstacle to the exercise of the freedoms guaranteed by those provisions.

Most observers had difficulties to immediately appreciate the impact of this judgment on the "real seat" doctrine as applied in private international law of companies. In the context of Community law, the establishment of the English private company in Denmark had to be regarded as a "branch". In the context of private international law of companies, however, it was in fact the "real seat" of the company, because it did business exclusively in Denmark. Consequently, the Danish authorities applied the minimum capital requirement derived from Danish company law to the English company on the basis of the company's "real seat" in Denmark. Since this was held to be incompatible with Community law, it was only logical to conclude, that a Member State is generally prevented from applying its domestic company law to a company validly incorporated in another Member State merely on the grounds that the "real seat" of such company is located within that Member State.

The correctness of this conclusion was clearly supported by the ECJ's judgment in the *Inspire Art* case.[9] Here the compatibility with Community law of a Dutch statute targeting "pseudo-foreign companies" (i.e., foreign companies doing exclusively business in the Netherlands) was at issue. According to this statute, certain Dutch company law rules (relating especially to minimum capital and directors' liability) were imposed upon a

---

[8] ECJ Case C-212/97 *Centros* [1999] ECR I-1459.

[9] ECJ Case C-167/01 *Inspire Art* [2003] ECR I-10155.

private company validly incorporated in England on the grounds that is was doing business exclusively in the Netherlands. The ECJ made it abundantly clear that the Dutch statute was incompatible with Community law. The Court held

> (105) [...] that Articles 43 EC and 48 EC preclude national legislation such as [the Dutch statute] which imposes on the exercise of freedom of secondary establishment in that State by a company formed in accordance with the law of another Member State certain conditions provided for in domestic law in respect of company formation relating to minimum capital and directors' liability. The reasons for which the company was formed in that other Member State, and the fact that it carries on its activities exclusively or almost exclusively in the Member State of establishment, do not deprive it of the right to invoke the freedom of establishment guaranteed by the Treaty, [...].

In the *Überseering* case,[10] the ECJ had to decide whether a transfer of a company's "real seat" from the Member State of incorporation (the Netherlands) to another Member State (Germany) allowed the latter Member State to subject the company to its domestic company laws to the effect that the foreign company was no longer "recognized" as a legal entity on the grounds that it could no longer be considered to have been incorporated under its "proper law" (even though the company continued to exist as a validly incorporated company within the Member State of incorporation). The ECJ held that

> (82) [...] the refusal by a host Member State ('B') to recognise the legal capacity of a company formed in accordance with the law of another Member State ('A') in which it has its registered office on the ground, in particular, that the company moved its actual centre of administration to Member State B [...], with the result that the company cannot, in Member State B, bring legal proceedings to defend rights under a contract unless it is reincorporated under the law of Member State B, constitutes a restriction on freedom of establishment which is, in principle, incompatible with Articles 43 EC and 48 EC.

This line of judgments makes it crystal clear, that Member States of the EU are no longer able to rely on the "real seat" doctrine in order to justify the application of their domestic company laws to foreign companies validly incorporated in another Member State. According to the ECJ's jurisprudence, a potential justification of the "real seat" doctrine can only be based on "overriding requirements relating to the general interest," provided it meets the proportionality test. No such justification was accepted

[10] ECJ Case C-208/00 *Überseering* [2002] ECR I-9919.

by the ECJ in the cases mentioned above. In particular, the Court has always rejected justifications based on considerations of creditor protection or abuse of the freedom of establishment.

The impact of Community law on Member States' private international law of companies is therefore quite drastic. Nevertheless, it is important to understand that the ECJ has not considered the "real seat" doctrine to be incompatible with Community law under all circumstances. The Court has decided that a Member State may, on the basis of the "real seat" doctrine, require a company incorporated domestically to also have a domestic "real seat" and threaten the dissolution and winding-up of the company in case it moves its "real seat" out of the Member State of incorporation. This question was put before the Court due to a request for a preliminary ruling submitted to the ECJ by the Court of Appeal of Szeged (Hungary) in the *Cartesio* case.[11]

This case concerned a limited partnership that seeked to transfer its operational headquarters from Hungary to Italy, but wished to remain registered in Hungary, so that its legal status continued to be governed by Hungarian law. However, the commercial court, in the exercise of its task of maintaining the commercial register, refused to enter the new address in the local register on the ground that the transfer was not possible under Hungarian law. It held that a firm that wishes to transfer its operational headquarters to another Member State must first be wound up in Hungary and then reconstituted under the law of that Member State. In the framework of the appeal proceedings, the Court of Appeal of Szeged (Hungary) has asked the ECJ for guidance in order to determine whether the relevant Hungarian legislation is compatible with the right to freedom of establishment.

The Advocate General squarely suggested to the Court that Articles 43 EC and 48 EC preclude national rules which make it impossible for a company constituted under national law to transfer its operational headquarters to another Member State. The ECJ did not follow the Advocate General's recommendation. Rather the Court, in its decision of 16 December 2008, approved of the compatibility of the Hungarian law based on the "real seat" doctrine with Community law and held that Member States are free to determine the connecting factor that links a domestic company to the domestic legal order.

In sum, as a matter of Community law, Member States are no longer free to shape their private international law rules applied to companies as they feel fit. They can no longer rely on the "real seat" doctrine as far as

---

[11] ECJ Case C-210/06 *Cartesio*, not yet published.

foreign companies are concerned which have been incorporated under the laws of another Member State. A domestic "real seat" can no longer be the legal basis for applying domestic company law as the "proper law." On the other hand, according to the *Cartesio* judgment, the "real seat" doctrine may continue to be applied to domestic companies. Member States are in any case not bound by Community law vis-à-vis states outside the Community. Consequently, the "real seat" doctrine may still be applied to foreign companies incorporated outside the Community but having their "real seat" within a Member State as well as to domestic companies having their "real seat" outside the Community, unless Member States are bound by bilateral treaties with third states to apply the "incorporation doctrine." A prominent example is the German–American Treaty of Friendship, Commerce and Shipping of 1954 in which the Federal Republic of Germany has committed itself to accept the application of the "incorporation doctrine" to companies incorporated in the United States.[12]

III. Towards a New Approach

It is highly questionable whether Member States are well advised if they continue to cling to the "real seat" doctrine even to the extent that Community law leaves them the freedom to do so. The private international law of companies is already compartmentalized to a considerable degree by the fact that distinctions are necessary between intra-Community relations, relations with third states regulated by bilateral treaties and relations with third states where no such treaties do exist. Conflicts of law rules for companies may vary accordingly. Following different approaches in different contexts may, however, give rise to much legal uncertainty and confusion. It is to be welcomed therefore that the German Ministry of Justice has commissioned a report on the reform of private international law of companies which was submitted to the ministry in 2006 by a special working group of experts.[13] On the basis of this report, the Ministry has presented its draft bill[14] which, once enacted, will for the first time

---

[12] See Article XXV(5) of the Treaty, Bundesgesetzblatt 1956 II 488.

[13] See Sonnenberger (ed.), *Vorschläge und Berichte zur Reform des europäischen und deutschen internationalen Gesellschaftsrechts* [Proposals and Reports on the reform of the European and German private international law of companies], 2007; an English version of the working group's legislative proposal can be found at pp. 65–122. See also *Sonnenberger/Bauer*, [2006] Recht der internationalen Wirtschaft (RIW), Beilage zu Heft 4.

[14] See footnote 1.

codify the German private international law rules for companies in a way which can only be regarded as revolutionary, because it replaces the "real seat doctrine" by the "incorporation doctrine."

The ministerial draft bill envisages an amendment of the private international law provisions contained in the German law introducing the Civil Code (Einführungsgesetz zum Bürgerlichen Gesetzbuch – EGBGB) by adding four new provisions: Article 10 EGBGB will contain the basic rule connecting the "proper law" of companies to the place of registration or the law of incorporation; Article 10a EGBGB will deal with international corporate restructurings (mergers, divisions, transfers of assets, changes of legal form), Article 10b EGBGB addresses international seat transfers, Article 11 (6) EGBGB deals with formal requirements for certain transactions, and Article 12 (2)–(3) EGBGB is about the protection of *bona fide* third parties. In the following, these new rules shall be analyzed in more detail.

III. 1. The Basic Conflicts of Law Rule

Article 10 EGBGB [as translated into English by the author] provides as follows:

> (1) Companies and firms[15] as well as associations and legal persons governed by private law are subject to the law of the state where they are registered in a public register. If they are not or have not yet been registered in a public register, they shall be subject to the law of the state under whose law they are organized.
>
> (2) The law applicable according to section 1 governs in particular
>
> 1. the legal nature, the legal capacity and the powers to act,
> 2. the formation and the dissolution,
> 3. the name and the firm name,
> 4. the organizational and financial constitution,
> 5. the powers of representation of the organs,
> 6. the acquisition and the loss of membership and the associated rights and obligations,
> 7. the liability of the company, firm, association or legal person as well as the liability of its members and of the members of its organs for debts of the company, firm, association or legal person,
> 8. the liability arising from the breach of obligations imposed by the law of companies, firms, associations or legal persons.

[15] The German term "Gesellschaft" has no equivalent in English; "companies and firms" are the terms used in Article 48 EC.

It must be emphasized at the outset that the ministerial draft bill in defining its scope *ratione personae* is intended to come as close as possible to Article 48 (2) EC-Treaty which defines "companies and firms" to mean "companies or firms constituted under civil or commercial law, including cooperative societies, and other legal persons governed by public or private law, save for those which are non-profit-making." The ministerial draft bill does, however, not include legal persons governed by public law. On the other hand, different from Article 48 (2) EC-Treaty, it covers not only entities which are profit-making, but also those which are not.

Article 10 (1) EGBGB incorporates the "incorporation" doctrine. The most straightforward application of this doctrine is contained in the second sentence of Article 10 (1) EGBGB where reference is made to "the law of the state according to which [a company is] organized" (i.e., incorporated). In case of companies, the application of this rule is practically limited to pre-incorporation companies which are intended to be (and in fact are required to be) registered in a public register but whose registration has "not yet" been completed. Then the law chosen by the founding shareholders for the incorporation of the company will be the "proper law" of that company. However, this law will remain to be the "proper law" of the company once the formation of the company is completed by its registration in a public register. This is so, because in order to be registered in a national public register and to emerge as a separate legal entity, a company must always have been formed according to the laws of the state to whose register the founding shareholders have applied for registration of the company. Consequently, the "incorporation doctrine" transpires even from the first sentence of Article 10 (1) EGBGB.

What is more, the jurisdiction of a public register is in principle determined by the registered office (i.e., the "legal seat") of a company as defined in its memorandum or articles of association. The location of the company's "legal seat" therefore determines the place of registration and at the same time the law according to which a company must be formed. In other words: Whether the place of registration in a public register or the law of incorporation is used as the connecting factor for the determination of the "proper law" of a company, in the end it is always the location of its "legal seat" which is controlling. It follows, that the ministerial draft bill on private international law of companies will move the German conflicts of law approach entirely away from using the "real seat" towards using the "legal seat" as the ultimate connecting factor for the determination of the "proper law" of companies. Nevertheless, the wording of Article 10

(1) EGBGB deliberately favors, for registered companies, the place of registration as the connecting factor, because this place is, in principle, most easily verifiable. Legal certainty is thereby enhanced.

The new Article 12 (3) EGBGB [as translated into English by the author] adds the following caveat in favor of *bona fide* third parties:

> (3) If a company, firm, association or legal person acts under the law of a state other than the one applicable according to Article 10, third parties who did not know or could not have been aware of the law applicable according to Article 10 may invoke this other law."

Consequently, a law different from the law of incorporation may be exceptionally applied vis-à-vis third parties to whom a company has misrepresented itself as an entity that has been incorporated under a different law.

It must be emphasized that, according to Article 10 (1) EGBGB no distinction is being made between companies incorporated in one of the Member States of the European Union, on the one hand, and companies incorporated outside the European Union, on the other. The new basic conflicts of law rule is designed to be of universal application. It is in line not only with the requirements of European Community law, but also with a large number of bilateral treaties in which the Federal Republic of Germany has granted the right of establishment of foreign companies and bound itself to the principles of non-discrimination and most-favoured nation treatment of foreign companies. The draft bill therefore contributes considerably to the simplification of private international law of companies, a legal field that is otherwise known for its enormous complexities.

III. 2. The Scope of Application of the Basic Rule

Naturally, the conflicts of law rule laid down in Article 10 (1) EGBGB applies to all matters that may be characterized as company law matters. Nevertheless, Article 10 (2) EGBGB contains a non-exhaustive list of issues which are expressly characterised as company law issues governed by the "proper law" of companies (the law of incorporation) as determined by the conflicts of law rule contained in Article 10 (1) EGBGB. Non-company law issues may be subject, according to their proper characterization, to the conflicts of law rules for contracts, torts, property, civil procedure, insolvency proceedings etc. The list contained in Article 10 (2) EGBGB is designed to provide as much legal certainty as possible.

Two well established principles transpire immediately from the wording of Article 10 (2) EGBGB: Firstly, German private international company law makes no distinction between the "recognition" of (foreign) companies and the determination of their valid incorporation according to the "proper law" to which they are subject; the existence of a company as a separate legal entity is simply regarded as a company law issue to be determined according to the "proper law" of companies (the law of incorporation) just as any other company law issue. Secondly, German private international law of companies does not distinguish between "internal" and "external" company law matters; therefore, the authority of directors to bind the company vis-à-vis third parties is a matter subject to the same "proper law" of the company as the company's internal governance structure.

According to Article 10 (2) EGBGB, the legal character of a company is to be determined according to its "proper law" (the law of incorporation). This clearly implies that the term "company" is not limited to entities which are known as companies under German law (such as, e.g., the French société anonyme simplifiée [SAS] or the English limited liability partnership [LLP]). Similarly, the capacity of a company and the powers of its directors are determined by the "proper law" of companies (the law of incorporation). Foreign company laws may, however, limit the company's capacity and the directors' powers to the company's objects. Such limitations are then in principle recognized as part of the "proper law" of the foreign company (the law of incorporation).[16]

However, German private international law protects third parties relying on the absence of any limitation to a company's capacity or directors' powers to the same extent as they are protected in case of natural persons. Article 12 (1) EGBGB protects *bona fide* third parties in case they deal with a foreign natural person who's capacity to contract is limited according to her "personal law" (the law of her home state). The latter person cannot invoke such limitations against the other contracting party, if at the time the contract was entered into both parties were present in a state where no such limitations prevailed. The new Article 12 (2) EGBGB [as translated into English by the author] extends this protection of *bona fide* third parties to companies:

> (2) If a contract is entered into by a company, firm, association or legal person and the organ or the member of the organ of the company, firm, association or legal person as

---

[16] A company's capacity to sue or to be sued is a procedural question which is subject to the applicable procedural rules as determined by the *lex fori* principle.

> well as the other contracting party are present within the same state, section 1 applies mutatis mutandis to the capacity and the powers of the company, firm, association or legal person as well as to the authority of the organ or the member of the organ to represent.

Other issues that are subject to the "proper law" of companies (the law of incorporation) include, of course, the formation of the company and, in particular, the company's firm name. The protection of a company's firm name against passing off or other violations by other companies is, however, not a matter of company law and therefore subject to other conflicts of law rules. Furthermore, the internal governance structure of a company is subject to the "proper law" of companies (the law of incorporation), including the company's organs and their powers, their composition, the appointment and removal of their members, these members' rights and duties, their liability for violations of their duties, the passing of board resolutions etc. Also the external position of board members regarding their authority to represent the company is subject to the "proper law" of companies (the law of incorporation). In this context, Article 12 (2) EGBGB may again come into play for the protection of *bona fide* third parties against potential limitations of board members' authority to bind the company.

A special problem is presented by the typical German model of workers' co-determination on the board level. It is questionable whether it can be characterised as a company law matter in the strict sense. The model presupposes the existence of a two-tier board structure (management board / supervisory board) which is typical for German public companies but is also mandatory for limited liability companies which are subject to the co-determination regime. In large enterprises with more than 2,000 employees, 50% of the supervisory board members have to be elected workers' representatives. However, the application of this model is expressly limited to companies incorporated under German company law. Consequently, the application of the German co-determination law always coincides with the German law of incorporation of a company.

The application of the "proper law" of companies (the law of incorporation) also extends to the position of shareholders, their rights and obligations, shareholders resolutions as well as the protection of minority shareholders. The transfer of shares is not exclusively a matter of company law though. Only their transferability and certain preconditions for a transfer are subject to the "proper law" of companies (the law of incorporation); the transfer itself is subject to other laws such as the law of contract (sales), capital market law, securities regulation etc. Similarly, the "proper law" of companies (the law of incorporation) determines the legality of certain contracts between the company and its shareholders (or board members) or among the shareholders themselves (e.g., voting agreements), whereas the contractual agreements as such are subject to the "proper law" of contracts.

Another important element of company law is the company's financial structure. Capital requirements (especially minimum capital requirements), payment of contributions, protection of companies' capital, payment of dividends, the status of shareholder loans granted to the company, changes of the company's capital etc. are therefore clearly issues which are subject to the "proper law" of companies (the law of incorporation).

The liability regime is also an indispensable element of the legal nature of a company and therefore subject to the "proper law" of companies (law of incorporation). In principle, shareholders are, according to the concept of "limited liability," only liable towards the company for payment of their contributions, but not towards the company's creditors for payment of the company's debts. Whether or not it is possible under exceptional circumstances to pierce the corporate veil, is to be determined according to the "proper law" of companies (the law of incorporation). However, direct liabilities of shareholders or directors based on other grounds (e.g., torts) are not within the scope of Article 10 (2) EGBGB, unless such liabilities arise from violations of company law duties.

Contrary to the report submitted by the working group of experts,[17] the ministerial draft bill does not include accounting rules in the list contained in Article 10 (2) EGBGB. This is due to the fact that such rules are not only imposed by company laws but also to a considerable extent by capital market laws, securities regulations and special industries regulations (such as banking laws). The ministry therefore felt that the draft bill should not subject accounting rules to one uniform conflicts of law rule. However, even though the characterization of accounting rules is context dependent, including accounting rules in Article 10 (2) EGBGB would have clarified that at least accounting rules imposed by company laws are within the scope of the "proper law" of companies. It would not in any way pre-empt other conflicts of law rules applicable to accounting rules imposed by other laws than company laws.

Finally, formal requirements for certain company law transactions are not necessarily subject to the "proper law" of companies; in principle the

---

[17] See Article 10a (1) no. 9, in: *Sonnenberger* (footnote 13), at p. 73.

rule *locus regit actum* is applicable. However, according to German jurisprudence, formal requirements for transactions affecting a company's constitution are exclusively subject to the "proper law" of companies. This principle is restated in Article 11 (6) EGBGB of the ministerial draft bill.

III. 3. International Seat Transfers (Change of the "Proper Law")

In the past, international (cross-border) seat transfers were always confronted with serious legal problems. The transfer of the company's "legal seat" from the state of incorporation to another state leads necessarily to a change of the company's "proper law." According to the "real seat doctrine", a transfer of the company's headquarters would lead to the same result. German law has always disapproved of such transactions. The change of a company's "proper law" was held to be legally impossible. The transfer by a German company of its seat to a foreign state always led to the dissolution and winding up of the company in Germany. The reverse transfer by a foreign company of its seat into Germany was considered equally impossible, because the company could not save its continuity as a legal person; it had to be re-incorporated in Germany as a newly established German company.

The ECJ's jurisprudence on the freedom of establishment mentioned above has to some extent overcome the obstacles that stood in the way of cross-border seat transfers. In the *Überseering* case[18] the ECJ held that the transfer by a company incorporated in another Member State of its "real seat" into Germany cannot lead to a change of the "proper law" of the company (as the "real seat doctrine" would have it); rather the company must continue to be recognized in Germany as a foreign company duly formed under the laws of the foreign state of incorporation. Whether a "real seat" transfer from Germany to another Member State may lead to a change of the "proper law" of an initially German company and, consequently, to the dissolution and winding up of the company in Germany, has now been positively decided by the ECJ in the *Cartesio* case mentioned above.

It is also true, however, that a cross-border transfer of a company's "legal seat" will normally always lead to a change of its "proper law." Whether the freedom of establishment of companies granted in Article 48 EC requires that Member States refrain from preventing or hindering such transaction, is an issue that the ECJ also touched in the *Cartesio* case. The

[18] See footnote 10.

Court expressed in an *obiter dictum* the view that Article 48 applies to such transactions, provided that the target State allows them.

The change of a company's "proper law" (law of incorporation) clearly involves two separate legal aspects: a conflicts of law aspect and a substantive company law aspect. The conflicts of law aspect relates to the question as to what exactly triggers a change of the "proper law" of a company. The answer to this question is quite simple: It is the transfer of the relevant connecting factor (i.e., the company' seat) from the state of incorporation to another jurisdiction that triggers the change of the "proper law." The substantive aspect relates, on the one hand, to the registration of the company in the target state without the company being required to be newly incorporated in that state and, on the other hand, the de-registration in the original state of incorporation without dissolution and winding up of the company there. In order for such transactions to be possible, national company laws must provide for the proper legal rules. It is precisely the lack of such rules which has up to now been responsible for the impossibility of a change of a company's "proper law" by way of an international seat transfer.

Article 10b EGBGB as proposed in the ministerial draft bill on the private international law of companies limits itself strictly to the conflicts of law aspect. [As translated into English by the author] it provides as follows:

> If a company, firm, association or legal person is entered into a public register in another state or if the organisation of the company, firm, association or legal person is in a recognisable way subjected to the law of another state, the law applicable according to Article 10 changes, provided the original and the new law admit such change without dissolution and re-incorporation and if the preconditions of both laws are fulfilled.

This provision merely states that a change of the "proper law" of a company is possible and that it is implemented, in case of a registered company or firm, by way of re-registration in another state. Since the place of registration is generally determined by the "legal seat", this amounts to providing that a transfer of the "legal seat" from the state of incorporation to another state is possible, if the relevant preconditions are fulfilled. The provision is silent, however, as to what these "preconditions" may be.

In this respect, the preparatory report of the working group of experts has been much more explicit. The provision proposed in the report[19]

---

[19] See Article 10d, in: *Sonnenberger* (footnote 13), p. 74–75. In the interest of the reader, it may be worth reproducing the full text of this Article:

(1) A company registered in Germany and founded under German law may change the applicable company law by relocating the place of registration relevant under Article 10(2) to another

specifies all the preconditions that would have to be fulfilled by a company "emigrating" from or "immigrating" into Germany. These preconditions are designed to protect the interests of members who did not consent to the change of the company's "proper law" as well as the interests of third parties, especially creditors. Furthermore, the experts' report provides for the necessary co-ordination of the registration and deregistration of the company in the states involved.

The reluctance of the ministerial draft bill to include such detailed rules on the implementation of a change of the "proper law" is apparently due to the fact that the EC Commission was, until recently, working on the proposal of a 14th European company law Directive on cross-border seat transfers. This directive would have been designed to harmonize

Member State of the EU or EEA, without having to transfer its actual seat. The requirements for deletion from the German register shall be governed by German law. The requirements for registration in the new state of registration shall be governed by the law of that state. The validity of a change of the applicable law shall be conditional on fulfilment of the measures prescribed by German company law with a view to protecting the rights of third parties and of members who did not consent to the change of applicable law. Creditors shall be publicly informed of the forthcoming change of applicable company law and invited to state their claims.

(2) A registered company which was founded under the law of a Member State of the EU or of the EEA may change the company law applicable to it by relocating its place of registration under Article 10(2) to Germany, without having to transfer its actual seat. The requirements for registration in Germany shall be governed by German law. The validity of a change of applicable law shall be conditional on the permissibility of the change under the hitherto applicable company law and fulfilment of the requirements prescribed by that law with a view to protecting the rights of third parties and of members who did not consent to the change of the applicable law. If authorisation is required under the law of the original state of registration, the company may be registered in Germany only upon presentation of such authorisation.

(3) If the rules of German law or of the law of another Member State of the EU or EEA by whose law the company wishes to be governed do not provide for registration, the company may change the applicable company law by subjecting its organisation to the law of another Member State of the EU or EEA in manner apparent to third parties. In the event of a move from Germany, paragraph 1, sentences 2, 4 and 5, shall apply and, in the event of a move to Germany, paragraph 2, sentence 3, shall apply *mutatis mutandis*.

(4) In the case provided for in paragraphs 1 and 2, the hitherto applicable company law shall apply until the company has been registered in its new place of registration. In the case provided for in paragraph 3, the hitherto applicable company law shall apply until the company's entry in the register of its former place of registration has been deleted.

(5) An non-registered company which has its seat, principle place of business or central administration in Germany or another Member State of the EU or the EEA and was founded under the law of one of those states may change the company law applicable to it by subjecting its organisation to the law of another Member State of the EU or EEA in a manner apparent to third parties, in particular by registering in another Member State. The applicable law will change when the resolution on reorganisation takes effect or when the company is registered in another member state of the EU or EEA. Rights of third parties arising prior to the change of applicable law shall continue to be determined on the basis of the hitherto applicable law. The law applicable to contractual obligations shall apply to changes, in the law applicable to companies which are not organised.

Member States' laws on the implementation of cross-border seat transfers and Germany would then have to transform the directive into its domestic legislation anyway. In the meantime, however, the EC Commission has dropped the project from its agenda as will be explained below. It will be for the German legislator, therefore, to introduce on its own initiative rules that make a cross-border seat transfer possible in practice.

III. 4. International Corporate Restructurings

The ministerial draft bill also contains a provision dealing with various kinds of international corporate restructurings, such as mergers, divisions, transfer of assets and transformation of legal form. The basic conflicts of law rule is contained in Article 10a (1) EGBGB which provides as follows [as translated into English by the author]:

> The preconditions, the procedure and the legal effects of a restructuring by way of merger, division, transfer of assets or transformation of legal form are, for each of the companies, firms, associations or legal persons involved, subject to the law applicable according to Article 10.

Article 10a (2) EGBGB specifies in more detail the scope of this provision, and Article 10a (3) EGBGB makes the legal effectiveness of a restructuring dependent upon the fulfilment of the requirements set out in the law applicable to the entity that emerges from such restructuring.

The proposal follows the general consensus that in case of a cross-border restructuring the laws applicable to each of the entities involved in the restructuring must be taken into consideration. This concept has also been codified in the 10th company law Directive on cross-border mergers of limited liability companies.[20] On the other hand, German law is still incomplete as far as rules are concerned that are indispensable for the implementation of cross-border restructurings. The German legislator has limited himself to transforming the 10th Directive on cross-border mergers. Rules for the implementation of other restructuring transactions are still missing. In this respect, the draft bill on private international law of companies is going merely half a step towards a satisfactory solution.

It needs to be emphasized that the ministerial draft bill makes a distinction that is not made in the preparatory expert report: According to the wording of Articles 10a and 10b EGBGB, a restructuring by way of trans-

---

[20] Directive 2005/56/EC of 26 October 2005, OJ L 310/1.

formation of legal form which is covered by Article 10a EGBGB is to be distinguished from a change of the "proper law" of a company which is covered by Article 10b EGBGB. Whereas the latter transaction leads to the transformation of a domestic company into an equivalent foreign company (e.g., a German Gesellschaft mit beschränkter Haftung [GmbH] is transformed into a French société à responsabilité limitée [SARL] due to a "legal seat" transfer from Germany to France), the transformation of legal form covered by Article 10a EGBGB implies a change of one company form into another company form (e.g., a German Gesellschaft mit beschränkter Haftung [GmbH] is transformed into a French société par actions [SA].

IV. The European Perspective

As has been explained above, companies' freedom of establishment is far from being fully implemented within the EC. Cross-border seat transfers and corporate restructurings still meet with a great variety of obstacles in spite of recent ECJ jurisprudence regarding the freedom of establishment of companies and the entering into force of the 10th company law Directive on cross-border merger. At present, the transfer of a company's "legal seat" is practically impossible, unless first a European Company (SE) is formed which may then transfer its registered office from the Member State of incorporation to another Member State.[21] Alternatively, the "legal seat" could be transferred if a company would form a subsidiary in the target state and then merge into the foreign subsidiary in accordance with the 10th company law Directive on cross-border mergers. Such transactions are complicated and very costly. Also, restructurings not covered by the 10th Directive are practically impossible.

It was to be hoped that at least the proposal of a 14th company law Directive on cross-border seat transfers would have improved the situation. However, the European Commission has published in December 2007 an impact assessment on this directive.[22] The document presents the pros and

---

[21] Article 8 (1) of the EC Regulation 1215/2001 of 8 October 2001 on the Statute for a European company (SE), OJ L 294/1 provides as follows: "The registered office of an SE may be transferred to another member State in accordance with paragraphs 2 to 13. Such a transfer shall not result in the winding up of the SE or in the creation of a new legal person." Paragraphs 2 to 13 then specify the procedural details of the seat transfer.

[22] Commission Staff Working Document, "Impact assessment on the Directive on the cross-border transfer of registered office", SEC(2007) 1707, available at http://ec.europa.eu/internal_market/company/seat-transfer/index_en.htm

cons of possible policy actions, also including an evaluation of the consequences of not undertaking any regulatory action in this field. The impact assessment has been validated by the Commission's impact assessment board. Having weighed the arguments advanced, Commissioner McCreevy has decided there is no need for action at EU level on this issue. The Commission (Directorate General Internal Market and Services) has therefore stopped work in this area. This appears to be due to the Commission's conviction that, before taking any further action, it should wait for further clarification of the EC-Treaty provisions on the freedom of establishment of companies and of existing legislation on cross-border mobility by the ECJ.

From the European Community's perspective, it would, however, clearly be worth considering the enactment, on the Community level, of conflicts of law rules on the law applicable to companies. This could be achieved by way of a Community regulation based on the powers granted in Articles 65(b) and 95 EC. Such regulation could be compared with the "Rome-I" Regulation on the law applicable to contractual obligations and the "Rome-II" Regulation on the law applicable to non-contractual obligations. The working group of experts commissioned by the German Ministry of Justice was expressly asked not to limit its work to German legislation, but to also consider rules which might be adopted on the Community level. The experts' report, having a Community regulation in mind, therefore also made proposals for some 10 Articles which could be enacted on the Community level.[23] These provisions do not differ in substance from the proposals for the German legislator. It is mainly the wording that had to be adjusted to the Community context.

V. Conclusion

The draft bill on the private international law of companies submitted by the German Ministry of Justice represents, for Germany, a totally new approach to the conflicts of law issues relating to companies. The shift away from the traditional "real seat doctrine" towards the "incorporation doctrine" is a major step towards international mobility of companies. At the same time, the draft bill is unnecessarily reluctant when it comes to rules that are necessary in order to make cross-border seat transfers or restructurings possible in practice. Except for cross-border mergers which are covered by the 10th

[23] See *Sonnenberger* (footnote 13), p. 69–72.

EC company law Directive, such rules are still missing. This is due to the fact that the ministerial draft bill limits itself too strictly to the conflicts of law issues. The Swiss Federal Code on Private International Law[24] which is also based on the "incorporation doctrine"[25] provides an excellent example as to how procedural and substantive rules for the implementation of cross-border seat transfers and restructurings can be codified even within the context of a law codifying conflicts of law rules.[26] So, in the end, the ministerial draft bill is to be welcomed, but at the same time it is to be hoped that the efforts to modernize the German private international law of companies will soon be completed.

It is also to be hoped, however, that the German proposals are taken seriously into consideration by the EC Commission. If the Community itself would introduce the "incorporation doctrine" into European private international law of companies, including the rules on cross-border seat-transfers and corporate restructurings, a big step forward towards implementing the freedom of establishment of companies in the Internal Market would be made. It is strongly recommended therefore that the Commission considers commissioning a report by a group of experts who could easily build on the ground prepared by the German group of experts that prepared the draft bill submitted by the German Ministry of Justice.

This perspective should, however, not be used by the German legislator as an excuse for non-action on the basis of the ministerial draft bill. One cannot exclude that the bill may meet with considerable opposition, especially when it comes to the German model of workers' involvement on the board level which, according to some, could be undermined by an enhanced international mobility of companies. It should be kept in mind, however, that only a small minority of "large" enterprises are subject to that model. Small and medium size enterprises that want to avail themselves of the freedom of establishment should not be taken hostage of that minority until workers' co-determination is appropriately taken care of. After all, the SE-Directive[27] as well as the 10th Directive on cross-border mergers[28] have demonstrated that an appropriate solution is possible even in this respect.

---

[24] Bundesgesetz über das Internationale Privatrecht (IPRG) of 18 December 1987 (SR 291).

[25] Article 154 IPRG.

[26] See Articles 161–164b IPRG.

[27] Directive 2001/86/EC of 8 October 2001 supplementing the Statute for a European company with regard to the involvement of employees, OJ L 294/22.

[28] See endnote 20.

The Impact of Community Law on the Determination of the Personal Law of Companies

LÁSZLÓ BURIÁN

I. Introduction

The impact of Community law on the national laws of the Member States is a well known phenomenon in Europe. It is a question of practical and theoretical interest. As time goes on, this impact is growing and Community law is gaining influence in new areas of law. One of these new areas is private law which, until recently, had hardly been influenced by European law. Another such new area is the law of conflicts or, as it is perhaps better known in continental legal systems, private international law ("PIL"). PIL has been a traditional branch of national law since the second half of the nineteenth century and it did not lose its national character during the twentieth century despite the growing number of multilateral and bilateral treaties. What treaties could not make in more than a hundred years, European law did in less than two decades. It penetrates into the traditional national system of private international law and often makes it more complicated. This phenomenon was well observed by the famous German professor of PIL Kurt Siehr some years ago. He emphasised that traditional PIL, despite its rather complicated choice of law rules and procedural aspects, has always been a comfortable area for practitioners, while national law could handle international cases according to its own principles but it loses its comfortable character as ever more parts are regulated by international treaties and by European law.[1] A growing number of PIL provisions of the Member States of the European Union are developing under the influence of a supranational system of law: European law. The influence of European law is complex. There is a direct

---

[1] Kurt Siehr, "Internationales Privatrecht in der Europäischen Union" in *Rozprawy Prawnicze Ksiega Pamiatkowa Profesora Maximiliana Pazdana* [Essays in honour of Professor Maksymilian Pazdan], Zakamycze Kraków 2005, p. 593.

influence by secondary legislation (regulations and directives) and there is an indirect influence by primary law. In the following paragraphs, I would like to focus on the influence of Community law on the conflicts rules regulating the nationality of companies.[2]

The conflicts rules which determine the nationality of entities with legal personality have long been characterised by two different approaches. One of them was the traditional approach of continental law. According to it, the personal law of companies should be determined by the law of the seat of the company (*lex situs*). The other one is characteristic of common law according to which the personal law of companies should be determined by the place of incorporation (*lex originis*). Both solutions are used and applied in the Member States of the European Union. The traditional continental choice of law rule, the *lex situs*, is followed by Germany, Austria, Greece, France, Belgium Luxemburg, Italy and Poland. The Netherlands, Denmark, England, Ireland, Spain, Portugal and Hungary on the other hand favour the law of the country of incorporation. The abovementioned division characterises not only European countries. It is a worldwide phenomenon. Neither of the two systems is perfect, neither is consistent in itself. The incorporation theory fails when no incorporation is required by a certain legal system. It does not give a perfect solution either when a company is registered in more than one country. The seat theory may also cast some doubts in cases when a company has more than one seat in different countries. Neither of the two theories can handle cases when the place of incorporation or the place of the seat is not identical with the place where the economic activities of a company can be located.

One might wonder why Hungary—a country with a traditional continental legal system—follows the traditional common law principle of incorporation. The incorporation rule is not an old choice of law rule of Hungarian PIL. The traditional Hungarian choice of law rule was the *lex situs* which had been developed by the practice of the Supreme Court of the Hungarian Kingdom—the Curia—at the beginning of the twentieth century. This approach was strongly supported by the theory between the two World Wars. István Szászy one of the most important theoreticians of Hungarian PIL of the twentieth century wrote in 1938: "The seat can not be fictitious since the legal person cannot put its centre of administration into a country to which it does not have an important and legally relevant

[2] Lajos Vékás, "Uniós alapvető szabadságok és közösségi nemzetközi kollíziós jog" *Európai Jog* 2005/1, 3–16.

link."[3] This standpoint was in harmony with the provision of section 211 of the Hungarian Act of Commerce 1875, according to which foreign companies had to prove that they had been legally established and commercially active in their countries of the registered seat in order to be registered in Hungary.[4] The proof of a real commercial activity in the country of the registered seat served as a guarantee and helped to avoid the registration of foreign letterbox companies in Hungary. All this is legal history. The present situation is different. Hungarian PIL gave up the traditional continental rule of the *lex situs* in 1979 when the Hungarian PIL Code (Law Decree 13. 1979) entered into force. The radical change in the Code was explained by referring to the consistency of the incorporation theory with the provisions of Hungarian substantive law and the solutions adopted in "the rest of European socialist countries." Section 18(2) the Code provides: "The personal law of a legal person is the law of the country on whose territory the legal person is incorporated." Subsection (3) of the same section states: "If a legal person is incorporated in more than one country, or if the law of the seat declared in the statutes of the legal person does not demand incorporation, the personal law of the legal person is the law of the seat declared in the statutes."[5] The *lex situs* is only a secondary choice of law rule applied in cases when incorporation does not create a certain link to a country. It applies to companies not incorporated at all, or incorporated in more countries at the same time.

As I have already pointed out, and as the provisions of the Hungarian Code suggest, neither of the two regimes is satisfactory. They have to be combined and complemented by a third choice of law rule—the centre of administration ("real seat"), which can be applied in cases when the company cannot be located in any country by using one of the two traditional choice of law principles. In such situations, section 18(4) provides the following: "If a legal person has no seat declared in the statutes, or has more than one seat, and has not been incorporated according to the law of any of the respective states, the personal law of the legal person is the law of the state on whose territory the central administration of the legal person takes place."

---

[3] István Szászy, *Magyar Nemzetközi Magánjog*, Budapest 1938, p. 228.

[4] István Szászy, *ibid.*

[5] The motives, the text and the reasons were published in English in 1982 by the Ministry of Justice: "*The Statutes of the People's Republic of Hungary,*" Law-Decree No. 13 of 1979 on Private International Law, with a commentary by Prof. Ferenc Mádl.

II. Private International Law versus Community Law

A relatively new question is the compatibility of the traditional national choice of law rules with Community law. Companies do have a right to the freedom of establishment according Article 48 EC. The multilateral treaty signed on 2 February 1968 on the mutual recognition of companies established under the law of another Member State did not enter into force because the Netherlands did not ratify it. The contents of the right to the freedom of establishment had to be clarified by the decisions of the European court of Justice ("ECJ"). The decision of the ECJ in *Daily Mail*[6] did not solve the problem. More than 10 years after *Daily Mail*, the debate flared up again after *Centros*[7] and *Überseering*.[8] The echo was Europe wide but the reaction of academics was especially strong in German legal literature and it had certain consequences in court practice too. The Germans tried to defend their traditional choice of law rule, the *lex situs*. Some of the proposed solutions and theoretical constructions like the *Überlagerungstheorie* by Sandrock,[9] or the qualification of foreign letterbox companies as *Offene Handelsgesellschaften* ("OHG") or *Gesellschaften bürgerlichen Rechts* ("GbR") proved to be provisional attempts[10] only in the light of the later decisions of the ECJ but there are still some open questions which have yet to be answered by the ECJ.

I do not want to go into the details of the above-mentioned theoretical debate. It is well known and was analysed by many authors in Hungarian legal literature both from the point of view of European law and of private international law.[11] I would like to raise some new aspects of the problem in Hungarian PIL. It seems to be *communis opinio* now that the traditional

---

[6] Case 81/87 *The Queen v. H.M. Treasury and Commissioners of Inland Revenue ex parte Daily Mail and General Trust PLC* [1988] ECR 5483.

[7] Case 212/97 *Centros Ltd. v. Erhvervs-og Selskabstyrelsen* [1999] ECR I-1459.

[8] Case 208/00 *Überseering BV v. Nordic Construction Baumanagement GmbH (NCC)* [2002] ECR I-9919.

[9] Otto Sandrock, *"Centros: Ein Etappensieg für die Üerlagerungstheorie"* BB 54 (1999) pp. 1337–1345.

[10] It is stated by Wulf Henning Roth with some regret: *"Internationales Gesellschaftsrecht nach Überseering,"* *IPRax* 2003/2, p. 117.

[11] See Lajos Vékás, *op. cit.* supra, Péter Metzinger, *"A de facto külföldi iráyítású társaságok székhelye és honossága az európai jog tükrében (de lege lata és de lege ferenda),"* *Európai Jog* 2006/3, pp. 17–26; Miklós Király, "A Daily Mailtől az Inspire Artig – az Európai Bíróság ítéleteinek hatása a társasági jog értékválasztásaira," in: *Egység és sokféleség. Az Európai Unió jogának hatása a kultúrára.* Budapest, 2007, pp. 207.

choice of law rule, the *lex situs* is not in conformity with European law[12] since it requires a company to dissolve itself when changing its seat to be recognised as a company in the country of its new seat. The solution of the Hungarian PIL—the incorporation rule—is theoretically in conformity with European law. For example, a company established under Dutch law and incorporated in the Netherlands has to be recognised as a Dutch company when it transfers its seat to Hungary and a Hungarian company can transfer its seat to Italy without dissolving itself under Hungarian law. As we shall see the practice is different. If the theory is correct, the modification of Hungarian PIL rules determining the personal law of companies by giving up the traditional *lex situs* and turning to the place of incorporation was a step in the right direction. Now we do not have to worry about the future of the *lex situs* rule and do not have to change the choice of law rules in order to achieve conformity with European law. The codifiers of the Hungarian PIL Code in the sixties and seventies could hardly have foreseen that the country would become a member of the EU but they nevertheless instinctively made a good decision. It does not happen often in Hungarian history.

However as we shall see the decisions of the ECJ do have some broader consequences for PIL. And not only PIL is affected but also the provisions of substantive law: the Companies Act and the Firms Act. A good example is the Hungarian case, *Cartesio*,[13] currently pending before the ECJ. In this case reference was made by a Hungarian appellate court for a preliminary ruling concerning the compatibility of Hungarian company law, firm regulations and PIL with the principle of the freedom of establishment in European law. Though no decision has so far been made, it seems to be clear that Hungarian company and firm law was—at least until its modification in 2007[14]—not compatible with the place of incorporation rule of the Hungarian PIL and this had caused problems in legal practice. I shall return to the *Cartesio* case later. In the following text, I would like to focus on some aspects on PIL which have not yet been discussed in Hungarian legal literature.

---

[12] This is the opinion of some German authors, like Gerald Spindler und Olaf Berner, *"Der Gläubigerschutz im Gesellschaftsrecht nach Inspire Art,"* *RIW* 2004/1, p. 7; Peter Behrens, *"Gemeinschaftsrechtliche Grenzen der Anwendung inländischen Gesellschaftsrechts auf Auslandsgesellschaften nach Inspire Art,"* *IPRax* 2004/1, p. 25.

[13] With the number as Case C-210/06. The judgment in this case was rendered by the ECJ after the submission of this article.

[14] Act V of 2006 on the Registration of Firms amended the former Act CXLV of 1997. The modification entered into force on 1 September 2007 with the *Cartesio* case still pending before the ECJ.

It should be emphasised that the problems in connection with movement of companies have arisen not only in situations when the country which the company intended to leave and the country where it intended to continue its activities had different choice of law rules, but also in cases when both countries followed the incorporation theory. This was the situation in *Daily Mail*, *Centros* and *Inspire Art*.[15] All countries playing a role in those cases (England, Holland and Denmark) follow the theory of incorporation. As I mentioned above, Hungarian PIL rules are theoretically compatible with European law. That is why the problem has not been discussed here as profoundly as in Germany, where some academics tried to prove that the traditional seat theory was not contrary to the freedom of establishment and European law did not require a change of the traditional German PIL rule.[16] I would like to put the question differently: Does the fact that Hungarian PIL follows the incorporation rule mean that the quoted decisions of the ECJ do not affect Hungarian PIL at all? We can hardly answer in the affirmative. A simple "Yes" would simplify the problem and not only because the Hungarian court misunderstood the meaning of the relevant provision of the Code. The provisions of section 18 on the personal law of companies should not be taken in isolation but should be interpreted in the context of the provisions of the General Part of the Code. As a consequence, I would like to analyse some aspects of the application of general provisions of Hungarian PIL.

III. Renvoi and the Freedom of Establishment

When focusing on some fundamental questions of the relationship and interactions between PIL and Community law in connection with the free movement of companies, Lajos Vékás has also mentioned among others the problem of renvoi. He said that the complicated question of the compatibility of the PIL rules with European law can be more complex when the role of renvoi in the different legal systems of Member States is taken into consideration.[17] Considering the two different approaches in the determination of the personal law of companies, one of the preconditions of

---

[15] C-167/01 *Kamer van Koophandel en Fabrieken voor Amsterdam v. Inspire Art Ltd.* [2003] ECR I-10155.

[16] Carl Baudenbacher, Dirk Buschle, *"Niederlassungsfreiheit für EWR-Gesellschaften nach Überseering," IPRax* 2004/1, p. 26.

[17] Lajos Vékás, *op. cit.* supra p. 4.

renvoi is fulfilled: since the Member States are practically divided into two groups in this respect, there is a real chance for reference back to the law of the forum or reference to a third law. The solutions, in reality, do not merely depend on the different facts but also on the different approaches to renvoi in the PIL of Member States. The handling of renvoi in Hungarian law is rather unique. The somewhat misleading main rule does not permit renvoi at all. The first sentence of section 4 provides: "If according to this Law Decree foreign law shall be applied, the substantive rules of the foreign law directly resolving the issue in dispute shall apply." The second sentence of the same section however permits the application of Hungarian law when the foreign choice of law rule points to Hungarian law: "If however, in a question at issue the foreign law refers to Hungarian law the latter shall apply." As we know renvoi can be helpful in restoring the international harmony of decisions when countries using different choice of law rules have a different attitude towards renvoi. This is the case in questions of the personal status of natural persons where the principles of domicile and nationality are applied. The total renvoi helps in treating natural persons the same way as their own national law does.[18] So, e.g., the personal law of a Danish citizen domiciled in Hungary shall be judged in Hungary and in Denmark according to Danish law: in Hungary because Danish PIL rules refer back to Hungarian law; and in Denmark because Danish courts follow the domicile principle and Danish PIL does not apply renvoi at all. This result cannot be reached in situations when the Danish citizen is domiciled in a third country because Hungarian PIL does not accept the reference to a third law. This rule should be altered in order to achieve the international harmony of decisions. As in the case of natural persons, an international harmony of decisions could also be achieved in connection with the status of companies and other legal entities. Thus Hungarian courts can apply the *lex situs* of a company in cases when it determines the personal law of a company which had been established in a country following the law of the seat principle and transferred its real seat to Hungary. Accordingly the personal law of the company shall be Hungarian law though Hungarian PIL follows the incorporation principle. That could, in certain circumstances, violate the freedom of establishment and be contrary to the European law. The situation is different in the *lex situs* countries which can apply the law of the place of in-

[18] That is why László Réczei argued for a restricted acceptance of the reference back in Hungarian law in personal law, though he was against renvoi in general. László Réczei, "A visszautalás," *Jogtudományi Közlöny* 1970/4, pp. 151–160.

corporation when accepting the renvoi. The free movement of companies could be attained, up to a certain degree, through applying the renvoi in *lex situs* countries and not applying it in *lex originis* (incorporation) countries. That would mean the total exclusion of renvoi in Hungarian law which would also put an end to the "*Heimwärtsstreben*" in this respect.

IV. Fraudulent Connection

Foreign letterbox companies (*Briefkastengesellschaften*) are companies whose personal law is the law of a foreign country where they are incorporated and their statutory seat is in that foreign country too, but their whole economic activity connects them domestically to the country where they have their center of administration. These companies are in fact not foreign companies and they could be treated as domestic companies which have created an artificial link to the country of their incorporation or statutory seat. Creating an artificial link or simulating a link to a foreign law in order to evade the application of the otherwise applicable law, is a phenomenon well known by PIL. The attitude of PIL to the fraudulent connection depends on the *lex fori*. Some of the countries (like France) treat it more severely, others (like Germany) are less severe and there are laws—like English or American law—which tolerate it and do not sanction such behaviour. Foreign letterbox companies are companies which can be regarded as textbook examples illustrating the fraudulent connection.

Hungarian PIL does not tolerate a fraudulent connection. Section 8(1) of the Code provides the following: "A foreign law emanating from a foreign element produced by the parties artificially or by simulation with the intention to circumvent the law otherwise applicable shall not apply." According to subsection 2 such connection should have no effect at all and the law otherwise applicable should apply. It means that foreign letterbox companies should be treated like Hungarian companies and their personal law should be Hungarian law.

In *Centros*- and *Inspire Art*-like situations one might discover an intention to evade domestic law by a fraudulent connection to a foreign law. A Hungarian forum could sanction this behaviour by not giving effect to the artificially-created foreign link and could treat those companies as Hungarian companies applying the provisions of section 8 of the Code. In such cases, it is irrelevant whether or not the conflicts rules of the country to which the foreign link had been created and the conflicts rules of the forum are different. A good example is the *Centros* case where both countries—England, the country where the company was incorporated and had its statutory seat and Denmark, where the registration of a branch office of the company was denied by Danish authorities—followed the incorporation rule. The Danish authorities denied the registration of a branch of Centros on the grounds that it had never even intended to be economically active in England and the only aim of establishing the company in England was to avoid less favourable Danish company law requirements. Since Denmark is also an incorporation country, the *Centros* case has no effect at all on the law of the seat principle.

The traditional Hungarian attitude towards a fraudulent connection would violate the freedom of establishment and be contrary to Community law in cases when a foreign letterbox company is artificially linked to a Member State of the Community. This also applies to EEA countries since the freedom of establishment is guaranteed for companies of EEA countries by virtue of Article 34 of the EEA Treaty.[19] It means for example that companies incorporated in Liechtenstein – a paradise for foreign letterbox companies – having no real link whatsoever to Liechtenstein can enjoy the freedom of establishment and can freely transfer their seat into any Member State without risking the suspicion of the evasion of the domestic law of the Member State in question. One must come to the conclusion that the evasion of law—a classical institution of PIL—cannot be applied in relation to EEA countries in the future.

V. *Ordre Public*

Just like evasion of law, *ordre public* (public policy) is also affected by Community law in the same context. A Member State could hardly refuse the registration of a branch or a subsidiary of a foreign letterbox company by invoking public policy. The freedom of establishment can be restricted on public policy grounds by virtue of Article 46 of the EC Treaty. That kind of public policy is not identical with the traditional public policy of the conflict of laws. This view, emphasised by Vékás in Hungarian legal literature, is correct.[20] Fundamental freedoms guaranteed by primary law can be restricted only in exceptional cases when it is required for protecting the public interest. The restrictions shall be proportional and non-discriminatory. The protection of creditors is an important goal of eminent

[19] See the analysis of Carl Baudenbacher-Dirk Buschle, *op. cit.* supra p. 29.
[20] Lajos Vékás, *op. cit.* supra p. 7.

public interest but one can hardly use it as an argument in order to restrict the freedom of establishment.[21]

Another question is whether the provisions of Hungarian company law could prevent a foreign company transferring its real seat to Hungary without being dissolved first and re-established according to Hungarian company law. Until recently, there was a discrepancy between Hungarian PIL and Hungarian company law in this respect. A domestic law can only require its application against conflicts rules in international cases, when the provisions of the domestic law are internationally mandatory. Such mandatory character cannot be imputed to Hungarian company law. This was the conclusion of the Hungarian Supreme Court in one of its recent decisions in a domestic case.[22] Though one might have serious doubts as to whether the so-called positive *ordre public* can be invoked in domestic cases, it seems quite clear that Hungarian company law provisions cannot be applied as internationally mandatory provisions against the applicable law and cannot serve as a tool in order to restrict the freedom of establishment.

VI. Qualification (Characterisation)

According to section 3(1) of the Hungarian 1979 PIL Code, a Hungarian forum shall apply the *lex fori* when legal qualification of the facts or legal relationships have to be judged in order to determine the applicable law. One of the important steps of qualification is the precise identification of the legally relevant facts in connection with the application of a certain choice of law rule. The range of the choice of law rule determining the personal law of companies is drawn by section 18 of the Hungarian Code. Section 18 provides that the relevant substantive questions determined by the personal law of legal persons are their legal capacity, their economic character, their personal rights and the legal relations of their members. The Code uses the term legal persons. This might cause trouble when the personal law of companies not having legal personality according Hungarian company law has to be determined. The Code has a special rule for the determination of the economic quality of private persons who carry out economic activity (section 14(1)). When determining the personal law of

[21] This view is shared by Maduro AG in his Opinion in the *Cartesio* case (Opinion, para. 32).

[22] Legfelsőbb Bíróság Gf.VI. 30848/1997/8: *BH* 1997, p. 489.

companies not having legal personality the application of section 18 seems to be the proper solution. This solution has been followed in the *Cartesio* case now pending before the ECJ.[23] Cartesio is a "*betéti társaság*" ("limited partnership") established under Hungarian law. Though a "*betéti társaság*" is not a legal person under Hungarian company law, there was no doubt about the application of section 18. There are situations however when the forum has the possibility of qualifying certain questions connected to company law as questions not belonging to company law and, as a consequence, not falling under section 18. The result of such a qualification may be the application of a law not identical with the law applicable under the company law statute.

Such juggling with the institution of qualification is a well-known phenomenon in PIL. There are certain legal institutions which might be sensitive in this respect. In German literature, bankruptcy is an example for different qualification.[24] There was a tendency in German PIL of the separate independent qualification of bankruptcy. Many situations formerly belonging to the grey zone of bankruptcy law and company law qualified as an institution of company law are qualified nowadays as independent of company law as being part of bankruptcy law. As a consequence the *lex fori* is applied under Article 4 of the Insolvency Regulation and not the law of the seat applicable under the company law statute. Some German authors expressed serious doubts whether this method could be helpful in avoiding the consequences of an unjust restriction on the right to freedom of establishment under the *lex fori*.[25] When company law claims are not qualified as company law issues and are not judged under the company law statute but rather under the *lex fori*, this does not mean that the application of the *lex fori* could lead to unnecessary restriction of the right to freedom of establishment. One can only hope that all this will not lead to a "race to the bottom" effect in the sphere of company law.[26]

---

[23] Case 210/06.

[24] Peter Mankowski, "Entwicklungen im internationalen Privat- und Prozessrecht 2004/2005 (Part I)," *RIW* 2005/7. pp. 468.

[25] Gerald Spindler, Olaf Berner, *op. cit.*, supra n. 12.

[26] On the "race to the bottom" effect, see Miklós Király, *op. cit.*, supra pp. 207–208.

VII. The *Cartesio* Case. A Possibility for the ECJ to Overrule its *Daily Mail* Decision

In the *Cartesio* case pending before the ECJ in a preliminary reference proceeding, the question is the compatibility of the provisions of Hungarian company law with Community law. This case differs from *Centros* and *Überseering* because it concerns the legal provisions of a country which the company intends to leave. In this respect, *Cartesio* is a parallel to *Daily Mail.* The question is not the compatibility of the choice of law rule of Hungarian PIL determining the personal law of companies but rather the compatibility of Hungarian company law and the regulation of firm proceedings with that of Hungarian PIL.

The facts of the case are the following: Cartesio, a "*betéti társaság*" ("limited partnership") constituted in accordance with Hungarian law has its registered seat in Baja (Bács-Kiskun county). It has two partners who are resident in Hungary and have Hungarian nationality. According to Hungarian law one of the partners is a limited partner, who is obliged to contribute a stipulated amount of capital and is liable only for that amount. The other partner is a general partner, who is liable for all debts of the limited partnership. On 11 November 2005, Cartesio submitted an application to the Bács-Kiskun County Court sitting as a commercial court to amend its registration in the local commercial register so as to record the address—21013 Gallarate (Italy), Via Roma No.16—as its new operational headquarters (real seat) of the company. The court however rejected the application. It held that Hungarian law did not offer companies the possibility of transferring their real seat to another Member State while retaining their legal status as a company governed by Hungarian law. Therefore, in order to change its operational headquarters, Cartesio first would have to be dissolved in Hungary and then reconstituted under Italian law. The reasoning of the court is important. The court found that both Hungarian and Italian law followed the law of the seat principle. It drew the attention of the applicant to the possibility of establishing a branch of the company in Italy while keeping its Hungarian nationality. The applicant did not share this view of the court. It emphasised that Hungarian law followed the principle of incorporation and, as a consequence, companies registered in Hungary could freely transfer their real seat to another country without being forced to change their personal status. The court found in its ruling that it was irrelevant whether the seat principle or the incorporation principle was followed by Hungarian PIL because both principles would lead to the application of Hungarian law. The court held that the problem could not be solved under the relevant provisions of Hungarian law and that there was no possibility of transferring the real seat while keeping the Hungarian nationality of the company under the then subsisting Hungarian legal provisions.[27]

In its appeal to the Szeged Regional Court of Appeal, Cartesio argued that the transfer of the real seat was in harmony with the provisions of Hungarian PIL. The main problem, according to Cartesio, was that although the nationality of the company was not influenced by the transfer of the real seat, Hungarian company law applied only to companies having their real and statutory seat in Hungary. Accordingly, a Hungarian company applying for the transfer of its seat abroad did not fall under Hungarian company law and so it could not apply for further registration in the Hungarian company register. Consequently, the transfer of the real seat was not blocked by the choice of law provisions of Hungarian PIL but by the substantive and procedural provisions of Hungarian law on companies and firms. In order to clarify the questions raised, the applicant proposed that the appellate court seek a preliminary ruling from the ECJ in order to determine whether the Hungarian law was compatible with the right to freedom of establishment constituted by EC law. The Szeged Regional Court of Appeal referred four questions to the ECJ for a preliminary ruling. Here I would like to deal with the fourth question only as relevant to the problem dealt with in this paper. The fourth question consists of three parts:

a) If a company, constituted under Hungarian company law and entered in the Hungarian commercial register, wishes to transfer its seat to another Member State of the European Union, is the regulation of this field within the scope of Community law or, in the absence of the harmonisation of laws, is national law exclusively applicable?
b) May a Hungarian company request transfer of its seat to another Member State of the European Union relying directly on Community law (Articles 43 [EC] and 48 [EC]? If the answer is affirmative, may the transfer of the seat be made subject to any kind of condition or authorisation by the Member State of origin or the host Member State?

[27] This view was shared by one of the judges of the Supreme Court too. Ursula Vezekényi, "A közösségi jog jelenléte a magyar társasági jogban," in *Gyakorló jogászként az Európai Unióban*, HVG-Orac Budapest 2004, p. 202.

c) May Articles 43 [EC] and 48 [EC] be interpreted as meaning that national rules or national practices which differentiate between commercial companies with respect to exercise of their rights, according to the Member State in which their seat is situated, are incompatible with Community law? May Articles 43 [EC] and 48 [EC] be interpreted as meaning that, in accordance with those articles, national rules or practices which prevent a Hungarian company from transferring its seat to another Member State of the European Union, are incompatible with Community law?

In the preliminary proceedings, the Hungarian government argued that the case fell outside the scope of Articles 43 EC and 48 EC. Ireland, Poland, Slovenia and the United Kingdom took the same view. On the other hand, Cartesio, the Commission and the Dutch government submitted that there had been a restriction on the right of establishment and that accordingly Articles 43 EC and 48 EC applied.

Maduro AG expressed the view in his Opinion that the case fell within the scope of the EC rules on the right to establishment. National rules that allowed a company to transfer its real seat only within the national territory amounted to discrimination against the exercise of the freedom of establishment. In those circumstances the Treaty rules on the right of establishment clearly applied. When analysing the case law of the ECJ since *Daily Mail*, he stressed his view that the ECJ's approach had become more refined and it rejected the argument that rules of national company law should fall outside the scope of the Treaty provisions on the right to establishment. He expressed his opinion that in the present state of Community law, Member States were free to choose whether they wanted to have a system of rules grounded in the real seat theory or in the incorporation theory. The result of this approach was that ECJ case-law typically respected national rules relating to companies regardless of whether they are based on the real seat theory or on the incorporation theory. However, at the same time, the effective exercise of the right to establishment implied that neither theory could be applied to its fullest logical extension. Maduro AG concluded that Member States did not enjoy an absolute freedom to determine the "life and death" of companies constituted under their domestic law, irrespective of the consequences for the freedom of establishment. He found that the restriction on the freedom of establishment could not be justified in the present case on grounds of general public interest neither on grounds of the prevention of abuse of fraudulent conduct nor even on grounds of the protection of creditors, minority shareholders, employees or tax authorities.

The Advocate General proposed that the ECJ should give the following answer to question 4 referred by the Szeged Regional Court of Appeal: "Articles 43 EC and 48 EC preclude national rules which make it impossible for a company constituted under national law to transfer its operational headquarters to another Member State."

It is probable that, partly as a consequence of the case pending before the ECJ, Hungary has already amended its Act on Firms. From 1 September 2007, companies have been free to transfer their centre of administration (real seat) to another Member State and only have to keep their statutory seat in Hungary so that they can remain under the regime of Hungarian company law. That means that Cartesio could move its real seat to Italy under present Hungarian law.[28]

The *Cartesio* case has not yet been decided by the ECJ. When deciding the case the ECJ will have an opportunity to confirm or to alter the *ratio decidendi* of its former decisions concerning the relationship of the national laws of Member States and the freedom of establishment. One might hope that the decision will give an answer to open questions in this troubled area of the interaction between national laws and Community law.

---

[28] A critique of the Opinion of Maduro AG is written by Péter Metzinger, "A társaságok és a szabad letelepedés (A Cartesio ügyben közzétett főtanácsnoki vélemény kritikája)," *Európai Jog* 2008/4, pp. 21–26. He criticises the following sentence of the Opinion: "Hungarian company law, so it would appear, is grounded in the 'real seat' theory…" He argues that company law cannot be grounded in any such theories since these are of a PIL nature. On the other hand, he says that the answer on the fourth question is correct.

Public Law, *Ordre Public* and Arbitration: A Procedural Scenario and a Suggestion

RICHARD M. BUXBAUM

I. Introduction

The ongoing discussion over the capability and the obligation of an arbitral tribunal to consider issues of public law and public policy has been enriched within the European Community by the complications generated by its federal nature.[1] That discussion expectably will also intensify in light of the current financial and economic crisis and the anticipated search for its resolution in a new level of national and international regulatory activity. It thus seems an appropriate time to revisit these questions of arbitrability of issues of substantial public-policy concern. The scope of the present effort, a tribute to Tibor Várady, whose work on international dispute resolution is a central and longstanding aspect of his intellectual and professional interests, does not permit broad coverage of these large issues. Fortunately, recent more ambitious treatments, in particular *Horn's* excellent overview and the publication of the Columbia Law School 2007 Symposium on the role of mandatory law in the arbitration process,[2] provide that broader context, both doctrinally and in policy terms, and allow this contribution to focus on some aspects specific to the US scene.

The privatization of law generated by landmark decisions of the US Supreme Court began with the Burger Court of the 1970s and can be marked by two specific trends. One is the cutback of the private action,

---

[1] The evolution of US jurisprudence in this field also was marked by resolution of important constitutional issues arising from the preemptive effect of federal legislation under the Supremacy Clause of the US Constitution. This development is briefly considered below.

[2] Norbert Horn, "Zwingendes Recht in der internationalen Schiedsgerichtsbarkeit," 2008 SchiedsVZ 209; Symposium, "Mandatory Rules of Law in International Arbitration," 18 Am. Rev. Int'l Arbitration 1 (2007).

once hailed as an important supplement to the governmental enforcement of regulatory legislation, by narrowing the scope of the implied-tort doctrine that is the bedrock of these actions. The other is the acceptance of arbitration to resolve disputes that hitherto had been considered the exclusive domain of the state's adjudicatory institutions.[3] The first applied whether the parties involved had a contractual relationship or not; the second, of course, applied only when parties to an agreement had chosen arbitration as their means of dispute resolution.[4]

One earlier development of similar import was relevant even at the outset only to international commerce and international investment; namely, the acceptance of forum derogation clauses. The two other developments identified above began on the domestic scene, but their relevance to international transactions quickly became apparent. In this paper I focus on the implications of the modern US jurisprudence for international transactions, leaving aside the important role in today's global markets of the private suit seeking (typically) compensatory relief for violations of public law. This judicial tendency in favor of arbitration is particularly marked in the law of the US and of many OECD nations, where even those non-arbitrability policies[5] that still may be found within the domestic sphere are increasingly likely to be relaxed in the transnational sphere.

All of these developments have been exhaustively examined and do not need further rehearsal here, but more recent expansions of their joint impact make a look at today's scene, in procedural as well as in substantive terms, newly relevant. In the United States, these developments find their clearest

---

[3] Some would argue that the characterization of the Federal Arbitration Act as an expression of a pro-arbitration policy preempting state-based rules of public-law non-arbitrability under the Supremacy Clause of the US Constitution did not necessarily lead to the "privatizing" of public-law norms enacted at the federal level. In my opinion the tenor of the times made all these developments of a piece.

[4] I put aside, though it is not irrelevant in this context, the gradual expansion of the duty to submit to arbitration imposed on parties not themselves signatories to the agreement but related in some fashion to the party so obligated. To this, see most recently William Park, Arbitral Jurisdiction and Non-signatories, in A. Rau, ed., Multiple Parties, Multiple Problems (forthcoming Oxford 2009).

[5] "Policies" instead of the more fine-grained distinctions between *ordre public*, procedural norms of mandatory character, and non-waivable public laws in the academic literature—see the full characterization spectrum in *Horn*—for the simple reason that in the US both the federal legislation and the jurisprudence tend to conflate all of these issues. The example of Stawski Distributing Co., Inc. v. Browary Zywiec S.A., 349 F.3d 1023 (7th Cir. 2003) (Easterbrook, J.), discussed below, is instructive in this regard.

statement in the 1974 *Scherk* and the 1985 *Mitsubishi* decisions.[6] But it is a specific recent decision of an important intermediate federal appellate court that has given new significance to *Mitsubishi*, to the point that courts and arbitral tribunals, not to mention academic and professional commentators, may find it worthwhile to reconsider the implications of the arbitrability of disputes centrally involving public-law norms.[7]

I limit myself to the US approach to this problem of mandatory laws and public policy controls,[8] and discuss the two contexts within which they are in play: the dispute over whether to require arbitration and the dispute over the scope of review of an award in the context of a proceeding to recognize and enforce it.

II. Public Law is Not Public Policy: Enforcing the Agreement to Arbitrate

This part of the discussion is based on and limited to the first stage of the two-stage scenario of judicial involvement in a challenge to the duty to arbitrate; namely, the effort of the party objecting to arbitration to avoid that process. In this setting, the challenger frequently initiates an action seeking a declaration that it is not required to submit the dispute to arbitration. Usually but not necessarily this is presented as a component of the complainant's effort to initiate litigation over its cause of action.[9] The

---

[6] Scherk v. Alberto-Culver Co., 417 U.S. 506 (1974); Mitsubishi Motors Corp. v. Soler Chrysler-Plymouth, Inc., 473 U.S. 614 (1985).

[7] This focus already is apparent in some of the academic literature; see, e.g., Karl Meessen, Economic Law in Globalizing Markets (the Hague 2004) at 313ff.

[8] The very designation "mandatory laws" is something of a latecomer to the US literature and jurisprudence. To the evolution of the concept, especially as to the distinction between laws mandatory in the purely domestic context and those mandatory even in the transnational context, see Patrick Borchers, "Categorical Exceptions to Party Autonomy in Private International Law," 82:1645 Tulane L. Rev. (2008).

Outside the US, this distinction finds its most salient recent formulation in the Rome I and Rome II Choice of Law Regulations; see Rome I Articles 3(3) and (4) and 9, Regulation (EC) 593/2008, OJ L177/6, July 4, 2008; and Rome II Articles 6(4), 8(4) and 16, Regulation (EC) 864/2007, OJ L199/40, July 31, 2007.

[9] An original action by the complainant, seeking to force the defendant to enter arbitration, may seem like an empty category, but is not. See the discussion of the *Mitsubishi* procedural context, infra. What was unusual in that case is that Mitsubishi had not yet initiated the Tokyo arbitration process at the time it went to court, though it did so a few days after filing the complaint seeking Soler's participation.

same challenge, of course, also may be raised as a defense to the proceeding brought by the party that seeks arbitration and requests a ruling mandating that submittal. The subject matter of these proceedings typically is an antitrust or a securities-regulation issue, though as we shall see the latter is an uncommon situation.[10]

While at least the challenger's objection to arbitration, as well as the opponent's demand for arbitration, may be brought in any forum which can exercise jurisdiction over the parties, the former case typically is brought in the forum to which an eventual arbitral award may be brought for recognition and enforcement.[11] In other words, art. II (3) of the New York Convention, with its reference to municipal law, comes into play. The party seeking arbitration may sue there, but it would not be unusual to seek that mandate before a court of the arbitration venue, or indeed before the courts of the party's domicile, assuming personal jurisdiction over the objecting party there.[12]

The recognition and enforcement of an eventual award is treated separately below. But it is, of course, in the air during the first phase, in particular when the court seized of the preliminary objection issue is the same court to which a later award may be presented for recognition and enforcement. And as is well-known, it is that connection, explicitly set forth in *Mitsubishi*, that distinguishes the US jurisprudence on this subject; it is this connection that now deserves to be revisited given the consequences it recently has generated.

The first element to consider is that court's problematic response to the objection that arbitral tribunals[13] were more likely than US courts to dispar-

---

[10] Consumer protection as a species of federal public law in the sense of its override of unfair contract terms is a third, more relevant within the European Community than in the United States though arising in a few situations there as well; to this more, below. Individual states may have a number of other categories the applicability of which is mandated even if their mandated non-arbitrability is not honored; to this, too, more below.

[11] That depends, of course, on whether the public-law issue is pleaded as a defense, since that in turn implies that an award against the objector normally will return to the objector's domicile for recognition and enforcement.

[12] Within the second of course there lies a separate possibility; that of challenging the foreign award in the arbitral forum's judicial system on the same ground.

A further subdivision distinguishes those cases in which the defendant appealed the award in the courts of the arbitral forum on similar grounds from those in which it did not do so (whether because it did not participate in the underlying arbitration and suffered a default award, or did but did not appeal).

[13] Especially those of non-US background.

age, subvert or ignore the public policy of private enforcement of antitrust and securities-regulation laws. The court simply asserts that "[i]nternational arbitrators frequently are drawn from the legal as well as the business community; where the dispute has an important legal component, the parties and the arbitral body with whose assistance they have agreed to settle their dispute can be expected to select arbitrators accordingly."[14] The unstated underlying assumption that a legally trained arbitrator is less likely to deprecate the values, policies, and doctrines of a rigorous antitrust law than an arbitrator coming from the business community is at the least questionable.[15] In part that is a consequence of the pool from which especially the repeat players are selected; in part it is a consequence of the distance of the arbitral tribunal from the state from which the public law at issue emanates (especially if more than one state's laws are involved).[16]

The second element is the famous Footnote 19 and following text, rejecting the argument of the US (as *amicus curiae*)[17] that the choice of Swiss law in the distribution agreement "raises the possibility that the arbitral tribunal will read this provision not simply to govern interpretation of the contract terms, but wholly displace American law even where it otherwise would apply."[18] Based (but only in part) on Mitsubishi's concession that American law applied to Soler's antitrust claims and that the recourse to arbitration had been submitted to and accepted by the arbitration panel on that basis, the court provided what over the years has turned out to be the cold comfort of referring to the chance for revisiting the dispute at the recognition and enforcement state.

In recent years, however, it is the subsequent statement, less frequently cited, that has turned out to be of decisive importance:

---

[14] *Mitsubishi*, supra n. 6, at 635.

[15] While Heinrich Kronstein's famous "Arbitration Is Power," NYU L. Rev. 38:661 (1963) may not be the last word on the subject, it remains an important starting point for a more empirically based discussion of this issue.

[16] This latter point is emphasized by *Horn*, supra n. 2, as the major "fact on the ground" in favor of a less focused engagement of an arbitral tribunal with the mandatory (non-waivable) laws either of the *lex contractus* or of the state with the closest connection to the matter at bar under whatever choice of law doctrines may be provided by the parties or chosen by the arbitrators.

[17] Given today's increasing deference to the primacy of the Executive Branch in foreign affairs, including foreign economic affairs, this rejection of the Executive's views on the problem posed by foreign arbitration of disputes non-trivially impacting US policy interests is itself an intriguing reflection on the temporal cycles of inter-branch relationships.

[18] *Mitsubishi*, supra n. 2, at 637 fn. 19.

> While the efficacy of the arbitral process requires that substantive review at the award-enforcement stage remain minimal, it would not require intrusive inquiry to ascertain that the tribunal took cognizance of the antitrust claims and actually decided them."[19]

The context underlying *Mitsubishi*, however, also needs to be taken into account. Doubtless there is a tendency, even in the judicial treatment of these matters, not to give full weight to an antitrust defense raised by a party charged with breach of a contract, a defense often thrown into the mix as a diversionary device. That distaste, in my view, explains at least a part of the *Mitsubishi* court's summary approach to the effort of Soler, the distributor, to prevent submission to the arbitral tribunal in the first place. But granting that point, the dictum that "the efficacy of the arbitral process requires that substantive review at the award-enforcement stage remain minimal" is immediately contextualized by the balance of the same statement, that "it would not require intrusive inquiry to ascertain that the tribunal took cognizance of the antitrust claims and actually decided them."

The judicial treatment of a problematic antitrust defense to a breach-of-contract claim has its limits. There is no automatic preclusion of its consideration—no estoppel doctrine preventing its being raised. Courts, at least US courts, generally have demonstrated appropriate sensitivity to the public interest in the appropriate consideration of such defenses. The training, functions, and limited role of arbitrators in similar situations suggests that a similar sensitivity to the public interest can not as readily be expected of the typical tribunal.[20] And whatever one's view of the anti-

---

[19] Id. at 638.

[20] Though a national court's view of a foreign mandatory law also can be problematical from this perspective. The attitude of Swiss courts towards violation of another state's anti-corruption legislation in the direct (and successful) appeal from a Swiss arbitration award that had voided the disputed procurement contract on that ground—Omnium de Traitement et de Valorisation—OTV c. Hilmarton, Supreme Court of Switzerland Decision of April 17, 1990, YB Com. Arb. XIX:214 (1994) finds a resonance in US judicial treatment of awards involving similar issues of foreign payments, questionable compliance with foreign boycott measures, and similar issues of international commercial relations. See especially Northrop Corporation v. Triad International Marketing S.A., 811 F.2d 1265 (9th Cir. 1986), resting in part on choice of law issues. For a full review of earlier situations, see Andrew Campbell, "Refusal to Enforce Foreign Arbitration Awards on Public Policy Grounds," 144 A.L.R.Fed. 481 (1998). Of course, that US courts also would disparage the EC's insistence that commercial-agent protection law rises to the level of rejection of arbitrability of non-compliant contracts in the context of the international *ordre public* (Ingmar GB Ltd. v. Eaton Leonard Technologies, Inc., ECJ Case C-381/98, 2000 E.C.R. I-9305) seems almost self-evident. *Borchers*, supra n. 8, at 1649 makes this point concerning the US view of much mandatory law.

trust defense in *Mitsubishi*, the context in which the antitrust objection had to be considered by the arbitral tribunal did not fall within any estoppel or unclean-hands objection based on its merely tactical use.[21]

The paradigm (though uncommon) situation in which the party seeking to avoid arbitration is the initiator of the litigation, and not merely responding to its opponent's effort to arbitrate a contract-breach dispute is the case of the investor who claims a violation of a provision of presumably mandatory capital-market law and uses this as the basis of its claim of a contract breach. The *Scherk* case[22] is a good and perhaps the only example: The purchaser of a corporation raised a Rule 10b-5 fraud claim against the seller of the securities representing its ownership, and sought to bring this dispute to a US court. It claimed that the non-arbitrability of claims based on the now-overturned judicial reading of the Securities Exchange Act to that effect permitted it to repudiate the arbitration provision provided for by the parties' agreement. The Supreme Court rejected the strategy[23] and in essence ordered arbitration, in this case without a specific savings clause concerning a possible use of the same argument as a defense against later recognition and enforcement of any award.[24]

The test of this second-stage defense did not occur in either case.[25] A recent case from an important federal circuit, however, finally has provided a first test of that second step.

---

[21] The *Baxter* dissent properly points out that "if Baxter had not raised the antitrust issue during arbitration, it would have risked being met with a defense of waiver to consideration of the issue here." Id. at 836, n. 3.

[22] Supra n. 6.

[23] Though again for reasons not unrelated to its doubts about the application of the substantive public law to a transaction that though formally achieved by the purchase of the shares representing the seller's 100% ownership of the companies was functionally the purchase of the company's assets. That this use of the heavy artillery of the securities-fraud norms might well lead an arbitral tribunal to reject if not to disregard that norm strikes me as at least equally plausible. Indeed, the assumption in *Scherk* that Rule 10b-5 applied to that transaction might well have been questionable under the later analysis in Landreth Timber Company v. Landreth, 471 U.S. 681 (1985).

[24] For a recent extension of this approach to a maritime employment agreement, a field long sacrosanct under maritime labor law, see Rogers v. Royal Caribbean Cruise Line, 547 F.3d 1148 (9th Cir. 2008).

[25] In *Scherk* the arbitral tribunal ruled against the claimant; thus, no award called for recognition and enforcement; in *Mitsubishi* Soler's post-arbitration bankruptcy mooted the recognition and enforcement of the award there.

III. Public Law is Not Public Policy: Recognition and Enforcement of the Award

The recent opinion of Judge Easterbrook in the *Baxter Laboratories* case[26] brought the significance of this quoted comment in the recognition-and-award phase to the fore.[27] *Baxter Laboratories* involved a breach-of-contract claim against the original licensor of certain patents, the licensee alleging that its world-wide rights were trespassed upon when that licensor, now the owner of a firm that allegedly had worked around these patents, produced and distributed the resultant products in its US home market. The license agreement itself had not called for arbitration, but a separate agreement calling for arbitration (in Japan) of any dispute arising out of the license agreement that might upset an undefined "original commercial arrangement" of the parties.

When the arbitral panel found that the new process did infringe on the original patent claims,[28] it rendered an award ordering the respondent, Baxter, to cease its relevant US activities. This generated an antitrust issue that had not been present in the case before then. Baxter responded with a request to the tribunal to reconsider, arguing that its order would, in the United States, result in market behavior not immunized under patent-license norms and thus create an antitrust problem. Its effort to have the arbitral panel review this issue was summarily rebuffed without reasons being given, the panel simply stating that the issue had been considered and by implication rejected.

The court considered the problem in the context of Baxter's claim that recognition and enforcement of the award in the US fell under the public-policy exception contained in art. V(2)(b) of the New York Convention. The majority's rebuff of this defense was as summary as was that of the arbitral tribunal's consideration of the substantive antitrust issue:

> The arbitral tribunal in this case 'took cognizance of the antitrust claims and actually decided them.' Ensuring this is as far as our review legitimately goes.[29]

---

[26] 315 F.3d 829 (7th Cir. 2003) (Easterbrook, J.), petition for rehearing en banc denied, 325 F.3d 954 (7th Cir. 2003), cert. denied, 540 U. S. 963 (2003).

[27] The EC parallel situation was the subject of a decision of the Cour d'Appel (Paris), Decision of Nov. 14, 2004 in Thalès Air Defense c. GIE Euromissile, (2005) 3 Rev. de l'arbitrage 751, discussed further below.

[28] The US member of the panel dissented from this finding. The dissenting judge in *Baxter*, while accepting that this was a finding which would withstand reversal under the normal deferential standards applicable to judicial review of arbitral awards, did find it "far-fetched." Id. at 836 fn. 6.

[29] Id. at 832.

Baxter Laboratories, part of the trend permitting even public-law disputes (however, that umbrella phrase may be defined) to be arbitrated, presents an interesting dilemma. That permission comes at a price: If "mere" errors of law by the arbitral tribunal cannot be reviewed, then even clear misreading of antitrust doctrine escapes control.[30]

If *Baxter Laboratories* becomes the bellwether of the future treatment of public-law issues within the art. V(2)(b) Convention defense, a reconsideration of the deferential standard of review generally recommended for that stage of the process[31] is called for. The cursory nature of judicial review of awards of an essentially commercial character is not automatically appropriate in the case of awards implicating a variety of (themselves more or less important) public-law issues. Rather, a more nuanced approach is called for, one that may well honor a two-track concept that distinguishes the *ordre public* international from the *ordre public* national but that engages in the balancing of the respective substantive policy implications of the latter defense[32] only after first achieving clarity on the degree of engagement of the arbitral tribunal with the particular domestic public law on which the challenge is based.

At least in the case of securities regulation, one major concession has to be made. Investor claims against brokerage firms based on Rule 10b-5 today universally have to go to arbitration,[33] indeed to an unusual form of arbitration that requires the investor to choose its appointed arbitrator from a panel presented by the sector's trade association. The judicial review of these awards—usually on direct appeal since the case to be dis-

---

[30] Indeed, *Horn*, (supra n. 2, at 219) emphasizes the fact that in *Thalès*, supra n. 27, the arbitral tribunal had not even considered the relevant EC antitrust legislation; yet the French court ordered the award's enforcement, on a technical reading of the margin of appreciation still allowed national courts on this issue by the same ECJ judgment that had characterized the antitrust legislation of the EC Treaty as being of mandatory application (Eco Swiss China Time Ltd v. Benetton International MV, ECR 1999:I-03055).

[31] Usually conceptualized under a notion of an *ordre public* international that faces a higher threshold of applicability than the *ordre public* national. This distinction has gained renewed salience in the choice of law arena; see *Borchers*, supra n. 8.

[32] In the usual sense of balancing the value of engagement in international trade and investment and the value of domestic public policies in at least a general if not commensurate sense. That, of course, itself varies from state to state. What the US Supreme Court allows in the area of forum derogation clauses, for example (paradigmatically in M/S Bremen v. Zapata Offshore Co., 407 U.S. 1 (1972)) is not necessarily what another national court might permit.

[33] In the sense that it is difficult to find a brokerage firm that will enter a customer relationship without requiring this element in the agreement creating the transaction or relationship.

cussed here results in an arbitral ruling against the investor—is if not as minimal as in a recognition and enforcement proceeding at least rudimentary and relatively tolerant of errors of fact and law. While I do not know of any empirical study quantifying the percentage of these actions initiated by foreign investors, their complaints would fall under the same system for resolution.

If that is the case, is there any reason to be more punctilious about international arbitration? The functionally persuasive response to that objection, in my opinion, lies in the institutional embeddedment of the domestic situation in the litigation equivalent of a deep and liquid capital market—in a well-developed domestic jurisprudence that reaches down to specific transaction types and behavioral events, and the professional competence of the arbitral panels involved in this high-volume dispute-resolution business. None of that architecture or professional specialization can be taken for granted in the international setting; more important, many of these disputes not only require attention to what is "foreign" law to the panel, but to law contestably claiming application to extraterritorial elements because of their claimed US conduct and effect.

The factually persuasive response is that *Scherk* events are rare for a reason. Direct investor fraud complaints are the subject of (mainly class) actions against issuers and insiders, and these do not occur in a context including contractual submission to arbitration. And *Scherk*-type complaints by a purchaser (or seller)[34] of an entire corporation or of the portion not yet owned by the purchaser by means of a securities transaction clearly are far less common than complaints about a share transaction involving only a portfolio investment.

These circumstances combine to permit a separate treatment of this type of claims from that given them in a purely domestic setting. And they suggest, further, that it is the antitrust question which within the mandatory law and *ordre public* context is the principal sector of current concern for the US judiciary.

Before developing the general argument in favor of closer judicial involvement of this sector in more detail, however, two other issues need to be presented. The first concerns the distinction between recourse to arbitration per se and acceptance by the arbitral tribunal of mandatory law—typically, that which is promulgated by the state of the domicile of the party objecting to the arbitration. This is particularly important, and prob-

[34] While uncommon, these can occur. See, e.g., the example of Vacold LLC v. Cerami, 545 F.3d 114 (2d Cir. 2008).

lematical, if that state uses its prescriptive jurisdiction to apply the substantive norm to conduct or events occurring outside its territory. While the particular extraterritorial reach may fall within the vague outer limits generally recognized under principles of public international law, many states—and therefore potentially many arbitral tribunals—may consider that reach illegitimate.[35]

The second issue is a specific federal one; namely, the acceptance or rejection by the central authority of prohibitions or limitations on the arbitrability of disputes promulgated by the subordinate authority if these are not limitations promulgated by the higher one. While this is today principally an issue within the European Community, two remnants of it remain in dispute in the United States, despite the general victory of federal principles of arbitrability already mentioned in the introduction to this paper. Coincidentally, each of these remnants recently has been involved in the further development of these NY Convention art. II(3) and V(2)(b) issues before US courts. Their current status may be of some comparative interest as the EC regime itself creates some space for Member States' discretion in accepting or rejecting attacks on awards on the basis of the arbitral tribunals handling of mandatory law or public policy issues.[36]

Each example—alcohol and insurance—arose in consequence of the US Supreme Court's Dormant Commerce Clause jurisprudence; namely, that state regulation of interstate commerce may violate the Commerce Clause even in the absence of federal legislation on the substantive issue under the affirmative grant of power of the Clause. The latter, of course, would result in the judicial prohibition of inconsistent state legislation, given the preemptive effect of the Supremacy Clause of the US Constitution. In the former case, however, the judiciary's rulings are considered legislative rather than constitutional, and explicit federal legislation authorizing or acquiescing in state regulation of the subject would be accepted. That is what happened as to these two examples. In the case of alcohol, a late-19th-century ruling of the Supreme Court[37] that the states

[35] There was a time, of course, when the opposite problem prevailed, when arbitral tribunals declined to hear cases involving important species of public law on the grounds of institutional competence to poach on what was once the exclusive territory of the courts. The revolution of 1975 largely ended that species of non liquet.

[36] See the discussion in text, supra n. 27; and, for a recent example suggesting that the French approach to judicial review of these issues is even more restrained now, see Cour de cassation (civ. 1), Decision of June 4, 2008, SNF SAS c. Cytec Industries BV, available at http://www.courdecassation.fr/jurisprudence_2/premiere_chambre_civ.

[37] Leisy v. Hardin, 135 U.S. 100 (1890).

could not bar interstate commerce in that sector was—by express invitation of the Court—immediately overturned by federal legislation[38] (later subsumed within the 21st Amendment to the Constitution) permitting states to exercise the option of banning the importation of alcohol from other states. In the case of insurance, a 1947 ruling of the Supreme Court[39] that declared the business of insurance to be commerce, reversing a 19th-century ruling to the contrary, in turn was reversed, after an intense lobbying effort by the insurance industry,[40] by Congressional legislation declaring that it was not interstate commerce and authorizing state regulation of the industry.[41]

This in turn led in time to the question whether the 21st Amendment, and the McCarran-Ferguson Act, also required acceptance of state statutes prohibiting or constraining the arbitrability of disputes between private actors arising from contracts that contained arbitration clauses. In the alcohol case, the already mentioned opinion in *Stawski*[42] used a narrow doctrinal distinction between choice of venue and choice of law to use the preemptive power of the Federal Arbitration Act to overrule the particular state's prohibition of arbitration.[43]

The insurance case is more complex and more serious in economic terms. Two federal appellate opinions, from 1995 and 2008 respectively, set the stage. In one,[44] the Kentucky Insurance Commissioner, as liquidator of a reinsurance company incorporated there, sued to require its cedents to pay past and future premiums; the dispute concerned the availability of a setoff defense to the cedents despite a state statute prohibiting setoffs against premiums owed an insolvent insurer. The reinsurance contracts at issue called for arbitration; in the case of foreign participants, apparently in London, thus bringing the role of the Convention into play. In the second case,[45] a private dispute among US and foreign insurers in

---

[38] Wilson Act of 1890, 27 U.S.C. §121.

[39] U.S. v. South-Eastern Unverwriters' Ass'n, 322 U.S. 533 (1944).

[40] Intense enough to lead the Congress to override President Truman's veto of that statute.

[41] McCarran-Ferguson Act, 15 U.S.C. §§1011ff.

[42] Supra n. 5.

[43] "Suppose that Illinois had attempted to require all disputes arising out of the Beer Industry Fair Dealing Act to be litigated in state court. Could such a statute block Zywiec from removing to federal court… Surely not….Yet a federal court would be a forum different from the one specified by Illinois law, just as arbitration occurs in a different forum." *Stawski*, at 1026.

[44] Stephens v. American International Ins. Co., 66 F.3d 41 (2d Cir. 1995).

[45] Safety Nat. Cas. Corp. v. Certain Underwriters at Lloyd's, London, 543 F.3d 744 (5th Cir. 2008).

the casualty-insurance field, with similar arbitration provisions, was involved. In both cases, an important preliminary question concerned the characterization of the transactions, since only the "business of insurance" would fall within the protective ambit of the McCarran-Ferguson Act. In *Stephens* that was a difficult problem, eventually decided in favor of coverage within the 'business" definition; in *Safety Nat. Cas.* the court assumed this fit.

Stephens made short shrift of the preemption issue, asserting that the NY Convention required an act of Congress to render it applicable within the municipal legal system. Since the McCarran-Ferguson Act specifies that "[n]o Act of Congress shall be construed to...supersede any law...regulating the business of insurance", "and since the Kentucky statute was held to regulate the business of insurance," the Convention was "simply inapplicable."[46] While some lower courts in other circuits questioned this syllogism, it was directly contradicted at the federal appellate level only in 2008. The court in the *Safety Nat. Cas.* case took a more detailed and nuanced if not a more persuasive approach to this conflict. Using the recent Supreme Court approach to the status of the Vienna Convention developed in Medellin v. Texas,[47] which in fact focused on the direct private enforcement of that Convention, it contrasted the language of the NY Convention requiring the courts of a Contracting State to "refer the parties to arbitration," finding in this at least an ambiguity. Then, in what amounts to little more than sleight of hand, it added:

> [E]ven if the Convention required legislation to implement it in United States courts, that does not mean that Congress an "Act of Congress," as that phrase is used in the McCarran-Ferguson Act, to include a treaty...The fact that a treaty stands on equal footing with legislation when implemented by Congress does not mean that it ceases to be a treaty and becomes an "Act of Congress."[48]

More interesting from a policy perspective now ascendant in the field of international relations generally, the court found the Supreme Court's approach in American Insurance Ass'n v. Garamendi[49] to be a persuasive if not direct precedent. In that case, after accepting the proposition that

---

[46] *Stephens*, supra n. 44, at 45.

[47] Medellin v. Texas, 129 S.Ct. 360 (2008). On the contested nature of this approach in *Medellin* itself, see Vásquez, "Treaties As Law of the Land: The Supreme Court and the Judicial Enforcement of Treaties," 122 Harv. L. Rev. 599 (2008) at 660ff.

[48] *Safety Nat.*, supra n. 45, at 750.

[49] American Insurance Ass'n v. Garamendi, 539 U.S. 396 (2003).

Executive Agreements not presented to the Senate for ratification[50] were as preemptive of conflicting state statutes under the Supremacy Clause as were Congressional enactments, the Supreme Court then disposed of California's anti-preemption argument, which also was based on the McCarran-Ferguson Act. Agreeing that the Act did intend to limit congressional preemption of the Dormant Commerce Clause artillery, it added:

> [A] federal statute directed to implied preemption by domestic commerce legislation cannot sensibly be construed to address preemption by executive conduct in foreign affairs.[51]

Based on this norm of essentially constitutional interpretation, the *Safety Nat.* court concluded that Congress did not, through its formulation of the insurance exemption, intend "to restrict the United States' ability to negotiate and implement a treaty that might affect some aspect of international insurance agreements…."[52]

With this ruling a conflict between federal circuits has been created that may eventually make its way to the Supreme Court for resolution. It may be a conflict of limited duration, if the insurance industry's recent efforts to obtain repeal of the McCarran-Ferguson Act and return the industry to unitary federal supervision succeeds. Nonetheless, while in the US context it may in time be no more than an interesting sidestream in the context of the larger discussion, this aspect of US state-federal relations may have some comparative value for the current evolution of the EC treatment of the subject of state efforts to limit the arbitrability of public-law issues.

That brings us to the basic dilemma between the duty to obey mandatory laws in substantive terms and the limited control of that duty by the judicial system either before or after arbitration has been pursued.

---

[50] For a recent full review of the use and status of these two forms of action in the convention field, see Oona Hathaway, Treaties' End: The Past, Present, and Future of International Lawmaking in the United States, 117:1236 Yale L. J. (2008).

[51] *Garamendi*, supra n. 49, at 428.

[52] Id. at 752. See also Goshawk Dedicated Limited v. Portsmouth Settlement Company I, Inc., 466 F.Supp. 1293 (N.D.Ga. 2006).

IV. Mandatory Laws and Judicial Review of Their Application in the Arbitral Process

The preemptive effect of the Federal Arbitration Act (as interpreted in the jurisprudence of the Supreme Court), once applied to international transactions despite their implications for the proper treatment of public-law issues, caused the courts concern as to its possible impact on both federal and state mandatory laws that by their terms could not be overridden by contracting parties' choice of (other) law. Both *Mitsubishi* and *Scherk*, after all, involved public laws that could not be avoided in this manner. In each case, the Supreme Court finessed that problem, when it arose in the preliminary battle over the duty to arbitrate, by finding "that a risk that arbitrators will not do their legal duty does not distinguish [these] disputes from any others." This is Judge Easterbrook's formulation of these holdings in the previously mentioned *Stawski* case.[53] Its phrasing passes rather lightly over some obvious issues such as the source of that "duty" and the evidence that it had been imposed on and accepted by the arbitration tribunal. In *Mitsubishi* the court found that latter agreement on the basis of the facts in the record, despite the contract's choice of Swiss law. In *Scherk*, the Supreme Court used a mix of policy arguments, including the possibility that the public law inherent in Rule 10b-5[54] might not reach the German seller's conduct, to deny plaintiff the litigation option. Given the procedural context of the case, it did not have to address the problem of later review of an award.

The point, however, is the distinction between the recourse to arbitration as a policy and the requirement that the otherwise applicable mandatory norms cannot be bypassed in the arbitration process. The best test of the situation is found when the applicable mandatory law has substantial extraterritorial reach. To the degree that arbitration takes place and the award rendered returns to the US for recognition and enforcement the check of a possible "bypass," while it may or not be cursory, at least will not question the legitimacy of the prescriptive jurisdiction claimed by the legislature when it made the relevant conduct actionable in substantive terms. That was not relevant in *Mitsubishi*, since the challenged anti-

---

[53] 349 F.3d at 1025.

[54] The agreement called for arbitration in Paris under ICC rules, and for the application of Illinois law to any dispute; but the US plaintiff's claim of fraud arose under Section 10(b) of the Securities Exchange Act (specifically, under Rule 10b-5), an exclusively federal cause of action.

competitive conduct there was well within the reach of any national antitrust law. It was, however, a significant issue in *Scherk*, since the alleged fraudulent behavior of the seller of the securities could be reached under US securities-regulation norms only on the basis of an "effects" test that by no means (at least at that time) was generally accepted.

This distinction—that is, the reach of prescriptive jurisdiction—illuminates the problem of judicial review of the applicability of mandatory norms in the arbitration setting. It would not be surprising to find at least a hidden if not overt repudiation by an arbitral tribunal of the US jurisprudence concerning the appropriate reach of a general norm, like that of Rule 10b-5, when its substantive violation is claimed in a context involving little connection to the US other than the domicile of the complainant.[55] Indeed, that is, basically, a statement of the facts in *Scherk*. What is the US court, reviewing the award under the minimal standards applicable in the recognition-and-enforcement context to do once the objector demonstrates even clear legal error, if "mere" legal error is not a ground for the rejection of an award in the ordinary commercial case involving only private-law norms? And if, as in *Scherk*, a finding for the defendant means that no award returns to the US court, and that court already has indicated that an objection to require arbitration of the investor-fraud dispute routinely will be dismissed, a further complication arises: What are the implications of that dismissal for a later effort to relitigate the dispute on the basis of the arbitral tribunal's allegedly erroneous or even non-existent findings, in terms of case or issue preclusion?

In my opinion a solution of this awkward dilemma in the US has to begin by revisiting the *Mitsubishi* opinion's Delphic statement that "it would not require intrusive inquiry to ascertain that the tribunal took cognizance of the antitrust claims and actually decided them." This statement says nothing about the way in which that "decision" was taken or about the level of inquiry into the degree of error in that decision, or even about the basic evidentiary documentation any appellate court would expect a trial court to have considered in a matter arising in this antitrust or securities context. If that is conceded—if *Baxter Laboratories*' reading of that phrase is deemed too narrow—then a level of review appropriate to the nature of the claim can develop; one which honors the dictates of effi-

---

[55] In the antitrust sector, at least, the U.S. Supreme Court itself has in a sense taken note of these concerns and used the policies of comity and respect for other approaches of other legal systems to mitigate this reaction. See in particular F. Hoffmann-La Roche Ltd. v. Empagran S.A., 542 U.S. 155 (2004), especially Part IV of the opinion.

ciency and speed in the recognition-and-enforcement context[56] but does not disparage the legislative value judgments inherent in that forum's catalogue of laws of mandatory application.[57]

But what of the *Scherk* type of situation, in which recognition and enforcement is not the issue? The proposed approach also implies that a court mandating recourse to arbitration over an objector's policy-based argument of non-arbitrability should not dismiss but retain jurisdiction over the matter, staying all proceedings until an award is made. If that award, as in *Scherk*, leaves nothing to recognize, the losing party (i.e., the original plaintiff in the dispute) should be permitted to reopen its original case. That court now would balance the *res judicata* or issue-preclusion effect of the award against the same dictates of efficiency and speed operative in the recognition and enforcement context. It would function, in other words, as an appellate court much as, in some jurisdictions, the courts of the arbitral forum might function.[58] Within the U.S. domestic system, the effectuation of such a process would lead to and require resolution of some complex issues of civil procedure, discussion of which is beyond the scope of this paper; but that "appellate" process in principle would be available for these purposes.[59] At the transnational level, of course, awkward issues of judicial conflicts akin to the anti-suit injunction conflicts might though need not arise; and yet other considerations of dilatory tactics and repeat litigation would have to be weighed by courts hearing such appeals and requests for de novo litigation. These, too, deserve more investigation than this brief presentation can undertake.

In any event, the practical effect of this approach should and would be on the arbitral process itself and its participants. The arbitral panel, wher-

---

[56] Note, however, that even today U.S. courts occasionally use a forum non conveniens defense to dismiss actions for recognition and enforcement of foreign awards (at least in the private sector). This unsettled issue is fully discussed in International Commercial Disputes Committee of the Association of the Bar of the City of New York, Lack of Jurisdiction and Forum Non Conveniens as Defenses to the Enforcement of Foreign Arbitration Awards, 15:407 Am. Rev. Int'l Arbitration (2004).

[57] Whether its own or those of another state deemed worthy of local honor—the *lois de police* issue.

[58] In this connection, note the judgment of the EC Court of First Instance, October 26, 2006, in C 168/05 (Mostaza Claro c. Centro Móvil Milenium, concerning the role of a "non-derogable" law argument as dictating reopening of that issue on appeal from an arbitral award though it was not raised before the tribunal.

[59] Indeed, a first such effort recently was launched, though it failed on the merits because of the full treatment of the defeated plaintiff's Rule 10b-5 claims by the Colombian arbitration tribunal. Bancol y Cia. v. Bancolombia S.A., 280 Fed.Appendix 85 (2d Cir. 2008).

ever situated, would be deliberating "in the shadow of the law;" as a result, the more transparent, factually intensive, and well-articulated its processes and awards, the more certain it and the award holder can be of respectful and expeditious treatment by the judicial system in either of the two described contexts.[60] In a world of global economic and financial networks—networks of the private actors and networks of the national, regional and international regulatory schemes and regulators—that approach in the long run might well be the principal basis of the continued vitality and legitimacy of arbitration as a system of dispute resolution.

[60] The call for more articulated and available awards is one made in many contexts, ranging from state-investor disputes (where it is on the whole honored) to commercial disputes where older summary practices had to be challenged. See, on this, Thomas Carbonneau, Rendering Arbitral Awards With Reasons, 23:579 Colum. J. Transnat'l L. (1985).

Forging American Arbitration Policy: Judicial Interpretation of the Federal Arbitration Act

RICHARD D. FREER[1]

I. Introduction

American courts inherited from their English forebears an antipathy to arbitration provisions. Judges viewed such agreements—as they viewed forum-selection clauses—to be invalid attempts to oust a tribunal of its authority.[2] Accordingly, at common law, American courts would not order enforcement of arbitration clauses. The American view has changed dramatically. The past generation, in particular, has seen full embrace of arbitration in a variety of contexts. With increasingly crowded dockets, one can hardly imagine a judge today who would not welcome a litigant's effort to leave the litigation stream and engage in alternative dispute resolution.

The sea change in the American judiciary's treatment of arbitration agreements traces back to 1925, when Congress passed the Federal Arbitration Act (FAA).[3] That legislation instructed the courts—at least, on the face of things, the federal courts—to enforce arbitration clauses. And it did much more. In 2008, the Supreme Court summarized the change eventually wrought by the FAA by saying that it

> establishes a national policy favoring arbitration when the parties contract for that mode of dispute resolution. The Act, which rests on Congress' authority under the

---

[1] It is my privilege to call Tibor Várady both my colleague and my friend.

[2] See, e.g., Cooper v. MRM Investment Co., 367 F.3d 493, 498 (6th Cir. 2004)(citations omitted)("At common law, American courts were loathe to order specific performance of an agreement to arbitrate, adopting the 'jealous notion held by the common law courts of England that arbitration agreements were nothing less than a drain on their own authority to settle disputes.' In response, Congress enacted the Federal Arbitration Act … 'to place arbitration agreements upon the same footing as other contracts.'").

[3] 9 U.S.C. §§ 1 to 14.

> Commerce Clause, supplies not simply a procedural framework applicable in federal courts; it also calls for the application, in state as well as federal courts, of federal substantive law regarding arbitration.[4]

This enthusiastic embrace was nothing new.[5] The Court had by then long made clear that arbitration could be denied only if "it may be said with positive assurance that the arbitration clause is not susceptible of an interpretation that covers the asserted dispute."[6]

The currrent state of affairs concerning arbitration under the FAA is not the result of the legislation alone. Indeed, no legislation ever gives the full story; that story is fleshed out by judicial interpretation and application of the statutory provisions. Although the central thrust of the FAA was clear, courts could surely have thwarted its impact by parsimonious interpretation. This is true in part because Congress failed to deal definitively with fundamental issues—including whether the FAA was to apply in state court proceedings and whether the Act provided federal subject matter jurisdiction. It fell to the courts to pick up the pieces left by the statutory language.

The purpose of this brief piece is to review selected topics on which the courts have been required to fashion rules that could have affected the impact of the FAA. These examples fall into two categories. First are matters addressed by the legislation, but unclearly. As to these, courts have had to engage in basic statutory interpretation. Second—and perhaps more interesting—are matters not addressed at all by the FAA. As to these, the courts have had to decide whether (and, if so, how) to fill in the gaps in the legislation. In both sets of examples, Congress probably should have been clearer. And in both sets, the courts have forged courses that generally promote a broad application of the FAA. In the end, the policy embodied in the FAA has been realized only because courts have been willing to step in to interpret and fill gaps as needed. We may put the

---

[4] Preston v. Ferrer, 128 S.Ct. 978, 981, (2008).

[5] "Section 2 [of the FAA] is a congressional declaration of a liberal federal policy favoring arbitration agreements, notwithstanding any state substantive or procedural policies to the contrary. The effect of the section is to create a body of federal substantive law of arbitrability, applicable to any arbitration agreement within the coverage of the Act.... The Arbitration Act establishes that, as a matter of federal law, any doubts concerning the scope of arbitrable issues should be resolved in favor of arbitration...." Moses H. Cone Memorial Hospital v. Mercury Const. Corp., 460 U.S. 1, 24–25 (1983).

[6] AT & T Technologies, Inc. v. Communications Workers of America, 475 U.S. 643, 650 (1986), quoting United Steelworkers of America v. Warrior & Gulf Navigation Co., 363 U.S. 574, 582–583 (1960).

examples in context by setting forth a brief overview of the main provisions of the FAA.

I. Brief Overview of the FAA

The FAA is based upon Congress's authority over interstate and international commerce. Although that authority is broad, it is not without limit, and Congress was careful not to attempt to federalize the whole of arbitration contract law. For example, § 2 of the FAA[7] makes an agreement to arbitrate specifically enforceable only if it is connected with a maritime transaction or a transaction involving foreign or interstate commerce. Even then, the Act expressly does not apply to contracts of employment of specified classes of workers engaged in interstate commerce.[8]

Chapter 2 of the FAA contemplates foreign arbitration.[9] The fact that a court in the United States may lack the power to enforce an injunction in a foreign forum is not an obstacle to its issuing an order compelling arbitration in a foreign country.[10] The federal policy favoring arbitration is said to have especial force in international disputes.[11]

Sections 3 and 4 are the centerpiece of the FAA. Specifically, § 3 requires a court in which suit has been brought "upon any issue referable to arbitration under an agreement in writing for such arbitration" to stay the court action pending arbitration once it is satisfied that the issue is arbitrable under the agreement. And § 4 provides a remedy for a party "aggrieved by the alleged failure, neglect, or refusal of another to arbitrate under a written agreement for arbitration." This provision, obviously,

---

[7] 9 U.S.C. § 2. The section number of each basic provision of the FAA corresponds to its placement in Title 9 of the United States Code (which contains the FAA). Thus, § 1 of the FAA is 9 U.S.C. § 1, § 2 of the FAA is 9 U.S.C. § 2, and so forth. For convenience, I will refer to the section numbers in the FAA, rather than by their formal designation in Title 9.

[8] 9 U.S.C. § 1: "[N]othing herein contained shall apply to contracts of employment of seamen, railroad employees, or any other class of workers engaged in foreign or interstate commerce."

[9] Chapter 2 of the FAA is found at 9 U.S.C. § 201 et seq.

[10] See, e.g., Intergen N.V. v. Grina, 344 F.3d 134, 142 (1st Cir. 2003).

[11] See, e.g., Paramedics Electro. v. GE Med. Sys., 369 F.3d 645, 654 (2d Cir. 2004)(federal policy favoring arbitration applies "with particular force in international disputes"); Laif X Sprl v. Axtel, S.A. de C.V., 310 F.Supp.2d 578, 581 (S.D. N.Y. 2004)(same).

permits a court to compel arbitration.[12] Together, these two sections ensure reference to arbitration in appropriate cases and that the benefits of the alternative forum will not be thwarted by ongoing litigation.

Sections 9, 10, and 11 provide a complete mechanism for judicial review of arbitration awards. Section 9 allows a judicial order enforcing an arbitration award. Section 10 allows a court to vacate an award, and § 11 allows an order modifying or correcting an award. Judicial review under each provision is expedited.[13] Not surprisingly, § 10 permits vacation of an award on very limited grounds. Specifically, a court may set aside an arbitration award only if (1) it was procured by corruption, fraud, or undue means; (2) an arbitrator displayed evident partiality or corruption; (3) an arbitrator engaged in misconduct by failing to postpone the hearing or in refusing to hear pertinent evidence or other misbehavior that prejudices the rights of a party; or (4) the arbitrator exceeded her powers.

In 1988, Congress added § 16 to the FAA, which specifies that certain judicial orders relating to arbitration are subject to judicial review.[14] The most significant part is § 16(a)(1)(B), which provides that the denial of a request for arbitration is, unlike most interlocutory rulings, immediately appealable.

Congress's basic goal in passing the FAA was clear: to put arbitration clauses "upon the same footing as other contracts," so as to render them "valid, irrevocable, and enforceable, save upon such grounds as exist at law or in equity for the revocation of any contract."[15] Under the Act, contracts of arbitration are to be as enforceable as any other contract, but not more so. Thus a court must be satisfied, based upon ordinary contract principles, that the parties intended to have the dispute resolved through arbitration rather than litigation.[16] Whether a contractual provision for

[12] The section provides in part that one so aggrieved "may petition any United States district court which, save for such agreement, would have jurisdiction under Title 28, in a civil action or in admiralty of the subject matter of a suit arising out of the controversy between the parties, for an order directing that such arbitration proceed in the manner provided for in such agreement." 9 U.S.C. § 4.

[13] "An application for any of these orders [under §§ 9, 10, or 11] will get streamlined treament as a motion, obviating the sparate contract action that would usually be necessary to enforce or tinker with an arbitral award in court." Hall Street Assocs., LLC v. Mattel, Inc., 128 S.Ct. 1396, 1402 (2008).

[14] 9 U.S.C. § 16, added by Act of Nov. 19, 1988, Pub.L. 100–702, § 1019, 102 Stat. 4670.

[15] EEOC v. Waffle House, Inc., 534 U.S. 279, 288–289 (2002).

[16] See, e.g., In re Continental Airlines, Inc., 484 F.3 173, 182 (3d Cir. 2007)("It is axiomatic that arbitration is a matter of contract.").

arbitration is valid is determined by general principles of contract law, usually under state law.[17] Accordingly, general contract defenses, such as fraud, may invalidate an arbitration agreement without contravening the FAA.[18]

Against this brief sketch, we turn to specific examples of unclarity in the FAA that could have limited its reach significantly.

II. Interpretations Concerning the Scope of the FAA

Section 1 of the FAA is an exemption provision. It makes clear that certain "contracts of employment" are not affected by the legislation. Obviously, then, Congress concluded that some employment contracts were not to benefit from the liberal pro-arbitration policy of the FAA. But Congress did not say that all contracts of employment were exempt—only particular ones. And it is here that the legislation suffers from uncertainty.

The exclusion extends to employment contracts "of seamen, railroad employees, [and] any other class of workers engaged in foreign or interstate commerce." The quoted phrase is interesting for the obvious juxtaposition of narrow and broad. While the provision starts with very specific types of employment, it ends with the broadest possible reference to congressional power under the commerce authority. No doubt many employees emphasized the latter language, attempting to have their employment disputes litigated rather than arbitrated. And at least the Ninth Circuit heard them. That court concluded that the exemption in § 1 applied to all employment contracts.[19] According to the Ninth Circuit, "Congress never intended for the FAA to apply to employment contracts of any sort."[20]

Other lower courts championed a more restrictive reading, however, and were ultimately vindicated by the Supreme Court. In 2001, the Court rejected the Ninth Circuit view and held that the limitation in § 1 applies only to employment contracts of transportation workers.[21] It reasoned that the broad language concerning "any other class of workers engaged in

[17] Ingle v. Circuit City Stores, Inc., 328 F.3d 1165, 1170 (9th Cir. 2003), cert. denied 540 U.S. 1160.

[18] Skirchak v. Dynamics Research Corp., 508 F.3d 49, 57–58 (1st Cir. 2007).

[19] Craft v. Campbell Soup Co., 177 F.3d 1083 (9th Cir. 1999).

[20] *Id.* at 1090.

[21] Circuit City Stores, Inc. v. Adams, 532 U.S. 105 (2001). Accordingly, the plaintiff in the case, who was not a transportation worker, was not exempted from application of the Act.

foreign or interstate commerce" had to be interpreted in light of the specific mention of seamen and railroad employees. Whatever one thinks of the rationale, there is no question that the holding ensured that the FAA can apply to the vast majority of employment contracts. Interestingly, it was not until 2001 that the issue was decided definitively.

Of greater potential importance is the question of whether the FAA was to apply in state courts. As a matter of policy, it seems obvious that it should. After all, what good is a statute that can be thwarted by the simple expedient of suing in state court? But the language of the FAA is not clear on this score.

Indeed, §§ 3 and 4, which permit courts to stay litigation and to compel arbitration, refer only to suits in federal court.[22] In the important case of *Moses H. Cone Memorial Hospital v. Mercury Construstion Corp.*,[23] the Court rescued the FAA by concluding that § 3 applied to state court litigation. It was not required to rule concerning § 4, but left no doubt that it should be decided the same way. The Court reasoned in part by incredulity: "Congress can hardly have meant that an agreement to arbitrate can be enforced against a party who attempts to litigate an arbitrable dispute in federal court, but not against one who sues on the same dispute in state court."[24]

It is rather surprising that legislation as important as the FAA would be bedeviled by such fundamental questions as these. In each case—concerning the exemption in § 1 and the application of the FAA in state court—the Court chose the path that led to broader application of the Act.

Section 10 of the FAA lists the bases on which a court may set aside an arbitration award. Courts have resolved two problems with that list, and have done so, interestingly, in different ways. First, Congress neglected to include "manifest disregard of the law" as a basis for vacating an award. Notwithstanding the principle of *expressio unius est exlusio alterius,* the courts have essentially engrafted this basis onto the list in § 10.[25] Second,

---

[22] Section 3 refers to stays of proceedings "[i]n any suit or proceeding ... brought in any of the courts of the United States...." Section 4 speaks of a petition to "any United States district court...." for an order compelling arbitration.

[23] 460 U.S. 1 (1983).

[24] *Id.,* at 27 n.34. As to § 4, the Court noted state authority for the proposition that it applies in state court. *Id.* at 27 n.35, citing Main v. Merrill Lynch, Pierce, Fenner & Smith Inc., 67 Cal.App.3d 19, 24–25, 136 Cal.Rptr. 378, 380–381 (1977).

[25] See, e.g., Hudson v. Conagra Poultry Co., 484 F.3d 496, 504 (8th Cir. 2007)(in addition to the statutory grounds for setting aside arbitration award under § 10, court will vacate award for manifest disregard of the law; none shown on the facts of this case, however);

however, is the question of whether the grounds listed in § 10 may be supplemented by contract. Lower courts had disagreed on the point.[26] In 2008, the Court held that the statutory grounds are exclusive and thus struck a parties' effort to allow vacation of an award for simple error of law.[27] In other words, in one way the statutory list was not exclusive, while as to another it was.

Finally, the relatively new provisions in § 16 for interlocutory review of various judicial orders concerning atbitration have created a problem. That section does not expressly require a party to take such an appeal and, ordinarily, failure to pursue an available interlocutory appeal does not result in forfeiture of the right to raise the issue subsequently. This is simply an example of congressional lack of foresight. The result, of course, is that the courts have to forge an answer for something Congress could have addressed. At least four courts of appeals have held that failure to pursue this interlocutory avenue promptly may, under certain circumstances, estop the demanding party from pursuing its claim of arbitrability.[28] Such

---

Duferco Int'l Steel Trading v. T. Klaveness Shipping A/S, 333 F.3d 383 (2d Cir. 2003); Marshall v. Green Giant Co., 942 F.2d 539 (8th Cir. 1991).

See also CACI Premier Tech., Inc. v. Faraci, 464 F.Supp.2d 527, 532 (E.D. Va. 2007)(manifest disregard of the law may satisfy statutory ground that arbitrator exceeded her power).

26 The Ninth and Tenth Circuits held that parties may not contract for judicial review based upon factors not included in §§ 10 and 11. Kyocera Corp. v. Prudential-Bache Trade Servs., Inc., 341 F.3d 987, 1000 (9th Cir. 2003); Bowen v. Amoco Pipeline Co., 254 F.3d 925, 936 (10th Cir. 2001).

In contrast, the First, Third, Fifth, and Sixth Circuits permitted parties to provide by contract for judicial review on terms not included in the statutes. Puerto Rico Tel. Co. v. U.S. Phone Mfg. Corp., 427 F.3d 21, 31 (1st Cir. 2005); Jacada 9Europe, Ltd. v. International Mktg. Strategies, Inc., 401 F.3d 701, 710 (6th Cir. 2005); Roadway Pkg. Sys., Inc. v., Kayser, 257 F.3d 287, 288 (3d Cir. 2001); Gateway Techs., Inc. v. MCI Telecomms. Corp., 64 F.3d 993, 997 (5th Cir. 1995).

27 Hall Street Assocs., LLC v. Mattel, Inc., 128 S.Ct. 1396, 1403–1406 (2008). The Court emphasized that its holding addressed only cases in which parties sought review under §§ 9, 10, or 11. "The FAA is not the only way into court for parties wanting review of arbitration awards: they may contemplate enforcement under state statutory or common law, for example, where judicial review of different scope is arguable." 128 S.Ct. at 1406. It remanded for consideration by the lower courts of whether such a non-FAA basis for review might apply.

28 Such estoppel is not automatic, however, and will be applied only upon a showing, inter alia, of prejudice to the other party. Colon v. R.K. Grace & Co., 358 F.3d 1, 4 (1st Cir. 2003); Cargill Ferrous Int'l v. Sea Phoenix MV, 325 F.3d 695, 700 (5th Cir. 2003); John Morrell & Co. v. United Food & Commercial Workers Int'l Union, 37 F.3d 1302, 1303 (8th Cir. 1994); Cotton v. Slone, 4 F.3d 176, 180 (2d Cir. 1993).

estoppel may make sense to avoid the waste of resources caused by a post-trial determination that the matter should have been arbitrated. These courts have been reluctant to impose an automatic waiver in this regard. Rather, the issue should be addressed on a case-by-case basis.[29]

In each of these examples, courts had to decide an issue which the FAA arguably addressed. In contrast, we turn now to topics on which the FAA simply says nothing.

III. Judicial Gap-Filling in Topics on Which the FAA is Silent

There are four important areas in which the courts have had to forge their way without any guidance in the FAA. Specifically, they are: (1) subject matter jurisdiction, (2) allocation of decision-making authority between the judge and the arbitrator, (3) how to proceed in cases presenting both arbitrable and non-arbitrable matters, and (4) how to handle statutory claims.

A. Subject Matter Jurisdiction

Although the FAA creates a body of substantive law concerning arbitration, it does not grant subject matter jurisdiction. This fact was especially clear with regard to §§ 3 and 4. The language of § 4 is explicit on the point[30] and § 3, allowing a stay of a pending action in favor of arbitration, necessarily is based upon the idea that there must be some jurisdictional basis for the action to be stayed.

But § 9 is far less clear. On its face, that provision could be read as granting the district courts jurisdiction for applications to enforce awards of arbitrators.[31] But it does not use language common to jurisdictional

---

[29] *Colon*, 358 F.3d at 4 (failure to pursue interlocutory appeal did not result in forfeiture of claim of arbitrability under the facts, where the district judge did not definitively deny the request for arbitration until after trial had begun.).

[30] Section 4 provides: that a party may petition "any United States district court which, save for such agreement, would have jurisdiction under Title 28, in a civil action or in admiralty of the subject matter of a suit arising out of the controversy between the parties...."

[31] Section 9 provides that if the parties in the arbitration agreement have specified the court that is to enforce awards, application shall be made to that court. The second sentence then provides: "If no court is specified in the agreement of the parties, then such application may be made to the United States court in and for the district within which such award was made." The third sentence of Section 9 refers to "jurisdiction" but in context plainly is speaking to personal, rather than subject matter, jurisdiction.

grants, and courts rather easily concluded that a case under § 9 should require an independent basis of subject matter jurisdiction. As one court noted, requiring independent jurisdictional grounds under §§ 3 and 4 but not under § 9 "would render the Arbitration Act—enacted as a single, coordinated piece of legislation in February, 1925—little more than an odd patchwork of individual statutes, bereft of any coherent plan."[32] Similarly, courts have concluded that neither § 10 nor § 11 of the FAA grants subject matter jurisdiction.[33]

Accordingly, for a federal court to entertain any suit related to arbitration, there must be an independent basis of jurisdiction.[34] Ordinarily, the jurisdictional basis will be diversity of citizenship, which requires, of course, that the case satisfy the citizenship and amount-in-controversy requirements of 28 U.S.C. § 1332(a). The latter mandates that the amount in controversy exceed $75,000. In determining the amount in controversy of a suit to compel arbitration, the court looks to the amount at stake in the arbitration—that is, the award that might reasonably result from an arbitration.[35]

In suits to confirm or vacate an arbitration award, however, there is an interesting question: to assess the amount in controversy, does the court

---

[32] Bangor & A. R. Co. v. Maine Cent. R. Co., 359 F.Supp. 261, 263 (D. D.C. 1973).

[33] Luong v. Circuit City Stores, Inc., 368 F.3d 1109, 1110–1111 n.3 (9th Cir. 2004)(though language of § 10 arguably creates jurisdiction, and thus the precedent is "quite an odd construct," the precedent is to the contrary and is clear); Greenberg v. Bear, Stearns & Co., 220 F.3d 22, 26 (2d Cir. 2000), cert. denied 531 U.S. 1075.

[34] "As for jurisdiction over controversies touching arbitration, the Act does nothing…." Hall Street Assocs., LLC v. Mattel, Inc., 128 S.Ct. 1396, 1402 (2008).

The Supreme Court explained in the *Moses Cone* case, 460 U.S. at 26, n. 32:

> The Arbitration Act is something of an anomaly in the field of federal-court jurisdiction. It creates a body of federal substantive law establishing and regulating the duty to honor an agreement to arbitrate, yet it does not create any independent federal-question jurisdiction under 28 U.S.C. § 1331 or otherwise. Section 4 provides for an order compelling arbitration only when the federal district court would have jurisdiction over a suit on the underlying dispute; hence, there must be diversity of citizenship or some other independent basis for federal jurisdiction before the order can issue.

[35] See, e.g., Advance Am. Servicing of Arkansas v. McGinnis, 526 F.3d 1170, 1173 (8th Cir. 2008)(lender's action to compel arbitration failed to invoke diversity of citizenship jurisdiction because disputed loans were valued at less than $1,000 and lender could not include amounts claimed by pending state-court class action); America's Moneyline, Inc. v. Coleman, 360 F.3d 782, 786–787 (7th Cir. 2004)(because arbitrator could not have awarded relief in excess of $75,000, case could not invoke diversity of citizenship jurisdiction).

look to the arbitration award itself or to some other figure? Obviously, if the award meets the amount requirement for a diversity case, a suit to compel or vacate presents no trouble—the amount requirement is satisfied. The problem arises when the award does not meet the amount requirement—including when the defendant wins the arbitration and the award is zero dollars. In such cases, looking to the amount of the award would mean that a defendant could never invoke diversity jurisdiction in a suit to confirm the award.[36] The matter may be complicated when a party seeks an order vacating an arbitration award and remanding the parties to a new arbitration.

The courts are not in agreement on how to deal with such cases. Some courts consider the arbitration award as the amount in controversy.[37] Others look to the amount of the underlying demand, at least if the party seeking to have the award vacated also seeks remand for new arbitration.[38] There is also some authority for looking to the amount of the underlying

---

[36] In Perpetual Secs., Inc. v. Tang, 290 F.3d 132, 136 (2d Cir. 2002), the arbitration award did not satisfy the amount in controversy requirement for diversity of citizenship jurisdiction. Though the court noted in passing that the claim would not invoke diversity, the parties had not raised the issue and the court focused instead on whether there was federal question jurisdiction. Two district courts have quite properly concluded, therefore, that this case should not be considered authority for the proposition that the amount of an arbitration award should always control. Doctor's Associates, Inc. v. Puskaritz, 2006 U.S.Dist.LEXIS 23208 (D. Conn. 2006); North American Thought Combine, Inc. v. Kelly, 249 F.Supp.2d 283, 285–286 (S.D. N.Y. 2003).

[37] See, e.g., Baltin v. Alaron Trading Corp., 128 F.3d 1466, 1472 (11th Cir. 1997). The court suggested, however, that had the plaintiffs requested modification that would have provided them with an increased recovery, the amount in controversy would include the increased amount sought plus the award recovery. *Id.* at 1472 n. 16.

See also Ford v. Hamilton Investments, Inc., 29 F.3d 255, 260 (6th Cir. 1994); Goodman v. CIBC Oppenheimer & Co., 131 F.Supp.2d 1180, 1184 (C.D. Cal. 2001).

See generally, Frost, *Welcome to the Jungle: Rethinking the Amount in Controversy in a Petition to Vacate an Arbitration Award Under the Federal Arbitration Act*, 32 Pepp.L.Rev. 227 (2005), in which the author concludes that the amount of the arbitration demand should control.

[38] See, e.g., Sirotzki v. New York Stock Exch., 347 F.3d 985, 989 (7th Cir. 2003)("The amount in controversy in a suit challenging an arbitration award includes the matter at stake in the arbitration, provided the plaintiff is seeking to reopen the arbitration."); Choice Hotels Int'l, Inc. v. Felizardo, 278 F.Supp.2d 590, 593–594 (D. Md. 2003)(amount of award sought to be avoided, plus amount to be obtained on remand to arbitration, met amount in controversy requirement for diversity of citizenship jurisdiction).

demand regardless of whether a party seeks a new arbitration.[39] It is imporant to contrast these cases, however, with one in which an underlying litigation invoked diversity of citizenship jurisdiction and was stayed pending arbitration. There, the jurisdiction invoked in the underlying litigation is retained, regardless of the amount of the arbitration award.[40]

The Ninth Circuit has had an especially difficult time with this issue. In *Luong v. Circuit City Stores, Inc.*,[41] the plaintiff sued for damages satisfying the amount in controversy requirement for diversity of citizenship jurisdiction. Granting defendant's motion, the district court compelled arbitration, which resulted in an award of zero dollars. The plaintiff then filed a separate case under § 10 of the FAA to vacate the award. The district court dismissed for lack of jurisdiction, holding that the amount in controversy was the arbitration award of zero dollars. Although the Ninth Circuit initially affirmed this decision, it later withdrew that opinion.[42] It then issued a new opinion in which it upheld federal question jurisdiction and elided the amount-in-controversy issue.[43]

In a different case, decided months later, in which the arbitration award was zero dollars, the Ninth Circuit upheld diversity jurisdiction.[44] There, after the parties submitted to arbitration, the plaintiff filed suit seeking to vacate the award and claiming damages on the underlying claim that would satisfy diversity jurisdiction. Though the plaintiff did not seek to reopen arbitration, the court considered the underlying claim—and not the arbitration award—to be the amount in controversy.

Such problems do not exist, of course, if the case invokes admiralty or federal question jurisdiction, for which there is no amount-in-controversy requirement. Many cases invoke such jurisdiction, such as claims for violation of various federal statutes.[45] More interestingly, it is arguable

[39] See, e.g., American Guar. Co. v. Caldwell, 72 F.2d 209, 211 (9th Cir. 1934). For modern discussion of the importance of this old case, see Theis Research, Inc. v. Brown & Bain, 400 F.3d 659, 664–665 (9th Cir. 2004).

[40] See Choice Hotels Int'l, Inc. v. Shiv Hospitality, LLC, 491 F.3d 171, 176 (4th Cir. 2007). The court relied upon the well-established principle that jurisdiction, once established, is not divested by acts of the parties.

[41] 356 F.3d 1188 (9th Cir. 2004).

[42] 368 F.3d 1113 (9th Cir. 2004).

[43] Luong v. Circuit City Stores, Inc., 368 F.3d 1109 (9th Cir. 2004). There is no amount-in-controversy requirement in cases that invoke federal question jurisdiction under 28 U.S.C. § 1331.

[44] Theis Research, Inc. v. Brown & Bain, 400 F.3d 659, 664–665 (9th Cir. 2004).

[45] See, e.g., Parilla v. IAP Worldwide Servs, VI, Inc., 368 F.3d 269, 274 (3d Cir. 2004)(claim for violation of Title VII invoked federal question jurisdiction, while

that the FAA may create a right, vindication of which invokes federal question jurisdiction. In this regard, the Eighth Circuit has held that the FAA creates a federal right that arbitration agreements will be enforceable and that efforts to litigate administratively claims that already had been arbitrated would interfere with that right and thus invoke federal-question jurisdiction.[46]

Similarly, the Second Circuit has held that an action to vacate an arbitration award may invoke federal question jurisdiction if it is based upon the arbitrator's manifest disregard of federal law.[47] In such a case, the federal court must determine what the federal law is and then determine whether the arbitrator manifestly disregarded it, a process that "so immerses the federal court in questions of federal law and their proper application that federal question subject matter jurisdiction is present."[48] Jurisdiction in such a case attaches even though the court ultimately determines that the arbitrator did not manifestly disregard federal law in making the arbitration decision.[49]

The courts' conclusion that the basic provisions of the FAA require an independent basis of federal subject matter jurisdiction may be bolstered by the fact that Congress knows how to grant federal jurisdiction when it wants to. For example, § 203 of the FAA provides federal subject matter jurisdiction over actions falling under the Convention on the Recognition and Enforcement of Foreign Arbitral Awards.[50]

---

related state-law claims invoked supplemental jurisdiction under 28 U.S.C. § 1367); America's Moneyline, Inc. v. Coleman, 360 F.3d 782, 785–786 (7th Cir. 2004) (in assessing whether claim under § 4 of the FAA invokes federal question jurisdiction, court assesses the matter as it does in any federal question case).

[46] Merrill Lynch, Pierce, Fenner and Smith v. Nixon, 210 F.3d 814, 817 (8th Cir. 2000), certi. denied 531 U.S. 958.

[47] Greenberg v. Bear, Stearns & Co., 220 F.3d 22, 25–28 (2d Cir. 2000), cert. denied 531 U.S. 1075. The court emphasized that the assertion must be the principal basis on which the arbitration decision is attacked and must be raised in good faith. *Id.* at 27.

[48] *Greenberg*, 220 F.3d at 27.

See also Biscanin v. Merrill Lynch & Co., Inc., 407 F.3d 905, 906–908 (8th Cir. 2005)(although Eighth Circuit "not certain" it agrees with the holding of the *Greenberg* case, it did not have to decide the question; action to set aside arbitration award on basis of arbitrator's alleged manifest disregard of law was so patently without merit that it failed to invoke federal question jurisdiction).

[49] *Greenberg*, 220 F.3d at 28–29.

[50] See, e.g., Credit Suisse First Boston, LLC v. Padilla, 326 F.Supp.2d 508, 510–511 (S.D. N.Y. 2004)(a dispute falls under that Convention when (1) there is a written agreement, (2) it provides for arbitration in the territory of a signatory of the Convention, (3) the contract concerns commercial subject matter, and (4) is not entirely domestic in scope).

B. Allocation of Decision-making Authority

One perennial question in arbitration is the allocation of initial decision-making authority on any particular issue. The FAA gives no guidance on the topic. The Supreme Court has long made clear that a "question of arbitrability" is to be decided by the court unless the parties clearly and unmistakably provide otherwise.[51] More recently, however, the Court has established that this "gateway" issue of arbitrability "has a ... limited scope."[52] For instance, the Court has held that the following issues do not raise questions of arbitrability and thus should (absent agreement to the contrary) be decided in the first instance by the arbitrator: whether a claim is barred by a temporal limitation contained in the arbitration rules of the National Association of Securities Dealers,[53] whether an arbitration agreement's limitation on recovery of punitive damages barred a claim for treble damages under RICO,[54] and whether an arbitration agreement forbids class arbitration.[55]

Generally, questions about arbitration procedure should be resolved in the first instance by the arbitrator.[56] Outside "the most distant of outer bounds," such as the use of undue means to procure an arbitration award, the Federal Arbitration Act does not regulate arbitration procedure.[57] The

---

[51] AT & T Technologies, Inc. v. Communications Workers, 475 U.S. 643, 649 (1986).
See also Howsam v. Dean Witter Reynolds, Inc., 537 U.S. 79, 83–85, (2002); In re Continental Airlines, Inc., 484 F.3 173, 182 (3d Cir. 2007); Poweragent v. Electronic Data Sys., 358 F.3d 1187, 1191–1193 (9th Cir. 2004)(arbitrability usually is decided by the court, not the arbitrator, unless there is clear evidence that the parties agreed to arbitrate the issue).

[52] Howsam v. Dean Witter Reynolds, Inc., 537 U.S. 79, 83 (2002).

[53] *Howsam,* 537 U.S. at 83. The Court noted other examples of issues to be decided (in the absence of agreement to the contrary) by the arbitrator: whether the first two steps of a grievance procedure were followed, where they were prerequisites to arbitration; allegations of waiver, delay, or similar defense; whether conditions precedent to arbitration were satisfied; and defenses such as laches, estoppel, and waiver.

[54] Pacificare Health Sys., Inc. v. Book, 538 U.S. 401, 407 (2003)("Given our presumption in favor of arbitration [cit.], we think the preliminary question whether the remedial limitations at issue here prohibit an award of RICO treble damages is not a question of arbitrability.").

[55] Green Tree Fin. Corp. v. Bazzle, 539 U.S. 444, 453–454 (2003)(plurality opinion).
See also Skirchak v. Dynamics Research Corp., 508 F.3d 49, 56 (1st Cir. 2007); Anderson v. Comcast Corp., 500 F.3d 66, 72 (1st Cir. 2007); Pedcor Mgt. v. Nations Personnel of Texas, 343 F.3d 355, 358–363 (5th Cir. 2003).

[56] Prima Paint Corp. v. Flood & Conklin Mfg. Co., 388 U.S. 395, 403–404 (1967).

[57] Sirotzky v. New York Stock Exch., 347 F.3d 985, 990 (7th Cir. 2003).

FAA does not require that parties be represented by lawyers, and the issue of whether lawyers—including a lawyer not licensed to practice in the state in which the arbitration proceeds—may participate is for the arbitrator, not the court, to decide.[58]

Another interesting issue is which forum—judicial or arbitral—is to decide questions relating to fraudulent inducement of an agreement to arbitrate. In *Prima Paint Corp. v. Flood & Conklin Manufacturing Co.*, the Supreme Court held that the court is to determine only "issues relating to the making and performance of the agreement to arbitrate."[59] In *Prima Paint*, a party to a case in federal court attacked the contract as a whole, and not simply the arbitration agreement contained within it, on the ground of fraudulent inducement. Because the attack was thus not on the "making" or "performance" of the arbitration clause itself, the issue was to be determined by the arbitrator and not the court. Accordingly, an argument that the arbitration clause itself is the result of fraudulent inducement is to be determined by the court,[60] while an argument that the overall contract is the result of fraudulent inducement is to be determined by the arbitrator. And an argument attacking the very existence of any contract is to be determined by the court.[61]

---

[58] Party losing at arbitration complained that lawyer for other side, licensed in another state, was permitted to engage in tactics that would violate rules of professional conduct in the forum state. While the argument "does suggest a way in which a litigant can be harmed by the unlicensed status of his opponent's lawyer," such procedural questions are to be decided by the arbitrator, not the court. *Sirotzky,* 347 F.3d at 990.

[59] 388 U.S. 395, 403–404 (1967). Because defense that entire contract was void for fraudulent inducement did not attack the "making" or "performance" of the agreement to arbitrate itself, court should order arbitration. FAA reflects "unmistakably clear congressional purpose that the arbitration procedure, when selected by the parties to a contract, be speedy and not subject to delay and obstruction by the courts." *Id.* at 404.

[60] See, e.g., Banc One Acceptance Corp. v. Hill, 367 F.3d 426, 430 (5th Cir. 2004)(validity of arbitration clause itself was for judicial determination); Highlands Wellmont Health v. John Deere Health, 350 F.3d 568, 575–576 (6th Cir. 2003)(court to address well-founded argument of fraud in the inducement of the arbitration clause itself, standing apart from the whole agreement); Bragg v. Linden Research, 487 F.Supp.2d 593, 605 n.15 (E.D. Pa. 2007)(determination of whether arbitration clause was unconscionable was to be made by court, not arbitrator).

[61] See, e.g., Will-Drill Resources, Inc. v. Samson Resources Co., 352 F.3d 211, 218 (5th Cir. 2003)(federal court must address the argument that not all parties signed the contract; such a defense calls into question the "very existence" of a contract and is for judicial determination, because if no contract ever came into existence, there was never any agreement to arbitrate); Banc One Acceptance Corp. v. Hill, 367 F.3d 426, 430–431 (5th Cir. 2004)(argument that no contract existed is to be distinguished from the "far

The Court amplified some of these basic points in cases decided in 2006 and 2008. In *Buckeye Check Cashing, Inc. v. Cardegna*,[62] the Court applied its holding in *Prima Paint* to a case in which the underlying litigation was filed in state court. That fact made no difference: when parties agree to arbitrate all disputes arising under their contract, questions concerning the validity of the entire contract are to be resolved in the first instance by the arbitrator, and not by a court.

A more interesting case is *Preston v. Ferrer*,[63] which involved a contract between a television actor and his attorney. The attorney invoked the arbitration provision of the contract in an effort to seek fees allegedly due under the contract. The actor petitioned a state administrative agency for a determination that the contract as a whole was invalid and unenforceable because the attorney was not a licensed talent agent under California law. A state court enjoined the attorney from proceeding with arbitration until the state administrative agency determined whether it had jurisdiction over the dispute. It concluded that state law vested the administrative agency with exclusive jurisdiction. The Supreme Court reversed. When a party attacks the validity of the entire contract—and not just the arbitration provision—the FAA supersedes state law that vests jurisdiction in another forum, either judicial or administrative.[64]

C. Mixed Arbitrable and Non-arbitrable Issues

Some lower courts concluded that if claims subject to arbitration were joined with nonarbitrable claims, and the claims were intertwined factually and legally, the court could deny arbitration even of the arbitrable claims and try all claims together. A unanimous Supreme Court rejected that

---

more common argument made by a party who does not challenge the existence of a contract, but rather attacks the enforceability of the agreement [by] alleging that the contract is void ab initio or voidable. Such a scenario calls for application of the severability doctrine contained in *Prima Paint*."); Runnin' Easy 3, Inc. v. Offshore Marine Towing, 314 F.Supp.2d 1246, 1251–1252 (S.D. Fla. 2004)(because party attacked validity of entire contract, not just arbitration clause, arbitrator would address question of fraudulent inducement).

[62] 546 U.S. 440 (2006). The Court later explained: "In [*Prima Paint*], we held that attacks on the validity of an entire contract, as distinct from atttacks aimed at the arbitration clause, are within the arbitrator's ken. The litigation in Prima Paint originated in federal court, but the same rule, we held in Buckeye, applies in state court." Preston v. Ferrer, 128 S.Ct. 978, 983–984 (2008).

[63] *Id.*.

[64] 128 S.Ct. at 982–988.

practice, and held that the courts have no such discretion. "[T]he Arbitration Act requires district courts to compel arbitration of pendent arbitrable claims when one of the parties files a motion to compel, even where the result would be the possibly inefficient maintenance of separate proceedings in different forums."[65] In that case that courts are free to decide for themselves what preclusive effect should be given to arbitration proceedings, and in framing a preclusion rule, can take into account the federal interests warranting protection.[66]

This situation is to be contrasted with one in which issues will remain in the judicial forum. Though § 3 speaks of a stay of "the trial of the action," which implies that the entire case be stayed, courts generally have concluded that non-arbitrable issues in the case need not be stayed, but may continue in litigation, notwithstanding a risk of piecemeal litigation. These courts have recognized an exception, however, when allowing litigation of non-arbitrable issues creates a risk of inconsistent rulings because the arbitration is likely to resolve issues material to the ongoing litigation.[67]

D. Federal Statutory Claims

There has always been some concern that certain federal statutory claims would somehow be diluted if subject to arbitration. That is, statutory claims should be sufficiently important to command litigation and, where appropriate, trial by jury. The Supreme Court has largely rejected this notion, and has upheld arbitration of a wide variety of statutory claims.[68]

---

[65] Dean Witter Reynolds Inc. v. Byrd, 470 U.S. 213, 217 (1985).

See also Hudson v. Conagra Poultry Co., 484 F.3d 496, 499–500 (8th Cir. 2007)("Under the Federal Arbitration Act, we generally construe broad language in a contractual arbitration provision to include tort claims arising from the contractual relationship, and we compel arbitration of such claims.").

[66] Dean Witter Reynolds Inc. v. Byrd, 470 U.S. 213, 221–225 (1985).

[67] See, e.g., Volkswagen of Am. v. Sud's of Peoria, 474 F.3d 966, 971–974 (7th Cir. 2007); American Recovery Corp. AgGrow Oils, LLC v. Natl. Union Fire Ins., 242 F.3d 777, 783 (8th Cir. 2001); American Recovery Corp. v. Computerized Thermal Imaging, Inc., 96 F.3d 88, 97 (4th Cir. 1996).

[68] See, e.g., Pacificare Health Sys., Inc. v. Book, 538 U.S. 401, 404–408 (2003)(RICO claims can be asserted in arbitration); Circuit City Stores, Inc. v. Adams, 532 U.S. 105, 109 (2001)(agreements to arbitrate employment disputes as a condition of employment are generally enforceable under the FAA).

See also In re Electric Machinery Enterprises, Inc., 479 F.3d 791, 796–797 (11th Cir. 2007)(bankruptcy); EEOC v. Woodmen of World Life Ins. Soc., 479 F.3d 561, 565 (8th Cir. 2007).

For example, an employee who agrees to arbitrate claims arising from her employment does not waive the protection of federal law, but merely substitutes an arbitral forum for a judicial forum for vindication of those claims.

It is imperative, however, that the arbitral forum provide effective vindication of the statutory claim.[69] For instance, in one case, an employer's arbitrator-selection process did not provide an effective substitute for a judicial forum in plaintiff's Title VII case.[70] And because Title VII permits recovery of punitive damages, an arbitration agreement's ban on such relief was unenforceable.[71] In some cases, parties have contended that fee-shifting clauses impose undue restrictions on their ability to obtain statutory relief. The courts have not spoken with one voice on the issue.[72] In 2000, the Court reversed a lower court holding that arbitration expense denied the plaintiff an effective forum. The Court noted that the holding was not based upon any evidence in the record, and held that the party asserting prohibitive expense has the burden of demonstrating the "likelihood of incurring such costs."[73]

Finally, the Court held that a predispute agreement to arbitrate claims arising under the Securities Act of 1933 is enforceable.[74] It had already reached that result with regard to claims under the Securities Exchange

---

[69] Gilmer v. Interstate/Johnson Lane Corp., 500 U.S. 20, 26, 28 (1991), quoting Mitsubishi Motors Corp. v. Soler Chrysler-Plymouth, Inc., 473 U.S. 614, 628 (1985). See also EEOC v. Woodmen of World Life Ins. Soc., 479 F.3d 561, 565 (8th Cir. 2007)(Title VII; "Arbitration agreements encompassing federal statutory claims are enforceable as long as the potential litigant can effectively vindicate her statutory rights through arbitration.").

[70] McMullen v. Meijer, Inc., 355 F.3d 485, 490–491 (6th Cir. 2004). The court of appeals remanded the case to district court to determine whether arbitrator selection provision of arbitration agreement should be severed, and the remainder of the provision enforced, or whether arbitration provision as a whole should be found unenforceable. *Id.* at 494–496.

[71] Hadnot v. Bay, Ltd., 344 F.3d 474, 478 n.14 (5th Cir. 2003). The court held that unenforceability of that clause did not vitiate the entire agreement to arbitrate.

[72] See, e.g., Faber v. Menard, Inc., 367 F.3d 1048, 1052–1054–1055 (8th Cir. 2004)(issue to be decided by arbitrator in first instance); Johnson v. Long John Silver's Restaurants, Inc., 320 F.Supp.2d 656, 667–670 (E.D. Tenn. 2004)(court not in a position to rule on the matter).

[73] Green Tree Fin. Corp.-Ala. v. Randolph, 531 U.S. 79, 92 (2000). See also EEOC v. Woodmen of World Life Ins. Soc., 479 F.3d 561, 566–567 (8th Cir. 2007)(cost of arbitration did not preclude plaintiff from vindicating her Title VII rights).

[74] Rodriguez de Quijas v. Shearson/American Express, Inc., 490 U.S. 477 (1989). In reaching this result the Court overruled its decision in Wilko v. Swan, 346 U.S. 427 (1953).

Act of 1934.[75] And it held that, at least in the international context, an agreement to arbitrate antitrust claims is valid and enforceable.[76]

Conclusion

American practice under the FAA is well established and embodies a strong commitment to alternative dispute resolution. Congress certainly deserves praise for its bold stand in 1925, but its drafting (as is often the case) left a great deal to be desired. In particular, there should be no uncertainty about jurisdiction, about the courts in which the Act is to apply, or as to the scope of the legislation's exclusions. In these and other particulars, the courts have ensured the effectiveness of the FAA by interpreting it (and filling gaps in it) in ways that support that Act's central policy.

[75] Shearson/American Exp., Inc. v. McMahon, 482 U.S. 220 (1987).

See also Scherk v. Alberto-Culver Co., 417 U.S. 506, 515–520 (1974)(Court ordered arbitration, pursuant to a provision embodied in an international agreement, of a claim arising under the 1934 Act even though it assumed that the Wilko rule would bar arbitration of a 1934 Act claim arising in a domestic context).

[76] Mitsubishi Motors Corp. v. Soler Chrysler-Plymouth, Inc., 473 U.S. 614 (1985). The Court found it unnecessary to decide whether, as many lower courts have held, antitrust claims arising from domestic transactions are not a proper subject of arbitration. *Id.* at 627.

The Decline of Free Thinking

GUY HAARSCHER

1. The Left, Free Thinking, and Religion

On March 14, 2007, Caroline Fourest, a journalist on *Charlie Hebdo*, a French satirical newspaper, gave a lecture on "the shock of prejudices." Groups of activist students who were ready to fight tried to prevent her from speaking. With great courage—I moderated the debate and can bear witness to this—she eventually succeeded in being listened to. One would expect that such an indefatigable advocate of secularism and free thinking was the victim of hecklers in a bigot—or even a fundamentalist—audience. But, perhaps surprisingly, the conference was taking place at the Free University of Brussels (ULB), an institution created in 1834, committed to the promotion of secularism, and making free thinking the very principle of its teaching and research.

On February 15, 2008, the Muslim public intellectual Tariq Ramadan participated at the ULB in a debate on "Islam and Enlightenment". The audience calmly listened to him, respecting his right to free speech, if not always agreeing with the content of his discourse. So the question which triggered my reflection in this article is the following: why should a genuine secularist be verbally assaulted today in the "temple of free thinking", whereas a Muslim religious preacher generates in the same place (and from the same persons) interest, support and even a sort of fascination?

Of course, such a way of asking the question is not totally adequate: it deliberately omits two key contextual elements, which obviously contributed to the polarization of the audience. When Tariq Ramadan spoke at the ULB in 2008 (it was not the first time), everybody kept in mind the refusal by the academic authorities, one year before, to authorize him to give a lecture on campus. On the other hand, Caroline Fourest works for *Charlie Hebdo*, whose director Philippe Val was sued for republishing the Muhammad cartoons (out of solidarity with the Danish journalists on the

Jyllands Posten, who were threatened by fanatics[1]). But it seems to me that these circumstances do not sufficiently explain the paradoxical difference of treatment between the two speakers, the secularist and the religious, in the so-called House of Free Thinking.[2] But above all, I would like to insist on the following point: if the Tariq Ramadan "affair" produced such an effect on campus and in the French-speaking part of Belgium, it was not only because free speech was at stake (one can defend the latter without necessarily approving the content of the considered discourse), but also because Tariq Ramadan generates, in some areas of the Left, more than simple sympathy. On the other hand, in another area of the Left, which Caroline Fourest represents very well, the positions taken by the Muslim intellectual are radically criticized.[3] To provisionally sum up the argument, let us say that Caroline Fourest and Tariq Ramadan generate contradictory passions which divide the Left (as well as other political currents). Why is it so? I would like to attempt here to show how, in my opinion, liberals who support Ramadan against Fourest are wrong. Has the Left learned nothing from its former failures?

2. Bringing "Billancourt" to Despair

As far as social questions are concerned, Tariq Ramadan belongs to the Left (he is a "liberal" in the American sense of the term). But he belongs to the Right as far as moral and religious problems are at stake. When a conservative religious movement also defends reactionary social positions, there is no risk that the Left will support it. But when that move-

---

[1] The cartoons were published on September 30, 2005. The very manipulated reaction got some impetus several months later. In France, the director of *Charlie Hebdo* was prosecuted on complaint notably by the French Council of Muslim Religion (*Conseil français du Culte musulman*) for having reproduced the cartoons. The trial took place on February 7 and 8, 2007. See M. Sifaoui, *L'affaire des caricatures. Dessins et manipulations* (Paris: Privé, 2006).

[2] I do not want to elaborate here on the reasons which convinced the Rector of the ULB that he had to forbid, at the end of February 2007, a lecture by Tariq Ramadan. I publicly supported the Rector's position for the following reason: it seemed to me that the conditions for an open debate were not met. I added that if they *had been* met, Tariq Ramadan should have been allowed to speak on campus (I myself debated two times with him in the past). As we have seen, he spoke at the ULB in 2008. See G. Haarscher, LE SOIR, Brussels, March 15, 2007.

[3] See C. Fourest, *Frère Tariq. Discours, stratégie et méthode de Tariq Ramadan* (Paris: Grasset, 2004).

ment is socially progressive and morally reactionary, which aspect should we privilege in a political struggle that always involves the necessity of "dirty hands", in the sense Sartre gave to the term? There is an old habit, in the extreme Left and in some areas of the moderate Left, of sacrificing "formal" or "bourgeois" liberties to the struggle against social inequalities, which is taking place, as Marx wrote, on the "real stage of the whole History". Indeed, one witnessed in the 19th and 20th centuries such an underestimation of the value of human rights, first by the author of *Das Kapital* himself, secondly by Communists: freedom of expression and of the press (including the right to impertinence), right to a fair trial, respect of democratic procedures, defense of critical reason and protection of dissidents were considered inessential. Communists and their fellow travellers had decided to link the legitimate struggle of the working class for social rights to an intransigent defense of the USSR, the "homeland of Socialism". However, the latter regime had violated all the rights mentioned above, as well as some social rights such as freedom of the unions. Again, as Sartre said, in one of his many brilliant phrases expressing aberrant political positions, one should not "bring Billancourt to despair". Billancourt was a big Renault car factory, built on the Seguin Island in Paris. It constituted the symbol of the working class struggle against the bourgeoisie, and Sartre's claim was that one should never deprive exploited people of their mobilizing myths. Even if the Soviet Union can be considered a totalitarian system (as an ever-increasing number of damning documents clearly showed), it nevertheless represented the hope of individuals oppressed by capitalism. Acknowledging the Soviet regime would have amounted to doing a big favor to the bourgeoisie by mellowing and demoralizing its opponents, that is, "bring them to despair."

Such a strategy constituted a serious attack on the basic presuppositions of free thinking, in that it involved the use of a rhetoric that unfortunately was destined for a bright future: the "double standard" strategy. Instead of examining in a critical way reality by calling a spade a spade (or a hangman a hangman, and a victim a victim), one tried to justify by all means the evil committed by one's "kins", and, conversely, one satanized even the most minor mistake made by the "other".[4] In May 1968, it

[4] "But the slave camps under the banner of liberty, the massacres that are justified by the love of man or a taste for super-humanity, in a sense, make the judgment impotent. On the day when the crime wears the clothes of innocence, it is innocence which is required to give its justifications, through a curious process of inversion that is characteristic of our times." A. Camus, *L'homme révolté* (Paris: Gallimard, 1951), coll. "Idées", p. 14.

seemed normal to the members of my generation to shout the famous slogan "CRS=SS"[5]. At the "Free Assembly" that had gathered at the Free University of Brussels in the follow-up of the Paris events, students showed no mercy to the "bourgeois" political and academic authorities. But at the same time, they idealized the Chinese cultural revolution, and followed the situation in Cuba by reading with almost religious devotion *Granma,* the official newspaper of a so-called "progressive" dictatorship.

But the indulgence towards recognized dictatorships and the naïveté of fellow travellers whom the Communists called, with their usual delicacy, "useful idiots" (the phrase comes from Lenin), did not directly raise the same problem for the values of free thinking. Indeed, such an exacerbated double standard language was evidence of the victory of prejudice over critical reason. But as far as criticism of religion was concerned, Communists were the most intransigent secularists: the denunciation of religion as the "opium of the people"[6] by the young Marx led to a radical criticism of Churches. We already know that, in the eyes of a certain Left, "formal liberties" did not measure up. Without a more sophisticated analysis, one could have the impression of being between "secularists", as the Communists were on the "right" side at the social level, that is, on the "real stage of History".

I do not suggest that such a position cannot be defended. The "social question", which addresses the class struggle and inequalities between rich and poor, is too often passed over in silence for the benefit of hollow discourses on human rights and democracy. But conversely, putting uni-

[5] The French *Compagnies Républicaines de Sécurité* (CRS) are a police force dedicated to intervening in public demonstrations and preserving security. It sometimes very brutally repressed the 1968 student movement in France. The comparison with the Nazi *Schutzstaffel* (SS) is really absurd: it conveys the impression that the organizers of the "final solution" were after all only brutal policemen. This results in a trivialization of the Holocaust.

[6] "Religion is the general theory of this world, its encyclopaedic compendium, its logic in popular form, its spiritual point d'honneur, it enthusiasm, its moral sanction, its solemn complement, and its universal basis of consolation and justification. It is the fantastic realization of the human essence since the human essence has not acquired any true reality. The struggle against religion is, therefore, indirectly the struggle against that world whose spiritual aroma is religion. Religious suffering is, at one and the same time, the expression of real suffering and a protest against real suffering. Religion is the sigh of the oppressed creature, the heart of a heartless world, and the soul of soulless conditions. It is the opium of the people." (K. Marx, "Contribution to the Critique of Hegel's Philosophy of Right, Deutsch-Französische Jahrbücher" [1844]), quoted by G. Haarscher, *L'ontologie de Marx* (Brussels: Editions de l'Université de Bruxelles, 1980).

laterally the emphasis on class and social conflicts might lead to dubious alliances, which their agents typically defend as a "lesser evil" in the struggle against the supposedly "main opponent". We have learned from the 20th century that social progress is definitely inseparable from an intransigent defense of civil and political rights. Communism did a great damage to the Left by allowing the Right to present itself as an almost exclusive advocate of freedom and human rights. I maintain that the theoretical and practical blindness of some on the Left is still present today. Of course, it would be wrong to identify Communism and Islamism with their respective extremist wings. There are radical versions of both, as well as those that are more tolerant and ready for dialogues. Without denying their distinctive qualities, I will only try to analyze some rhetorical strategies that attest the persistence of a certain mentality in both.

Since its creation, the Free University of Brussels (ULB) has been at the vanguard of the struggle against Catholicism as the established religion in Belgium. Catholicism was opposed to free thinking and the freedom of science. It invoked the argument of authority: one could not challenge a thesis that was divinely guaranteed. By the same token, Catholicism opposed secularism and prevented the State from acting for the whole people (*laos*)[7] by transforming it into a kind of "private property" of a part of the population (the one that adhered to the "right", i.e., official religion). When Communism penetrated the mentalities of some professors (and many students), it did not challenge—at least *prima facie*—the secularist values of the ULB. Communists advocated radically anticlerical positions that included an attack on religion itself (and not only on its politicization). Many did not see—or did not want to see—that the USSR could only claim to be secularist by creating a deleterious illusion: official atheism and the persecution of the religious people only inverted the terms of all religious inquisitions. Instead of excluding non-believers or the heterodox from society, the Party excluded and persecuted believers. But in the specific Belgian historical and political context, Communism looked, at least in a superficial way, like an ally of liberals in the struggle against Catholicism. Admittedly, Communism has been called a secular religion: in many regards, the kind of universal emancipation it promised constituted a transposition of religion. Salvation would exist on this Earth, at the

[7] The English word "secularism" corresponds to te French "laïcité". The latter is built on the Greek notion of *laos*. State and society should not be monopolized by a *part of* the *laos*, that is, an official religion. Of course, *laïcité* and secularism have generated many controversies on both sides of the Atlantic.

end of History.[8] It is indeed for that very reason that Marx called religion a drug: by transforming the social evil (exploitation of the proletariat and economic inequalities) into a metaphysical destiny (man, the sinner in the eyes of God), it took away responsibility from the oppressors and calmed the sufferings of "the insulted and the humiliated"[9] by painting in glowing colors an artificial paradise.[10] But Communism also secularized Christian religion in another way: the official ideology was the embodiment of the absolute truth (as are the Ways of Providence in Christian theodicy), and the Party was always right. The denial of freedom for the Unions paradoxically counted in favor of the (future) rights of workers; the Gulag, considered to be a "progressive" instrument of Terror, was supposed to only repress the enemies of Revolution. Those who denounced the totalitarian abuses of Communism (as, in France, Albert Camus had courageously done) were labelled henchmen of the people because they supposedly defamed the Great Proletarian Revolution. They played, the argument goes, into the hands of the advocates of the bourgeoisie and the status quo. In *L'homme révolté*, Camus reminded us that Ignatius of Loyola, the founder of the Jesuit order, claimed that he was able to believe that something was black (even if he saw it white) if the Church would ask him to do that.[11] By the same token, secularized religion required from its "soldiers" to consider "black" (progressive) what any candid assessment would have considered "white" (reactionary).

I could go on listing—after so many others—the Communist borrowings from Christian theology. But it remains that secular religion is not immediately recognizable *as religion*: one sometimes needs a significant effort of thought to be able to detect behind the "façade"—the denunciation of the opium of the people and the defense of atheism—a transformed version of at least some aspects of Christianity. Which aspects? The better and the worse: the idea of a universal fraternity, that is, the naive (but respectable) readiness to take the Gospel at its word and to carry out on Earth the Sermon on the Mountain; but also the unbearable dogmatism of

---

[8] Raymon Aron calls "secular religions the doctrines which take in the souls of our contemporaries the place of the vanished faith and situate in this world, in a remote future, under the form of a social order to be created, the salvation of humanity." See R. Aron, *L'Âge des Empires et L'avenir de la France*, (Paris: Éditions Défense de la France, 1946), p. 288. My translation.

[9] This is the title of a famous novel by Dostoyevsky.

[10] See Baudelaire's *Les Paradis artificiels*.

[11] "I must always, in order not to get lost, be ready to believe to be black what I see white." Ignatius of Loyola, *Spiritual exercices*, quoted by A. Camus, *L'homme révolté*, p. 289.

a Church which is always right because the Ways of the Lord (or of the Communist Party of the USSR) are by definition inscrutable. During the Cold War, at the time when the Catholic Church made its *aggiornamento* during the Second Vatican Council, secular-minded people remained suspicious. In short, when the "real" Church was engaged in a process of liberalization (that was admittedly partial), one mistrusted it sometimes more than the secular "Church", which maintained its hold, even if the Soviet Union after Stalin was, making due allowances, more "open" than before.

Today, after 1989 and the implosion of the Soviet system, the situation looks very different. This time, we are witnessing—to use French sociologist Gilles Kepel's terminology—a real "revenge of God".[12] Admittedly, the phenomenon is very complex. But it is incontestable that the process of "recolonization of the public space" (Habermas) by often radical religious currents exists today in many parts of the world. I make the hypothesis that those members of the Left who have learnt nothing from the experience of Communism act today towards Muslim religion as they acted towards the late secular religion of the Party. Why *Muslim* religion? I do not want to antagonize those who would blame me for stigmatizing Islam. I do not intend to do that. Quite the contrary: the main aim of this article consists in trying to rebut a kind of charge that is very often made nowadays. I shall go back to that point later on. What I maintain here is only the following simple idea: some Islamist militants embody, in varying degrees of radicalism, a struggle against the West, the United States, neo-colonialism, etc. Such a struggle is certainly open to criticism, in its aims as well as in its means. But Islamist militants undeniably possess a popular basis and are able to mobilize huge crowds. They fight the power of America; their hate of the United States touches the right chord and appeals to the old anti-Americanism that was inherited from Communism, but also goes back a very long time in history, notably in France and French-speaking Belgium.[13] Moreover, the most visible minorities in Western Europe are Muslim, and they are often poor, discriminated, oppressed, and humiliated; sometimes even a quite explicit form of racism (especially since the attacks of 9/11) is present. In short, both at the global and the local levels, a certain form of Muslim political and religious pro-

---

[12] See G. Kepel, *La revanche de Dieu. Chrétiens, juifs et musulmans à la reconquête du monde* (Paris: Editions du Seuil, 1991).

[13] See P. Roger, *L'ennemi américain. Généalogie de l'antiaméricanisme français* (Paris: Editions du Seuil, 2002).

test awakes in the Left old feelings of solidarity that unfortunately involve a deleterious lack of vigilance.

So what are the consequences for free thinking? For the unbeliever Sartre, atheism was "a cruel, long and exacting enterprise," which involved the necessity of "systematically thinking against myself to the point of measuring the evidence of an idea by the displeasure it caused me."[14] The problem consisted in getting rid of any religious remnant. Sartre deluded himself in two ways. First, his series of articles entitled *Les communistes et la paix* ("Communists and peace"), which were masterfully criticized by the then very young Claude Lefort[15], embodies in a caricatured way the idea of the fellow traveller (or of the useful idiot), who is blind to the worst ravages of religion, provided the latter disguises itself by taking on the appearance of a secular ideology. Secondly, Sartre wrongly believed that one should be systematically trying to free oneself from any trace of Christianity.[16] He failed to see that religions, being human creations, have carried along the better and the worse of human condition. The Sermon on the Mountain embodies a spiritual revolution that was betrayed by the Constantinian Church (already an established religion) as well as by the secularist Communist "Church". But if Sartre, who was in so many respects so subtle and sophisticated, did not see the worst of religion behind the proclaimed atheism of the political "Commissar", it is because he was obsessed by the social question, which in a sense blocked his intellectual view: "Marxism", he wrote in 1960 in the *Critique of Dialectical Reason*, "is the impassable horizon of our time". Generally speaking, if the Left I call "captive" cannot recognize oppression, intolerance and bigotry inherent in some currents of radical Islamism, it is because in the name of the class struggle, it takes almost spontaneously the side of the declared opponents of the United States, considered to be the embodiment of inequality, oppression, and economic exploitation.

---

[14] J.-P. Sartre, *Les Mots* (Paris : Gallimard, 1964), coll. "Folio", at 211.

[15] J.-P. Sartre, *Les communistes et la paix* (I), Les Temps Modernes, nr. 81 (1952), at 1–50; *Les communistes et la paix* (II), Les Temps Modernes, nr. 84 and nr. 85 (1952), at 695–763 ; *Les communistes et la paix* (III), Les Temps Modernes, nr. 101 (1954), pp. 1731–1819 ; *Réponse à Lefort*, Les Temps Modernes, nr. 89 (1953), at 1571–1629. C. Lefort, *Le marxisme et Sartre*, Les Temps Modernes, nr. 89 (1953).

[16] See M. Onfray, *Traité d'athéologie* (Paris : Grasset, 2005).

3. Poisoning the Source

Such an indulgence would be hardly thinkable towards, for instance, French Catholic integrism, or American Protestant fundamentalism. Indeed, the latter religious currents are clearly rightist, on the moral as well as on the social plane. Conversely, several Muslim currents generate a certain amount of sympathy in the Left because they are supposed to represent the "damned of the Earth", "our" poor, "our" oppressed: they are clearly on the Right as far as moral questions are concerned, but they are on the Left as far as social problems are at stake. Formerly, at the time of the Cold War, those who dared denounce the Soviet totalitarianism as such (or the Chinese and Cuban forms of secular religion) were rejected as Rightists, and even labelled "Fascists", which was enough to radically delegitimize their criticisms. I shall call that strategy—by using an expression coined by René Girard—the "poisoning of the source". It consists, in the case when one does not want to take into account the embarrassing content of a criticism, in casting a doubt on the integrity of the person who makes it: if an individual who has a bad reputation defends a position, the latter does not even have to be rebutted on the merits in order to be annihilated. Communists were the masters in the art of poisoning the source: if a "Fascist" developed any thesis, the latter could not be taken seriously into consideration because the opprobrium heaped on the enunciator was almost automatically transferred to the content of the statement. Now the benefits of such an attitude are rather obvious: it allows the "poisoner" to bypass the criticism by disqualifying the person. One does not have to discuss with a Fascist: what he says necessarily comes within the province of Fascism.

Such "benefits" have not at all been lost today, and the strategy of poisoning the source continues to exercise its eminently perverse effects on certain minds. I shall take two very controversial contemporary examples of such a strategy. First, I shall envisage the question of the prohibition of religious ostensible signs: in public school for the pupils, and elsewhere for those who exercise public authority (in particular when the latter involves a contact with the population). Secondly, I shall briefly mention the affair of the Danish cartoons, which generated well-known reactions in the Muslim world.

3.1. Ostensible Religious Signs at School

The question of the "veil" has generated, since it appeared in the school context in France in 1989, unending controversies which have divided the Left as well as the Right. Wearing a religious sign is obviously covered by the right to freedom of religion. It should be authorized in open societies except in extreme cases (for instance the Burqua is a garment that covers the whole body and the face, and generates in particular—but not only—security problems, given that one cannot recognize the person behind it). It seems to me that, regardless of such an extreme situation, the prohibition of the veil would only be legitimate in two cases. The first is related to the school context: the authorities are entitled to impose on non-adult pupils a certain number of rules, as admittedly students in high school are not yet ready to exercise their autonomy in the full sense of the term (in particular because they are still vulnerable and easily influenced). The second case concerns the holders of a public office, as they should give the population an appearance of neutrality that reflects their expected impartiality. Of course, both these arguments do not necessarily involve the prohibition of religious signs, but they make it plausible and justifiable by good reasons. In the public schools of the City of Brussels, for instance, the prohibition of political and religious signs was decided well before there were Muslim "communities" in that town—so the latter could not, by definition, feel targeted by such a measure. One can understand that teachers must enjoy a certain amount of authority, and may organize—if they find it appropriate—an ordered debate in which, indeed, each individual retains his or her freedom of expression and opinion. But it must be a discussion in which nobody will *a priori* define a label of belonging, especially an intangible religious Truth. Political positions do not possess, in a democratic secular framework, such a categorical character, but again they must yield to the force of the better argument. In that context, the pupil does not speak "as such or such", but as an individual who is supposed to be able to use reason and is the bearer of rights, as well as the bearer of responsibilities. Moreover, if some supplementary elements are present, such as pressures exercised on the young female students, the prohibition will still be more legitimate. Actually, this is one of the main reasons why the French Stasi Commission finally opted in favor of a statute prohibiting religious ostensible signs in public school.

Now one can be of a different opinion and maintain, in spite of these arguments, that it would be better, all things considered, to enter dialogue with the girls and their families than to prohibit the veil. As long, the argument goes, as there are no breaches of the order in school, and the curriculum or the rights of other students are not challenged, wearing an ostensible religious sign should, according to that opinion, be authorized. Such a position would probably be adopted by the US courts, and it was taken by the French *Conseil d'Etat* (the highest administrative jurisdiction) in 1989, when the then Minister for National Education, Lionel Jospin, being confronted with the problem of the veil, had asked for an advisory opinion. But 15 years later, notably at the request of the school authorities (who were compelled to take decisions on a case by case basis that were from time to time struck down by administrative tribunals), and because of the radicalization of Islamist pressures (and the danger they created for the integration of the concerned pupils), France decided to legislate and to prohibit ostensible religious signs in public school. Now one can think that this was a bad policy and that other countries should certainly not pass the same kind of legislation. One could even dream of an idyllic situation, in which a civil servant wearing an ostensible sign would not generate in a citizen's mind a negative reaction—a fear, or at least a feeling of partiality. But we live in a much too "harsh" world for such an idealization to make sense, and therefore, the appearance of impartiality of someone in position of public authority is, it seems to me, required. Concerning the pupils at school, I am convinced by the abovementioned arguments in favor of prohibition, but I respect those who think differently on the topic.

Now the converse is absolutely not true. In a recent book,[17] several authors defend the thesis that those who take position in favor of the prohibition of the veil in public school are *racists.*[18] There is no doubt that such a rhetorical strategy falls within the domain of the "poisoning of the source".

This is an important point, even an essential one for democracy. I do not label "fundamentalists" those who, after due reflection, decide to oppose the prohibition of the veil. Of course, some of them *are* radicals. But the authors of the mentioned book must be considered interlocutors in a normal democratic debate: it is unavoidable that, in the political and intellectual arena, various interpretations of human rights and secularism will be in confrontation. But the converse, as I said, is not true: those who have spoken in favour of the prohibition are treated by some authors of *Du bon usage de la laïcité* ("The right use of secularism") as racists. Could one imagine a more efficient poisoning of the source? Racism is not only a position that is rightly considered devoid of any legitimacy in our democratic space, but even racist *speech* has been made a crime in several European countries (notably France and Belgium). Affirming that a secularist who would take position on an eminently controversial topic of public

[17] M. Jacquemain & N. Rosa-Rosso, *Du bon usage de la laïcité* (Brussels: Edition Aden, 2008).

[18] See *Du bon usage de la laïcité*, at 35–48 and 75–100. The position taken by Marc Jacquemain, one of the editors of the book, is slightly more nuanced.

interest (the presence of religion in public school) is *ipso facto* a racist, is untenable for at least two major reasons. *Either* the notion is understood in a strict sense—the racist is the one who "fragments" humanity in *a priori* hierarchical categories and wants to oppress or at least discriminate against inferior "races"—and then one necessarily obtains an absurd position: many secularists who oppose the wearing of the veil at school are anti-racist militants who simply take also very seriously the struggle against religious bigotry. *Or* one uses the concept of racism in a vague, so to say watered-down, sense, and therefore one does the antiracist struggle a disservice. Indeed, a strategy constantly used by the extreme right consists in deliberately distorting the notions in order to introduce confusion into the debate: clarity would put it at a disadvantage. There are of course too many racist attitudes, but elementary intellectual probity consists in not trivializing too much the most important concepts underpinning the struggle for human rights. Again, I do not consider that all those who happen to defend the right to wear the veil at school are fundamentalists: some are legitimate interlocutors with whom I happen to disagree.

Let me summarize the argument made by those who want to identify the prohibition of the veil with a racist attitude: "If you refuse the wearing of the veil at school—even if you want to defend young Muslim women, who are often the most vulnerable among the vulnerable—it is because you dislike Islam (you are overwhelmed by an irrational fear of that religion—an islamo*phobia*)." And—to make a link between this and the time of the Cold War—you despise the poor and the people who are "different". But let us be clear: the racist is horrified by the perspective of a Europe in which people from the "Maghreb" (to use a simplifying expression) would become the majority in 2050. The secular-minded person who does not accept the veil at school has no objections or misgivings concerning the "genetic" composition of the population in the future: what is important to him is the way the inhabitants of Western Europe (whoever they are) will envisage their mutual relationships and will—or will not—take the ideals of liberal democracy and human rights seriously. So the poisoning of the source is definitely a perverse strategy.

3.2. The "Chilling" of Speech

But the problem becomes still more dramatic in the context of free speech being confronted with the requests for censorship coming from religious currents. The same confusion is present here, but it is pushed to the extreme. In democracy, reasoning is often made from a short-sighted point of view, and decisions are hastily taken. The time of political action is not the time of the Platonic longest detour. Today there are many people who opine that the main danger comes from "too much" (as opposed to "not enough") freedom of expression. The danger allegedly consists in that the members of various communities could be easily offended in their convictions or "sensitivities". Thus, criticism should be limited to speech that would not gratuitously insult others. Such are the claims made by a vague and omnipresent current labelled political correctness. This position may reflect some good intentions: why hurt the feelings of our neighbor? But a reflection undoubtedly shows that its perverse effects are quite formidable and often underestimated. First, who is that "Other" whose convictions and sensitivities should be respected? In religious matters, such a demand consists in saying that one should not blaspheme, that is, insult or defame a divinity that is venerated by a part of the population (the *laos*). But in pluralist societies, religious groups are numerous, and they often disagree with each other (even inside the same confession). If freedom of speech should be limited by the claim of necessary respect for—notably religious—"sensitivities", the whole intellectual debate would be weakened. One must correctly assess such a threat. Many among us think that the major danger associated with free speech is exaggeration, which consists in going "too far" in a vigorous democratic discussion, by gratuitously offending people. So, in a debate, one should avoid all what would unnecessarily hurt others in their convictions. Of course, one would still be allowed to criticize religions and ideologies, but freedom of speech should be balanced against the respect of beliefs. I showed elsewhere[19] that such an application of the political correctness doctrine would inevitably lead (to use the language of the US Supreme Court) to a *chilling effect*: many citizens, being desirous to express themselves, would give up, out of fear of sanctions. Now the danger threatening our democratic societies does probably not consist in the (always possible) exaggeration, but in its opposite: conformism, hypocrisy, and the temptation of gregariousness.

Democracy is worthy of its name only when citizens can freely speak without any form of intimidation. If they think that expressing their views

[19] See G. Haarscher, "Free speech, religion, and the right to caricature," in A. Sajo, ed., *Censorial sensitivities : free speech and religion in a fundamentalist world* (Utrecht: Eleven International Publishing, 2006) at 309–328; G. Haarscher, "Rhetoric and its abuses: how to oppose liberal democracy while speaking its language," in J. Mootz III, Jr., ed., *Recalling Vico's Lament: the Role of Prudence in Law and Legal Education* (Chicago: Chicago-Kent Law Review, Volume 83, Number 3, 2008) at 1225–1259.

on a given topic will get them into trouble, they will prefer to remain silent, and this will amount to a loss for the democratic liveliness of our societies. On this point, I can only refer to my other articles. I just want here to rapidly summarize the argument. Individual defamation and insult are as such abuses of freedom of expression; but recognizing this cannot involve an immunization of *ideas*—notably religious ones—from criticism, or even from the use of caricature. The great weight of religions in society and the dangers they create for individual and collective autonomy, as well as the element of absoluteness that they often contain, obviously constitute subjects of general interest. If, in pluralist societies, the criticism of religion (or atheism, or any body of ideas) were not totally free, freedom of expression would depend on the "heckler's veto", that is, on those who, for various reasons and on a subjective basis, would pretend that they are shocked or offended. I showed elsewhere that such a threat for free speech—a vital principle of our democracies—has at least taken so far two distinct forms. First, one does not speak any more of blasphemy ("defamation" of God) but of an exaggerated attack on the other's convictions. The relationship, which was so to say vertical (blasphemer/God) becomes horizontal as it opposes this time the one who exercises his right to free speech and the one who, being offended, considers that such an use of the right to free speech violates his own right to religious freedom. But that reasoning is eminently fallacious: the principle of religious liberty in no way involves the right that speech even virulently critical on beliefs be prohibited by law.

Such an argumentative strategy consists thus in not mentioning anymore blasphemy. The terms of the conflict between freedom of expression and religious dogmatism should be reformulated, to shape it into a conflict that is *internal to the system of human rights*: between freedom of expression and religious freedom, that is, between *two liberties*. But all this amounts to a sophism, as freedom of religion and worship is independent of the right to criticize religions. It seems to me that the courts, even the European Court of Human Rights[20], have often too easily accepted such a politically correct argument par excellence. The Strasbourg Court has not declared the laws prohibiting blasphemy contrary to the European Convention on Human Rights: it has accepted up to a certain point the "translation" of such repressive legal provisions into the language of human rights. In short, a "defamed" God is not mentioned any more, but one puts

[20] See references in footnote 19.

the emphasis on human communities whose members are supposedly gratuitously offended.

But a second rhetorical strategy is commonly used today, which takes us immediately back to the "poisoning of the source". The argument runs as follows: if you criticize a religion in such a virulent way, it is because you dislike those who practise it; you are overwhelmed by an irrational fear, a phobia: you are an islamophobe (or a christianophobe, judeophobe, "atheiophobe", etc.). In short, the one who exercises his right to free speech in an "exaggerated" or "caricatured" way is a racist. We have seen that such an argument is very often used in contemporary debates. It aims at discrediting the opponent, as we rightly consider in Europe that racism does not constitute an "opinion".

4. A Brief Conclusion

The crisis of free thinking is not to be denied. But it has to be seriously assessed, in order for us to be able to consolidate the intellectual foundations of democracy in the 21st century. In this text I gave some examples of the rhetorical strategies that definitely weaken the public debate: being indulgent towards fundamentalism because it is supposed to be the ideology of the poor and the oppressed; poisoning the source of the discourse in order not to be submitted to the force of the better argument; and finally, adopting the rhetorical strategy of the "wolf in the sheepfold" by defending the wearing of the veil or the prohibition of blasphemy in the name of freedom of religion, and human rights in general.

Questions of Arbitration and the Case Law of the European Court of Justice

ATTILA HARMATHY

The topic of the present paper is related to one of the main fields of activity of Tibor Várady: international commercial arbitration. When choosing the topic of the paper the intention was to pay tribute to him in this way, too, in the collection of papers published in his honour.

International commercial arbitration is not in the forefront of the activity of the European Court of Justice. Nevertheless, it cannot be neglected. The competence of the Court to proceed as an arbitral tribunal is based on the European Community Treaty (the Treaty). According to Article 238 of the Treaty:

> The Court of Justice shall have jurisdiction to give judgment pursuant to any arbitration clause contained in a contract concluded by or on behalf of the Community, whether that contract be governed by public or private law.

There are a considerable number of cases in which the Court proceeded on basis of an arbitration agreement of the parties and taking position in questions of arbitration. There are, however, judgments of the Court not based on arbitration agreement, expressing principles having a great importance for international arbitration proceedings taking place in the Member States of the European Union. Some of the judgements have aroused great interest among lawyers; some others seem to have remained nearly unnoticed. The paper outlines some of the principles having an importance, expressed in the case law of the Court.

1. Arbitration Agreement

a/ The Court examined the problem of validity of arbitration agreement in the *Claro* case referring to the conflicting principles of public policy and efficiency of arbitration proceedings.[1] The case concerned a mobile telephone contract made between the claimant and the respondent. The contract contained an arbitration clause. The claimant initiated arbitration proceedings and the respondent presented arguments on the merits of the dispute without any reference to the nullity of the arbitration clause (in accordance with the Spanish law implementing Council Directive 93/113/EC of 5 April 1993 on unfair terms in consumer contracts mentioning in the annex the unfair arbitration clause). The award was against the respondent who contested the award before the competent court, which decided to refer a question for a preliminary ruling. The Court took into consideration that the consumer protection under the Directive is based on the idea that the consumer is in a weak position vis-à-vis the seller or supplier, as regards both his bargaining power and his level of knowledge. According to settled case-law the imbalance shall be corrected by positive action of national courts. Thus, the Court explained the conflicting principles in the following way:

- on the one side, there is the interest of efficient arbitration proceedings requiring a limited review of arbitration awards and annulling or refusing to recognise an award only in exceptional cases,
- on the other side, it is necessary to grant an application for annulment of an arbitration award where the application is based on failure to observe national rules of public policy or in a similar way to comply with Community rules.[2]

The Court was of the opinion that the mandatory provision of the Directive has a particular importance and ruled that a national court seized of an action for annulment of an arbitration award must determine whether the arbitration agreement is void and annul that award where that agreement contains an unfair term, even though the consumer has not pleaded that invalidity in the course of the arbitration proceedings, but only in that of the action for annulment.

The consequence of the decision is that arbitral tribunal has to decide on the nullity of the arbitration agreement on its own motion if it considers that the agreement is in contradiction with the mandatory rule of the Directive. A similar question is put in connection with enforcement of an award of an arbitral tribunal not examining that some terms of the contract were contrary to the rules of the European Community Treaty on competition.

---

[1] C-168/05 *Mostaza Claro* [2006] ECR I-10421, judgment given on 27 April 2006.

[2] Pp. 34–35.

The decision has met angry reaction. A commentator of the decision was of the opinion that the solution accepted by the Court "would turn the arbitration clock back by several decades and destroy the established principle that State courts may not review the legal merits of a case."[3] It seems that the French reaction was more polite but not positive either. In a case the French *Cour de cassation* dismissed the appeal for rejecting the enforcement as there was no manifest and flagrant violation of the Community rules. In the French legal literature the question has been put whether this attitude can be applied in general in connection with the judicial control of awards.[4] This opinion is based on the general principles of civil procedure. It is to be noted that it has some backing in another decision of the Court.[5] In the *Renault* case the Court stated that the enforcement of a decision emanating from another Contracting State cannot be refused solely on the ground of considering the Community law to have been misapplied. An error of law such as alleged in the proceedings does not constitute a manifest breach of a rule of law.[6] It is questionable whether the reference to this decision is a strong enough argument from the point of view of the Court as there are other decisions of the Court with similar position as in *Claro* (some of them will be mentioned later).

b/ In the *Rich*-case the validity of an arbitration agreement was discussed in connection with the Convention of 27 September 1968 on Jurisdiction and the Enforcement of Judgments in Civil and Commercial Matters.[7] (The decision is not of simple historical interest as the rule of the Convention is the same as that of Article 1 paragraph 2 (d) of Council Regulation (EC) No 44/2001 of 22 December 2001 on jurisdiction and the recognition and enforcement of judgments in civil and commercial matters.)

The question referred to the Court for preliminary ruling was whether exclusion of arbitration from the sphere of application of the Convention extends to proceedings pending before a national court concerning the appointment of an arbitrator and, if so, whether that exclusion also applies where in those proceedings a preliminary issue is raised as to whether an arbitration agreement exists or is valid. The Court has stated that it would

---

[3] Case C-168/05, *Elisa María Mostaza Claro v. Centro Móvil Milenium SL*, judgment of the Court of Justice, Comment by Chr. Liebscher, *Common Market Law Review* 2008. 556.

[4] *Sentance arbitrale et ordre public international*, Cour de cassation, 1re civ., 4 juin 2008, Obsérvation de Xavier Delpech, *Recueil Dalloz* 2008. 1686.

[5] C-38/98, *Renault* [2000] ECR-I. 2973, judgment given on 11 May 2000.

[6] Pp. 33–34

[7] C-190/89, *Rich* [1991] ECR-I. 3855, judgment given on 25 July 1991.

be contrary to the legal certainty to vary according to a preliminary issue. Consequently, the exclusion provided for in the Convention extends to litigation pending before a national court concerning the appointment of an arbitrator, even if the existence or validity of an arbitration agreement is a preliminary issue in that litigation.[8]

c/ The existence of an arbitration clause was discussed in a case where the Court acted as an arbitration court.[9] The claim was based on an arbitration clause in accordance with rules of the Treaty. The respondent submitted a counterclaim alleging that he had made an agreement with the claimant and asked the Court to set off the claim against the counterclaim. The claimant denied the existence of the agreement.

The Court pointed out that the question whether the Court has jurisdiction to hear and determine a counterclaim and to consider whether it is admissible, must be assessed solely in the light of the rules of the Treaty. The jurisdiction of the Court derogates from the ordinary rules of law and must therefore be given a restrictive interpretation. The Court came to the conclusion that it has jurisdiction to hear and determine a counterclaim arising only from the same contract or facts on which the claim is based.[10] The decision reflects the special position of the Court and does not take into consideration the interests as they are accepted in the ordinary rules of procedure.

2. Arbitrability

It has been correctly stated by Várady, Barceló and von Mehren that the issue of arbitrability is considered as one of the most important preliminary questions in the arbitration proceedings. There has been a reluctance to allow arbitration in spheres where there is a strong public interest at stake.[11] There are many uncertainties, problems in connection with arbitrability. As competition has a special importance in the Community law, arbitrability of disputes involving application of competition law has become an important question. The International Chamber of Commerce Commission on Arbitration established a Task Force on Arbitrating Com-

[8] Pp. 27–29

[9] C-426/85, *Commission* v. *Zoubek*, [1986] ECR. 457, judgment given on 18 December 1986

[10] Pp. 10.11.

[11] T. Várady, J. J. Barceló, A. T. von Mehren, *International Commercial Arbitration*, 3 ed. St. Paul, MN, 2006. 217.

petition Law Issues in 2003. The Task Force took into consideration that the role of arbitration is growing although the principle of party autonomy and public policy can come into conflict.[12] Some questions were considered by the Court, too, although the way how the problem was approached, was not directly from the point of view of arbitrability.

a/ The role of competition has been controversial in international arbitration but there is a tendency of admitting arbitration in most fields of the law of competition.[13] The problem of taking into consideration public policy has become important in parallel way.[14] The law of competition plays an important role in the Community Law and its natural consequence is that public policy in connection with competition law has appeared in decisions of the Court.

The case *Eco Swiss* is one of the cases which are often referred to.[15] The Court examined the question whether an arbitration award neglecting the prohibition laid down in Article 85 of the Treaty should be annulled or its enforcement should be refused. The Court has emphatically put in the decision that where domestic rules of procedure require a national court to grant an application for annulment of an arbitration award on an application founded on failure to observe national rules of public policy, it must also grant such an application where it is founded on failure to comply with the prohibition laid down in the Treaty. The decision stated that the provisions of Article 85 of the Treaty may be regarded as a matter of public policy within the meaning of the New York Convention of 1958 on the Recognition and Enforcement of Foreign Arbitral Awards.[16]

The Court has made it clear in the decision that when reviewing an arbitral award ordinary courts have to interpret the rules on competition of the Treaty. Therefore, the ordinary courts when asked to determine the validity of an arbitration award have the possibility to refer questions, if necessary, to the Court of Justice for a preliminary ruling.[17] At the same time, the Court reinforced its position taken in the *Nordsee* case according

---

[12] J. Bridgeman, "The Arbitrability of Competition Law Disputes," *European Business Law Review* 2008, 147–148.

[13] B. D. Ehle, "Arbitration as a Dispute Resolution Mechanism in Mergers and Acquisitions," *Comparative Law Yearbook of International Business*, 2005, 303.

[14] G. Blanke, The Role of EC Competition Law in International Arbitration: A *Plaidoyer*, *European Bussiness Law Review*, 2005, 169–171.

[15] *Eco Swiss China Time Ltd.* v *Benetton International NV* C-126/97 [1999] ECR-I 03055, judgment given on 1 June 1999.

[16] Pp. 36–39.

[17] P. 40.

to which an arbitral tribunal is not a court within the meaning of Article 177 of the Treaty.[18] In the *Nordsee* case this argument was decisive for coming to the conclusion that the Court has no jurisdiction to give a ruling on the questions referred to it by an arbitrator (arbitral tribunal).[19]

In a similar way, as in the case *Claro*, there are opinions published in the legal literature which are not in favour of the decision of *Eco Swiss* and would prefer the application of the principle of the *Renault* decision according to which the annulment or refusal of enforcement of an arbitral award takes place in case of a manifest breach of a rule of law.[20] It has also been explained that instead of a control of awards exercised by courts it would be better to allow arbitrators to submit questions to the Court for a preliminary ruling in order to achieve uniform application of the economic policy.[21] The position of the Court seems to be a strict interpretation of Article 234 (ex Article 177) of the Treaty, which may be in connection with the workload of the Court.

b/ An interesting question of arbitrability has been raised in a dispute concerning pre-contractual liability. In the case *Tacconi* the claimant brought an action in an ordinary court for making good all the damage caused by breaching the duty to act honestly and in good faith infringing the claimant's legitimate expectations relying on the conclusion of a contract.[22] The respondent pleaded that the court had no jurisdiction because of the arbitration clause of the contract. The Italian Supreme Court referred questions to the Court for preliminary ruling. One of the questions concerned the interpretation of pre-contractual liability under the Brussels Convention of 1968 on Jurisdiction and Enforcement of Judgments in Civil and Commercial Matters.

The starting point of the decision is that "that the expressions 'matters relating to a contract' and 'matters relating to tort, delict or quasi-delict' in Article 5(1) and (3) of the Brussels Convention are to be interpreted independently, having regard primarily to the objectives and general scheme of the Convention. Those expressions cannot therefore be taken as simple references to the national law of one or the other of the Contracting States

---

[18] P. 34.

[19] Operative part of the judgment given on 23 March 1982 in the case C-102/81, [1982] ECR 01095.

[20] A. Mourre, "Note," *Journal de Dorit International* 2005, 370.

[21] S. Jarvin, "The sources and limits of the arbitrator's powers," in: J. D. M. Lew, ed., *Contemporary Problems In International Arbitration*, Dordrecht, Boston, Lancaster, 1987, 69.

[22] C-334/00, [2002] R-I, 7357, judgment given on 17 September 2002.

concerned."[23] In this way the Court wanted to achieve a uniform interpretation of the rules. The Court was of the opinion that "the obligation to make good the damage allegedly caused by the unjustified breaking off of negotiations could derive only from breach of rules of law, in particular the rule which requires the parties to act in good faith in negotiations with a view to the formation of a contract." Thus, the Court ruled that an action founded on pre-contractual liability is a matter relating to tort, delict or quasi-delict within the meaning of the Brussels convention.[24]

It is regrettable that the Court did not follow advocate general Geelhoed's opinion. The advocate general analysed the UNIDROIT principles of international commercial contracts and its part on breaking off negotiations in bad faith. He has pointed to the fact that this was the first time that the Court had to deal with this problem and that the Conventions laid down no rules on pre-contractual liability. The advocate general referred to national legal systems saying that the Court may use national laws as a source of inspiration when answering questions referred to it.[25] His conclusion was that if the party has assumed an obligation towards the other party, it must be regarded as falling within the scope of matters relating to a contract.[26]

c/ Another aspect of arbitrability was decided by the Court in connection with "civil matters" under the Brussels Convention of 1968.[27] The question referred to the Court for a preliminary ruling was whether a legal action under a right of recourse under the law on general assistance brought by a municipality entitled to seek recovery against a person liable to pay maintenance was a civil matter within the meaning of the Convention?

In this case also the Court was of the opinion that the question should be interpreted in an autonomous way. The decisive element was whether the claimant, a public authority, acted in the exercise of its public powers.[28] Another important element was whether the right to recourse was governed by ordinary law.[29] In this case one can observe that although the Court has emphasized that the interpretation is aiming at an autonomous meaning of civil and public matters in the Brussels Convention, nevertheless, national legal concepts were taken as a basis of the decision.

---

[23] P. 19.

[24] Pp. 25, 27.

[25] Pp. 55, 57, 58.

[26] P. 86.

[27] *Gemeente Steenbergen* v *Baten* C-271/00, [2002] ECR-I. 10489 judgment given on 14 November 2002.

[28] Pp. 28, 30.

[29] P. 37.

3. Language of Documents

A recent decision is not connected with arbitration; nevertheless, the questions raised may be of interest for arbitral proceedings, too. The Claimant pursued damages. It lodged the application in English but the annexes were in German. The respondent refused to accept the application. The question referred to the Court for preliminary ruling concerned the interpretation of Article 8(1) of Council Regulation (EC) No 1348/2000 of 29 May 2000 on the service in the Member States of judicial and extrajudicial documents in civil or commercial matters.[30] The Court of First Instance of the European Communities has taken the view that in a direct action all documents annexed to the pleadings of the other parties, including the interveners, must, in principle, be translated into the language of the case. The Court explained that the answer depends on the nature of a given document. As far as the documents are concerned which initiate the proceedings, the possibility of refusing documents is confined to exceptional cases. However, the right of defence cannot be undermined. Therefore, the Court has stated that the addressee of a document instituting proceedings which is to be served does not have the right to refuse to accept that document, provided that it enables the addressee to assert his rights in legal proceedings in the Member State of transmission, where annexes are attached to that document consisting of documentary evidence which is not in the language of the Member State addressed or in a language of the Member State of transmission which the addressee understands, but which has a purely evidential function and is not necessary for understanding the subject-matter of the claim and the cause of action. It is for the national court to determine whether the content of the document instituting the proceedings is sufficient to enable the defendant to assert his rights or whether it is necessary for the party instituting the proceedings to remedy the fact that a necessary annex has not been translated.[31]

The above few examples which were outlined can show that arbitrators also have to study the case law of the Court. At the same time it would seem to be useful if meeting of judges and the exchange of views would not be restricted to judges of the Court and of Supreme Court judges but arbitrators would be involved as well.

---

[30] *Ingenieurbüro Michael Weiss und Partner GbR* v *Industrie und Handelskammer Berlin* C-14/07 judgment given on 8 May 2008.

[31] P. 78.

Recognition of a Recognition Judgment Within the European Union: "Double *Exequatur*" and the Public Policy Barrier[1]

PETER HAY

I. Recognition of Recognition Judgments as a Public Policy Issue

"Enforcement measures do not travel," Justice Ginsburg wrote in a majority opinion.[2] They are local, not exportable. Strictly speaking, substantive adjudications of course also "do not travel," in the sense of enjoying extraterritorial force or effect. Absent a constitutional or treaty-based command, recognition of a foreign judgment, including the range of its effects, is a matter of comity, as Justice Gray restated over a hundred years ago.[3] States extend comity and accord recognition as a matter of self-interest which, in turn, finds expression in commonly shared notions of res judicata.[4] They differ with respect to preconditions that must be fulfilled for recognition (for instance, with respect to the issuing court's jurisdiction or that the foreign system accord reciprocity to similar local judgments). As a result, they therefore diverge as to the kind and extent of review to which they subject the foreign judgment. However, most legal systems today purport not to review the foreign judgment on the merits, e.g., to exclude a *révision au fond*.[5]

---

[1] For a preliminary comment on this subject, see Hay, Guest Editorial, September 2008, www.conflictoflaws.net.

[2] Baker v. General Motors Corp., 522 U.S. 222, 235 (1998). See also Restatement (Second) of Conflict of Laws § 99 (1972) ("The local law of the forum determines the methods by which the judgment of another state is enforced").

[3] Hilton v. Guyot, 159 U.S. 113 (1895).

[4] See Millar, The Historical Relation of Estoppel by Record to Res Judicata, 35 Ill. L. Rev. 41 (1940).

[5] See Cheshire, North & Fawcett, Private International Law 539, 615, 628 (Fawcett & Carruthers, eds., 14th ed. 2008).

What about foreign decrees that themselves accord recognition to, and permit enforcement of, a foreign judgment (i.e., a judgment of a third country)? Are they "enforcement measures [that] do not travel" or "judgments" like any other and to be treated as such for recognition purposes?

Conceptual differences between civil law and common law judgment recognition law resulted in an easy—but by no means self evident—answer. The civil law *recognizes* the foreign judgment and then *declares it enforceable*: the declaration of enforceability—the *exequatur*—does not transform the foreign judgment into a local one, but permits its enforcement (as a foreign judgment) in the local territory. The sovereign grants permission. While recognition and enforceability are separate, the former usually takes place for purposes of the latter, and the latter is a sovereign act, operative only within the issuing sovereign's territory. There are different—and interchangeable—ways to describe what happened: The forum's act is an enforcement measure (i.e., something to be characterized as "procedural"), or: it is, by its own terms, self-limited to the issuing state's territory, or: as a sovereign act it could not even purport to create effects in another sovereign's territory. The result is the same: an *exequatur* does not travel, recognized long ago by the European mantra of "exequatur sur exequatur ne vaut."[6] In the framework of judgment recognition in the European Community, this civilian tradition then leads to the conclusion that an *exequatur* issued in one member state with respect to a non-member state judgment is not a "judgment" that falls under the recognition command of the EC Brussels-I Regulation on Jurisdiction and Recognition of Judgments in Civil and Commercial Matters.[7]

The sovereignty concern—independent from its function as explaining the *exequatur* as self-limited in its effect—also finds expression in the argument that a *foreign exequatur* cannot be permitted to produce local effects because it might prejudice local public policy-based review. This argument unnecessarily complicates—or obscures—the problem. The role of local public policy concerns is a general problem in judgment recognition, by no means limited to the *exequatur*: the question is whether local public permits review of the foreign judgment—for its observance of procedural standards, for its substance, or both. Where do review for public

[6] Kegel, Exequatur sur exequatur ne vaut, in Festschrift für Müller-Freienfels 377 (1986), a maxim by him attributed to Gavalda in Clunet 1935, 113.

[7] Regulation (EC) O. 44/2001, O.J. 2001, L 012/1 (hereinafter: "Brussels-I Regulation"). See nn. 11–14 infra.

policy and rejection of *révision au fond* intersect?[8] Can a foreign judgment ever be preclusive of an issue as against a local public policy objection? Because of the central role of the public policy objection, it is best treated as such: as an overarching issue. It is not peculiar to the question of the effect of an *exequatur*.

The common law does not share the civil law's conceptual difficulty. A foreign judgment has no effect of its own domestically (the same as in the civil law). It is a *claim* on which suit is brought.[9] Examination of the "claim" involves the traditional defenses to judgment recognition—from

---

[8] See Hay, "On Merger and Preclusion in U.S. Foreign Judgment Recognition," in Schütze ed., *Einheit und Vielfalt des Rechts—Festschrift für Reinhold Geimer* 323, 332 (2002); Bundesgerichtshof, June 23, 2005, IX ZB 64/04.

[9] Some common law countries, for instance the United Kingdom, also provide, by statute, for the registration of judgments of foreign countries with which they maintain treaty relations to that effect or which have been designated by local authority as beneficiaries of the registration procedure. The text describes the traditional common law method. The result is the same regardless of procedure: the foreign judgment now has the same standing and effect as a local judgment. See Dicey, Morris & Collins, *Conflict of Laws* 645–46 (14th ed. 2006); Cheshire, North & Fawcett, supra n. 5, at 584. However, an amendment to the 1933 Foreign Judgments (Reciprocal Enforcement) Act (added by the 1982 Civil Jurisdiction and Judgments Act) provides (Sec. 1(2A)) that the registration procedures do not apply to a judgment entered in a country to which the Act applies that was entered upon another judgment and "having as [its] object the enforcement of that judgment." The registration procedure thus resembles a civilian *exequatur* and treats foreign recognition judgments also as such. *But see* Morgan Stanley & Co. v. Pilot Lead Investments Ltd., [2006] HKLRD 731 (High Ct., Hong Kong): The Foreign Judgments (Reciprocal Enforcement) Ordinance, Cap 19 (FJREO), does not contain a provision similar to Sec. 1(2A) of the English Act (supra). "In the absence of any provision similar to section 2A, th[e] practice of 'laundering' foreign judgments, however undesirable it may be, is permissible under FJREO." At para. 26.

A more differentiated approach was adopted by two decisions in Australia and Papua New Guinea: recognition by *registration* of a third-country judgment in the first state was not a *judgment on the merits* (i.e., it was only an enforcement measure, like a European *exequatur*) and therefore not entitled to registration in the second state. Reported by Molloy, Registering a Registered Foreign Judgment, 81 Aust. L. J. 760 (2007). Reaching the same conclusion: Smart, Conflict of Laws: Enforcing a Judgment on a Judgment?, 81 Aust. L. J. 349 (2007). An Canadian decision, reported by Smart at nn. 30–34, arrived at the same conclusion with respect to a New Jersey judgment giving Full Faith and Credit to a Florida judgment: Frederick A. Jones, Inc. v. Toronto General Ins. Co., [1933] 2 DLR 660 (Ont. Ct. App.). This decision misperceives the nature of recognition by means of a *new* judgment, entered in consequence of the American Full Faith and Credit command, as distinguished from the registration of the first state's judgment for purposes of local enforcement (i.e., like an *exequatur*). See infra at n. 59 et seq., also with respect to international judgments.

the jurisdiction of the rendering court, to objections on procedural due process grounds, to public policy defenses. At the end, the successful foreign judgment creditor obtains a *domestic judgment* (not only a declaration of enforceability of the *foreign* judgment).[10] The obvious question, at this point, must then be: does the recognition command of European Community law apply to an English judgment recognizing, say, an American judgment?[11]

The Brussels-I Regulation defines broadly: the recognition command extends to "... any judgment, whatever the judgment may be called, including a decree, order, decision, or writ of execution ...." (Art. 32). Nonetheless, even this broad formulation arguably may not justify importing national law definitions, but requires a "Community meaning." The Court of Justice has not spoken to the issue.[12] The literature has overwhelmingly assumed that *exequatur*-notions apply and that recognition judgments are therefore not in turn entitled to recognition, regardless of their nature and effect in the country of rendition.[13] Advocate General Lenz finds textual

---

[10] Dicey, Morris & Collins, supra, 570; Scoles, Hay, Borchers & Symeonides, Conflict of Laws § 24.3 et seq. (4th ed. 2004).

[11] American judgments do not benefit from the English registration procedure (supra n. 9); their recognition and enforcement follows the common law method. Cheshire, North & Fawcett, supra n. 5, 579 n. 515; Dicey, Morris & Collins (supra, at 9) and Cheshire, North & Fawcett, supra, at 600) nevertheless conclude that a judgment upon a judgment is outside the purview of the European recognition command. See also Clarke v. Fennoscandia Ltd. et al., [2003] SCLR 894, [2004] SC 197, [2004] ScotCS 209 (Outer House, Ct of Sessions, Scotland, 2003) at paras. 31–34. Viewed from the English perspective, this may be correct when recognition is sought for a civil-law *exequatur*, given its nature in the country of rendition. It does not follow that the same should be true when recognition is sought in another EC state for an English *judgment* (at common law, as distinguished from a registered judgment, see supra n. 9) that recognizes a third-country judgment. It is therefore does not convince when Cheshire, North & Fawcett state (loc.cit.), that "the Regulation is only concerned with recognition of judgments *given in Member States* and is not intended to affect the recognition of judgments given in non-Member States" (original emphasis).

[12] In Case C-129/92 (Owens Bank Ltd. v. Bracco), [1994] ECR 1, the Court did not decide the point but dealt with matters now covered by Arts. 27–28 of the Brussels-I Regulation. Advocate General Lenz did address the point in his Submissions (at No. 20 et seq.) and concluded that an exequatur of an exequatur was not envisioned by the (then) Brussels Convention (forerunner of the Brussels-I Regulation).

[13] See Wautelet, in Magnus & Mankowski (eds.), Brussels I Regulation, Art. 32 annos. 32, 35 (2007). See also Rauscher in Rauscher & Heiderhoff (eds.), Europäisches Zivilprozessrecht, Art. 32, Brussels-I Regulation, anno. 14 (2006). For a forceful early statement, see Kegel, supra n. 6.

support for the conclusion that recognition is territorially limited in the language of what is now Art. 38(1) of the Brussels-I Regulation, viz. that the judgment "has been declared enforceable *there*" (emphasis added).[14] The language cited seems scant support: absent a recognition command in a higher norm, any judgment is only enforceable where rendered ("there"). The precise question is to what the recognition command attaches. The reference to "enforceable there" is therefore perhaps best understood in the meaning of "binding," "effective," as distinguished from preliminary. The Brussels-IIa Regulation (on jurisdiction and judgment recognition in divorce and custody matters) states it well when it provides for the enforcement of a judgment "which is enforceable in that Member State and *has been served* ...."[15]

The (civilian) view that recognition of a non-member state's judgment is essentially a procedural matter and hence not entitled to recognition, in turn will treat English and Irish judgments differently depending on whether they are based on an original claim or on a claim seeking recognition of a third-country judgment. To be sure, third-country defendants also are not covered by the Brussels I Regulation's jurisdictional rules, thus permitting member states to apply different standards from those that obtain with regard to EU defendants. But third-country parties and claims are therefore not necessarily outside the Regulation's scope. A judgment rendered against a non-EU defendant, even one based on a member state's exorbitant rule of jurisdiction,[16] is a "judgment of a member state" and

Isolated voices differ. See Kegel, previous n., at nn. 6 and 10, particularly Schütze, Die Doppelexequierung ausländischer Zivilurteile, 77 ZZP 3287 (1964). See also Baumbach/Lauterbach/Albers/*Hartmann*, ZPO, §328 anno. 10 (67th ed. 2009), with reference to Schütze. More recently, the Oberlandesgericht Frankfurt noted, in a different context, that in cases in which "the arbitration award is fully incorporated in the court's judgment of confirmation ('doctrine of merger' in Anglo-American law) such a judgment may be declared enforceable." Decree of 13 July 2005, 20 W 239/04, at No. 18 (author's translation).

14 Supra n. 12. See likewise Schlosser, Doppelexequatur zu Schiedssprüchen und ausländischen Gerichtsentscheidungen, [1985] IPRax 141, 143 (answering Schütze, previous n.).

15 Regulation (EC) No. 2201/2003, Concerning Jurisdiction and Enforcement of Judgments in Matrimonial Matters and Matters of Parental Responsibility, [2000] O.J. L 338/1 [hereinafter: "Brussels-IIa Regulation"], Art. 28(1), emphasis added.

16 Art. 3 of the Brussels-I Regulation restricts assertion of jurisdiction over EU defendants to the jurisdictional bases the Regulation provides and, in the Regulation's Annex I, proscribes specified bases of jurisdiction under the national law of the member states, such as jurisdiction based on the presence of assets of the defendant unrelated to the claim (e.g., under German law) or assertion of transient jurisdiction (e.g., under English and

entitled to recognition, subject only to the defenses contained in the Brussels-I Regulation. Despite different jurisdictional underpinnings, judgments rendered against EU and non-EU defendants alike benefit from the Regulation's recognition command.[17] What then justifies differentiating between judgments on the basis of whether they adjudicate a claim or recognize a judgment?

It has been suggested that exclusion of recognition judgments from the inter-EU recognition command is needed to permit review by the present (recognizing) court that the original court observed principles of procedural due process and to guard against violations of the forum's public policy.[18] According to this view, mandating recognition within the European Community is justified because the Brussels-I Regulation provides common (procedural) standards; but a third-country judgment might not satisfy these standards and should not benefit from recognition by another member state (the specter of "judgment laundering"). As Kegel wrote in a more general context, "one trusts one's friends, but not the friends of one's friends."[19] A Texas court expressed similar concerns when it refused recognition to a Louisiana judgment recognizing a Canadian judgment: to hold differently would recognize the Canadian judgment through the "back door."[20] In the particular American context, this decision must be regarded as wrong[21] (a point to be revisited later). However, it serves to illustrate that, underlying the whole discussion of when and how much recognition is due a foreign determination, the concern with local public policy and the danger of its circumvention through forum shopping for judgment laundering[22] looms largest. The concern is pervasive.

Irish law). Art. 4, in contrast, expressly leaves to member states whether to assert such bases of jurisdiction in litigation against non-EU defendants.

[17] For criticism of these effects on third-country defendants, see Cheshire, North & Fawcett, supra n. 5 at 635 and references cited there.

[18] Wautelet, supra n. 13, at anno. 34.

[19] Supra n. 6, at 392 (author's translation).

[20] Reading & Bates Constr. Co. v. Baker Energy Resources Corp., 976 S.W.2d 702, 715 (Tex.App. 1998).

[21] See Scoles, Hay, Borchers & Symeonides, supra n. 10, § 24.13 n. 7.

[22] Forum shopping is usually associated with the search for the most desirable forum for jurisdiction or for litigational or applicable-law advantages. The present discussion shows another application. In general and in the abstract, there is nothing either startling or wrong with a party seeking the advantages of one of two or more equally available legal systems. See Juenger, What's Wrong With Forum Shopping?, 18 Sydney L. Rev. 5 (1994).

If public policy is at the heart of it all, what difference does it make to call another state's recognition of a third-country judgment a (territorially limited) *exequatur* rather than to treat it as a judgment that is itself entitled to recognition, subject to the usual defenses? By regarding the prior country's recognition a non-recognizable *exequatur*, the original third-country judgment remains open for review; in contrast, treating the prior country's recognition as a *judgment* limits local review to that judgment. In the latter case, Community law requires that one must "trust one's friends," in Kegel's words (supra). What Kegel does not ask or pursue is why trusting one's friends does not include trusting them to have undertaken a proper review of *their* friends' judgments before recognizing them. The question can therefore be put yet more narrowly: who undertakes the public policy review—must it always be the present forum? Internationally, the answer is undoubtedly "yes." This follows from the territorially-focused, discretionary judgment-recognition practice of states, only observing more or

---

Forum shopping, in an original action, can of course be unduly burdensome to the other party or to the chosen, but only minimally involved forum. In the common law, the possibility of a dismissal for *forum non conveniens* supplies a corrective. See Hay, Weintraub & Borchers, Conflict of Laws—Cases and Materials ch. 4 (13th ed. 2009); J. Harris, The Brussels I Regulation and the Re-Emergence of the English Common Law, [4-2008] Eur.Legal Forum I-181, I-183. Narrowly drawn jurisdictional rules, such as in the EC, limit forum shopping at the outset. In both systems, the forum state's public policy also sets limits. It finds expression, for purposes of the present discussion, both in concrete rules for the denial of judgment recognition (for instance, those of Art. 34(2-4) Brussels-I Regulation and § 328 German ZPO) or in the general public policy defense, common to all legal systems (see, e.g., Art. 34(1) Brussels-I Regulation).

These objections do not apply in the present context: the presence of assets against which enforcement is being sought provides both the reason and the link for suit in this forum. "Laundering" suggests something "bad." But this paints with too broad a brush: "[I]t is not at all clear why this should be considered an improper evasion. The creditor in pursuing assets in the first executing jurisdiction has a real and genuine interest in proceeding against assets there. If his judgment remains unsatisfied, why is it improper to proceed to further legal recovery in the most advantageous way? The subjective element of the notion of *fraude à la loi* is therefore lacking." Glenn, Exequatur sur exequatur (Doppelexequatur) in Europe and North America, in: Basedow, Drobnig, Ellger, Hopt, Kötz, Kulms, Mestmäcker (eds.), Aufbruch nach Europa 705, 711 (2001). See also Juenger, La Convention de Bruxelles du 27 septembre 1968 et la courtoisie internationale, [1983] Revue critique de dr. int. priv. 37, 48. This view, of course, does not address the case of an action brought in the original jurisdiction to gain an advantage under its law (i.e., the usual case of forum shopping), such as punitive damages, that could not have been obtained in the state in which a recognition judgment is now sought to be enforced and which would not have recognized the original judgment. See further infra at n. 74 et seq.

less self-defined limits of comity.[23] But what about states bound together by and subject to higher norms for judicial jurisdiction and judgment recognition, such as the European Community and the United States?

II. The Public Policy Defense and the *Exequatur* in the European Community

The Brussels-I Regulation details grounds for the non-recognition of member state judgments in Art. 34. Of the provision's four paragraphs, only one (subsection 3) is not public policy-related: as between inconsistent judgments, the prior in time takes precedence when neither is a judgment of the forum. Subsection 1 states the general (traditional) public policy exception, while subsections 2 and 4 are particular applications: precedence of the forum's own inconsistent judgment, regardless whether prior or subsequent to the judgment sought to be enforced (subsec. 4) and non-recognition of default judgments when the defendant was not notified in time defend (subsec. 2).[24] The second of these reflects public policy principles in that it posits a right to be heard, to a day in court. A German court of appeals saw it this way when it expanded subsec. 2 by reliance on the general provision of subsec. 1 and held that extremely late notice constituted such a hardship for the party as to amount to a denial of access to justice.[25] Other courts have been more restrictive. Thus, courts did not find Art. 34(2) to be applicable when a claim was added in the first proceeding without additional notice to that effect or when remedies had been available but not exhausted after initial failure to give proper notice.[26]

---

[23] Supra at n. 3.

[24] While not directly applicable (because not yet in force at the relevant time), the provision was applied as expressing governing "principles" and interpreted by the Spanish Supreme Court. It adopted the view that non-recognition under this provision "is limited to cases were non-appearance was unintentional," e.g., because of non-notification, and did not include intentional non-appearance. Re Recognition of a Canon Law Judgment, Judgment of October 24, 2007, [2008] I.L.Pr. 31, at no. 39 (Spanish Tribunale Suprema).

[25] Oberlandesgericht Zweibrücken, May 10, 2005, 3 W 165/04, [2005] RIW 779, [2006] IPRax 487.

[26] See Oberlandesgericht Köln, January 12, 2004, IPRspr. 2004, No. 156, 340–347; Oberlandesgericht Frankfurt, December 16, 2004, OLG-Report Frankfurt 2005, 962-964; Bundesgerichtshof, December 12, 2007, XII ZB 240/05, [2008] Eur. Legal Forum II-8, with anno. by Calabresi-Scholz. In Krombach v. Bamberski, Case C-7/98, [2000] ECR I-1935, the Court of Justice had indicated that a defendant must litigate jurisdictional

Art. 34(1)—the general public policy exception—needs interpretation. Art. 34(2-4) leaves little or no leeway for interpretation. But, as the example of the decision with the extremely late notice shows, national courts may give public policy an expansive meaning. The only express limitation on such national action is Art. 35 which precludes resort to public policy to justify an otherwise proscribed review of the rendering court's jurisdiction. Other limits on national court use of the exception have to come from the Court of Justice as it performs its function as the authoritative interpreter of Community law.

The public policy exception to judgment recognition is narrow. As Art. 34(2) and its possible extensions show, it addresses primarily concerns of "procedural due process," in American terms.[27] Moreover, under the Brussels-I Regulation objections to the recognition and enforcement of a judgment have been moved from the trial level in the recognizing state (as under the predecessor Brussels Convention) to the appellate level.[28] Nonetheless, and despite the streamlining in the Brussels-I Regulation, obtaining crossborder recognition and enforcement of a judgment by *exequatur*

---

objections in the first court or lose them (see art. 35(1). Unlike in American law, for instance, the defendant does not have the option to default in the first court and then litigate his objection to that court's jurisdiction in the second court. The two courts of appeal in the decisions cited seem to believe that *Krombach* extends to the factual situations presented in their cases. If so, would not Art. 35(1) also preclude the result reached by the Oberlandesgericht Zweibrücken, previous n.? On balance, it seems that the Zweibrücken decision is right and the Köln and Frankfurt decisions unduly restrictive. The former properly limits the prohibition of Art. 35(1) to questions of jurisdiction, while the latter go beyond the language of the provision and the issue decided in *Krombach* and thereby end up with a narrow interpretation of Art, 34(2). With no provision other than Art. 34(2) addressing problems of procedural due process, Art. 34(1), the general public policy defense, is the logical source for the protection of such of rights as access to justice and an opportunity to be heard. See Hay, The Development of the Public Policy Barrier to Judgment Recognition Within the European Community, 7 Eur. Legal Forum I-289, 292 (6-2007). To regard Art. 34(1) to encompass protection of such rights would also be consistent with the obligations of all member states as parties to the European Convention on Human Rights and with the incorporation of human rights law into Community law. Art. 6(2), Treaty on European Union. See also Cheshire, North & Fawcett, supra n. 5, at 613, and infra at n. 66–69. For a slightly less restrictive application of Art. 34(2) by the ECJ, see Case C-283/05 (ASML Netherlands BV v. Semiconductor Industry Services GmbH (SEMIS)), [2006] ECR I-12041, [2008] IPRax 519, with critical anno. by Geimer, id. at 498.

[27] See Hay, previous n. Cf. also Borchers, *Jones v. Flowers*, An Essay on a Unified Theory of Procedural Due Process, 40 Creighton L. Rev. 343, 346 et seq. (2007).

[28] See Arts. 33(1), 38(1), 41, 42–45.

or by suit on the judgment (as at common law) can be time-consuming and, especially for small claims, prohibitively expensive.

The Commission has favored abolition of the *exequatur* for some time, favoring direct enforceability of the first state's judgment in the second.[29] Three specialized Regulations[30] now expressly dispense with the requirement of an *exequatur*. They are the European Enforcement Order Regulation,[31] the European Order for Payments Procedure Regulation,[32] and the European Small Claims Procedure Regulation,[33] in force in all EU states except Denmark. The first of these provides for the certification, by the court of rendition, of a judgment concerning an "uncontested claim" as constituting a "European Enforcement Order." An "uncontested claim" includes claims to which the defendant did not respond, that is, in which a default judgment issued. The Regulation provides strict standards for notice to the defendant to be observed by the court of rendition (Art. 12 et seq.), but limits courts of the state of enforcement to refuse enforcement

---

[29] See Frattini, European Area of Civil Justice—Has the Community Reached the Limits?, [2006] ZeuP 225, 233. See also Van der Grinten, Abolishing Exequatur in the European Union: An Alternative, in van der Grinten & Heukels (eds.), Crossing Borders 71 (2006).

[30] For brief discussion, see Cunniberti, The First Stage of the Abolition of the Exequatur in the European Union, 14 Colum. J. Eur. L. 371 (2008). In addition, the Brussels-IIa Regulation, supra n. 15, dispenses with the need for a declaration of enforceability with respect to decisions ordering the return of a child: Art. 42(1). For an illustration that streamlining enforcement procedures does not necessarily bring about speedy and effective enforcement when national procedures can be invoked to bring about delay, see Case C-195/08 PPU (Rinau), [2008] ECR __, anno. by Schulz, [2008] ZFamR 1732. See also infra at n. 38.

[31] Regulation (EC) No. 805/2004, [2004] O.J. L 143/15, Art. 5. For discussion, see Gerling, Die Gleichstellung ausländischer mit inländischen Vollstreckungstiteln nach der Verordnung zur Einführung eines Europäischen Vollstreckungstitels für unbestrittene Forderungen (Diss. Köln 2005); Bittmann, Die Voraussetzungen der Zwangsvollstrekkung eines Europäischen Vollstreckungstitels, [2008] IPRax 445. For early comment, see Geimer, Das Brüssel I-System und seine Fortentwicklung im Lichte der Beschlüsse von Tampere, in: Kiss & Varga (eds.), Magister artis boni et aequi—Studia in honorem Német János 229, 237 et seq. (2003).

[32] Regulation (EC) No. 1896/2006, [2006] O.J. L 399/1, Art. 19.

[33] Regulation (EC) No. 861/2007, [2007] O.J. L 199/1, Art. 20(1). For brief discussion of this and the European Payments Order Regulation, see Hess & Bittmann, Zur Europäischen Mahnverfahrens- und Bagatellverordnung, [2008] IPRax 305. For discussion of all three Regulations, particularly also in the present context, see Freitag, Anerkennung und Rechtskraft europäischer Titel nach EuVTVO, EuMahnVO und EuBagatellVO, in: Baetge, von Hein & von Hinden (eds.), Die richtige Ordnung—Festschrift für Jan Kropholler 759 (2008).

only in the case of an earlier inconsistent judgment (their own[34] or that of another state) (Art. 21). A stay may be granted if, inter alia, an appeal is pending in the state of rendition. As this brief summary shows, the judgment debtor virtually has no defenses—under the Regulation—*in the state of enforcement*, he must bring them in the state of rendition. That means that the state of enforcement cannot refuse recognition and enforcement on public policy grounds, as under Art. 34(1), Brussels-I Regulation. Only if and when the judgment creditor "contests" the claim in the state of rendition,[35] the automatic mechanism of the Enforcement Order Regulation no longer applies; at that point, the Brussels-I Regulation does.[36] Again, the question arises: what if a member state recognizes a claim arising from a third-country judgment—can such a claim become the subject of an European Enforcement Order? What if the claim arising under the third-country judgment, for instance for support,[37] was recognized by *judgment* in a member state, such as in the United Kingdom?

The other two Regulations providing for an abolition of the *exequatur* parallel the Enforcement Order Regulation in their enforcement provisions (no review in the second state, except in the case of inconsistent orders), but—by their nature—are unlikely to involve the problem of the recognition of third country determinations. The Small Claims Procedure Regulation seeks to expedite the usual Brussels-I procedure for cases not exceeding 2,000 Euro. It is essentially a written procedure. The European Pay-

---

[34] The Brussels-I Regulation also gives priority to *subsequent* forum judgments as a concession to forum public policy concerns. The Enforcement Order Regulation, as well as the other two mentioned in the text, drop the forum preference and limit the ground for refusal to the traditional European rule regarding judgment priority.

[35] As has been noted, the Enforcement Order Regulation provides a strong incentive for the defendant to appear in the state of suit, thereby perhaps extending its jurisdictional reach beyond that contemplated by the Brussels-I Regulation. Geimer, Internationales Prozessrecht anno. 3182 (5th ed. 2005). However, even the Brussels-I Regulation precludes review of the rendering court's jurisdiction in most cases. When review is permitted (e.g., in consumer cases), it is limited to a review of the law (excluding jurisdictional facts). Art. 35(2). The further restriction brought about by the Enforcement Order Regulation thus relates to the Art. 34 defenses of the Brussels-I Regulation. See also next n.

[36] It is an interesting question to what extent use of the Enforcement Order mechanism will reduce use of the Brussels-I Regulation recognition procedure. See Mankowski, Wie viel Bedeutung verliert die EuGVVO durch den Europäischen Vollstreckungstitel ?, in Baetge et al., supra 33, 829.

[37] For the applicability of the Regulation to support orders, see R. Wagner, Das Gesetz zur Durchführung der Verordnung (RG) Nr. 805/2004 zum Europäischen Vollstreckungstitel—unter besonderer Berücksichtigung der Vollstreckungsabwehrklage, [2005] IPrax 401, 409.

ment Order was introduced to facilitate collection of pecuniary obligations now due and payable; jurisdiction is governed by the rules of Brussels-I, with consumers subject to jurisdiction only at their domicile (Art. 6); the resulting order, once again, is enforceable without an *exequatur*.

The new Regulations all provide that, to quote the Enforcement Order Regulation, the judgment declared enforceable by the state of rendition "shall be enforced under the same conditions as a judgment handed down in the Member State of enforcement" (Art. 20(1)). Does this provision permit use of national-law procedures that might prevent enforcement of the order? The German action to prevent execution (*Vollstreckungsabwehrklage*)[38] permits the judgment debtor to raise matters that may have arisen after conclusion of final (oral) argument in the original action, for instance that the judgment has meanwhile been assigned to another. There is argument that such a remedy exists under German national law with respect to *all* judgments and that its use with respect to Enforcement Orders thus falls within Art. 20(1). This view would accept the consequence of non-uniform results, in the sense that a particular European Enforcement Order may be subject to such an action in Germany to block its enforcement, while it is enforceable in another member state.[39] However, while part of the procedural body of law concerned with enforcement and execution, the *Vollstreckungsabwehrklage* seeks to establish that the judgment is not entitled to enforcement. The circumstance that such an action can be brought as a preemptive measure in advance of attempted execution does not alter its nature as a defense against liability pursuant to the judgment. If the Enforcement Order Regulation—and indeed the Brussels-I Regulation itself—refer defenses to the court of rendition, national-law differences seem to be acceptable only (within the meaning of Art.

[38] § 767(2) Code of Civil Procedure (ZPO).

[39] R. Wagner, supra n. 37, at 405, 407–08, also dismissing (in n. 95) the possibility of "limping recognition decisions," as raised by Hess, [2004] IPRax 493, 494, as "far less troublesome" than limping marriages (author's transl.). Avoiding *both* would no doubt be desirable.

For the view that the *Vollstreckungsabwehrklage* (and Art. 12(1) of the German statute (the AVAG) implementing EU procedural law) are compatible with the enforcement provisions of the Brussels-I Regulation (and, presumably, the Enforcement Order Regulation), see Bundesgerichtshof, Decision of 14 March 2007, XII ZB 174/04, at no. 22 et seq., BGHZ 171, 310, [2008] IPRax 38; Zöller-*Herget*, ZPO § 767 anno. 6 (27th ed. 2009). In contrast, Geimer believes that Art. 45(1), Brussels-I Regulation, clearly proscribes such a remedy, except perhaps for liquidated amounts (the appellate court may consider "only ... one of the grounds specified" in the Regulation itself): Zöller-*Geimer*, ZPO, Appendix I, EuGVVO anno. 1 (27th ed. 2009). The present discussion shares the latter view.

20(1)) as they address the *manner* of enforcement and execution, without affecting the obligation established by the judgment or order.[40]

The results this far: The Brussels-I Regulation requires most defenses to be raised in the first state, but preserves a limited[41] public policy exception for application by the court of the enforcement jurisdiction. The Enforcement Order, Payment Order, and Small Claims Regulations, in contrast, leave virtually no review function for the second state. What happens to the second state's public policy concerns and does such a limitation on the ability to review action by the court of rendition raise concerns under national constitutional law? And what is the effect of these issues on the question about recognition of recognition judgments of the first state? Brief consideration of another model may help in addressing these questions in a subsequent section.

III. An Alternative Model: *Res Judicata*, Full Faith and Credit, and System Standards

The United States presents a relevant alternative model: with no national law in most areas of private law and civil procedure,[42] there is need for inter-system accommodation with respect to jurisdiction of courts and the

[40] From this perspective, the decision of the German Oberlandesgericht (OLG) Düsseldorf of May 6, 2008, I-3 W 36/08, [2008-4] Eur. Legal F. II-106, interpreting a payment as satisfying the payment obligation established by the Dutch judgment and not as applying to a different obligation, as urged by the judgment creditor, clearly gave relief that is within the province of the rendering court and impermissible action for the court of enforcement to undertake. It is another question whether the court of enforcement *should have* the power to grant the same relief as the rendering court could give. This may be desirable (infra, text following n. 80), but Art. 43 et seq. of the Brussels-I Regulation do not so provide now. It is not a case where the foreign judgment comes in through the "back door" (supra n. 20): local defenses do.

It has also been suggested that to bar the *Vollstreckungsabwehrklage* would be at odds with Art. 22(5) of the Brussels-I Regulation. Wagner, previous n. at 408. That provision, however, merely provides that each member state shall have exclusive jurisdiction over measures of enforcement and execution within its territory. The view expressed in the text does not ignore Art. 22(5). It regards the *Vollstreckungsklage*, regardless of how characterized in national law, as touching upon the substance of the obligation and not merely the manner of its enforcement. For comparison, see Restatement (Second) of Conflict of Laws § 99 (1972), quoted in n. 2 supra.

[41] For the view that the public policy exception of Art. 34(1), Brussels-I Regulation is very limited indeed, see Hay, supra n. 26.

[42] Hay, Law of the United States nos. 17-24 (2d ed. 2005); same: Hay, US-amerikanisches Recht nos. 19–24 (4th ed. 2008).

recognition and enforcement of their judgments. Without a national approach, individual states deal individually with third-country judgments, thus also raising the question of the inter-system recognition of recognition judgments.[43]

Federal constitutional standards limit the exercise of state court judicial jurisdiction,[44] as does the Brussels-I Regulation—in a much more concrete manner[45]—in the EU. The federal Constitution's "Full Faith and Credit Clause" (Art. 4 Sec. 1) prescribes interstate judgment recognition and the federal implementation statute specifies that this means that the judgment must be given the same effect as it has in the state "from which [it was] taken."[46] The latter provision imports the rendering jurisdiction's rules of res judicata: in an action, in which both parties participate, issues that were or could have been raised are now precluded, that is, cannot be raised again in the second court.[47] There are no additional *local* remedies:[48] the remedy is appeal in the court of rendition. With respect to jurisdiction and substantive matters the result is thus similar to that in the EU.[49] However, since the result is based on principles of *res judicata* and not on a rule of higher (federal) law, an American court of enforcement may entertain those defenses that could still be raised in the state of rendition under that state's law. Ultimate review of compliance with jurisdictional standards lies with the U.S. Supreme Court and in the EC Court of Justice, respectively; review of issues of substantive (private) law is the province of state and national supreme courts, respectively. In the United

---

[43] For a general overview, see Scoles, Hay, Borchers & Symeonides, supra n. 10, § 24.8 et seq. (4th ed. 2004).

[44] See, e.g., Shaffer v. Heitner, 433 U.S. 186, 212, 97 S.Ct. 2569, 2584 (1977): "all assertions of state court jurisdiction must be evaluated according to [federal law] standards ..."

[45] The primary limitation of American federal constitutional law is the Due Process Clause of the 14th Amendment of the federal Constitution, in the current interpretation by the U.S. Supreme Court. There is some room for state to state differences within that limit. The Brussels-I Regulation, in contrast, provides formulated jurisdictional rules. As a result, jurisdictional standards in the U.S. state law and the EU will often coincide, but, in some cases, may also differ: the American exercise of general jurisdiction on the basis of "doing continous and systematic business" has no EU counterpart, except perhaps for Art. 15(2), Brussels-I Regulation (jurisdiction over the foreign parent on the basis of the activity of the local branch for the protection of the consumer-purchaser from the latter).

[46] 28 U.S.C.A. § 1738; for this point and the following discussion, see also Hay, supra n. 42 (Law...), at nos. 201–209, 215–217.

[47] See Treinies v. Sunshine Mining Co., 308 U.S. 66 (1939).

[48] *But see* next n.

[49] For the EU, see Arts. 35–36, Brussels-I Regulation.

States, the procedure is the common-law method of suit upon the first judgment (treating it as a claim), resulting in a new local judgment.[50]

What about public policy? In Anglo-American law, the claim advanced by the plaintiff "merges" in the resulting judgment[51] and it is the latter which now becomes the claim for which recognition is sought in the second state. If the first judgment reduces a claim to an award of a sum of money, the claim for recognition purposes is for money, the underlying claim is now irrelevant, even if—for public policy reasons—it could not have been brought in the second state as an original matter: the judgment is entitled to recognition.[52]

The Full Faith and Credit Clause deal with interstate recognition. State law applies to the recognition of international judgments. In many respects, state practice, especially also in application of a Uniform Law,[53] parallels interstate recognition practice. Major differences lie in the inapplicability of the "merger"-doctrine to international judgments[54] and lesser preclusion as a result of res judicata. Lesser preclusion results from the circumstance that certain issues, for instance, compliance with American due process standards, could not have been litigated in the foreign action and therefore can not be precluded, but are open for review in the second (American) court. The inapplicability of the "merger"-doctrine leaves the underlying claim in place. Both differences combine to leave foreign-country judgments more susceptible to review than domestic (sister-state) judgments. This is true, especially, with respect to objections to the foreign judgment on public policy grounds.[55] Review on these grounds may range, for instance, from objections to a foreign system's placing the bur-

---

[50] Supra n. 42, loc. cit and at no. 213. As an alternative, many states provide for a summary procedure for the registration of a sister-state judgment: Uniform Foreign-Country Money Judgment Recognition Act (1962 and 2005 Revision). This statute permits the assertion of local defenses in addition to those available under the law of the state of rendition: use of the summary procedure is voluntary; the judgment creditor using it opts for speed at the risk of exposure to additional defenses. This procedure will not be pursued further in the subsequent discussion.

[51] Scoles, Hay, Borchers & Symeonides, supra n. 10, §§ 24. 1, 24. 3; Hay, supra n. 42, nos. 202, 213.

[52] Fauntleroy v. Lum, 210 U.S. 230 (1908), discussed in Scoles, Hay, Borchers & Symeonides, supra n. 10, § 24.20.

[53] Supra n. 50 and Scoles, Hay, Borchers & Symeonides, supra n. 10, § 24.36.

[54] Id. at §§ 24.3, 24.41.

[55] For comprehensive review, wih references, see Hay, Comments on Public Policy in Current American Conflicts Law, in Baetge, von Hein & von Hinden (eds.), Die richtige Ordnung—Festschrift für Jan Kropholler 89 (2008).

den of proof on the defendant in a defamation action[56] to a general inquiry into the fairness and impartiality of the foreign legal system.[57] More recently, a more restrained application of local standards has been adopted by some decisions: it is not compliance with American due process law that is required, but observance of an "international concept of due process"—a lesser standard that focuses on basic and widely shared values and standards of fairness.[58]

With respect to the recognition of recognition judgments, differences in interstate practice on the recognition of foreign country judgments are not relevant. The foreign judgment has not been "declared enforceable," in the sense of an *exequatur*, but a local judgment has been issued (which, in fact, now exists side by side with the judgment it recognizes[59]), regardless of whether this is the result of a recognition proceeding at common law or under the Uniform Act. The recognizing judgment is judgment like any other: it—and not the foreign country judgment through the "back door," as one court erroneously held[60]—is now entitled to interstate recognition under the command of the Full Faith and Credit Clause and its implementing statute. It may be, of course, that the foreign country should not have been recognized in the first place, for instance because the foreign court's assertion of jurisdiction or conduct of the proceeding violated American concepts of due process or because the result of the foreign

---

[56] Matusevich v. Telnikoff, 877 F.Supp. 1 (D.D.C. 1995). See also Bachchan v. India Abroad Publications, Inc., 154 Misc.2d 228, 585 N.Y.S.2d 661 (1992).

[57] See Bank Melli Iran v. Pahlavi, 58 F.3d 1406, 1410, 1411-12 (9th Cir. 1995); Bridgeway Corp. V. Citibank, 201 F.3d 134, 139, 141 (2d Cir. 2000). See also S.C. Chimexim S.S. v. Velco Enterprises, Ltd.., 36 F.Supp.2d 206, 208 (S.D.N.Y. 19990, judgment reinstated, 2004 U.S. Dist. LEXIS 2603 (recognizing a Romanian judgment after review of the countries progress from a communism "to a free market economy" and noting its judiciary has "outstanding ... graduates of the law schools." For criticism of the sometimes rather political reviews of foreign systems or the application of American constitutional standards, see Caroline, Political Judging: When Due Process Goes International, 48 Wm. & Mary L. Rev. 1159 (2007). See also Rosen, Exporting the Constitution, 53 Emory L. J. 171, 198 (2004); Rosen, Should "Unamerican" Foreign Judgments be Enforced?, 88 Minn. L.Rev. 783 (2004).

[58] Society of Lloyd's v. Ashenden, 233 F.3d 473, 477 (7th Cir. 2000). For discussion and comparison with the *effet atténué*, see Hay, supra n. 55, at 92–97.

[59] Judgments, unlike claims, do not merge in judgments in Anglo-American practice. Supra n. 54. As a result, the judgment creditor remains free to seek enforcement of either judgment. Depending on how limitations are characterized, this may be a consideration, for instance, if one of them, especially the recognizing judgment, should become time barred.

[60] Supra nn. 20–21.

litigation (the judgment itself) violated the public policy of the (recognizing) forum. These matters, as discussed above, should have been raised in the recognizing forum; they are now precluded. Not precluded in the present (second) forum: the jurisdiction of the (first) recognizing forum and resort to local public policy concerns. However, if the recognizing (first) court had jurisdiction *or* the objecting party participated, the jurisdictional inquiry is either precluded as well or resolved against the objector. A public policy objection would need to find the sister state's judgment to violate public policy—not for what it did (recognition), but for what it awards, e.g. the payment of money. On these grounds, the objection is likely to fail; the recognition judgment is entitled to recognition interstate.

IV. Public Policy and Full Faith and Credit in the European Community

As discussed, the Brussels-I Regulation limits review by the recognizing court to the issue of priority as between inconsistent judgments, to lack of notice in time to defend, and to public policy concerns, and shifts consideration of all of these to the appellate level. With the express exclusion of review for jurisdiction and increasingly shared principles of substantive law, the public policy defense is likely to be no more than another instrument for the safeguarding of procedural due process.[61] It has been suggested that the Brussels-I mechanism could perhaps do without it.[62] The three specialized Regulations (Enforcement Order, Payments Order, and Small Claims Procedure) retain only a provision on inconsistent orders and make no mention of a public policy defense.

An early article, commenting on the Brussels Convention, precursor of the Brussels-I Regulation, proclaimed that "Full Faith and Credit Comes

---

[61] Hay, supra n. 26. See also Hohloch, Zur Bedeutung des Ordre public-Arguments im Vollstreckbarerklärungsverfahren, in Baetge et. al., supra n. 55, 809; Leipold, Zum anerkennungsrechtlichen ordre public, in: Hohloch, Frank & Schlechtriem (eds.), Festschrift für Hans Stoll 625, 644 (2001); Martiny, Die Zunkunft des europäischen ordre public im Internationalen Privat- und Zivilverfahrensrecht, in: Coester, Martiny, Prinz von Sachsen Gessaphe (eds.), Privatrecht in Europa—Vielfalt, Kollision, Kooperation—Festschrift für Hans Jürgen Sonnenberger 523, at 528, 541, 547 (2004).

[62] See Laptew, Abschaffung der anerkennungsrechtlichen Ordre public-Kontrolle in Osteuropa: Vorbild für die EU?, IPRax 2004, 495. See also Hohloch, previous n.; Sujecki, Die Möglichkeiten und Grenzen der Abschaffung des *ordre public*-Vorbehalts im Europäischen Zivilprozessrecht, [2008] ZEuP 458.

to the Common Market."[63] Did it? In fact, in some respects the EU has gone beyond the American Full Faith and Credit model. This is so because EU law precludes the use of defenses in the recognizing court that the rendering court would still permit, thereby relegating litigation of all objections to the latter.[64] This being so, can one really maintain that recognition judgments are not entitled to recognition—just by calling them not to be a "judgment," but only an *exequatur* which, in the three new Regulations, has been abolished?

A potent argument, at least in the past, has been the fear that objectionable third-country judgments might circumvent local public policy review by being laundered in another member state. American awards of punitive damages, considered offensive by most EC member states, are the most frequently cited example.[65] However, public policy as a ground for refusal of recognition has largely disappeared in inter-EU recognition except for issues of procedural due process, as discussed earlier. Yet procedural due process is not the reason why recognition of recognition judgments is being opposed (see the punitive damage example). And if procedural due process (in the third-country judicial proceeding) were an issue, EU standards of procedural due process would require an opportunity to litigate that issue in the (first) recognizing court. That court, in turn, is bound by the principles of EU law and the procedural due process guarantees of Art. 6 of the Human Rights Convention.[66]

Another basic difference between the EU and American approaches—in addition to relegating most defenses to proceedings in the court of rendition—is the absence, in formal rules or in legal tradition, of binding common standards. In its *Krombach* decision,[67] the Court of Justice (ECJ) spoke of a *Community* ordre public, informed by written Community law, human

---

[63] Bartlett, Full Faith and Credit Comes to the Common Market: An Analysis of the Provisions of the Convention on Jurisdiction and Enforcement of Judgments in Civil and Commercial Matters, 24 Int'l & Comp. L. Q. 44 (1975).

[64] It goes beyond the American model because the latter only requires the recognizing court to give the judgment the effect it has in the state in which it was rendered. Supra at n. 46. See also text following n. 82.

[65] See Quarta, Recognition and Enforcement of U.S. Punitive Damages Awards in Continental Europe: The Italian Supreme Court's Veto, 31 Hastings Int'l & Comp. L. Rev. 753 (2008); Lopez de Gonzalo, Punitive Damages e ordine pubblico, 44 Rivista dir. int. priv. e proc. 77 (2008). See also infra n. 74.

[66] See *Krombach, supra* n. 26.

[67] Supra n. 26.

rights law principles (such as the rights to be heard and to a fair hearing), and principles of constitutional law common to the member states. The German *Bundesgerichtshof*, which had submitted the case to the ECJ under the preliminary reference procedure, however, chose to decide the case on the basis of (substantively identical) safeguards of *German* constitutional law.[68] *Community* principles of public policy, as recognized or established by the ECJ, as well as the standards of the Human Rights Convention (invoked by the ECJ in *Krombach*), are applied by national courts. There is no mechanism for individual litigants to seek review by the ECJ of a national court's failure to observe such principles or standards: national cases come to the ECJ only by reference from national courts for preliminary rulings.[69] The abolition of the *exequatur* in the three new Regulations and the shift of virtually all review functions to the court of rendition and away from the courts of the state of enforcement was therefore seen as a *sea change* in the EC's law of judgment recognition and enforcement.[70] Indeed, concerns were expressed that the relinquishment of any review competence on the part of the local court of enforcement might not be compatible with guarantees of national constitutional law.[71]

V. Application: Recognition of Recognition Judgments?

If there existed minimum standards, commonly shared and observed, there can be little doubt that a member state's recognition of a third-country judgment should itself be entitled to recognition. From this would also follow that the first court could bring about this result in an appropriate

---

[68] BGHZ 144, 390, 392 (2000).

[69] Art. 234 EC Treaty. Possible alternative avenues for relief that an aggrieved party might pursue is a national action on national constitutional law grounds, if available, or recourse to the European Human Rights Commission and Court: Martiny, supra n. 61, 546; Rauscher, supra n. 13, Intro. to EGVOllstrTVO annos. 36, 41.

[70] See, e.g., Kohler, Von der EuGVVO zum Europäischen Vollstreckungstitel, in: Reichelt & Rechberger (eds.), Europäisches Kollisionsrecht 63, 75 (2004) ("a leap into the dark," author's transl); Rauscher, supra n. 13, Intro. to EG-VollstrTitelVO annos. 13-14.

[71] See Kohler, previous n., at 76. For brief discussion, see also Geimer, supra n. 31, at 239 (finding the concerns to be unfounded); Rauscher, supra n. 13, Intro. to EGVollstrTVO anno. 33. Cunniberti, supra n. 30, adds—and notes with concern—that abolition of the exequatur, combined with a review on other grounds by the state of enforcement, also precludes review of compliance with requirements of the European Human Rights Convention (see supra nn. 26, 69–70) by the latter state's courts. For an extensive bibliography, see Sujecki, supra n. 62, at 458 n. 5.

case by means of a European Enforcement Order. The reason for resisting the first court's acting as a "transformation court"[72] cannot be the nature of that court's act as not constituting a "judgment," at least not in those cases in which it *is* a judgment under the court of rendition's own law. By definition that includes an Enforcement Order issued for a member state's judgment. The real reason for resistance must be sought in the increased loss of control by the court of enforcement. To rephrase Kegel's observation[73] in the EC context: it is not that one "does not trust the friends of one's friends"—it is that one does not even trust one's friends! Because these "friends" might let in an unpalatable third-country judgment, such as one awarding punitive damages.

Punitive (or "exemplary") damages are not unknown in the national law of EU countries.[74] The United Kingdom might also recognize an American judgment awarding them.[75] If the judgment were an original one under English law, it would be entitled to recognition.[76] If, in contrast, the judgment recognizes an American judgment, current opinion would deny it recognition in another EC state. The incongruity is obvious. What

[72] See Glenn, supra n. 22, at 710–11 with references, using the example—in the context of the North American Free Trade Area (NAFTA)—of a Mexican judgment, recognized in Texas, and then to be recognized in California under Full Faith and Credit principles. To the same effect, Glenn, The Morris Lecture: Conflicting Laws in a Common Market? The NAFTA Experiment," 76 Chi.-Kent L. Rev. 1789, 1817–18 (2001) (discussing the use of a "transformative" judgment to assure recognition of a U.S. judgment imposing liability for asbestos damage in the face of contrary Canadian provincial legislation). The last example is of course precisely the type of case envisioned by those who oppose recognition of recognition judgments on the ground of "judgment laundering." See supra at nn. 19–22 and infra at n. 79.

[73] Supra n. 6.

[74] See also Hay, Entschädigung und andere Zwecke, in Hohloch, Frank & Schlechtriem (eds.), Festschrift für Hans Stoll 521, 523 et seq. (2001).

[75] See SA Consortium General Textiles v. Sun and Sand Agencies Ltd., [1978] 1 Q.B. 279, 299-300 (obiter dictum: recognition of French award of punitive damages would not violate English public policy but award in question was considered to be compensatory, hence statement is not part of holding); Lewis v. Eliades, [2004] 1 All E.R. 1196 at para. 50, [2004] 1 W.L.R. 692 at para. 50 (Court of Appeal) (court will not enforce a foreign judgment for a penalty, meaning a sum of money payable to the state, rather than to a private party). For discussion of exemplary damages in English law, see also Cassell & Co. v. Broome, [1972] A.C. 1027, Kuddus v. Chief Constable of Leicestershire, [2001] UKHL 29, [2002] A.C. 122 (H.L.).

[76] In the absence of procedural irregularities or inconsistent judgments, Arts. 34 (2–4) of the Brussels-I Regulation would not apply. The general public-policy defense of Art. 34(1) also does not apply to a money judgment lest the court were to engage in a review of the content and underlying basis of the judgment which is proscribed by Art. 36.

lurks beneath is the fear that review by the first recognizing state may not have been stringent enough, to which one might suggest two answers: First, local public policy cannot insist that foreign law and procedure (here, the first recognizing state's) mirror one's own. Differences in law do not touch upon essential values (as public policy exceptions are usually framed),[77] just as, in the choice of the applicable law, local "interests" do not make for a policy or mandatory rule requiring use of local law and rejection of the other.[78] Second, commonality of values and standards would serve to alleviate the reluctance to accept a sister state's court as the "transformation court," in substitution for oneself, that translates the third-country judgment into a domestic one. Many have emphasized the need for more trust and commonality of values in interstate procedure and judicial cooperation in the EC in the context of the changes brought about by the three new Regulations.[79] This holds true for the particular issue of the recognition of recognition judgments: there are no analytic reasons that speak against it. All that is needed is "trusting one's friends."[80]

---

[77] See, e.g., § 328(1) No. 4 German Code of Civil Procedure (ZPO); Decision of the Oberlandesgericht Zweibrücken, supra n. 25, at para. 26 ("manifest violation of an essential legal principle of the recognizing state," author's transl.).

[78] Compare introductory Recital (37) to the Rome-I Regulation on the Law Applicable to Contractual Obligations, Regulation (EC) 593/2008, [2008] O.J. L 177/6: "The concept of 'overriding mandatory provisions' should be distinguished from the expression 'provisions that cannot be derogated from by agreement' and should be construed restrictively." See also *Bundesgerichtshof*, in [2006] NJW 762, with anno. by Weller, id. at 1247; Borchers, Categorical Exceptions to Party Autonomy in Private International Law, 82 Tul. L. Rev. 1645 (2008). Cf. also Parsons & Whittemore Overseas Co. v. Société Générale de l'Industrie du Papier (RAKTA), 508 F.2d 969, 974 (1974): "To read the public policy defense as a parochial device protective of national political interests would seriously undermine the [New York Arbitration] Convention's utility." *But see*, for a more forum-centered approach, Carlier, L'utilisation de la *lex fori* dans la résolution des conflits de lois no. 160 et seq. (at p. 96 et seq.), Diss. Lille (2008).

[79] See Kohler, Das Prinzip der gegenseitigen Anerkennung in Zivilsachen im europäischen Justizraum, [2005-II] ZSR 263, 285. Introductory Recital (18) to the European Enforcement Order Regulation posits that mutual trust among the member states permits made adoption of the Regulation and its elimination of controls on the part of the state of enforcement possible. To some, this is a projection into the future, a fictitious assumption to justify the result. Rauscher, supra n. 13, VollstrTVO anno. 15.

[80] If there were true commonality of values, "trusting one's friends" would be easy. The example of punitive damages, however, shows that differences may be expected to continue to exist: While the draft of the (Rome-II) Regulation on the Law Applicable to Non-Contractual Obligations had stipulated that an otherwise applicable law should not be applied if it provided for punitive damages because this would offend "Community public policy" (Art. 24 of the Proposal, COM(2003)0427(final)), the final text of the

To come full circle: "trusting one's friends" should be a two-way street. In the EU, that would require a change in existing law so as to permit the enforcing court to entertain the same defenses that are available in the rendering court. The German *Vollstreckungsabwehrklage*, criticized earlier,[81] could take cognizance of pre- or post-judgment defenses available in the state of rendition, but not of defenses available under German law.[82] This is the Full Faith and Credit model. It might alleviate some of the concerns of the enforcing court discussed here. It also has the advantage of convenience for the judgment debtor, while not placing any burden on the judgment creditor who, after all, is present and seeking enforcement. Its price is the risk of error and less uniformity of result when the enforcing court applies foreign law. This would be the trust that the rendering court extends to the court of enforcement.

Rome-II Regulation drops this provision. Instead, Art. 26 merely contains a general public policy defense. Regulation (EC) No. 864/2007, [2007] O.J. L 199/40. Instead, the Introductory Recital (32) specifies (i.e. sanctions in advance) that a member state may regard punitive damages as contrary to its public policy. The change took account of English concerns. See von Hein, [2007] Versicherungsrecht 440, 443.

Not having to apply a law because of strong public policy objections, is one thing, to gainsay elements of another court's determination that otherwise satisfies all requirements of fairness, is quite another. Differences in substantive law (which includes damages in European practice) should not matter: the proscription of a review (Art. 36, Brussels-I) addresses this. Art. 25 of the Brussels-IIa Regulation, supra n. 15, is quite explicit in its particular context: recognition may not be refused because "the law of [the recognizing forum] would not allow divorce, legal separation or marriage annulment on the same facts."

81 Supra text following n. 39.

82 In support of its view that the *Vollstreckungsabwehrklage* is compatible with Community law, the Bundesgerichtshof showed that similar remedies exist in a number of other member states. Supra n. 39, at nos. 32–35. Existence of such remedies does not prove the point of course. Instead, the existence of post-judgment remedies in the *particular* state in which the judgment in question was rendered should justify use by the state of enforcement of procedural *mechanisms* available under its own law (e.g., the *Vollstreckungsabwehrklage* in Germany or similar remedies elsewhere) to take cognizanze of defenses that would be cognizable *under the law of the state of rendition*. This is quite different from consideration of defenses under the *lex fori*.

European Union Legislation and Private International Law: A View from Hungary

LÁSZLÓ KECSKÉS

Introductory remarks

1. I met Professor Tibor Várady in the early eighties when he was teaching private international law at the Law School of the University of Novi Sad. I was responsible for the same subject at the Law School of the University of Pécs. Our universities nourished modest contacts, despite the rather cold political circumstances. Várady's guest lectures in Pécs used to attract huge interest, and he never failed to impress the audience by the depth of his knowledge and the ability to convey even the most sophisticated theoretical problems in a clear and accessible manner. Tibor's intellectual excellence and his warm personality would always make scientific and humanistic concerns equally important. During the early nineties we both had held governmental positions in our countries. While Tibor was the Minister of Justice of Yugoslavia, I was working in the Hungarian Ministry of Justice as a Deputy Secretary of State. Although this was the time of political tensions in Central Eastern Europe, our official cooperation was always based on the mutual respect and the shared concern for justice. The world and our region have changed since then. International judicial cooperation today is becoming increasingly independent of state jurisdictions. We are approaching a relatively optimal situation in this field, something we could earlier only dream about. Tibor and I often participate together in international arbitration cases. It is always my honour to be his co-arbitrator. I always learn a lot from these hearings and cases. It is well known that Professor Várady's scientific interest lies—beside international arbitration—in the field of private international law. This is why I decided to contribute to this volume with a paper that explores one particular question of Hungarian private international law. The subject of my analysis is a recent amendment to the Hungarian Statute on Private International Law in light of the new EU legislations that regulates

judicial cooperation in civil law and commercial law cases. I put forward a proposal to apply, instead of the strict terminological dichotomy between civil law and commercial law, the broader notion and terminology of 'civilistic' judicature. In the usage I propose, the term 'civilistic' covers a very broad area of civil law, including commercial law, labour law, family law, civil procedural law and private international law.

2. After Hungary's accession to the EU, the legal material that used to be structured in multilateral treaties with EU member states was transformed into EU regulations. On 1 May 2004 the following Council regulations became effective in Hungary: (i) the Council Regulation (EC) No 1346/2000 of 29 May 2000 on insolvency proceedings; (ii) the Council Regulation (EC) No 1347/2000 of 29 May 2000 on jurisdiction and the recognition and enforcement of judgments in matrimonial matters and matters of parental responsibility for children of both spouses; (iii) the Council Regulation (EC) No 1348/2000 of 29 May 2000 on service in the member states of judicial and extrajudicial documents in civil or commercial matters; (iv) the Council Regulation (EC) No 44/2001 of 22 December 2000 on jurisdiction and the recognition and enforcement of judgments in civil and commercial matters; and (v) the Council Regulation (EC) No 1206/2001 of 28 May 2001 on cooperation between the courts of the member states in the taking of evidence in civil or commercial matters.

Further, the Council Regulation (EC) No. 2201/2003 of 27 November 2003 concerning jurisdiction and the recognition and enforcement of judgments in matrimonial matters and the matters of parental responsibility became operative on 1 August 2004 and repealed the Regulation (EC) No. 1347/2000, under the condition that certain provisions of the new regulation were not to be effective until 1 March 2005. The Regulation (EC) No. 805/2004 of the European Parliament and the Council of 21 April 2004, which entered into force on 21 January 2005 (although a significant part of the regulation did not come into effect until 21 October 2005), created an European Enforcement Order for use in respect of uncontested claims.[1]

One can argue that there is little novelty in respect of the contents of the Community regulations created after the Treaty of Amsterdam became effective on 1 May 1999, because, with the exception of one regulation, all the other regulations were based on earlier international treaties. Let

[1] This paper does not deal with Regulation (EC) No 861/2007 of the European Parliament and the Council of 11 July 2007 establishing a European Small Claims Procedure as this regulation was completed after the manuscript was finalized on 1 September 2006.

me provide some examples. Council Regulation (EC) No. 44/2001 of 22 December 2000 is almost a complete copy of the Brussels I Convention signed on 27 September 1968, which entered into force on 1 February 1973, as amended on several occasions thereafter.

The Council Regulation (EC) No. 1347/2000 of 29 May 2000 was content-wise the same as the Brussels II Convention signed on 28 May 1998. This regulation only covered parental responsibility for spouses, children of their own and with regard to divorce actions and never came into force. It was repealed by the Council Regulation (EC) No. 2201/2003 of 27 November 2003, as suggested by France.

The Council Regulation (EC) No. 1348/2000 of 29 May 2000 is very much based on the Hague Convention of 15 November 1965 on the Service Abroad of Judicial and Extrajudicial Documents in Civil or Commercial Matters.

A significant portion of the provisions of the Council Regulation (EC) No. 1346/2000 of 29 May 2000 on insolvency proceedings is based on the EC Madrid Agreement of 1995.[2]

As an exception to the intensive wave of Community regulations regarding the "civilistic" judicature that began in 2000, the Regulation (EC) No. 805/2004 of the European Parliament and the Council of 21 April 2004 creating a European Enforcement Order for uncontested claims stands alone. This Regulation is unprecedented in earlier community legislation or international conventions. Its founding premises—the acknowledgement of the "European enforcement title", the examination in the originating country and the execution of proceedings in the country of enforcement without separate exequatur proceedings—can be traced back to an international colloquium held in Paris in 1993.[3]

---

[2] Cf. *Nagy, Adrienn:* Az európai fizetésképtelenségi eljárások során hozott határozatok elismerése az Európai Unió tagállamaiban [Recognition of judgments issued in European insolvency proceedings in the member states of the European Union], Collega, 2005/5, pg. 26–27.

[3] See also *Harsági, Viktória:* Rendelet a nem vitatott követelések végrehajtásáról [Regulation on enforcement of uncontested claims], in: *Kengyel, Miklós–Harsági, Viktória:* Európai Polgári Eljárásjog [The law of European civil proceedings], Budapest 2006, (to be published at Osiris Kiadó) Unit VII, p. 148; *Nagy, Csongor István:* Az Európai Unió nemzetközi magánjoga [The private international law of the European Union]. HVG-ORAC Kiadó, Budapest, 2006.

Fading formulae of separated branches of law—But legal terminologies are still important!

Until the middle of the 20th century it was common that the recognition and enforcement of foreign judgments and decisions were regulated in civil procedural codes—and in other laws attached to these civil procedural codes. Since the middle of the 20th century, the revaluation of this issue and the recognition of its similarities with private international law matters have led to the current situation, where the private international law codes regulate recognition and enforcement of foreign judgments and decisions. For instance, the Swiss Private International Law of 1987 (IPRG) expresses even in its structure that the jurisdiction, the law of conflicts aimed at establishing the applicable material law, and the norms for recognition and enforcement of foreign judgments and decisions are considered as three equally important issues of private international law and international civil procedural law; The Italian Act of 1995 indicates that it covers private international law and international civil procedural law.[4] The classical dogmatic view of separated branches of law pales in being gradually replaced by complex regulations distinguished by overlapping of different fields of law. The issue of judicial cooperation in civil and commercial cases is regulated by four relatively autonomous fields of law, each having a separate name, with some viewing each field of law as being a separate branch of law. Such separate fields are as follows: private international law, international civil procedural law, European civil procedural law and civil procedural law of the EU.

In certain countries, in certain periods of time, there have been and still are views pursuant to which international civil procedural law is handled separately from the material of private international law. Among the member states of the EU, this tendency is present in Germany and Portugal. There is undoubtedly a thematic overlap between the two fields of law, demonstrated by the fact that the issue of the institution of jurisdiction is an essential topic of both fields. Beyond questions of jurisdiction, the other significant aspect of the institutions of private international law is the problem of the applicable law. Besides jurisdiction, international civil procedural law considers the recognition and execution of foreign

[4] See also *Brávácz, Ottóné–Szőcs, Tibor:* Jogviták határok nélkül. Joghatóság, külföldi határozatok elismerése és végrehajtása polgári ügyekben [Legal disputes without boundaries: jurisdiction, recognition and enforcement of foreign judgments in civil cases], HVG-ORAC Kiadó, Budapest, 2003. pp. 29–30.

judgments and decisions, as well as some certain other additional international rules of proceedings, as the main parts of the institutional system of this relatively separate area of law.

The outline of the aforementioned topical and thematic overlaps of private international law and international civil procedural law area as follows:

Private international law	*International civil procedural law*
a) Jurisdiction	a) Jurisdiction
b) Applicable law	b) Recognition and execution of foreign judgments and decisions
	c) Other international rules and regulations of proceedings

One can easily recognize that jurisdiction is an essential thematic unit of both private international law and international civil procedural law.

Obviously, there is a difference between international civil procedural law and European civil procedural law from the point of view of the geographical scope of the territoriality of the two fields of law. The former field, referring to the whole phrase, is of a wider scope, as it also includes the regulatory materials of European civil procedural law. The regulatory materials of the law of the latter field are embodied in the documents of the Hague Conference of Private International Law, in the so-called Hague Conventions. The Lugano Convention concluded in 1988 also belongs to this group, as the EFTA countries participated in it along with the states which were members of the EC at that time. The thematically matching conventions of the Council of Europe are also included here. These include for example "The European Convention on Information of Foreign Law," adopted in 1968, and the convention adopted in Istanbul of 1990, entitled "The European Convention on Certain International Aspects of Bankruptcy."

It seems important to separate the material of European civil procedural law from EU civil procedural law. The latter exclusively refers to the member states of the EU—in some cases, with restrictions (e.g., Denmark)—and has lately been developing by the EU rapidly, especially since the Treaty of Amsterdam became effective on 1 May 1999. Civil procedural law of the EU is, of course, part of the European civil procedural law.

A peculiarity of the judicial cooperation in civil and commercial matters is that the theoretical considerations and tenets which clearly relate to private international law and had determined the new conceptions concerning the evaluation of applicable law recently fundamentally influenced the procedural thinking about jurisdiction. New connecting factors appear as important rules in the newly created EU regulations of civil proceedings, which connecting factors had been ripened and strengthened as important exception rules earlier—over decades since the 1960s—within the instruments of private international law. Such an important connecting factor is, for example, the place where the damage (harmful event) occurred. This connecting factor developed as an exception to the famous classical connecting factor of *lex loci delicti commissi*. As The Council Regulation (EC) No. 44/2001 of 22 December 2000 on jurisdiction and the recognition and enforcement of judgments in civil and commercial matters stipulates in Section 3 of Article 5, a person domiciled in an EU member state may be sued in matters relating to tort, delict or quasi-delict in the courts of the place where the harmful event occurred or may occur, even in another EU member state. Also, the process described as the downfall of the "seat theory" in the development of private international law affects the newer legal provisions of procedural law. Besides the registered address, the branch, agency or other establishment becomes important as a connecting factor of procedural law and the establishment of jurisdiction. The Regulation No. 44/2001 further stipulates (Section 5 of Article 5), that a person domiciled in an EU member state may be sued in another EU member state in a dispute arising from the operations of such a branch, agency or other establishment, in the courts of the place in which the branch, agency or other establishment is situated.[5]

My thesis is also that in the newer law of European civil proceedings and in regulations of EU civil procedural law, the goal is to ensure the recognition and enforcement of foreign judgments and decisions. Accordingly, the harmonization of jurisdictional rules is simply the means to that end.

[5] See also *Nemessányi, Zoltán:* A székhely elv alkonya? [The downfall of the residence theory?], Daily Mail – Centros – Überseering, in: Európai jog 2003/6, pp. 16–24; *Vékás, Lajos:* Uniós alapvető szabadságok és közösségi nemzetközi kollíziós jog [Basic liberties of the European Union and international Community law of conflicts], in: Európai Jog 2005/1, pp. 3–16.

Civil Cases vs. Civil and Commercial Cases: 'Civilistic Cases' as a Possible Alternative

In the development of EU law, the legal terminology of the regulations of private international law and that of the civil procedural law affecting civil law applications, there has been some sloppiness. We can see both the expressions "civil cases" and "civil and commercial cases" in a historically changing environment. However, the primary legislation of the EU, with few exceptions, uses the term "civil cases." Contrary to this are the Brussels I Convention and its ancillary regulations. The secondary EU legislation based on this convention consistently uses the terminology "civil and commercial cases."

In this relative order that is seemingly promising there is a serious flaw. The third indented paragraph of Section 65(a) of the EC Treaty, amended by way of the Treaty of Amsterdam, uses the phrase "civil and commercial cases" in a rather rule-breaking manner. It is difficult to base a theory on an inconsistently worded positive law.

The expression "civil and commercial cases"[6] made its way into the terminology of the Community law during the preparation for the Brussels I Convention. Allegedly, the drafters of this convention wanted to favor the French legal culture by also mentioning the scope of "commercial cases," since in the development of the French private law there has always been and still is a respect for the relative separation of commercial law.[7]

In my view, the terminological sloppiness could be eliminated if the expression "civilistic" cases would be used in all cases by EU law, and we would not enter the realm of uncertainty created by the confusing terms "civil cases" vs. "civil and commercial cases."

By the application of the term "civilistic cases," we can reach a more unified interpretation than by using the earlier and confusingly outlined terms.

---

[6] See also in more detail, *Garamvölgyi, Róbert – Nemessányi, Zoltán:* Lezárult a verseny a nemzetközi magánjogi jogalkotásban? Az EK nemzetközi magánjogi jogalkotási hatáskörének változása az alapító szerződésektől az Alkotmányig [Has the competition concluded in private international law legislation? Changes in the scope of the private international law legislation of the EC from the founding conventions to the Constitution], in: Európai Jog 2004/6, pp. 22–25.

[7] See also, *Geimer, Reinhold–Schütze, Rolf:* Europäisches Zivilverfahrensrecht. 2nd edition, Munich 2004. p. 71; see also, *Kengyel, Miklós–Harsági, Viktória:* Európai Polgári Eljárásjog [The right of European civil proceedings], Osiris Kiadó, Budapest, 2006. p. 65.

In the Brussels I Convention and in Council Regulation (EC) No. 44/2001 of 22 December 2000 repealing the previous one, there are numerous notions and expressions that may have a different meaning in each and every EU member state. If we want to reach the goal that the regulations create the same rights and obligations for EU member states and the affected persons, then notions and expressions are not to be considered as references to the inner legal norms of EU member states, but rather are to be considered in an autonomous way, interpreted in common for all EU member states. In the view of the Court of Justice of the European Communities: "In the interpretation of the concept of civil and commercial matters, reference must be made not to the law of one of the states concerned, but first to the objectives and scheme of the convention and secondly, to the general principles which stem from the corpus of the national legal systems."[8] Only a common European interpretation can ensure the unified application of the convention. In the lack of such interpretation, EU member states may be able to narrow or expand the applicable scope of the convention in accordance with their actual interests. EU member states could also use the means of "requalification", meaning that, by way of the modification of national law, the material effect of the treaty may be modified and, therefore, EU member states could establish the extent of the rights and obligations burdened onto EU member states by the treaty.[9]

Reinhold Geimer proposes to outline the concepts of "civil and commercial" matters on the basis of the pan-European legal tradition. His argument is that the continental legal systems, notwithstanding their different law development, belong to the Roman-Germanic family of law; therefore, common European roots of the different national solutions can be found.[10]

Using a unified interpretation, it follows that the civil law classification of Article 1 of the Brussels I Convention does not assume that the subject

---

[8] See also, Judgment of the Court of 14 October 1976. - LTU Lufttransportunternehmen GmbH & Co. KG v Eurocontrol. Case 29-76. (ECR 1976, 01541.) No. 5., *Kengyel, Miklós–Harsági, Viktória:* Európai Polgári Eljárásjog [The law of European civil proceedings], Osiris Kiadó, Budapest, 2006. p. 64.

[9] See also, *Geimer, Reinhold–Schütze, Rolf:* Europäisches Zivilverfahrensrecht. 2nd edition. Munich, 2004. pp. 66–67; Schack, Haimo: Internationales Zivilverfahrensrecht 3rd edition, Munich, 2002. p. 43; *Kengyel Miklós–Harsági Viktória:* Európai Polgári Eljárásjog [The law of European civil proceedings], Osiris Kiadó, Budapest, 2006. p. 64.

[10] See also, *Geimer, Reinhold–Schütze, Rolf:* Europäisches Zivilverfahrensrecht. 2nd edition, Munich 2004. p. 67; *Kengyel, Miklós–Harsági, Viktória:* Európai Polgári Eljárásjog [The law of European civil proceedings], Osiris Kiadó, Budapest, 2006. p. 64.

of the legal dispute is classified as private law in accordance with the legal system of all EU member states. If that was an assumption, the applicable territory would be reduced to the smallest common denominator that would not comply with what the convention is aimed at.[11]

The use of the terminology "civilistic" cases on the EU level seems promising, especially since with its help we can understand and describe the areas of private international law and the law of civil proceedings in the field that poses numerous new problems, with one such area being labor law[12] and another such area being family law.

Hungarian Attempts and Uncertainties

Hungarian diplomatic activities before 1990, at the time of the one-party socialist system, were very one-sided in the course of international cooperation in civil law matters. Hungary concluded legal aid agreements with the "national democratic" (socialist) countries. These agreements included rules on recognition and enforcement of foreign judgments in respect of civil law matters. From the western countries such agreements were made only with the Federal Republic of Germany, France, Greece, and Cyprus.

During the course of the preparatory negotiations for Hungary's Accession Agreement with the European Community (December 1990–November 1991), the issue of judicial cooperation in civil matters was a topic of discussion. At the beginning of the negotiations the Community pointed to the discriminative provisions in the Hungarian law regarding the deposit of a security for the procedural costs of foreign claimants. These provisions were repealed only much later.[13]

---

[11] See also, *Geimer, Reinhold–Schütze, Rolf:* Europäisches Zivilverfahrensrecht. 2nd edition Munich 2004. p. 70; *Kengyel, Miklós–Harsági, Viktória:* Európai Polgári Eljárásjog [The law of European civil proceedings], Osiris Kiadó, Budapest, 2006. p. 65.

[12] See 21. *Garamvölgyi, Róbert–Nemessányi, Zoltán:* A közösségi jog hatása a nemzetközi magánjogra. Beszámoló "A nemzetközi magánjog és az üzleti jog újabb fejleményei" című trieri konferenciáról [The effect of community law on international private law: Report of the Trier conference titled "The latest developments of private international law and business law"], in: Európai Jog 2005/5. pp. 42–44.

[13] Act LXXX of 2003 amended Section 85(5) of Act III of 1952 On Civil Procedure, so that in accordance with the new text, a citizen of a member state of the European Union and a citizen rightfully residing in a member state of the European Union…cannot be obliged to deposit a security. See also, for more details, *Osztovits, András:* A perköltségbiztosíték közösségi jogi szabályai – észrevételek a Fővárosi Ítélőtábla Polgári Kollégiumának ajánlásához [The community law regulations of security—Comments to the

During the technical consultations accompanying negotiations, the Hungarian delegation tried to determine how willing the Community was to open the Brussels I Convention of 1968 to the potential new members. However, the Community made it clear that the Lugano Convention of 1988 was intended to apply in the future member states.

Therefore, Hungarian diplomacy of justice turned towards the Lugano Convention which is an agreement applying to both EC member states and EFTA countries. This Convention, by way of its Articles 60 and 62, contained an accession option for other countries. In accordance with Article 60(c) of the Lugano Convention, the states that are invited to join by way of Article 62(1)(b) may participate as contracting parties.[14] After diplomatic preparations that lasted several years, the Hungarian Government announced its intention to become a party to the Lugano Convention in December 1997. In accordance with Government Resolution No. 2392/1997 (XII.3.),

> the Government
>
> 1. agrees that the Republic of Hungary join the Convention on jurisdiction and the enforcement of judgments in civil and commercial matters, signed in Lugano on 16 September 1988;
>
> 2. authorizes the minister of foreign affairs or the person appointed by such person to submit the Notifications required for accession of the Republic of Hungary set out in *Annex 1*, and the declarations set out in *Annex 2* to the Swiss Federal Council, as the Depositary of the Convention, with regard to the rules and regulations of the accession proceedings set out in the Convention;
>
> 3. authorizes the minister of justice to make a proposal to the Parliament in order to consolidate the Convention, if the Depositary of the Convention invites the Republic of Hungary to accede;
>
> 4. trusts the minister of justice to review the Hungarian legal provisions affecting the subject of the Convention—of the nature of private international law, civil proceedings law and enforcement law—and to make proposals for modification and amendment thereof as needed.[15]

---

recommendation of the Civil Section of the Metropolitan Court of Appeal], in: Európai Jog 2005/V., p. 3.

[14] See also *Kengyel, Miklós:* Magyarország a Luganói Egyezmény kapujában [Hungary on the doorstep of the Lugano Convention], in: A magyar polgári eljárásjog a kilencvenes években és az EU jogharmonizáció. Dr. Németh János egyetemi tanár tiszteletére, 40 éves oktatói jubileuma alkalmából [Hungarian civil law in the 1990s and EU legislative harmonization. In honor of professor János Németh, on the 40th anniversary of his teaching position], (ed.: *Papp, Zsuzsanna*), ELTE Eötvös Kiadó, Budapest, 2003. p. 32.

[15] See also *Kengyel, Miklós:* Magyarország a Luganói Egyezmény Kapujában [Hungary on the doorstep of the Lugano Convention], in: A magyar polgári eljárásjog a kilencvenes években és az EU jogharmonizáció. Dr. Németh János egyetemi tanár tiszteletére, 40 éves oktatói jubileuma alkalmából [Hungarian civil law in the 1990s and EU legislative

Hungarian diplomatic attempts were successful. The Government of the Republic of Finland—with the support of the Government of the Republic of Austria—requested that the Swiss Federal Council, as the Depositary of the Convention, on 18 November 1996, issues an invitation to Hungary for accession to the Convention. This fact was communicated to the Hungarian Embassy in Switzerland by the Swiss Federal Ministry of Foreign Affairs in a letter of 29 November 1996. In the following step, the Government of the Republic of Hungary issued the notifications and declarations prescribed by Article 63 of the Convention.[16]

The accession of Hungary to the Lugano Convention was cancelled, partly due to the diplomatic hesitancy of Hungary arising from the state of the EU accession negotiations, meaning that Hungary was at the gate of the Lugano Convention, but never entered. (From the Eastern European new member states only Poland acceded to the Lugano Convention in 2000.)

The invitation of Hungary to accede was approved by most of the countries who were parties to the Lugano Convention, primarily by those states with which Hungary had a significant relationship in respect of legal aid. However, Hungarian accession could not take place because certain EU member states did not find the time appropriate for the extension of the Lugano Convention (primarily with regard to the impending review of the Brussels I Convention and the Lugano Convention).[17]

---

harmonization. In honor of professor János Németh, on the 40th anniversary of his teaching position], (ed.: *Papp, Zsuzsanna*), ELTE Eötvös Kiadó, Budapest, 2003. p. 29. See also: *Brávácz, Ottóné–Szőcs, Tibor:* Jogviták határok nélkül. Joghatóság, külföldi határozatok elismerése és végrehajtása polgári ügyekben [Legal disputes without boundaries: Jurisdiction, recognition and enforcement of foreign judgments in civil cases], HVG-ORAC Kiadó, Budapest, 2003. pg. 33.

[16] See also *Kengyel, Miklós:* Magyarország a Luganói Egyezmény kapujában. [Hungary on the doorstep of the Lugano Convention], in: A magyar polgári eljárásjog a kilencvenes években és az EU jogharmonizáció. Dr. Németh János egyetemi tanár tiszteletére, 40 éves oktatói jubileuma alkalmából [Hungarian civil law in the 1990s and EU legislative harmonization. In honor of professor János Németh, on the 40th anniversary of his teaching position], (ed.: *Papp, Zsuzsanna*), ELTE Eötvös Kiadó, Budapest, 2003. pp. 41–42. See also *Brávácz, Ottóné–Szőcs, Tibor:* Jogviták határok nélkül. Joghatóság, külföldi határozatok elismerése és végrehajtása polgári ügyekben [Legal disputes without boundaries: Jurisdiction, recognition and enforcement of foreign judgments in civil cases], HVG-ORAC Kiadó, Budapest, 2003. pg. 33.

[17] See also, *Brávácz, Ottóné–Szőcs, Tibor:* Jogviták határok nélkül. Joghatóság, külföldi határozatok elismerése és végrehajtása polgári ügyekben [Legal disputes without boundaries: Jurisdiction, recognition and enforcement of foreign judgments in civil cases], HVG-ORAC Kiadó, Budapest, 2003. p. 33.

The Special Nature of Council Regulation (EC) No. 44/2001 of 22 December 2000 and the Code of Hungarian Private International Law

The most significant piece of the regulation materials, taking up 260 printed pages, comprising of five regulations (so far) affecting the „civilistic" area of law, is undoubtedly the Council Regulation (EC) No. 44/2001 of 22 December 2000 on jurisdiction and the recognition and enforcement of judgments in civil and commercial matters. Regulations subsequently enacted used the Council Regulation (EC) No. 44/2001 as a foundation. This is confirmed by way of referencing provisions.[18]

In the future, it can be expected that new Community regulations relating to civil law application will also be founded based on Council Regulation No. 44/2001. In addition to specific provisions of these regulations, literature of jurisprudence often emphasizes the universal nature of Council Regulation No. 44/2001.[19]

Although Hungary did not join the Lugano Convention, Act CX of 2000 was passed, which amended the Hungarian Statute on Private International Law in the sense of this Convention. This Act took into consideration—by way of a confusing reference—that the issue of the judicial cooperation in civil and commercial matters has been revaluated

[18] In Article 27, for example, Regulation (EC) No. 805/2004 of the European Parliament and the Council of 21 April 2004, creating a European Enforcement Order for Uncontested Claims, states the following: "This Regulation shall not affect the possibility of seeking recognition and enforcement, in accordance with Regulation (EC) No 44/2001, of a judgment, a court settlement or an authentic instrument on an uncontested claim. Preamble Sections 9 and 11 of Council Regulation (EC) No 2201/2003 of 27 November 2003 concerning jurisdiction and the recognition and enforcement of judgments in matrimonial matters and the matters of parental responsibility, provide for observance of certain sections of Council Regulation (EC) No 44/2001. The third sentence of Section 9 says that "Measures relating to the child's property which do not concern the protection of the child should continue to be governed by Council Regulation (EC) No 44/2001 of 22 December 2000 on jurisdiction and the recognition and enforcement of judgments in civil and commercial matters". Section 11 thereof states the following: "Maintenance obligations are excluded from the scope of this Regulation as these are already covered by Council Regulation No 44/2001. The courts having jurisdiction under this Regulation will generally have jurisdiction to rule on maintenance obligations by application of Article 5(2) of Council Regulation No 44/2001."

[19] See also, *Kengyel, Miklós–Harsági, Viktória:* Európai Polgári Eljárásjog [The law of European civil proceedings], Osiris Kiadó, Budapest, 2006. p. 63.

in the European Union since the Treaty of Amsterdam entered into force.[20]

To support my criticism, let me provide several examples. Section 57 of Act integrates a hard and "recuperative" provision into the Hungarian law, to which there is no similar provision in the Lugano Convention or Council Regulation No. 44/2001. Section 57 of the Hungarian code violates even the basic principles of the aforementioned legal documents. As a result of the amendment of Act CX of 2000, Section 57 of the Hungarian private international law code contains the following text: "Hungarian courts shall have jurisdiction in lawsuits under property law where the defendant has no domicile or residence in Hungary but does have assets in Hungary that can be attached. Any claim due a defendant shall be considered as the defendant's asset in Hungary if the residence of the person owing the claim is in Hungary or if the claim is secured by a thing situated in Hungary." This provision was meant to facilitate more effective legal actions against foreigners who have a tendency to run up debt and then leave it behind by "disappearing," with an essentially similar provision being found in the Act on the Code of Civil Procedure. During the amendment of the Hungarian Private International Law Code in 2000, when the text of the new Section 57 was formulated, the example used was the aforementioned Section 32(3) of the Code of Civil Procedure.[21] Jurisdiction based upon the place of the object in question is intended to make the domestic enforcement of a claim of a plaintiff possible. But it is not a requirement for requisition: given that the domestic judgment is granted, it would not be possible to enforce this claim abroad. An example would be a case where the defendant resides in a state, or the assets to be included in the enforcement of a claim are in a state where the Hungarian court judgment cannot be enforced due to the lack of an international agreement or due to the lack of reciprocity.[22]

---

[20] At the time of the preparation of Act CX of 2000, the Hungarian law harmonization activities were thematized and determined by the then in-progress accession negotiations. See also: *Kecskés, László:* EU-jog és jogharmonizáció [EU law and law harmonization], expanded second edition, HVG-ORAC Kiadó, Budapest, 2005. pp. 750–770.

[21] See also *Brávácz, Ottóné–Szőcs, Tibor:* Jogviták határok nélkül. Joghatóság, külföldi határozatok elismerése és végrehajtása polgári ügyekben [Legal disputes without boundaries: Jurisdiction, recognition and enforcement of foreign judgments in civil cases], HVG-ORAC Kiadó, Budapest, 2003. p. 78.

[22] See also *Brávácz, Ottóné–Szőcs, Tibor:* Jogviták határok nélkül. Joghatóság, külföldi határozatok elismerése és végrehajtása polgári ügyekben [Legal disputes without boundaries: Jurisdiction, recognition and enforcement of foreign judgments in civil cases], HVG-ORAC Kiadó, Budapest, 2003. p. 79.

Neither Council Regulation (EC) No. 44/2001, nor its precedents, the Brussels I Convention or the Lugano Convention, acknowledge such jurisdiction, and they expressly ban the application of such "exorbitant" (connectionless) jurisdiction. Council Regulation (EC) No. 44/2001 and Brussels I Convention both guarantee that a judgment issued in a state can be enforced in another state, and that is why there is no need to protect the interests of a plaintiff for the domestic enforcement of his claim by providing him with such jurisdictional ground.[23]

Article 3(2) of the Lugano Convention excludes the "exorbitant" jurisdictional grounds. Peter Schlosser pointed out that there are "connectionless" jurisdictional bases in the national law of every nation, the application of which would be in opposition with the objectives of the Lugano Convention. Article 3(2) of the Lugano Convention lists those strict exorbitant jurisdiction provisions, grouped by contracting states that may not be applicable against persons domiciled in a contracting state.[24] It is not by chance that, in accordance with Article 3(2) of Council Regulation (EC) No. 44/2001; such jurisdiction may not be applied against persons domiciled in an EU member state, based on Annex I of Council Regulation (EC) No. 44/2001. In this annex, Council Regulation (EC) No. 44/2001 lists the rules and regulations of EU member states that are too strict from a jurisdictional point of view. In respect of the persons domiciled in a contracting state, in accordance with Council Regulation (EC) No. 44/2001, a significant benefit is that the strict "exorbitant" jurisdictional rules cannot be applied against such persons.[25]

---

[23] See also *Brávácz, Ottóné–Szőcs, Tibor:* Jogviták határok nélkül. Joghatóság, külföldi határozatok elismerése és végrehajtása polgári ügyekben [Legal disputes without boundaries: Jurisdiction, recognition and enforcement of foreign judgments in civil cases], Budapest, 2003. pp. 79–80.

[24] See also *Schlosser, Peter:* Bericht zum EuGVÜ vom 9.10.1978.: Abl. 5 3. 1979. Nr. C.59,88. quoted in *Kengyel Miklós:* Magyarország a Luganói Egyezmény kapujában [Hungary on the doorstep of the Lugano Convention], in: A magyar polgári eljárásjog a kilencvenes években és az EU jogharmonizáció. Dr. Németh János egyetemi tanár tiszteletére, 40 éves oktatói jubileuma alkalmából [Hungarian civil law in the 1990s and EU legislative harmonization. In honor of professor János Németh, on the 40th anniversary of his teaching position], (ed.: *Papp, Zsuzsanna*), ELTE Eötvös Kiadó, Budapest, 2003. pp. 34–35.

[25] Neither the Brussels I Convention nor Council Regulation (EC) No 44/2001 oblige the EU member states to cancel the jurisdiction clauses of their autonomous jurisdictional regulations of their national right as they pertain to the location of the defendant's assets that can be seized; the application of such jurisdictional regulations is expressly allowed in cases when the domicile of the defendant is located in a "third state" (in a state out-

In certain articles of the Lugano Convention, by applying asymmetrical regulation methods, more advantageous positions are made available to subjects of law (parties) in a weaker position: in Article 5, for contracts of employment; in Articles 7–12, for matters of insurance; and in Articles 13–15, for matters related to consumer contracts.

In the third part of Council Regulation (EC) No. 44/2001 for matters related to insurance (Articles 8–14), in the fourth part for matters related to consumer contracts (Articles 15–17) and in the fifth part for matters related to individual contracts of employment (Articles 18–21), more advantageous positions are made available to subjects of law (parties) in a weaker position, by way of the application of asymmetrical regulation methods.

In respect of this concept of protecting the "weaker party," there is a little reflected, even if only outlined, in the Hungarian private international law code amended by Act CX of 2000 related to legal disputes arising in respect of consumer contracts and contracts of employment, but the protection regarding insurance matters is not included.

Content and length wise, the Hungarian rules related to legal disputes arising from consumer contracts and employment contracts cannot be even remotely equivalent with the relevant rules of Council Regulation (EC) No. 44/2001, the lack of protection of "weaker parties" in insurance matters in Hungarian regulation is unusually conspicuous.

It is also strange that some years after having forgotten about insurance matters in terms of the scope of jurisdictional regulations, through Section 139 of Act XLVIII of 2004, which entered into force on 10 June 2004, insurance matters were given attention in connection with the rules of the applicable law. Since 10 June 2004, Section 25(k) of the Hungarian private international law code has contained a provision indicating that with respect to insurance policies—in the case of the absence of another provision indicating otherwise—the applicable law shall be the law of the state where the insurer is domiciled or where its base of operations is. This regulation is more advantageous to "weaker parties" in insurance matters,

side the EU member states). The member states may also apply such jurisdiction clause against defendants domiciled in a third state. The majority of the exorbitant jurisdictional regulations on the so-called "blacklist" of Article 3(2) concerns jurisdiction based on the Hungarian assets of the defendant, similar to Section 57 of the Hungarian private international law codex. See also *Brávácz, Ottóné–Szőcs, Tibor*: Jogviták határok nélkül. Joghatóság, külföldi határozatok elismerése és végrehajtása polgári ügyekben [Legal disputes without boundaries. Jurisdiction, recognition and enforcement of foreign judgments in civil cases], HVG-ORAC Kiadó, Budapest, 2003. p. 80.

compared to the earlier regulation, in that the "separate provision of law" may make it possible to change the law dictated by the state where the insurer is domiciled or where its base of operations is.

The Lugano Convention and the Council Regulation (EC) No. 44/2001 do not contain any excluded jurisdictional regulations, Act CX of 2000 amended the earlier Hungarian regulation by extending the excluded jurisdiction grounds, in spite of the declared law harmonization intentions.[26]

In part 6 of Council Regulation (EC) No. 44/2001 (Article 22), immunity of the state did not impact the list of exclusive jurisdictional reasons that are regulated in the 5 points indicated therein.

In contrast to the above, the regulations of the Hungarian private international law code relating to exclusive jurisdiction that content wise do not comply with the regulations of Council Regulation (EC) No. 44/2001 contain rules that reflect state immunity.[27]

Due to the aforementioned issues, the current rules of the Hungarian private international law code regarding jurisdiction issues and the recognition and enforcement of foreign judgments are controversial, and the application of these rules may be hampered by way of Council Regulation (EC) No. 44/2001. The idea that the probability of difficulties arising in respect of the application of the Hungarian rules is increased by the rather special direct effect of Council Regulation (EC) No. 44/2001. The direct effect of this regulation, as that of the other community regulations, is undisputable. But in respect of direct applicability, several problems are worth mentioning.

Such problems are related to the following: in Chapter VII of Council Regulation (EC) No. 44/2001, under title "Relations with other instruments", Article 67 states as follows: "This Regulation shall not prejudice the application of provisions governing jurisdiction and the recognition and enforcement of judgments in specific matters which are contained in Community instruments or in national legislation harmonized pursuant to such instruments"[28]

[26] See also Sections 62/C., 62/D. and 62/E of the Hungarian private international law codex (Law-Decree 13 of 1979).

[27] See also Sections 62/A. and 62/B of the Hungarian private international law codex (Law-Decree 13 of 1979), enrolled by Act CX of 2000, entering into force on 1 May 2001.

[28] The commentary edited by *Wopera – Wallacher* does not deal with an explanation of Article 67 of Council Regulation (EC) No. 44/2001; only the normative text is included. See also *Wopera, Zsuzsa–Wallacher, Lajos* (Eds.): Polgári eljárásjogi szabályok az Európai Unió jogában [Civil procedural rules in the law of the European Union], Buda-

Article 67 of Council Regulation (EC) No. 44/2001 contains two passages:

The first: This Regulation shall not prejudice the application of [the other *(the author)*] provisions [regulations *(the author)*] contained in community instruments.

From this excerpt, it is obvious that this regulation counts on the thematic overlap and the thematic obstruction behind such overlapping phenomenon of the Community Regulations related to judicial cooperation in civil and commercial matters.

The thematic obstruction is evident, if we examine for example the institutions regulated by Council Regulation (EC) No. 44/2001 and Regulation (EC) No. 805/2004 of the European Parliament and the Council of 21 April 2004 creating a European Enforcement Order for uncontested claims—where we find parallel elements on the lists. The recognition and enforcement section of Council Regulation (EC) No. 44/2001 refers to any decision issued by the court of an EU member state, regardless of its name, including a judgment, order, payment order or writ of execution, and the establishment of costs and expenses by an officer of the court.[29]

Regulation (EC) No. 805/2004 of the European Parliament and the Council creating a European Enforcement Order for uncontested claims, whose applicability is limited to debtors or defendants who are non-responsive to a certain extent, applies to any decision issued by a court of an EU member state, regardless of its name, including a judgment, order, payment order or writ of execution, and the establishment of costs and expenses by an officer of the court.[30] In addition to the previous list, it also refers to public documents and settlements.[31] This thematic obstruc-

---

pest, 2006. p. 205. The commentary of *Kengyel–Harsági* explains in two short paragraphs, in a rather dubious manner, that the terminology of "preference" (elsőbbség) is mistakenly used instead of "primariness" (elsődlegesség). The following is also included: "The rules of the regulation on jurisdiction and on recognition and enforcement of judgments replace the national provisions of law". However, Community law cannot take over the role of the internal law of member states. Such opinion has been confirmed by the Court of Justice of the European Communities, which said that national procedural rules can be applied "until the practical efficiency of the regulation is impaired". See also *Kengyel, Miklós–Harsági, Viktória:* Európai polgári eljárásjog [The law of European civil proceedings], Budapest, 2006. p. 60.

[29] See also Articles 57–58 of Council Regulation (EC) No 44/2001.

[30] See also Article 4 of Regulation (EC) No. 805/2004 of the European Parliament and the Council.

[31] See also Articles 24–25 of Regulation (EC) No. 805/2004 of the European Parliament and the Council.

tion within the scope of the regulated subjects will evidently intensify, when the long-awaited European Union regulation related to the European payment order will have been finalized.[32]

The first passage of Article 67 of Council Regulation (EC) No. 44/2001, which states "This Regulation shall not prejudice provisions in Community instruments...," means that this regulation partially returns the application courtesy of the other Community regulations being in a thematic relationship with it. With respect to the "universal" nature of Council Regulation (EC) No. 44/2001, it follows that this courtesy cannot be at the same level with the courtesy provided to this council regulation by the aforementioned other Community Regulations. If it was not so, the universality of Council Regulation (EC) No. 44/2001 would not make sense, and we would be reminded of the small humorous scene of two gentleman wishing to use the same revolving door, and who, after a series of courteous acts of letting the other use the door first, bump into each other.

Whereas the first passage of Article 67 of Council Regulation (EC) No. 44/2001 deals with the relationship of sources of Community law, the second passage of this article regulates a different dimension: the relationship of the legal systems of community law and domestic laws of EU member states.

The second passage of Article 67 states that this regulation does not affect the "application of provisions governing jurisdiction and the recognition and enforcement of judgments in specific matters which are contained in Community instruments or in national legislation harmonized pursuant to such instruments." This rule can be interpreted to mean that Council Regulation (EC) No. 44/2001 holds back its direct applicability to a certain extent, against the jurisdiction and foreign judgment recognition and enforcement rules of the domestic legal systems of EU member states.

This special nature of Council Regulation (EC) No. 44/2001 may, at first reading, mean that the application of jurisdictional rules in the Hungarian private international law code[33] and the rules of recognition and

---

[32] The translation differences of the text of Council Regulation (EC) No. 44/2001 and Regulation (EC) No. 805/2004 of the European Parliament and the Council are conspicuous and confusing.

[33] See also Chapter IX of the Hungarian private international law codex (Law-Decree 13 of 1979), enacted by Act CX of 2000 with an entry into force date of 1 May 2001, so that the regulations on jurisdiction are to be used in the case of proceedings commenced after 1 May 2001.

enforcement of foreign judgments[34] are not affected by Council Regulation (EC) No. 44/2001. This is not true, though, as the jurisdictional regulations in Hungarian private international law code and the rules of recognition and enforcement of foreign judgments are not harmonized in an EU law sense. As it has been already stated above, Act CX of 2000, as a law harmonization product, is imperfect and false. Here, two more reasons of a legal nature can be brought up to prove that the "law harmonization" created by Act CX of 2000 cannot be considered as law harmonization in an EU law sense.

These two reasons are related to the harmonization goals mentioned by the ministerial reasoning of Act CX of 2000, the Lugano Convention of 1998 and the draft of Council Regulation (EC) No. 44/2001 available to the codifiers at the time of the preparation of the Hungarian Act CX of 2000. Due to the legal status of the Lugano Convention, it cannot be considered as a law harmonization goal from a purely EU law standpoint, since it is a multilateral international agreement concluded by and between EU member states and non-EU member states. The earlier draft of Council Regulation (EC) No. 44/2001 cannot be considered as a law harmonization goal either, since in a draft format it was not a source of Community law.

Since jurisdictional rules in the Hungarian private international law code and the rules of the recognition and enforcement of foreign judgments of this code are not qualified as harmonized fields of law from an EU law standpoint, in my view, Council Regulation (EC) No. 44/2001 does not hold back its direct applicability against the aforementioned Hungarian rules. Hungarian lawyers, therefore, rightly consider a direct effect of Council Regulation (EC) No. 44/2001.

If we oversimplify the problem: should any doubts occur as to whether the jurisdictional rules of the Hungarian private international law code or Council Regulation (EC) No. 44/2001 are to be applied, the application of the rules of the latter are advisable to resolve any EU-related private international law issue. When the jurisdictional rules and the recognition and enforcement of foreign judgments rules of the Hungarian private international law code are really harmonized with the relevant EU law sources,

---

[34] See also Chapter XI of the Hungarian private international law codex (Law-Decree 13 of 1979), enacted by Act CX of 2000 with an entry into force date of 1 May 2001, so that the regulations on recognition and enforcement of foreign judgments are to be applied in the case of decisions that entered into force after 1 May 2001 in accordance with the law of the state in which they were issued.

then it will be significant from the Hungarian point of view also, what kind of fine-tuning adjustments have been made by the Court of Justice of the European Communities in its judgments in respect of jurisdiction and the recognition of foreign judgments to the legal systems of EU member states and Community law.

With respect to the personal scope of the effect of Council Regulation (EC) No. 44/2001, differentiation is needed between the norms of jurisdiction and the rules for the recognition and enforcement of foreign judgments in Chapter III. In accordance with the main rule, the norms of jurisdiction are to be applied if the defendant has a domicile in the EU, while the rules referring to the recognition and enforcement of judgments are to be applied in the case of all decisions that were issued by the court of any EU member state having competence under the territorial regime of council Regulation (EC.) No. 44/2001. In respect of the latter, the domicile of the defendant is irrelevant. For example, if a Hungarian person initiates proceedings against an American defendant in front of a French court, the French court will establish its jurisdiction in accordance with its own national jurisdictional regulations. If the French court rules against the American defendant, the Hungarian plaintiff can require the recognition and enforcement of this judgment in any EU member state in accordance with Council Regulation (EC) No 44/2001.[35]

Council Regulation (EC) No. 44/2001 does not create a unified legal regime fully superseding EU member states domestic jurisdictional regulations: in accordance with the main rule, it sets jurisdictional rules only in relation one EU member state and another EU member state. On the one hand, this means that—in accordance with the main rule - Council Regulation (EC) No. 44/2001 can only be applied if the defendant has a domicile in an EU member state. Therefore, if a Hungarian plaintiff sues an Ukrainian defendant in a Hungarian court, then the Hungarian court examines if it has jurisdiction based on the Hungarian private international law code, provided that there is no valid international agreement relevant to the issue. However, if a Hungarian plaintiff sues an Austrian defendant, the rules of Council Regulation (EC) No. 44/2001 are to be used, though there is an exception to this rule. From the wording of Article 22 on exclusive jurisdiction, it follows that exclusive jurisdictional rules are set, but not only in respect of the case where the defendant has a domicile in the EU: this article is formulated in the following way: "The following courts shall have exclu-

[35] See also *Nagy, Csongor István:* Az Európai Unió Nemzetközi Magánjoga [The private international law of the European Union] Budapest. HVG-ORAC 2006. pg. 45–46.

sive jurisdiction, regardless of domicile..." Another exception to the above main rule is Article 23 of Council Regulation (EC) No. 44/2001 on prorogation of jurisdiction, that is to be applied when one or more of the parties are domiciled in any EU member state: thus, it is not necessary that the defendant be the party who is domiciled in the EU. Article 23 is also applicable if only the plaintiff is domiciled in an EU member state. Articles 27-28 on the pendency of actions and related actions are not only to be applied if the jurisdiction of the court is based on Council Regulation (EC) No. 44/2001, but also in the case where the court acts based on its own, national jurisdictional regulations, though the matter itself is within the scope of the effect of Council Regulation (EC) No 44/2001.[36]

The jurisdictional rules of Council Regulation (EC) No. 44/2001 do not supersede national legal rules in all cases. One of the goals of this regulation is to ensure the proper legal framework for commerce within the European Union and protect the persons having a domicile in the EU against the strict and exorbitant jurisdictional regulations of other EU member states. As a result of this, the jurisdictional rules of Council Regulation (EC) No. 44/2001 shall only be applied—as a main rule—where the defendant has a domicile in one of the EU member states, in other cases national jurisdictional regulations will still be in force. In the Wolfgang Brenner and Peter Noller v. Dean Witter Reynolds, Inc. case[37] the Court of Justice of the European Communities ruled that in accordance with the main rule, the Brussels I Convention cannot be applied if the defendant has no domicile in a member state of the EU, and that national jurisdictional regulations are to be applied in such case.[38-39]

Article 69 of Council Regulation (EC) No. 44/2001 lists all the bilateral or multilateral conventions or treaties concluded by and between EU member states that are superseded by Council Regulation (EC) No. 44/2001, though these conventions and treaties remain in force with regard to proceedings not within the scope of the regulation, and these conventions and treaties remaining in force with regard those decisions which had been made before the coming into force of the regulation and those

---

[36] See also *Nagy, Csongor István:* Az Európai Unió Nemzetközi Magánjoga [The private international law of the European Union], Budapest, HVG-ORAC 2006. pp. 41–43.

[37] C-318/93 Wolfgang Brenner and Peter Noller v Dean Witter Reynolds Inc., [1994] ECR I-4275., quoted in: *Nagy, Csongor István:* Az Európai Unió Nemzetközi Magánjoga [The private international law of the European Union], Budapest, HVG-ORAC 2006. p. 46.

[38] Sections 17 and 19 of Council Regulation (EC) No. 44/2001.

[39] See also *Nagy, Csongor István:* Az Európai Unió Nemzetközi Magánjoga [The private international law of the European Union], Budapest, HVG-ORAC 2006. pp. 45–47.

public documents that were prepared in accordance with formal requirements or were registered as public documents also remain in force.[40]

Article 71 is an exception though, in accordance with which Council Regulation (EC) No. 44/2001 shall not affect any conventions to which EU member states are parties and which, in relation to particular matters, govern jurisdiction or the recognition or enforcement of judgments. With a view to its uniform interpretation, actions are to be taken in the following manner: (a) this regulation shall not prevent a court of an EU member state, which is a party to a convention on a particular matter, from assuming jurisdiction in accordance with that convention, even where the defendant is domiciled in another EU member state which is not a party to that convention. The court hearing the action shall, in any event, apply Article 26 of the regulation. (b) Judgments issued in an EU member state by a court in the exercise of jurisdiction provided for in a convention on a particular matter shall be recognized and enforced in other EU member states in accordance with this regulation. Where a convention, on a particular matter, to which both the EU member state of origin and the EU member state addressed are parties, lays down conditions for the recognition or enforcement of foreign judgments, those conditions shall apply. In any event, the provisions of this regulation which concern the procedure for the recognition and enforcement of foreign judgments may be applied.[41]

The EU seemingly does not want its norms on jurisdiction and norms on the recognition and enforcement of foreign judgments to fully supersede EU member states' national rules. The EU accepts the differences between EU member states' national legal rules, the lack of consistency of these norms and the content wise colorful and open regulation material of the private international law of these countries, which are not EU member states.

The European Union is aiming to develop a unified judicial region composed only of states within its boundaries. Its approach is essentially similar to the approach adopted in the 1980s and 1990s. As much as it protected the closed nature of the regulating regime of the Brussels I Convention, thus, the legal boundaries of the EU—and referred "outside enquirers" to the Lugano Convention—the European Union also reacts in the same way at present, in that it overlooks the regulation differences of the relations outside the European Union.

[40] See also Article 70 of Council Regulation (EC) No. 44/2001.

[41] See also *Nagy, Csongor István:* Az Európai Unió nemzetközi magánjoga. [The private international law of the European Union], Budapest, HVG-ORAC 2006. pp. 42–44.

Constitutional Democracy: Outline of a Defense

János Kis

Theorists of democracy tend to agree that majority rule is morally acceptable only if it is limited by the rights of the individual. But the content and scope of individual rights are controversial, and this raises the question, who should decide what the proper limits of majority decisions are.

Majoritarians respond: the majority should decide through its representatives. Their opponents argue that majoritarian decision-making must be subjected to constitutional constraints and, that enforcement of those constraints must be delegated to some independent body, possibly to courts.

In its perhaps most popular version, the criticism of the majoritarian conception presents the problem as one of balancing values and striking a compromise. Majority rule is a true political value, it is said. But individual rights are of a fundamental value. The decisions of the majority may threaten those rights, and when the threat becomes effective, the courts must step in. When the Justices strike down legislation, a moral price is paid, democracy is diminished. But it is a general fact of the human condition that values tend to conflict and that compromises are unavoidable.

Ronald Dworkin claims that the compromise view is shallow. Majoritarianism offers a political theory that explains how a community should decide what rights it has to respect. The compromise thesis leaves that theory alone, and so it is unable to show how non-elected and non-accountable judges can be justified at all to overrule the decisions of the elected representatives of the people. Thus, Dworkin concludes, the majoritarian thesis must be attacked at its very premises.

The majoritarian conception of democracy judges the fairness of the political process by looking at its procedural characteristics alone. Majority rule is fair, it holds, because it gives all citizens an equal chance to determine the outcome of collective decisions. It introduces no bias in the way the process translates individual preferences into collective decisions, and this is what fairness requires from collective decision-making under conflict and disagreement.

This view is objectionably narrow, Dworkin argues. Collective decisions distribute burdens and benefits over a community. Suppose that what the losers lose is not just a variable component of their well-being, but a right that defines a threshold condition for their status as equals. Or suppose that the same people end up as losers in an endless series of successives votes. In both cases, the voting system allows the collective decision to impose unfair burdens on these people.

When we ask the question whether a particular decision-making process treats all voters as equals, the intrinsic properties of the procedure are not everything. What matters is whether the procedure treats individuals as equals overall, not just in terms of its formal characteristics, but first of all in terms of the substantive decisions it is likely to produce.

When a voting system departs from pure procedural fairness without diminishing the status of any single citizen, and with the aim of protecting persistently disadvantaged groups against unfair outcomes, no moral cost is paid, Dworkin insists. If so, then the requirement of special majorities, characteristic of constitutionalism, is not intrinsically offensive to the principle of treating ctizens as equals.

But majoritarianism has a further claim, too, that argues for majority rule in a different sense. Political equality must hold, majoritarians remind us, not only among citizens horizontally, but also in the vertical relationship between ordinary citizens and their officials. There is no government without its officials having immense powers that ordinary citizens do not have. The asymmetries of power built in the structure of any conceivable government are a serious problem from the point of view of political equality, and they cannot be justified unless certain reverse asymmetries obtain, majoritarians claim. The officials who make the ultimate decisions on the law of the community must be collectively authorized to do so by all those who are bound by the law. They must use their power in the service of the community from which they get authorization, and they must be accountable to it. In other words, in a community of equals, the ultimate decisions are met by the elected representatives of the people. This is the idea of majority rule as representative government.

Dworkin's answer to the argument for representative government goes very deep. It is based on a thoroughgoing revision of the standard account of collective action and collective agency. Suspicion about attributing personhood, beliefs, intentions or desires to groups tempts us to interpret collective action reductively, in terms of individual acts aggregated in a certain way. Dworkin labels this model of collective action *statistical*. Although the statistical model works well with regard to certain kinds of collective action such as, for example, setting the price of a commodity on a competitive market, it is not capable to account for the adoption and execution of collective political decisions. Democratic politics cannot be properly understood unless we ascribe its processes to a distinct collective agency.

Such ascriptions need not attribute metaphysical personhood to communities. Consider voting in a legislature. There is no legislative decision without there being a winning coalition of individual law-makers, but the decision is owned by the legislature as a body not just the winners. We say, "The Parliament adopted law L." According to the model Dworkin calls statistical, this sentence can be translated with no loss of meaning into the following one: "The majority of the MPs voted for law L." But clearly, it cannot. The decision belongs to the Parliament, not to the majority of its members. Once a group has a decision-making rule, that rule identifies a minimal coalition of participants whose concurring vote decides the issue for the entire group. Any group that is in possession of decision-making and decision-enforcing rules is capable of acting as a distinct collective agency. Collective action understood on this second model is called by Dworkin communal.

Collective decisions have no value, however, unless they bind all the community members, not only those who voted in favor of them. But someone whose status in the community is that of a social and moral inferior is not obligated to obey its collective decisions. He is not a genuine member at all. Genuine members enjoy equal symbolic recognition of membership, they have an equal part in the community's public life, their interests are being given equal consideration by the communal decisions, and their independence in matters of conscience and conviction is duly respected. True communities are communities of genuine members. And only true communities are capable of meeting collective decisions that are binding for all.

That I am bound by the decisions of my community may be understood in two very different ways, the argument continues. On the first reading, those decisions limit my freedom, but I am morally required to comply with them. On the second reading, the decisions of my community are not liberty-limiting at all, because in a deep sense they are my own decisions.

If I am a genuine member of my community, then I have to see myself as having a part in the collective responsibility for communal decisions and actions. I have a reason to feel that my own responsibility as individual is at stake in what the community, as a distinct agent, has done, even if I did not contribute to it, or, perhaps, dissented from it. Genuine members are equal partners in collective self-government. Dworkin calls this the *partnership conception* of democracy.

We are now only one step away from his conclusion concerning the role of judicial review in a well-ordered democracy. On the statistical model, citizens cannot be said to have a part in official decisions unless they could participate in at least the election of the decision-makers. Citizens, upon this reading, are justified to consider themselves to be the ultimate authors of the decisions taken by their elected representatives. But they are not justified to think themselves to be the ultimate authors of judicial rulings because the courts are insulated from the electoral process.

On the communal model, the contrast dissolves. Suppose the role of constitutional adjudication is restricted to preventing the majoritarian decisions from invading the moral rights of the individuals. Then the judicial rulings, provided that they are accurate, secure their own democratic credentials. They make sure that citizens have an equal moral status as members of the community. By the same token, they also make sure that they themselves are in some relevant sense the decisions of the whole community in which all citizens have their part. So, the communal model explains judicial review as enhancing popular self-government without detracting anything from it.

This is a powerful and inspiring conception. But I am not sure it is defensible as it now stands. It is not clear to me, in particular, how much burden the distinction between statistical and communal collective action is capable to carry.

Dworkin's idea of communal action has two components. First, it identifies groups as primary units of responsibility. Second, it entails that collective responsibility, even if it is primarily incumbent on a group as a whole, has implications for the members—the genuine members—of the group. It is this second, distributive component of collective responsibility that allows individuals to bear vicarious responsibility for what their group as a distinct agency does. But one must be careful to distinguish clearly between two questions regarding the distributive implications of group responsibility. The first question is forward-looking, and it asks, who are liable to assume the costs of rectifying the harm that may have been collectively caused. The second question is backward-looking, and it asks, who have to assume moral responsibility for the causation of the harm. The fact that a person belongs to the first group does not automatically make the same person belong to the second. At one point in *Law's Empire*, Dworkin raises the question who should contribute to the compensation of victims harmed by corporate action. And he answers that covering the costs is the shareholders' responsibility. But when he explains why the shareholders are responsible for compensating the victims, he does not claim that they in some way own the corporate decisions. He rather argues that a principle of fairness binds shareholders to contribute. "If someone shares in the gains of another's action he must also share the responsibility for wrongs that that other person does."

Fairness, however, may bind anybody with regard to the consequences of the acts of anybody else. It does not presuppose any special relationship between the two agents beyond one of them accepting benefits produced by the other. And it certainly does not involve that the decisions of the producer of benefits are in some relevant sense owned by the beneficiary.

If this is true, however, then we seem to be back to the compromise thesis. The outcome of judicial review may improve the moral quality of democracy, but this improvement seems to come at a moral cost in terms of the procedure. To the extent that judges are not elected officials accountable to the electorate, their political decisions do not bear the mark of popular authorship, and this is a loss to be regretted.

Does it follow that we have to choose between settling on the compromise view and returning to pure majoritarianism? I think it does not. We have not examined yet a further argument, implicit in the way Dworkin lays out his partnership conception. Dworkin himself has never contemplated the possibility to fully develop this argument. But I believe it is worthy of some attention.

"Constraints on majority will might well expand any particular individual's control over his own fate." On a superficial reading, this statement appears to be just another version of the traditional view of rights as bulwarks against the tyranny of the majority. But Dworkin has something else in mind. For here is how he continues: "On the communal reading, liberty is a matter not of any relation between government and citizens one by one, but rather of the relation between government and the whole citizenry understood collectively. Positive liberty, so understood, is the state of affairs when 'the people' rule their officials, at least in the final analysis, rather than vice versa..." In other words, by obeying the constitution, the people enable themselves to rule their officials. The constitutional regime imposes disabilities on representative government, and it instructs courts to enforce those disabilities. The courts are insulated from the electoral process as much as possible, and so by delegating the task of interpreting and enforcing the constraints to them, the community ties its own hands. But self-binding is a means of self-empowering.

The idea of self-binding as self-empowering originates with the analysis of individual action. Individual preferences sometimes change cyclically, due to temporary losses of control of the person over his choices and acts. In a sober state, he may want that if he gets drunk he does not drive his car. But he knows that once drunken, he will want to drive home. He also knows that the next day, sober again, he will regret to have done what he wanted to do in his drunken state. So he gets control over his drunken self by disabling it: when he arrives to the party where he knows he will drink a lot, he gives the keys of his car to a friend whom he instructs not to return them before the next day. Some authors interpret communal self-binding on this analogy. In its calm moments, the community understands that, from time to time, it undergoes experiences of collective panic and hysteria. In the states of such collective mental disorders, it takes decisions it cannot acknowledge as its own once in a calm state again. So it disables itself from adopting such decisions, and instructs courts to enforce t`ose self-imposed disabilities.

There are serious problems with this account of collective self-binding. But I don't need to examine those problems now because I will not follow the model of preference inconsistency over time that the analogy from individual action suggests.

Nor do I base my argument on the assumption that popular majorities adopt persistent attitudes towards certain minorities that, as democrats, they are supposed to disown: group hatred, prejudice, and the like. Such phenomena raise serious problems for democratic theory, to be sure, but the account of judicial review I am about to propose cannot begin by appealing to them. Wanting a social group to be segregated from and subordinated to the majority hardly qualifies as a case in treating individuals as fellow citizens. Such an attitude is not a controversial expression but a declared enemy of a sense of community between equals.

So I suggest that, in the beginning, we set aside these ugly facts, and imagine a society united by an honest aspiration to be a true community. Presumably, in such a society, the majority's settled views on individual rights reflect the outcome of good-faith public debates. Given such favorable conditions, can there still be a need for the community to tie its hands in order to be truly self-governing? Yes, there can, but communal self-binding is not needed in order to overrule the settded views of the majority. Rather, it is needed in order to help them prevail.

I guess you find this claim bizarre. If the aim is that the settled views of the majority prevail, why not to allow the majority to take its decisions unencumbered by constitutional constraints?

The answer is that abandoned to itself, representative government is likely to produce paradoxical outcomes. But its vulnerability to such outcomes is made invisible by the approach typically taken by both majoritarians and non-majoritarians.

The majoritarian as well as the partnership conception interpret the democratic process as one aiming to resolve practical disagreements through common deliberation and collective decision-making. This, of course, is essential for any minimally plausible and attractve account of democracy. But in modern, representative democracies the processes through which conflicts and disagreements are getting resolved are at the same time processes of competition for power, and this aspect of democratic politics is not given serious enough attention by either the majoritarian or the partnership account.

Perhaps the reason why normative conceptions of democracy tend to bracket out the aspect of competition for power is that they try to identify the ideal of democratic politics. In other words, both the majoritarian and the partnership conceptions aspire to occupy the domain of what Rawls calls ideal theory while competition for power seems to pertain to the domain of non-ideal theory.

But this is not exactly the case. With all its well-known weaknesses, the democratic competition for power is significantly different from power struggles in non-democratic polities. The electoral process not only pacifies the struggle for power; it puts it in the service of the democratic community in a deeper sense. Under favorable circumstances, the competition for elected office is a powerful tool of clarifying the controversial public issues, of elucidating the nature of disagreements on them, and of enabling the citizenry to take enlightened choices. So it is a mistake to set democratic power struggles aside as belonging to mere non-ideal theory. They have their own ideals, fully integrated to the broad ideal of democratic politics.

But they have paradoxical implications as well. I will briefly discuss one of the different mechanisms that are responsible for such implications. The phenomenon I will describe is due to the fact that legislative power in a democracy is distributed between government and opposition, but it is distributed in an asymmetrical manner.

Let me illustrate. Freedom of speech has a core that is uncontested in modern democracies. Nobody would deny that public criticism of government is of value and that deserves protection. Democratic parties surely would not deny this. But at any point in time, they are asymmetrically positioned with regard to this valuable asset. Freedom of speech is a friend of the opposition in its struggle for gaining power, and for the same reason, it is an embarrassment to the government. Imagine a two-party system, and suppose that, in the long run, the two parties spend roughly equal times in government and in opposition. Then, their short-term interests cancel out each other, and what remains is the joint commitment to freedom of speech. But law is made in the short term, and it is made by the party in government. To be in government provides one with an incentive against adopting laws that widen the protected domain of speech, and for adopting laws that narrow that domain. So, other things being equal, there is some likelihood that while in government, a party will pass some law abridging freedom of speech, even though it will regret that move once in opposition. The opposition may vehemently object to the law when it is adopted. But it has no means of unmaking it before it comes to government. Once in government, however, its interests change. They may not be fully reversed, because a complete break with its previous anti-abridgment position would damage its reputation as a trustworthy political agent. But they certainly shift because freedom of speech is now a weapon in the hands of its competitor. So there is some likelihood that the new government will not restore the status quo ante. Rather, it is likely to legislate some compromise. Although, in the long run, all the players support freedom of speech, the legislative acts add up to a trend towards abridging it. To contain that undesirable tendency, the community does well to declare that the legislature shall not make law abridging freedom of speech, and to assign to courts the task of enforcing that disability. It has reason for tying its hands in order to have what it aims to: freedom of speech.

One might object that this story covers political speech only, and freedom of political speech belongs to the procedural rules that constitute the practice of democratic politics. Even majoritarians may concede that the task of supervising the observance of democratic procedures can be delegated to courts. What gain is derived from getting a new justification for what is already generally accepted? Well, the justification can be extended to rights that are not identified as constitutive of the democratic procedure. Let me remind you of the defeats privacy rights suffer in this decade all over the democratic world. This unglorious process fits well, I think, the explanatory scheme I am offering. Furthermore, the paradox-generating mechanism that I tried to outline is but one in a family of related mechanisms. For example, the logic of electoral coalition-building predicts that legislation is often less permissive on moral issues (such as abortion or assisted termination of life) than the general public. But I cannot continue the unpacking of my suggestion on this occasion. It is time for me to take stock.

The conception of communal self-binding takes much of the partnership conception for granted. It accepts the idea of true political community as a community of equals. It accepts that, in a community of equals, pure procedural fairness cannot be the right standard of collective decision-making: a more complex standard is needed, one that integrates procedural and substantive considerations. It shares the ambition of building a theory of democracy that makes room for constitutional disabilities and judicial review without ending up with the compromise thesis. But it does not rely on the ambiguous idea of vicarious responsibility. It agrees that the decisions of the judiciary to strike down legislation are owned by the community, but it does not justify this claim by automatically attributing official decisions to all those whose equal status they respect and make respected. Judicial decisions are owned by the community, it believes, because they are means of communal self-binding governed by the aim to overcome the paradoxes of representative government.

Here is a second example. Elections for representative government cannot deal with separate policy issues separately. The competing parties must build up broad electoral coalitions along the various different issues. Simplifying a bit, let us group the big issues into two main categories: socio-economic (employment, inflation, wages, welfare, and taxes), and moral (abortion, assisted termination of life, stem cell research, gay marriage, etc.). Let us suppose, in accordance with our general assumption, that the community adopts its settled views on the basis of good-faith public debate. Let us add, however, two further assumptions. First, most voters give priority to the socio-economic issues over the moral ones. And, second, there may be passionate ideological minorities unwilling to sacrifice their views on the moral issues for the sake of progress, however significnt, in the socio-economic domain. If the difference between the majority and the minority on the socio-economic issues is not larger than the size of the passionate minority, then no government can be formed without including the representatives of this minority. (Depending on whether the electoral system is proportional or majoritarian, the coalition may be built as an alliance of separate parties after the election, or as an intra-party coalition before the election. This is a technical detail.) The upshot is that a representative government may occupy positions on individual moral rights that are systematically different from the settled views of the majority. Under such conditions, disability rules and judicial review help the majority views to prevail over the distorting effects of representative politics.

This brief account does not address all the paradoxes of representative government that call for communal self-binding in order to make representative government more democratic. But is provides, or so I hope, a hint at how the communal self-binding defense of judicial review might work.

The European Dream and its Evolution in the Architecture of the Treaties of Integration

FERENC MÁDL

> "Thou who didst waken from his summer dreams
> The blue Mediterranean, ...
>
> Drive my dead thoughts over the universe
> Like withered leaves to quicken a new birth!
> And, by the incantation of this verse,
>
> Scatter, as from an unextinguished hearth
> Ashes and sparks, my words among mankind!
> Be through my lips to unawakened Earth
>
> The trumpet of a prophecy! O Wind,
> If Winter comes, can Spring be far behind?"
>
> *P. B. Shelley: Ode to the West Wind*

I. A Message from Afar

The European cultural and political heritage radiates well founded messages to us. The early *European dream* teaches us that a just and efficient legal system is needed to respond to the challenges of the protection and further development of the core European values of human dignity; so that this may increasingly satisfy what once was created and foreseen for all men, and then held to be good (Gen. I,1,31).

These spiritual and political lessons and messages are emanating from the Ten Commandments, from the Sermon on the Mount, from works and experience of the creative scholars of the European ethical, political and legal thinking and historic law-making, such as Plato, Aristotle, Justinian, St. Augustine, Charles the Great, Thomas More, Erasmus. Notwithstanding all the doctrinaire differences among them, they were deeply concerned with man's social, political, cultural and legal well being. In their major works they came, *i.a.*, to the conclusion that comprehensive structures of legal norms with their actual operation were needed to make society and the active coexistence of nations work.

Plato (427–347 B.C.) in his major works *The State* and *The Laws* used the language of philosophy to conceive features and comprehensive structures of an ideal state. There he explored forms of state and state organization, values and viable rules of social and individual behavior, good legislation, judiciary and public order, equality among men. One of Plato's intentions was to convince men, communities and society to create and live under a just and viable legal system.

Emperor Justinian (ruling 527–565 A.D.)—assisted by some of the most brilliant thinkers of his time—enacted the big *Corpus Juris Civilis* (the *Codex Justinianus*, the *Digesta* and the *Institutiones*). This legal architecture—which would prove strongly influential on the subsequent European legal development—was meant to and really served the goals of the legal unity and effective functioning of the Roman Empire.

Charles the Great (712–814 A.D.) was very deeply influenced by the readings of St. Augustine's *De civitate Dei* (413–426), the book that depicted and projected the Christian spiritual, legal, and ethical values to the proper functioning of the Carolingian empire.

The *Utopia* (1516) has been described by the author Thomas More (1477–1535), the knowledgeable citizen and chief justice of London, as a description of an ideal, that is the "most perfect form of state." More's goal was to specify moral requirements for good laws and institutions, which would guarantee justice in actual coexistence of citizens, communities and cities of the state.

When Erasmus of Rotterdam (1466–1536)—friend of Thomas More, and his spiritual and political ally—strived for unity of Europe and the *Ecclesia Universalis*, he also came up with an ideal legal construct, which he named the 'United States of Europe.'

Napoleon is claimed to have said that the many battles he won would fade away with the passing of time, but that people will never forget his Code. No question, *Code Napoleon* (1804) had a deep impact on harmonization of the evolution of the personal and property relationships in civil society.

The above messages demonstrate the overwhelming creativity of the European spiritual, legal and political thinking in developing comprehensive instruments—laws, codes, treaties, conventions, regulatory schemes, jurisprudential books—that importantly contributed to the political, legal, social, economic and cultural structuration of the European communities.

Contemporary Europe responded correspondingly to the above messages, gradually—in a long, historical process that was not free of controversies—leaning towards a more perfect integration. The following comprehensive survey of the construction of the treaties in the legal architecture of the European integration presents an overview of this spectacular path. In the last chapter special attention will be paid to the new elements of the Treaty of Lisbon as the most recent reform answer to the particular challenges of the development of the European Union.

II. The Idea of Europe and the Architecture of the European Integration

After the Thirty Years' War and the Peace of Westphalia (1648)—in the process of reconciliation and the renewal of the European moral and cultural values, in an effort to provide for stable political relations—the early European dream, the idea of a Christian Europe, was once again conceived of as the driving force of lasting peace.

Something similar emerged in Europe also after World War II. Having experienced the trauma of the two world wars, the political elites recognized and acknowledged the historical importance of the crossroad. They agreed that a lasting peace would require not only the revival of the traditional European moral values, but also the institutionalization of the economic, political and cultural cooperation, in order to close the book on the history of the disastrous violent divisions.

They also envisaged that a process of institutionalization would unfold under the banner of the European integration. To set the foundations for opening such a process, inter-governmental treaties were foreseen. These treaties should depict the architecture in full appearance; they should spell out the objectives and principles of common activities, decision-making and implementation rules; the dispute-resolving fora; the role of the member states in the accession and decision-making procedures; the competence concerning the policies and other areas coming within the framework and aims of the integration philosophy; the logic of the co-operation with third countries and international organizations.

Such an ambitious goal required serious efforts and careful coordination of steps to be undertaken. Europe would not be born with one blow or in one day, claimed Robert Schuman in his book *Pour l'Europe* (Genève, 1990) and the *Schuman Declaration* (Paris, May 9, 1950). The *Schumann Declaration* solemnly announced that France and Germany, with the participation of other states, would erect an institution pioneering the idea of a new Europe. Four centuries after Erasmus and Westphalia, with the strong belief in the early European dream, they would start building the road of European integration in the spirit of reconciliation, solidarity and co-operation. On April 18, 1951 Belgium, France, Germany, Italy, Luxemburg and the Netherlands signed in Paris the *Treaty Establishing the European Coal and Steel Community* (ECSC). This was followed by the Rome Treaties signed by the same six states in 1957: the *Treaty Establishing the European Economic Community* (EEC Treaty) and the *Treaty establishing the European Atomic Energy Community* (EAEC Treaty), respectively. So did it start.

The full story is long and well known. In a comprehensive manual *Constitutional Law of the European Union* (London, 2005) K. Lenaerts and P. Van Nuffel offer, among other things, a concise summary of the treaties, followed by an analysis of the waves of the accession treaties and the amending treaties. These are: the accession treaties of Denmark, Ireland, the United Kingdom (1972); Greece (1979); Portugal, Spain (1985); Sweden, Finland, Austria (1994); ten accessions by the Accession Treaty of Athens, 2003 (Czech Republic, Estonia, Cyprus, Letonia, Latvia, Hungary, Malta, Poland, Slovakia, Slovenia); Romania and Bulgaria acceded in 2007. The amending treaties are the *Maastricht Treaty of the European Union* (1992), the *Amsterdam Treaty* (1997) and the *Nice Treaty* (2001). The last step for the time being is—after the abortive *Constitutional Treaty* (Rome, 2004)—the *Treaty of Lisbon* (2007).

The establishing and amending treaties and the corresponding academic writing reveal: 1. the goals of the European integration; 2. its areas: social, economic, political and cultural; 3. legal and institutional architecture of the; 4. goals, ways and means of further development.

III. The Architecture of the European Integration—Evolution of the Treaties

III. 1. The Founding Treaties

Three treaties provide the foundations for the European integration: *The Treaty Establishing European Coal and Steel Community* (ECSC, 1951); *The Treaty Establishing the European Economic Community* (EEC, 1957); *The Treaty Establishing the European Atomic Energy Community* (EAEC, 1957).

The European Economic Community Treaty (EEC, 1957) created the original map of the growing road system of the European integration. Its Parts I–VI identify the principles, objectives and fields of action (common market, customs union, the 'four freedoms'—free movement of persons, goods, services and capital), gradual development of common policies in the areas of agriculture, transport, economic competition, social policies, and trade, through approximation of the relevant laws; the institutions, their structure, composition, competence, decision-making procedures; the association with overseas countries and territories; legal personality and the regime of ownership. It is established that the Treaty shall not take precedence over the rules of the Member States governing the regime of property ownership (Art. 222), the international relations of the Community (Art 228), and the accession of new members (Art. 237).

III. 2. The Single European Act, 1986

With the accession of Denmark, the United Kingdom and Ireland (1972), the nine Member States of the Community signed in Luxembourg on February 17, 1986 and in The Hague on February 28, 1986 respectively, the *Single European Act* (SEA). This brought new dimensions to the evolution of the European architecture.

This Act—while amending the three funding treaties—adds a number of important new elements: the institution of the European Political Cooperation for a common development and implementation of a European foreign policy (Title III); the enhancement of the common European market (Art. 13); the co-operation towards the envisaged Economic and Monetary Union (Art. 20); the establishment of the European Council, composed of the heads of states and prime ministers of the Member States, and the President of the Commission (Title I, Art. 2); the development of the relations among the Member States shall lead to the establishment of the European Union, as envisaged in the *Stuttgart Declaration* of June 19, 1983 (Preamble).

III. 3. A New Stage: Treaty on the European Union (TEU, Maastricht, 1992)

"By this Treaty the High Contracting Parties establish among themselves a European Union" (Article A). Following the accession of Denmark, Ireland and the United Kingdom in 1972, Greece in 1979, Portugal and Spain in 1985, the twelve Contracting Parties announce in the Article A, that "this Treaty marks a new stage in the process of creating an ever closer union among the peoples of Europe."

It marks a new stage for several reasons.

It extends the integration process to twelve countries. In establishing the European Union with substantial amending of the three founding treaties (ECSC, EEC, EAEC), the Treaty represents a step towards a different political structure.

The Treaty contains VII Titles with Articles A to K, as well as 17 Protocols and 33 Declarations.

In Title I, the *Common Provisions* declare the establishment of the European Union, a new political and legal entity. The *Provisions* spell out the objectives of the Union, and establish that it shall be served by a single institutional framework, while respecting and building upon the *acquis communuataire*. The European Council shall provide the Union with the necessary impetus for its development and shall define the general political guidelines thereof. The Union shall respect subsidiarity principle and the national identities of its Member States, as well as the fundamental rights guaranteed by the European Convention of 1950. The further objectives include the establishment of an economic and monetary union, ultimately including a single currency, develop common foreign and security policy, introduce the citizenship of the Union, and provide a basis for the cooperation in justice and home affairs.

In Title II under Article G of the Union Treaty the *Provisions Amending the Treaty Establishing the European Economic Community with a View to Establishing the European Community* are set out.

Taken together, these Provisions and the amending-complementing provisions of the founding treaties, demonstrate that the integration process evolved far beyond a *European Economic Community* only. The process has led to the establishment of the European Community (EC), and accordingly, as Article G, title II declares, the term 'European Economic Community' shall be replaced (throughout the Treaty) by the term 'European Community'.

The "new stage" elements extend to many of the altogether 248 Articles of the EEC Treaty, through 86 amendments by the EU Treaty, and relevant EU Treaty provisions. They include: elections of the members of the European Parliament (EEC, Art. 137–138); the extension of the qualified majority voting respecting the consensus requirements where so defined by the Treaty (EU, Art. "J.3"); the legislative co-operation and joint decision procedures of the Parliament, the Council and the Commission (EU, Art. "K"); the Ombudsman (EEC, Art. 138e); the Committee of the Regions (EEC, Art. 198a); Court of Auditors (EEC Art. 188); the Economic and Monetary Union (EU Art. B., EEC Art. 102a, 105ff); the excessive deficit procedure, and the convergence criteria (EEC, Art. 104c, Protocol on the Statute of the European Monetary Institutes, Art. 12, Protocol on the Excessive Deficit Procedure, Protocol on the Convergence,

EEC Art. 109j); institutions in partly renewed regulation (System of the Central Bank of Europe, the European Investment Bank, EEC Art. 4a, 4b).

These important developments brought quite a number of policies under community competence: education, culture, public health, research and technology, consumer protection, environment, trans-European networks, energy, etc. (EEC Art. 126, 128, 129, 130).

"New stage" elements are coming to the fore also in the rest of the EU Treaty Titles: in Title III *Provisions Amending the Treaty Establishing the European Coal and Steel Community*; in Title IV *Provisions Amending the Treaty Establishing the European Atomic Energy Community*; in Title V, Art. 7 of the *EU Treaty Provisions on a Common Foreign and Security Policy*; in Title VI, Art. K of the *EU Treaty Provisions on Cooperation in the Fields of Justice and Home Affairs*; in Title VII, Art. L-S *Final Provisions*, extending ratification requirements of this Treaty to the application and admission procedures for new membership.

No doubt, the *Treaty on the European Union* designed an unprecedented large area of competence, tasks and activities with extended legislative and executive responsibilities to the European Union and the European Community.

III. 4. The Treaty of Amsterdam (1997) and the Treaty of Nice (2001)

After the accession of Austria, Finland and Sweden in 1994, two treaties were added to the European architecture: The *Treaty of Amsterdam* and the *Treaty of Nice*.

These two Treaties modify the *Treaty on the European Union* (TE) and the preceding treaties establishing the European Communities (ECSC, EEC, EAEC). The new Treaties also add new elements. The most significant changes are in the following areas: the European social policy; protection of the employees; visa, asylum, customs and immigration regulations; the European Regional Development Fund.

Since the accession of the ten new Member States to the Union in Athens in 2003 (and the more recent accession of Romania and Bulgaria in 2007), the family of twenty-seven countries lives now within the regime constructed by the above treaties.

III. 5. Reforms and Changes Towards a Stronger Europe—Enlargement, Efficiency, More Democracy and Better Governance

III. 5. a) Towards a Constitution for Europe

One could have thought that with the Maastricht Treaty the legal and political development and treaty making would calm down—for a while, it looked as if the European integration has approached perfection.

However, we have seen that the idea of reform was foreseen right at the beginning by the founding treaties, followed by comprehensive processes of development. Accordingly, reforms were welcome by the very nature of the European integration and treaty making process.

With the accession of the ten new Member States in Athens 2003, the enlargement process imposed a comprehensive challenge to the identity, institutional structure and the political and social processes within the Union.

Reform challenges were especially pertinent in the following areas: transparency and efficiency of governance; new decision-making and voting procedures, principally in the law-making sphere; the active role of the Member States in the EU institutions; the elections to the European Parliament and other efforts to overcome the democracy deficit; strengthening foreign policy and security responsibilities; streamlining and providing for better coherence in the spheres of the primary and secondary sources of law; regulating and balancing the competences, policies and activities assumed increasingly by the Union; the evolution of the Economic and Monetary Union; the accommodation of the Charter of the Fundamental Rights of the Union as the binding European law.

All these issues converged on the demand for a new comprehensive treaty. The first task of a new treaty would be to integrate the values, structure, organization and substantive elements accomplished so far. Second, it should introduce new institutional elements demanded by the present stage of development. Third, it should help the citizens and communities of the Union to reach a higher moral and material level in their quality of life.

In response, the European Council on its 2001 December summit meeting established the European Convention, with the task to elaborate a new treaty. The Convention penned the *Draft Treaty Establishing a Constitution for Europe*, and submitted it to the President of the European Council in Rome on July 18, 2003. On October 29, 2004 the *Draft* was signed by the authorized representatives of the 25 Member States.

One of the main reform considerations was that the new Treaty should integrate and consolidate in one instrument the founding and all the amending treaties and instruments which brought about and regulated the functioning of the EU as it evolved and worked so far. Thus all treaty and community law norms in force would be codified in one Act, the Constitution. However, history thought of it differently.

III. 5. b) Towards the Reform Treaty of Lisbon

The destiny of the *Treaty Establishing a Constitution for Europe* is known. To enter into force by November 1, 2006 as foreseen by the Treaty, all Member States' ratification was required. Though ratified by eighteen Member States, after the rejection of the referendum in France and The Netherlands, the rest of the needed ratifications did not follow. By November 1, 2006 it became evident, that the Constitutional Treaty has no chance to get into force.

This shock, however, did not do away with the need for a reform. The Member States remained convinced that the reform of the EU architecture must be brought to a good end, and that it required a new reform treaty. A new reform treaty would have to do what the Union meant to accomplish with the original constitutional reform treaty.

On its meeting in Brussels on June 21–22, 2007, the European Council decided to give the Intergovernmental Conference the Mandate to prepare a new treaty. In this Mandate, the almost complete structure and almost all vital content elements of the envisaged new treaty—hereinafter called "Reform Treaty"—were projected. It was also held that under the Portugal Presidency the text of the Draft shall be finalized by the Intergovernmental Conference, then submitted for consideration to the High Contracting Parties and signed by them by the end of the Portugal Presidency in 2007 in Lisbon. This indeed happened when the EU heads of states and governments, meeting in Lisbon on December 13, 2007, signed the reform Treaty of Lisbon 2007, the full title of which is the *Treaty of Lisbon Amending the Treaty on the European Union and the Treaty Establishing the European Community.*

When venturing a short picture of the reasons and features of the outcome of the reform process—the failure of the Constitutional Treaty and the successful coming about of the Treaty of Lisbon—one should refer to few factors of this development.

The name of the original Act—*The Constitution for Europe*—seemed to be too much for many. A single constitution-type corpus of law instead of a multitude of founding and amending treaties, would have more than symbolized what was really not expected to come about—a uniform state structure, a sort of European 'super-state', instead of a federation of nations.

In its July 2007 Mandate, the European Council extended the unequivocal instruction that a codified constitution, which would have replaced all former treaties, "is abandoned." In its stead came the demand for a Reform Treaty, which shall contain the treaties in force as amended so far, as well as the innovations of the Constitutional Treaty as specified by the Mandate. The *Reform Treaty* shall have "two substantive clauses," which shall modify and complement the *Treaty on European Union* (TEU) on the one hand, and the amended *Treaty Establishing the European Community* (TEC) on the other hand; the *Treaty of European Union* shall keep its name, while the *Treaty on the European Community* shall hereinafter be named the *Treaty on the Functioning of the European Union* (TFEU); the word "Community" shall be replaced throughout the Treaty by the term "Union". The amended Treaties constitute the foundation of the Union, but they shall have no constitutional character. They shall leave unaddressed the question of the state-type symbols or denominations (Union foreign minister, flag, hymn). The Union shall exercise more constraint in assuming policy competences.

Once this treaty-making philosophy returned to the tradition of building the reforms on what was accomplished before—on the valid treaties—the traditional inner structure of the Treaties was of course also to be honored, with their preambles, values-objectives, parts, titles, chapters, sections, articles, final provisions, ratification procedures, signatures, protocols and declarations. Viewed from this perspective, the *Treaty of Lisbon* shows at the first sight a traditional but skeleton-like appearance: 7 Articles altogether, the preamble containing the list of the heads of states and governments who signed the *Treaty*; Article 1 introduces and amends the *Treaty on European Union*; Article 2 introduces and amends the *Treaty of the Functioning of the European Union*; Articles 3–7 cover closing provisions on ratification requirements, etc.

To give a schematic picture, the *Consolidated Version of the Treaty on European Union* (Official Journal of the European Union, 9.5.2008) contains 55 Articles, the *Consolidated Version of the Treaty on the Functioning of the European Union* (OJ, 9.5.2008) contains 358 Articles, while the *Treaty of Lisbon* has 37 Protocols and 65 Declarations (J.O. 9.5.2008). What the *Maastricht Treaty* brought about both in terms of structure and content with its amended 53 Articles and then consolidated in the version

(Journal Officiel, 29.12.2006) of the *European Union Treaty*, and with the 314 amended and the consolidated text *Articles of the Treaty of the European Community* (J.O. 29.12.2006), was to be amended and incorporated correspondingly into the Treaty of Lisbon. It may be interesting to note that The *Maastricht Treaty* contains 86 amendments to the *Treaty of the European Community*, while the *Treaty of Lisbon* has 295(!) amendments to the same instrument (Article 2).

In this equation of the structures and numbers on the one hand, and the content-specific elements on the other hand, we find the architecture of the European integration as evolved in the treaties and offered to the "tenants". This legal structure is now providing for the architecture of the European dream.

III. 5. c) Areas of Major Reforms Revisited

The analysis on the evolution of the European integration treaties, and the present status of the architecture as shown by the *Treaty of Lisbon,* offer a picture of the legal dynamics and the legal structure of the European Union. It also tells us about the reforms through which the development manifested itself.

The most important reform can be identified when comparing the *Lisbon Treaty* amendments (61 amendment) to the 295 amendments to the *Treaty of the Functioning of the European Union*. No doubt, the amending process of the Treaty of Lisbon was by far more successful than its predecessors both as regards the numbers of the Articles and the many substantive norms therein. In this section I will explore a few areas affected by these legal changes.

Moral values must be seen as the pillar of the European architecture—Europe needs a soul, too, claimed Jacques Delors, former President of the EU Commission, in a discussion about the introduction of values into the envisaged *Constitutional Treaty*. The *Treaty of Lisbon* has now enshrined the well-tried values and principles of the Christian European heritage, the European humanist values, the social values and political principles of democracy. Though not spelling out explicitly the Christian inspiration of Europe, but in substance honoring it, both the *Draft Treaty Establishing a Constitution for Europe* and the *Treaty of Lisbon* are explicitly "drawing inspiration from the cultural, religious and humanist inheritance of Europe, from which have developed the universal values of the inviolable and inalienable rights of the human person, freedom, democracy, equality and the rule of law."

In agreement with these value claims, the *Charter of Fundamental Rights of the European Union* was declared in Nice, on December 7, 2000, by the Presidents of the European Parliament, the Council and the Commission. It will become binding law by virtue of Article 6 of the *Treaty of Lisbon*, which says that "the Charter shall have the same legal value as the treaties." The Charter covers such values and rights as human dignity and right to life; right to liberty and security; respect for private and family life; freedom of thought, conscience and religion; freedom of assembly and of association; right to education, right to property; freedom to conduct business; solidarity, social security and social assistance; right to vote and stand as candidate at elections, and rights to other values of similar social importance.

TEU Article 6 (3) states that "fundamental rights... as they result (also) from the constitutional traditions common to the Member States, shall constitute general principles of the Union law."

Norms that formulate democratic principles are affirmed in the TEU Title II, Articles 9–10 and TFEU Article 17: equality of citizens should be observed; every national of a Member State shall be a citizen of the Union; the EU citizenship shall be additional to national citizenship and shall not replace it; functioning of the Union shall be based on the principle of representative democracy; the citizens' rights as set out in TFEU Article 20 (2) shall not be exclusive—the Council, acting unanimously and upon the consent of the Parliament, new rights; such added provisions however require the approval by the Member States.

TEU Article 11 (4) and TFEU Article 20 (2d) introduces the *citizens' right to petition* to the Parliament, which includes the right of legislative initiative: not less than one million citizens who are nationals of a significant number of Member States, may invite the Commission to submit their appropriate proposal to the Parliament.

In the *institutional, especially decision-making, area,* reforms of the *Treaty of Lisbon* include the following: the "Parliament shall jointly with the Council, exercise legislative and budgetary functions ..., it shall elect the President of the Commission" (TEU Article 14 (1); from 2009 onwards, the number of MPs shall be limited to 750+1 (TEU Article 14 (2)); "the European Council—consisting of the Heads of State and Government of the Member States, together with its President and the President of the Commission—shall provide the Union with the necessary impetus for its development and shall define the general political directions and priorities thereof; it shall not exercise legislative functions" (TEU Article 15 (1); "the European Council, acting by qualified majority, with the agreement of the President of the Commission, shall appoint the High Representative of the Union for Foreign Affairs and Security Policy" (TEU Article 18); the Council—consisting of a representative of each Member State—shall, jointly with the European Parliament, exercise legislative and budgetary functions, and act by qualified majority except where the Treaties provide otherwise; as from 1 November 2014, a qualified majority shall be defined as at least 55% of the members of the Council, comprising at least fifteen of them and representing Member States comprising at least 65% of the population of the Union (TEU Article 16); the Presidency of the Council shall be held by Member State representatives in the Council on the basis of equal rotation (TEU Article 16 (9)); from 1 November 2014 the European Commission—as foreseen by TEU Article 17 (5)—will be composed of a number of members corresponding to two-thirds of the number of the Member States; the Commission President is now elected by a majority of Member States of the European Parliament on a proposal from the European Council, acting by qualified majority (TEU Article 14).

Subsidiarity, national interests and the role of National Parliaments in the Union emphasize the requirement of balance. TEU Article 5 (3) establishes that "the institutions of the Union shall apply the principle of subsidiarity as laid down in the Protocol on the application of the principles of subsidiarity and proportionality; National Parliaments ensure compliance … in accordance with the procedure set out in that Protocol" (TEU Protocol No 1). The new treaty Protocol provides efficient control mechanism for the subsidiarity principle. In case of violation of the principle, the majority of Parliaments can refer their case directly to the EU Court of Justice.

TEU Article 47 declares that *"the Union shall have legal personality,"* which until now had only the European Community and Euratom. The EU may thus conclude international agreements in all of its areas of competence, unless specified contradictions emerge.

Strategic reform efforts and developments evolved—and gave impetus to their actual implementation—in three other major areas: *co-decisions* of the Council and the Parliament; the voting in the Council where *areas were moved to qualified majority*; *the competence* regulation.

TEU Article 14 provides that "the European Parliament shall, jointly with the Council exercise legislative and budgetary functions," that is, make community law legal acts in *co-decision procedure*. This provision aims at improving the quality of legislation, strengthening laws' capacity to accomplish stated goals, and elevating democratic legitimacy of the Union.

Both the draft Constitution and the *Treaty of Lisbon* accommodated a very important reform element: *moving the areas to qualified majority* when voting in the Council. This goes hand in hand with the ordinary legislative procedure, the co-decision with the Parliament. Thus, the qualified majority voting has become the general rule—with specified exceptions.

The *Treaty of Lisbon* defines a *clear division of competences* between the Union and the Member States. The *Treaty* distinguishes between the exclusive, the shared and the supporting competences. TEU Article 5 (2) provides that "under the principle of conferral the Union shall act only within the limits of the competences conferred upon it by the Member States in the Treaties to attain the objectives set out therein; competences not conferred upon the Union in the Treaties remain with the Member States." The domains in which the Union has exclusive competence, those with shared competences and those with supporting competencies (e.g. in the areas of research, technological development and space) are covered under TFEU Articles 3-4.

The strong reform value of the competence regime becomes manifest in the extensive appearance of the "Union Policies and Internal Actions" (TFEU Titles I-XXIV), where the development-oriented responsibilities and tasks are expected to materialize (e.g., with regard to more efficient shaping of and accession to the Eurozone in the Treaty regulations, TFEU Part Three, TITLE VIII).

Future-oriented reforms have been closely attended in the *Treaty*, providing for the accommodation of *new policies* in the Union: energy, sport, tourism, civil protection, European Research Area, and administrative cooperation (TFEU Articles 165, 179, 194, 196).

IV. An Epilogue

The *Editorial* in the Special Edition of *Europolitics* (7 November 2007, p.3) holds that "The Treaty of Lisbon is presented as the *sine qua non* for the proper functioning of a Union of 27 member states, enabling it to adopt policies that will gave it greater control over its own destiny and make it more influential on a rapidly evolving global stage."

This Epilogue is perhaps not overoptimistic when—after all what has been accomplished in the process of conceiving and erecting the architecture of the European dream—one is inclined to give justice to this *sine qua non* judgment.

This value and role of the Treaty is presented by history along the roads of which the builders followed their long way—always listening to and adjusting their steps and actions to the actual needs and challenges emerging on the road—led by the intention to provide a framework for a possible better life of men and women, communities and nations of Europe.

Europa, this royal beauty of Phoenicia—symbolizing what emerged to become the European dream—started her destiny-driven mission from the early Mediterranean, riding then on the back of the Bull Zeus all over Europe, following his historic adventure until he arrived to the farthest Western point of the continent, at Lisbon, the site where the new Treaty of the architecture for a stronger Europe has been signed by the 27 Member States of the European Union.

"Non-Signatories" and the Long Arm of Arbitral Jurisdiction

VLADIMIR PAVIĆ

1. Introduction

Every "traditional" dispute resolution mechanism, be it litigation or arbitration, has a design built around compromise.

Litigation offers reassuring permanence of court offices, dignity and solemnity of the judicial apparatus and the promise that any mistakes of the lower tier might be rectified at a higher instance. At the same time, rectification might come at a high cost in time, money and subpar quality of decision making. In addition, the resulting judgment may be declared by a judge who is not necessarily well versed in the subject-matter and who is imposed on the parties by the state's "invisible hand."

Arbitration promises a relatively relaxed, flexible procedural surrounding, swift delivery of the final award and very limited opportunities for review. Judgment is handed over by those regarded by the parties to be true experts fit for the job. However, setting arbitration in motion requires undertaking certain preparatory steps by the parties. The cornerstone of arbitration proceedings, since the very beginning, has been the arbitration agreement. It is the arbitration agreement that provides mandate for the arbitrators, determines the scope of the subject-matters they can rule on, and sometimes even sets a map of procedural and substantive rules to be followed. Arbitration agreement is the beginning and the end of all things arbitral, so much so that it is often regarded as the single most important and defining feature of arbitration.[1]

---

[1] French Cour de cassation, 27 July 1937, Roses v. Moller et Cie I Dalloz 25 (1938). For overview of discussion on contractual nature of arbitration see Fouchard/Gaillard/Goldman, On International Commercial Arbitration, sec. 44–57; J. Lew, L. Mistelis, S. Kroell, Comparative International Commercial Arbitration, Kluwer Law International 2003, p. 77 et seq. with further references.

However, the view on what the essence of arbitration is has been anything but uniform. A fair number of authors pointed out that while the whole process is about delivering justice and contracted for and organized privately, its end result is to produce a decision whose standing equals court judgment. It was submitted that the primary feature of arbitration is to displace jurisdiction of state courts, and that this mission was more important than the means of accomplishing it.[2]

As it often happens, both sides ("jurisdictionalists" and "contractualists") were right to a certain degree. Arbitration did take off because states actually allowed it to take off, and it was permitted to develop in the shadow of the existing systems of the judiciary. At the same time, this alternative way of settling disputes could only be initiated if there was agreement of the parties to resort to it. It was a way of asking parties if they "really, truly want" to displace regular recourse to courts. This trade-off promised them a relaxed and supposedly less costly procedure, after the initial transaction costs of concluding an arbitration agreement.

As arbitration became a primary dispute resolution choice of those engaged in international transactions, the limitations of such a compromise design began to show. Litigation could quickly attract additional parties with rights and obligations inextricably linked to the original controversy. Attraction of jurisdiction is a powerful tool of the judiciary which can greatly maximize its efficiency. Yet this possibility was denied to the arbitrators: they could adjudicate only a dispute between the parties to the arbitration agreement. In most cases this meant that there was a total of two parties unambiguously opting out of court adjudication. However, just as the models used by economists cannot possibly capture the complexity of everyday interactions, the two-party design of the arbitration agreement is every now and then less than adequate when it comes to encompassing transactions that involve several actors.

One way of dealing with this problem is to anticipate it. If the web of relationships is complex (as it often is in, e.g. construction projects), so should be the pertinent clause. Drafting arbitration agreements for possible multi-party arbitration is anything but straightforward. Its goal is to

[2] The most forceful jurisdictional argument was probably made by F. A. Mann in "Lex Facit Arbitrum," in P. Sanders, ed., *Liber Amicorum Martin Domke*, The Hague 1957, p. 158 et seq. As far as case law is concerned, the high water mark so far is perhaps a judgment of the Supreme Court of Columbia commented in A. M. Garro, "The Colombia Supreme Court Holds Unconstitutional the Participation of Foreign Arbitrators Under the New Arbitration Law," *1 American Review of International Arbitration* 594 (1990).

test the original two-party design of arbitration without seriously distorting it—and so is the *Anpassung* of provisions related to appointment of arbitrators and other matters.[3]

Another way of dealing with the problem is to cooperate: if the dispute clearly seems to reach the parties not having concluded the arbitration agreement originally, there is nothing to stop them from executing another one and embracing arbitration as their preferred method of dispute settlement. However, expecting a potential debtor to submit to arbitration and forego a potentially time-wasting jurisdictional challenge might prove too optimistic.

The final way of testing the limits of arbitral design is, therefore, confrontational. As a rule, an arbitration agreement should be in writing or evidenced in writing—more often than not this also means that the parties have affixed their signatures to it. There are generally two possible scenarios for the entities not appearing to be parties to the arbitration agreement to enter the stage: one is the role of the claimant, alone or alongside the party whose participation is non-contestable; another is at the receiving end, as the sole or an additional respondent. Given the traditional setting of "an agreement in writing, signed by both parties," such third parties have repeatedly been referred to as "non-signatories."

This paper will try to shed some light on the pattern of "extension": not on the situation where one of the parties (through different mechanisms) is replaced by another party stepping into its shoes, but rather a situation where a third party appears before arbitration *despite* the fact that it does not appear as a party to the arbitration agreement.[4] This either happens when a third party attempts to join the side of the claimant, alongside original claimants—or, even more controversially, where the claimant tries to reach beyond the obvious respondents and get to the solvent companies which are not the named parties of the arbitration agreement.

---

[3] The raw data routinely presented at arbitration conferences suggests that, at least when it comes to major institutional arbitration centers, the multiparty disputes are nowadays a rule rather than exception.

[4] For other aspects of arbitration despite the parties see T. Várady, "Arbitration Despite the Parties," in M. Sumampouw et al. eds., *Law and Reality, Essays on national and international procedural law in Honour of Cornelis Carel Albert Voskuil*, The Hague 1992, p. 351.

2. Is the Signature Relevant at All?

Traditionally, paramount importance has been accorded to a written arbitration agreement. Therefore, it is only logical that the first line of defense of non-signatories would be formal: they have not signed the agreement, hence there is no written form evidencing their consent. Basically, this amounts to declaring that extension of the arbitration agreement to a non-signatory is a contradiction in terms.

However, the signature itself has already been abandoned as the formal prerequisite to an effective arbitration agreement. The 1958 New York Convention provided that the term "agreement in writing" includes:

> (...) arbitral clause in a contract or an arbitration agreement, signed by the parties or contained in an exchange of letters or telegrams.[5]

It appears that the agreement to arbitrate has to be evidenced in writing, but need not be accompanied by signatures, at least not in the traditional sense of physical alteration or imposition made on paper or comparable material. The second milestone of modern arbitration, 1985 UNCITRAL Model Law on International Commercial Arbitration (Model Law), further relaxed the writing requirement by providing that the agreement may be contained in, *inter alia*:

> (...) exchange of letters, telex, telegrams or other means of telecommunications which provide a record of the agreement, or in exchange of statements of claim and defense in which the existence of an agreement is alleged by one party and not denied by another.[6]

Liberalisation of form requirements gained additional ground in the 2006 Model Law revision: there are now two options to the model. According to the first one, a written agreement exists if it was recorded in any form, regardless of the form of initial conclusion (oral, by conduct, or otherwise). The second option is even more radical and basically amounts to doing away with the requirement of writing altogether.[7]

---

[5] New York Convention, Article II.2. See generally N. Kaplan, "Is the Need for Writing as Expressed in the New York Convention and the Model Law out of Step with Commercial Practice?" [1996] 12 *Arbitration International* 1, 27; M.M. Cohen, "Arbitration 'Agreements in Writing': Notes in the Margin of the Sixth Goff Lecture" [1997] 13 *Arbitration International* 3, 273.

[6] Article 7 of the 1986 version of the Model Law.

[7] Article 7, Options I and II of the 2006 version of the Model Law.

Most of the jurisdictions still impose somewhat more stringent requirements of writing. However, even in such circumstances, bringing a party which does not appear as a signatory to the written arbitration agreement has proved to be less difficult as of lately. The Swiss Supreme Court had to address the "no agreement in writing" defense of non-signatory respondents. When deciding a similar issue in the context of forum selection clauses, it decided that the requirement of writing was impossible to circumvent.[8] However, in a recent decision the relevance of writing and signature was all but dispensed with when it came to non-signatories of the arbitration agreement.

In that case, three companies entered into a written agreement containing the arbitration clause.[9] Subsequently the fourth, non-signatory party, repeatedly interfered with performance and implementation of the originally concluded contract. Should such a party be bound to the terms of the contract? One of the defenses invoked was that, on the face of it, there was no written piece evidencing its consent to be bound by the arbitration agreement. The court disagreed and held that formal requirements (contained in Article 178(1) of the Swiss PIL[10]) need only be satisfied with regard to the *initial* conclusion of the arbitration agreement. The issue of *ratione personae* scope of the arbitration clause was, therefore, not regarded as an issue of formal, but rather of material validity. Consequently, as long as the clause initially satisfied the requirement of form, its extension to non-signatories cannot be objected to on purely formal grounds.[11]

This solution came under a forceful attack, and the primary objection was that it created two distinctly different sets of formal requirements, at least in the Swiss law: one applicable to the initial consent to arbitrate (requiring evidence in writing), and another to subsequent extension (which appeared to require no written evidence).[12] In essence, critics of the decision called for uniform formal requirements: if the original consent had at least to be "evidenced in writing," so should the potential sub-

[8] DTF 119 II 394.

[9] DTF 129 III 727.

[10] "Concerning form, an arbitration agreement is valid if it is made in writing, by telegram, telex, telecopier or any other means of communication that permits it to be evidenced by text."

[11] Some US courts have followed a similar reasoning, see the case law of the Second Circuit in *Fisser v. International Bank*, 82 F.2d 231 (2nd Cir. 1960), Interocean *Shipping Co. v. National Shipping and Trading Corp.*, 523 F.2d 527 (2nd Cir. 1975).

[12] J. Poudret, S. Besson, *Comparative Law of International Commercial Arbitration*, London 2007, p. 221.

sequent consent bringing another party to arbitration. Otherwise, the cardinal principle of form requirements covering all *essentialia negotii* would be overridden, since the identity of the parties to the contract would not have to satisfy the requirement of form.[13]

However, a strict application of formal requirements to all signatories would create effects not consistent with the goals of introducing the written form in the first place. There are various ways in which contractual obligations may be transferred to another party (assumption, assignment, transfer). Since transfer of such obligations is usually not subject to any formalities, an unintended consequence of a uniform formal regime would be that the obligation (or the entire contract) would indeed be transferred to another party, and yet the arbitration agreement would not. A uniform treatment would be justified if the subject matter of the contract was the reason for imposing formal requirements (e.g. transfer of real estate).[14]

Accepting the lack of formalities as a bar to the extension of an arbitration agreement to non-signatories would in effect prevent extension (as defined in this paper) altogether. However, those exceptions do happen rather frequently in arbitral practice. The essence of controversy then becomes not the signature, writing or the lack thereof, but rather the indispensable requirement of the parties" consent. Although the roadmap of such extensions is highly casuistic, it is possible to discern some of the recurring patterns.

3. The "Real Parties"

If the matter is not one of form, then everything usually boils down to the notion of "consent." Tribunals have been increasingly eager to broaden their jurisdictional scope to include the parties that are not parties to the contract. Justification for such an extension was highly dependent on the particular fact patterns. However, if any generalization could be made, it is that two components were required: the first one was objective—that a non-signatory took "active and substantial part" in the negotiation and/or performance of the main contract, or that it had "interfered" with it.[15] In

[13] Habegger, op.cit., p. 403.

[14] DTF 110 II 342.; D. Girsberger, Art 165 CO N 9 in Honsell, Vogt & Wiegand, eds., *Kommentar zum Schweizerischen Privatrecht, Obligationenrecht I*, 2nd ed., 1996.

[15] On interference as a sufficient reason for extension see DFT 129 III 727 (4P.115/2003), ASA Bulletin 2/2004, 364.

addition, this objective element has to give rise to a subjective element: precisely because of its involvement with the contract, the signatory was aware of the existence of arbitration agreement and its contents.[16]

In practice, however, observance of these two minimal requirements for extension resulted in rather different approaches and outcomes.

3. 1. "Group of Companies"

The most controversial of those was the extension over non-signatories based on the "groups of companies" doctrine, which is sometimes used to bring non-signatories into arbitration. The case that started it all was the ICC interim award in *Dow Chemical*.[17] The parent company of the entire Dow Chemical "network" appeared as a claimant alongside its other subsidiaries that actually signed the agreement. When the parent company's *locus standi* was objected to, the tribunal cleared the ground for the parent in two steps. First, it determined that the arbitration agreement was not to be examined in accordance with any particular national law (including the French law, as the law of the seat). This allowed the tribunal to circumvent different legal personalities of the companies and concentrate on what it labeled as "usages": the fact that those dealing with vast multinationals are expected to deal with the whole group at once, no matter which particular company within the group actually negotiated. The group was "economic reality" and, given that the parent company participated in the negotiation and conclusion of the contract, and completely controlled the operations of its subsidiaries, the extension was justified.

This was, however, a situation where the "group of companies" presented itself on the side of the claimant. When they find themselves in the roles of the respondents, those same groups are much keener on asserting the distinct and separate legal personalities of their subsidiaries. However, once the door was opened in *Dow Chemical*, it was hard to close it, and another French case, *Sponsor v. Lestrade*, saw the extension of arbitration agreement over the parent company since it had participated in the con-

[16] B. Stucki, "Extension of Arbitration Agreements to Non-Signatories," paper presented at ASA Below 40 Conference held on September 29, 2006., http://www.arbitration-ch.org/below-40/pdf/extension-bs.pdf *sec* 14.

[17] ICC Award no. 4131, upheld by Paris Cour d'appel, October 21, 1983, Rev. Arb 1084, p. 98 (Chapelle). For a detailed analysis see S. Gravel, P. Peterson, "French Law and Arbitration Clauses—Distinguishing Scope from Validity: Comment on ICC case no 6519 Final Award" (1992) *McGill Law Journal* 510.

clusion and performance of the contract, inspiring and masterminding the whole deal.[18]

Invoking the "group of companies" doctrine has remained, to a great extent, a kind of legal alchemy, and is essentially restricted to France. Only in France do the courts view arbitration agreements as subject to no particular national law. Consequently, once their validity is to be determined purely on the basis of the "will of the parties" and "international usages," it is tempting to find consent where there was none, and usage where there was hardly any.

Development of the "group of companies" doctrine follows a pattern reminiscent of the reforms recorded in ancient legal regimes: the one where rites involving bronze tablets and solemn oaths were replaced by simple, down-to-earth promises. Old constructs are sacrificed in favor of economic reality. However, there is more to the "group of companies" than that—it sacrifices the very notion of a separate legal personality. Traditionally, the veil of a legal personality was lifted only when it came to fraud; the "group of companies" doctrine practically lifts it even where there was no wrongdoing. It comes as no surprise that other major arbitral jurisdictions reject the notion of the "group of companies."[19]

However, once one embarks on such an approach to extension, two further dilemmas await: the first is whether it works both ways, i.e. whether it can be utilized for a parent to bind subsidiaries just as it can be applied in the situations where the parent appears as a non-signatory. Consistent with the *Dow Chemical* case, there are reports that other tribunals have also answered affirmatively.[20]

The other dilemma is whether the "group of companies" doctrine dispenses with the requirement of consent altogether. In other words, is the link alone, the common economic roof and the "chain of command," enough to draw in other entities within the group? Does participation in the group create a presumption that all the members consented to all arbitration clauses signed by other members, or is consent still to be determined independently? In the *Sarhank* case, a tribunal sitting in Cairo and, subsequently, the Second Circuit Court in the U.S. took opposing views. The tribunal's justification for

[18] Pau Cour d'appel, Rev. Arb. 1988., p. 153 (Chapelle).

[19] J. Poudret, S. Besson, op.cit. pp. 220 et seq.; S. P. Woolhouse, "Group of Companies Doctrine and English Arbitration Law," 20 *Arbitration International* (2004) 435; *City of London v. Sancheti* [2008] EWCA Civ 1283, overturning *Roussel-Uclaf v GD Searle & Co Ltd* [1978] 1 Lloyd's Rep 225.

[20] J. Savage, T. A. Leen, "Family Ties: when arbitration agreements bind non-signatory affiliate companies," *Asian Dispute Review* (2003) 16, p. 17.

extending jurisdiction over the signatory's parent company was founded on the impression that "contractual relations cannot take place without the consent of the parent company." The U.S. court disagreed, stating that certain "objective intention to agree to arbitrate" had to be present.[21]

Tribunals (even those based outside France) might at times be persuaded by the reasoning of the *Dow Chemicals*. However, their liberalism does not fare well with the courts of the *lex loci arbitri*. In *Peterson Farms*, a London-based tribunal extended jurisdiction on the basis of "group of companies." However, an English court later overturned this jurisdictional stretch on two accounts: one was that the issue of the parties" consent had to be examined in accordance with a national law. The second was that none of the potentially applicable substantive frameworks (those of England or Arkansas) knew of such doctrine.[22]

It would be hard to see this doctrine flourishing outside France, even if its restrained aspect, where a common economic group represents an indication, rather than a presumption, of a tacit approval of the arbitration agreement by the other members of the group, is advocated. The application of the doctrine in its original form is possible only if the arbitration agreement is free of any national law constraints and examined in the light of more ethereal legal notions, such as "transnational law" or "*lex mercatoria.*" Once the examination is reverted to the realm of national law, the notions of "common economic destiny" would have to be substantiated under some of the already available and tested legal institutions. The list of invoked principles and theories is extensive, and certainly non-exclusive,[23] with several of them deserving further investigation.

3. 2. Agency

There are several mechanisms in place that to a different degree justify the arbitration agreement extension to parties who not originally signing it.

---

[21] *Sarhank v. Oracle Corporation*, 404 F.3d 657 (2nd Cir. 2005) at 662.

[22] *Peterson Farms Inc. v. C&M Farming Ltd* (2004) All. E.R. (D) 50, 67.

[23] According to J. M. Hosking, there are at least twelve bases on which extension is attempted or carried out (in addition to the "group of companies" doctrine): assignment, subrogation, third party beneficiary, novation, incorporation by reference, agency, estoppel/equitable estoppel, assumption of obligation, succession, "single economic transaction" and equity. See J. Hosking, "Non-Signatories and International Arbitration in the United States: the Quest for Consent," *Arbitration International*, Vol. 20 No. 3 (2004) 289, 290. Not all of those made it to this paper, not only because different denomination sometimes obscures reliance on similar or almost identical grounds for extension.

Unquestionably, a successor company taking over inherits the rights and obligations that the predecessor enjoyed. The effects of such universal succession among juridical persons are usually determined pursuant to either the law of the place of incorporation, or pursuant to the provisions of the jurisdiction where the seats are located.[24]

Another possibility to include a party not named in the arbitration agreement would be under the provisions of agency.[25] Unlike the "group of companies" doctrine, this is a fairly traditional concept which may be used to go beyond and reach for the principal (but it would rarely be possible to use it to reach downwards, to the subsidiary of a company having signed the agreement). Still, the rules in this area differ so much among various jurisdictions and are so complex that a tribunal might be excused for taking a shortcut and shunning away the conflict of law rules.

One approach is based on filtering agency (explicit or apparent) through the prism of applicable national rules. Tribunals indeed sometimes distinguish among rules applicable to the arbitration agreement itself, rules applicable to the agent's capacity to bind the principal, and those applicable to certain formal aspects of the agency relationship (such as the form of authorization and impact of the lack of form on binding the principal).[26]

Even more importantly, it is probably the applicable national law which would also answer whether, and under what conditions, the agent was vested with apparent authority.[27] If the agency was disclosed, the agreement would bind the principal only—for someone appearing as a claimant this will, for the most part, be satisfactory if the principal alone is sufficient to meet terms of the award sought. If the agency was apparent, it might be possible for the claimant to drag in both the principal and the agent, but only if the agent also acted in its name.[28] However, such justification should not act as a covert replacement of the group of companies doctrine. Although all corporations do represent their owners to some degree, this does not subject all owners to the agreements of their corpora-

[24] A. Redfern, M. Hunter, op.cit. at 3–36.

[25] C. B. Lamm, J. A. Aqua, "Defining the party—who is a proper party in an international arbitration before the American arbitration association and other international institutions," 34 *The George Washington International Law Review* (2003) 721 at 724 et seq.

[26] ICC case no 5832 (1988) Journal du Droit International 1198.

[27] Some advocate that apparent authority is a general principle of international commerce and that there is no need to get into conflict methodology and examine national rules to judge its effects, see Ch. Jarrosson, *La Notion d'arbitrage*, Paris 1987, pp. 225 et seq.

[28] J. Poudret, S. Besson, op.cit. p. 212.

tions.[29] While agency is a well-established fiduciary relationship, it is always recommendable to exercise caution when confronted with an agent. One court even suggested that agency, due to its complexity and initially unpredictable outcomes for those involved,

> "(...) should be a danger signal, and like a railroad crossing, suggests a duty to stop, look and listen."[30]

Finding middle ground might be difficult. On the one hand, the impression on the third party might be sufficiently strong to warrant finding that there was an apparent authority: e.g. if both the principal and agent use identical logos, utilize one another's form contract, and bring into play the term "branch" to describe their relationship. Even if they are separate legal entities, this creates an apparent mandate in the eyes of a third party.[31] However, at the same time, a party relying on apparent authority without at least investing purported powers of representation might later find it hard to compel non-signatory to arbitrate.[32]

3. 3. Extension without Consent

Reaching beyond the signatories is, in most of the cases, the issue of consent and contract. The "group of companies" doctrine is a borderline case: while still usually founded on consent, it uses "economic reality" as a tool with which to overcome the difficulties related to the proof of intent.[33] However, including a non-signatory is sometimes not an issue of its consent, but rather a sanction for its behavior. Here, again, traditional concepts are used, together with the inevitable hodgepodge of comparative legal terminology and the resulting terror of nuances.

"Piercing of the corporate veil" has been frequently mentioned in the context of the "group of companies" doctrine.[34] However, mixing the two

---

[29] C.A. Corrie, "Challenges in International Arbitation for Non-Signatories," *Comparative Law Yearbook of International Business*, Vol. 29 (2007) 45, at p. 54.

[30] *Racicky v. Farmland Industries Inc.*, 328 F.3d 389, 393 (8th Cir., 2003).

[31] T. Zuberbuehler, "Non-Signatories and the Consensus to Arbitrate," *ASA Bulletin*, 26, No.1 (2008), 18 at 20.

[32] Ibid. at 21.

[33] See, e.g. classification of the "group of companies" doctrine as the extension not based on consent in D. Vidal, "The Extension of Arbitration Agreements within Groups of Companies: The Alter Ego Doctrine in Arbitral and Court Decisions," *ICC International Court of Arbitration Bulletin* Vol. 16 No. 2 (2005) 63 at pp. 70–71.

[34] A. Redfern, M. Hunter, op.cit. at 3–31.

is not necessary: piercing is an extreme remedy for situations where the company owner abuses the separation of legal persons. If the company invokes legal separation as a liability shield, corporate veil is pierced in order to prevent unjust results. Similar concepts are argued in the United States under the headings of "confusion" and "fraud" in order to achieve the same result—getting to the real owners. Although piercing the veil does lead to the arbitration clause extension to a non-signatory owner, there have been occasional observations that the arbitration clause extension is not a proper sanction for liability.[35] Moreover, piercing is an extreme remedy also from the point of view of (usually) the claimant. Once the veil is pierced, the owners of the pierced entity will be liable *instead*, rather than alongside it.

The principle of estoppel (or *venire contra factum proprium*) has also been often invoked in order to bring a non-signatory into arbitration. One is not allowed to contradict itself to the detriment of others. Or as the common law theory of equitable estoppel would put it, equitable estoppel precludes a party from asserting rights it would otherwise have where such assertion would be contrary to equity.[36] This usually amounts to situations where a party has been deriving a direct (and not merely incidental) benefit from the contract signed by someone else, provided that the non-signatory had sufficient information about the existence and content of the arbitration clause and failed to object to it.[37]

The outer limits of the extension without consent may be found in the ICC cases 7604 and 7610 (1995). There, a claimant initiated arbitration not only against the company which had actually signed the contract, but also against its parent company as a second respondent. The extension was sought on the basis that the parent company had participated in the negotiation and performance of the contract. Such a construction was rejected. Instead, the extension was granted on another basis: in a dispute initiated before an Algerian court, the parent company objected to the jurisdiction of the court and submitted that all the parties had agreed to submit the dispute to the ICC. The Tribunal concluded that the second

---

[35] T. Zuberbuehler, op.cit. 28.

[36] *First Union Commercial Corp.* vs. *Nelson, Mullins, Riley & Scarborough* (*In re Varat Enters., Inc.*), 81 F.3d 1310, 1317 (4th Cir. 1996); *Lowery* vs. *Stovall*, 92 F.3d 219, 223 (4th Cir. 1996). *Grigson v. Creative Artists Agency, LLC*, 210 F.3d 524 (5th Cir. 2004). See also A. A. Hui, "Equitable Estoppel and the Compulsion of Arbitration," 60 *Vanderbilt Law Review* (2007) 711.

[37] A. Redfern, M. Hunter at 3–32 with further references.

respondent could not have it both ways, and that its objection to the court jurisdiction precluded it from objecting to the jurisdiction of the tribunal.[38]

4. Subsequent Court Control

The justifications offered above are among those that are, to a different degree, founded on law. However, it is always tempting to substantiate one's pleadings with the depiction of adverse (or beneficial) consequences that might stem from a tribunal's decision to grant or refuse extension of jurisdiction over a non-signatory. Thus it is not uncommon for a party pleading for extension to base its argument on equity, efficiency of the entire justice process, or on similar considerations. Absent express *ex aequo et bono* mandate, arbitrators are generally not allowed to wander into equity territory while ignoring the letter of applicable rules. Taking the equity shortcut is tempting, not only because it is technically easier than applying the law. On the other hand, arbitrators do not operate in a world of their own, and resolution of disputes is certainly not irreconcilable with the idea of fairness.[39]

Therefore, when confronted with the vague notions of equity, efficiency of procedure and avoidance of multiple fora, arbitrators are well advised not to base their jurisdictional decision solely on such considerations. Instead, various policy reasons may be invoked as additional, supporting and persuasive grounds which should, in the eyes of parties and courts, cement the foundations of the decision to extend jurisdiction.[40]

The final award is usually subject to two filters: one at the seat of arbitration and another at the place of recognition and enforcement.[41] While the latter type of control is carried out in an almost uniform manner (under the New York Convention Article V provisions), the former is subject to relatively disparate systems which are increasingly being harmonized

---

[38] For further details, see B. Hanoitau, *Complex Arbitrations, Kluwer Law International*, 2006, p. 62.

[39] T. Zuberbuehler, op.cit. 30.

[40] B. Hanoitau, op.cit 48 cites an unpublished *ad hoc* award which did exactly that—used equity as oblique justification for a legal conclusion it arrived at.

[41] In addition, if the objection to jurisdiction over non-signatory has been dealt with in a separate (preliminary, interim) decision, it is generally possible to challenge such decision before courts of the *lex loci arbitri* even before the final award is given. *Brevitatis causae*, this avenue of challenging decision to extend jurisdiction has not been dealt with in this paper.

pursuant to the growing popularity of the UNCITRAL Model Law. Still, the discrepancies remain. When arbitrators are based in a country whose legal system has a liberal attitude towards bringing non-signatories into arbitration, resulting awards might prove to be unenforceable in other jurisdictions. Conversely, if arbitrators disregard conservative attitude of *lex loci arbitri* in favour of a liberal approach of the likely enforcement jurisdictions, they risk the award being quashed immediately in the proceeding for setting aside.

Attempting annulment or refusing enforcement on the grounds that one was not a party to the arbitration agreement is open only to the party not having entered the fray itself. A non-signatory party, once it clears any objections from the opposite side and joins the proceedings, is estopped from later claiming that it was not a party to the original agreement.

On the face of it, one of the possible grounds that a non-signatory may invoke against the arbitral award is contained in Article V 1(a) of the NYC and Article 34 (2) (a) (ii) of the Model Law, that is, that the award, *inter alia*, is based on invalidity of the arbitration agreement. Logically, this reason for setting aside would also be applicable where the agreement did not exist at all—at least from the perspective of one of the parties. However, it has been submitted that the wording of those provisions does not allow for sanctioning of excess jurisdiction established over a non-signatory, but only for determination whether the agreement was formally and materially valid to start with.[42] This, in effect, means that the "validity" is examined *in abstracto*. There are, however, certain national legislations where this basis for annulment is worded in such a manner that it actually encompasses a wider set of jurisdictional insufficiencies.[43] If a non-signatory invokes invalidity (understood broadly) or lack of jurisdiction (if so formulated) as grounds for setting aside, court will have to assess this in accordance with the law of the country of the arbitration seat (since parties rarely choose the law applicable to arbitration agreement, even implicitly).

Another ground which might be invoked is the one contained in Article V 1(c) of the NYC and Article 34(2)(a)(iii) of the Model Law: that the award is dealing with

> (...) a difference not contemplated by or falling within the terms of the submission to arbitration, or it contains decisions on matters beyond the scope of the submission to arbitration, (...).

---

[42] J. Poudret, S. Besson, op.cit. p. 729.

[43] English Arbitration Act, sec. 67: Swiss Private International Law Art. 190(2)(b).

At first glance, the wording plainly means that the tribunal should not rule beyond prayers of relief of the parties (*ultra petita*) or decide on a subject matter which falls outside of the matter conferred to the tribunal by the parties (*extra potestatem*). Again, a logical extension of this reason for annulment/refusal of recognition would be to allow it to sanction not only the infraction appearing to be in excess of the requested relief or outside the subject matter conferred, but also to jurisdictional overreach which has been exercised against a person not having been a party to the arbitration agreement. In other words, since a party has never submitted to arbitration, there could be no "terms of submission" which would cover its participation.[44] This is the only reason of opposition explicitly mentioning the possibility of partial annulment or partial recognition, so that the excess is eliminated and the "sound" part of the award is allowed to stand.[45] However, deciding on what "excess" is in cases involving non-signatories might be more difficult than it looks on the face of it. Where a non-signatory is found to be jointly liable together with a signatory, the separation is not difficult.

There could be an additional, if erroneous, way to disguise challenge based on the lack of arbitration agreement (at least towards a party) as a "lack of arbitrability." The proper basis of challenge under the Model Law and opposition in the system of the NYC is the lack of "subject-matter arbitrability"[46] and not of the "ordinary arbitrability" (which would cover validity, existence and scope).[47] It is not, then, that the subject matter was not effectively submitted to arbitration, but rather that the subject-matter itself is not capable of being settled by arbitration. In other words, the award would be deficient even if the lack of signature (and consent) was not an issue at all.

Finally, one could attempt to argue that the enforcement of awards which are not consent-based is contrary to public policy. Although this

---

[44] As observed with regard to erroneous Sarhank decision on at least two occasions. See B. H. Garfinkel, D. Iherlihy, "Looking for Law in All the Wrong Places: The Second Circuit's Decision in Sarhank Group v. Oracle Corporation," 20–6 *Mealey's International Arbitration Report* (2005) 12; B. Hanoitau, op.cit. 231.

[45] However, the fact that this was mentioned explicitly only in respect to this ground does not mean that other grounds cannot be used to exact minimal damage and annul or refuse recognition only with respect of a part of the award, if it is separable from the rest. See J. Poudret, S. Besson op.cit. p. 874.

[46] Article V(2)(a) of the New York Convention.

[47] The term "ordinary arbitrability" and its scope is borrowed from J. J. Barceló III, "Anti-Foreign-Suit Injunctions to Enforce Arbitration Agreements," Cornell Law School research paper No. 07-024, http://ssrn.com/abstract=1030403

ground for annulment and/or non-enforcement to be examined *ex officio*, it is more likely to be introduced by the resisting party than by the court eager to substitute it as ground for annulment instead of the one invoked by the party. When that happens, the court in charge of annulment will use *lex fori* public policy as guidance. The same can be expected of the recognition and enforcement court in another country, although in that case the use of less stringent "international public policy" test has been advocated for quite some time when foreign decisions are scrutinized.[48] Public policy is argued "when points fail,"[49] and it is not easy to see why its efficiency against the awards involving non-signatories would not be particularly impressive. In countries which openly favour extension concepts which are predominantly economic (e.g. France), public policy challenge might be worthless.

5. Concluding Remarks

One would be hard pressed not to be ambivalent towards the ever repeating efforts of the parties to extend the arbitration agreement so that its scope includes the parties that have not affixed their signatures to it. This ambivalence is the inevitable consequence of the friction between two parallel pillars of arbitration: its contractual basis and its "judicial" aspirations.

There is a lot to be said in favor of reaching beyond signatories, especially when it comes to procedural efficiency and overall efficiency of the distribution of justice. If one rigidly sticks to the two-party model and ignores the reality behind these two clear manifestations of willingness to arbitrate, the tribunal will end up not really arbitrating the proper controversy, and will instead adjudicate a mere fragment of it. The efficiency argument is powerful, and it has gained steadily in importance as the arbitration grew in stature.

However, there are limitations to this argument, one of the most important being the consent of the parties. There are ways to work around the requirement of signature or even written form in order to reach an equitable and just result. However, this should not be done at the expense of

[48] Sometimes this is explicitly spelled out in domestic legislation (which, pursuant to article VII of the NYC, can be availed of): Article 1498 and 1502 of the. Even when the legislator has not introduced such distinction, courts have underlined it, see e.g. BGH 18. 01. 1990. XVII YBCA 503 (1992). See also Fouchard/Gaillard/Goldman at sec. 1711.

[49] *Richardson v. Melish* 2 Bing 229, 252 (1824).

sound legal reasoning, and the shortcuts involving concepts not grounded in law are not destined to do well in all of the major arbitration jurisdictions. At the same time, there will be sound legal approaches which might not invoke the parties" consent as justification to extend the operation of the clause. The further one gets from the notion of "consent" and firm legal reasoning, the slimmer the chances that the award will fare well after being rendered.

Somewhat surprisingly, the two main arbitration documents (the UNCITRAL Model Law and the New York Convention) are not equipped with tools specifically designed to deal with unjust extension of the scope of the clause. It is possible, however, to found a successful challenge on the basis of their provisions—it is just that it does not appear to be as straightforward as it is in the case of other alleged irregularities. Naturally, the way in which some of the Model Law jurisdictions (and some jurisdictions which have not followed the Model Law way) have phrased their grounds of annulment allows for easier choice. The broader the notion of challenge ("jurisdiction"), the more it will hold. The implementation of the New York Convention and operation of its Article VII prevent this at the stage of recognition and enforcement, and the opposing party may not expect anything but the original wording of the treaty.

These differences underline the importance of the seat chosen. Given that the breadth of control will vary more at the annulment stage than at the ones of recognition and enforcement, and given the different attitudes among major arbitral jurisdictions towards certain aspects and justifications for arbitration agreement extension, the initial choice of seat will to a great extent determine the later dynamics of deliberation and the willingness of the tribunal to go beyond the letter of the agreement.

The Pendulum Swings Back: The Cooperative Approach of German Courts to International Service of Process

HANS-ERIC RASMUSSEN-BONNE

1. Introduction

As the German Federal Minister of Justice points out in the new brochure "Law—Made in Germany," Law is becoming an important competitive factor and export good in an era of accelerated economic globalization.[1] This publication is the German "Me too"—reaction to the earlier English equivalent "England and Wales. The jurisdiction of choice,"[2] which has considerably annoyed German professional organizations.[3] Both initiatives trumpet the success story of one's own law as being the ultimate and preferable source of a predictable and reliable legal system. These publications are mainly sponsored marketing measures and strive to take or keep the lead in the "fight for the applicable law" or—less sensational—in the competition of national legal systems in a globalized world. They are informative but sound a wrong note and do not advance the necessary judicial cooperation in international legal transactions. The legal community should rather devote more time and energy to understanding the differences of legal systems,[4] discussing and drafting model laws dealing

---

[1] The brochure has been published by the German Federal Chamber of civil law notaries (*Bundesnotarkammer*), German Federal Bar (*Bundesrechtsanwaltskammer*), German Bar Association (*Deutscher Anwaltsverein*), German Notaries' Association (*Deutscher Notarverein*) and German Judges Association (*Deutscher Richterbund*).

[2] http://www.lawsociety.org.uk/documents/downloads/jurisdiction_of_choice_brochure.pdf.

[3] See the interview "Das deutsche Recht hat an Boden verloren" with *Hartmut Kilger*, president of the German Bar Asscociation in Frankfurter Allgemeine Zeitung of December 27, 2008, 12.

[4] Such as *Várady/Barceló/von Mehren*, International Commercial Arbitration. A Transnational Perspective, 3. ed. 2006; ALI/Unidroit Principles and Rules of Transnational Civil Procedure, 2006; *Krätzschmar*, "Der deutsch-amerikanische Rechtsverkehr—mehr als nur ein 'Justizkonflikt,'" in *Rasmussen-Bonne/Freer/Lüke/Weitnauer*, Balancing of Interests. Liber Amicorum Peter Hay (2005), 241; dealing with systemic differences be-

with international issues, such as the Convention for the International Sale of Goods, the various UNCITRAL model laws, the New York Convention on the Recognition and Enforcement of Foreign Arbitral Awards, and last, but not least the Convention on the Service Abroad of Judicial and Extrajudicial Documents in Civil and Commercial Matters (Hague Service Convention)[5] than to put up such fences. Model laws and conventions underline the need for and are instruments of international cooperation, if they are interpreted in accordance with their international origin.

The following remarks reflect upon the current status of the cooperation between Germany and the United States in the area of service of process in Civil and Commercial matters. The Hague Service Convention is designed to simplify intergovernmental judicial assistance. Its Contracting states decided to support the enforcement of foreign claims to jurisdiction resulting from the engagement in global legal transactions. Therefore, the Hague Service Convention shall—within limits to be discussed hereinafter—not be used as a battlefield for fights about legal institutions unknown to the other Contracting states' law.

Furthermore, the article focuses on the increasing relevance of direct postal service permitted under certain conditions by Art. 10 of the Hague Service Convention, Art. 14 of the Regulation (EC) 1393/2007, and by § 183 of the German Code of Civil Procedure (*Zivilprozeßordnung—ZPO*). Lastly, the article wants to develop the latest position of German Courts regarding service of process in the judicial cooperation between the United States and Germany. In this regard, it is of special interest whether the defense by the plaintiff that the statement of claim itself shows an egregious abuse of law is an argument effectively to block service. In this context, the responsibilities of the Central Authorities involved in the service process require some clarification.

---

tween U.S. and German Law and instruments to deal with them; *Stürner*, "Die verweigerte Zustellungshilfe für U.S.—Klagen oder der Schuss übers Grab," JZ 2006, 60, with a detailed analysis of the formal requirements of an action, notice pleading and service of process under U.S. Civil Procedure. To this end, the BVerfG has begun to publish English press releases and English versions of some decisions on its website http://www.bundesverfassungsgericht.de /en/index.html in October 2004.

[5] Federal Law Gazette (*Bundesgesetzblatt*) 1977 II, p. 1452.

II. The Rediscovery of Cooperation

II. 1. The Bertelsmann-Napster Case

In 2003, the Second Senate of the Federal Constitutional Court (*Bundesverfassungsgericht –BverfG*) had granted an interim order to protect the German media company Bertelsmann AG from service of a class action complaint filed by several music publishers and song writers in the United States District Court for the Southern District of New York.[6] The plaintiffs claimed $17 billion in compensatory damages on the theory that Bertelsmann had, by giving loans to the internet file-sharing platform Napster, prolonged its existence and contributed to the infringement of the plaintiffs' copyrights. The employees of Bertelsmann in Gütersloh/Germany refused to accept the service of process and such refusal triggered litigation before German courts with regard to legality of the service. In these proceedings, Bertelsmann argued that service of process should be rejected on the basis of Art. 13 of the Hague Service Convention which allows the requested state to refuse the service request "if it deems that compliance would infringe its sovereignty or security." The BVerfG found some merit in this argument and granted an interim order blocking service without hearing the American plaintiff. The interim order was prolonged several times. It was finally rescinded after Bertelsmann withdrew its constitutional complaint ("*Verfassungsbeschwerde*") in November 2005 and the parties settled the case not only through payments but also by means of Mergers & Acquisitions redistributing the market shares in the music industry. Therefore, the issues raised by the interim order were left unanswered by the Constitutional Court.[7] The Bertelsmann case has attracted a great deal of academic and business lawyers' comments;[8] most commentators perceived it as an unexpected

---

[6] 2 BvR 1198/2003, order of July 25, 2003, BVerfGE 108, 238 = NJW 2003, 2598.

[7] For a comprehensive contribution in English on the development of the proceedings, the legal issues and the settlement see *von Hein*, "Recent German Jurisprudence on Cooperation with the United States in Civil and Commercial Matters—A Defense of Sovereignty or Judicial Protectionism?," 101, in *Gottschalk/Michaels/Rühl/von Hein*, eds., Conflict of Laws in a Globalized World, 2007; *von Hein* is also the coauthor of an expert opinion on American law of service of process asked for by the BVerfG in the Bertelsmann-Napster case (*Hopt/Kulms/von Hein*, Rechtshilfe und Rechtsstaat, 2006).

[8] Comprehensive references at *Rasmussen-Bonne*, "Zum Stand der Rechtshilfepraxis bei Zustellungsersuchen von US-Schadensersatzklagen nach dem Beschluss des Bundesverfassungsgerichts vom 25. Juli 2003," 323, Fn. 4, in *Rasmussen-Bonne/Freer/Lüke/*

and surprising departure from a 1994 ruling of the First Senate which had displayed a rather liberal attitude ruling that the possible risk of having to pay punitive damages in an unspecified amount would not be a reason to block service.[9]

German Higher Regional Courts of Appeal (*Oberlandesgericht-OLG*) had responded to this interim order in the Bertelsmann case by either prohibiting to execute the service order and to transmit the certificate of service or at least staying proceedings involving American requests for service of process.[10] The OLG Koblenz took a more radical approach in its decision of June 27, 2005.[11] It denied the applicability of the Hague Service Convention in a class action brought by consumers and advocacy groups against various pharmaceutical companies, among them Boehringer Ingelheim GmbH & Co. KG ("Boehringer") in Minnesota federal Court. The action asserted several antitrust violations and sought treble damages. The Koblenz court declared the claim for treble damages not to be a "civil and commercial matter" within the scope of Art. 1 of the Hague Service Convention. In its view, such claims would rather belong to the realm of public law. At a minimum, service of process would violate German sovereignty. The U.S. proceedings seemed to have been initiated only to exert media pressure upon Boehringer: This fact alone should have prevented the U.S. Court from requesting service in the first place.[12]

Weitnauer, Balancing of Interests—Liber Amicorum Peter Hay, 2005; and *Schack*, "Ein unnötiger transatlantischer Justizkonflikt: die internationale Zustellung und das Bundesverfassungsgericht," AG 2006, 823; *Stürner* (supra Fn. 4); *Hopt/Kulms/v. Hein*, "Zur Zustellung einer US-amerikanischen Class Action in Deutschland," ZIP 2006, 973; *Koch/Horlach/Thiel*, "US-Sammelklage gegen deutsches Unternehmen," RIW 2006, 356; *Hess*, "Transatlantische Justizkonflikte," AG 2006, 809; *Schwung*, "Transatlantische Justizkonflikte aus Unternehmenssicht," AG 2006, 818 (from a business perspective).

[9] 1 BvR 1279/1994, order of December 7, 1994, BVerfGE 91, 335 = NJW 1995, 649; English analysis by *Lenhardt*, "Service of U.S. Punitive Damages Complaint passes Constitutional Muster in Germany," 29, Vand. J. Transnat'l Law 291 (2006).

[10] E.g. prohibiting to execute the service order and to transmit the certificate of service: OLG Hamburg, Order of May 11, 2004, 2 VA 3/04; OLG Naumburg, Order of October 12, 2004, 4 VA 1/04; Staying proceedings until final decision of the BVerfG: OLG Frankfurt, Orders of October 24, 2004, 20 VA 4/04 and 20 VA 5/04; see *Rasmussen-Bonne* (supra Fn. 8), 329 et seq. for case summaries and discussion.

[11] 12 VA 2/04, Order of June 27, 2005, IPRax 2006, p. 25; *Koch/Horlach/Thiel*, US-Sammelklage gegen deutsches Unternehmen, RIW 206, 356; *Piekenbrock*, Zur Zustellung kartellrechtlicher *treble damages*—Klagen in Deutschland, IPRax 2006, 4.

[12] 12 VA 2/04; IPRax 2006, 25, 34: Plaintiffs themselves would call their own conduct only "de facto legal."

Since the parties finally settled the case when a final US-judgment was rendered, the German Federal Court of Justice (*Bundesgerichtshof-BGH*) did not rule upon these issues.[13] However, several OLG had already clarified that they did not intend to follow the approach of the Koblenz court.[14]

II. 2. Recent Orders of the BVerfG

In contrast, the first chamber of the Second Senate of the BVerfG, which had granted the interim order in the Bertelsmann-Napster case, ruled on January 24, 2007 that service in an action for punitive damages did not violate "essential principles of a free state governed by the rule of law" ("*unverzichtbare Grundsätze eines freiheitlichen Rechtsstaats*"),[15] that is, fundamental constitutional principles. It did not admit the constitutional complaint for decision. The particularities of U.S. law, such as pre-trial discovery and the American rule on costs were insufficient reasons for blocking service. However, the Court left the door open for cases where the action itself and its service in Germany would appear from the outset to abuse the law.[16]

In another order of June 14, 2007,[17] rendered by the same chamber of the Second Senate, the Court confirmed its return to the rulings for class action lawsuits of the First Senate of 1994. The Court held that service of

[13] See *Stürner/Müller*, Aktuelle Entwicklungstendenzen im deutsch-amerikanischen Rechtshilfeverkehr, IPRax 2008, 339, 341 and Fn. 19.

[14] Either explicitly rejecting or distinguishing the Koblenz ruling are OLG Celle, 16 VA 4/05, order of July 20, 2006, JURIS = IPRspr 2006, Nr. 170; OLG München, 9 VA 03/04, order of June 7, 2006, IPRspr 2006, Nr. 168, 378; OLG Düsseldorf, I-3 VA 12/05, 3 VA 12/05, Order of April 21, 2006, JURIS = NJW-RR 2007, 640; OLG Naumburg, 4 VA 1/04, Order of February 9, 2006, JURIS = IPRspr 2006, Nr. 165, 357 and OLG Naumburg, 4 VA 1/05, Order of February 13, 2006 (unreported) continuing the stayed proceedings of supra Fn. 10 and granting the service request; OLG Frankfurt, order of March 30, 2006 (withdrawal of the complaint of supra Fn. 10); OLG Karlsruhe 10 VA 10/03, 1/04 and 13/03 of September 14, 2006 (unreported).

[15] 2 BvR 1133/04, RIW 2007, 211.

[16] Ibid, 212.

[17] 2 BvR 2247- 2249/06, Order of June 14, 2007, WM 2007, 1392 = NJW 2007, 3709 consolidating the constitutional complaints against the decisions of OLG Karlsruhe (supra Fn. 14). English version is downloadable at http//www.bverfg.de/entscheidungen/rk20070614_2bvr224706en.html. The complainants had also filed extraordinary complaints based on obvious illegality against the orders for service with the Federal Court of Justice (*Bundesgerichtshof-BGH*). The BGH dismissed these complaints in its orders IV AR (VZ) 2/07 of March 28, 2007, IPRax 2008, 349 as inadmissible; see on this issue *Stürner/Müller* (supra Fn. 13), 340.

an action based on a tort involving a multitude of injured parties without individual members of the class actively involved in the litigation did not violate fundamental constitutional principles. The Court stated further that compliance with international law limits by German state institutions when interpreting and applying Article 13 of the Hague Service Convention were not an end in itself; instead, only such compliance would ensure that the Hague Service Convention would also be honored by other Contracting States. Finally, adherence would help to avoid resort to others methods of service which would make the legal position of German defendants considerably more burdensome.

These decisions were applauded by most commentators[18] as a welcomed return to the 1994 ruling of the First Senate.

The most recent order of the Second Senate confirms and summarizes the earlier rulings.[19] Service may be refused if the objective and the specific circumstances of the legal action indicate that there has been an obvious abuse of process from the outset. Under these circumstances, service would violate fundamental constitutional principles. Indications of the commission of an abuse of process could usually be seen in the following facts which must be obvious from the outset:

- There is obviously no basis for the amount of the claim lodged; or
- The defendant is obviously not linked to the conduct of the complaint; or
- Significant (including media) pressure has been built up in order to compel the defendant to agree to an unfair settlement.[20]

The Court ruled that it were neither initially obvious that there was no basis for the amount of the claim nor that the claim appeared to be without any basis from the outset nor that the complainant could not have been involved in the challenged cartel agreement.[21] The Court stated explicitly

[18] *von Hein*, "BVerfG gestattet Zustellung einer US-amerikanischen Klage auf Punitive Damages," RIW 2007, 249; *Geimer*, WuB VII C § 13 HZÜ 1.07; *Stürner/Müller* (supra Fn. 13); critical annotation by *Stadler*, JZ 2007, 1047.

[19] 2 BvR 1739/06, 2 BvR 1811/06, order of September 4, 2008, downloadable only in German under http://www.bundesverfassungsgericht.de/entscheidungen/rk20080904_2bvr173906.html. The complaints were also not admitted because the complainants had not previously filed complaints pursuant to § 29a of the Act on the Matters of Non-Contentious Jurisdiction (*Gesetz über die Angelegenheiten der freiwilligen Gerichtsbarkeit—FGG)* against the orders alleging that it did not receive a hearing (*Anhörungsrüge*).

[20] Ibid, N. 19.

[21] Order of September 4, 2008 (supra Fn. 19), N. 21.

that it would not admit any further constitutional complaints against service of a foreign action under the Hague Service Convention for decision unless the objective and the specific circumstances of the legal action suggest that the limits of a violation of essential principles of a free state governed by the rule of law are exceeded.[22]

III. The Function of Service of Process: Due Process of Law versus Exercise of Sovereign Administrative Authority

Service of process, whether in a national or an international case, must find the balance between the plaintiff's interest to obtain access to justice in the individual case ("*Justizgewährung*") and the defendant's interest in timely and efficient information. Perfected service, that is, service of the statement of claim upon the defendant leads to "*lis pendens*" under German law. Service must be completed to comply with procedural and substantive requirements as to time, and therefore is in the plaintiff's interests. The defendant obtains notice of the proceedings initiated against him through service which enables him to defend himself against the action. In this regard, service ensures due process and a fair trial. These interests are common ground in all civilized legal systems and are also pertinent in the area of judgment recognition.[23]

In an international case, the parties' interests are pronounced. The plaintiff is primarily interested in a fast service of the action upon the defendant domiciled abroad to ensure that he can prosecute his claims in his local court thereafter. Moreover, he needs reliable documentation of the service upon the foreign defendant as proof of service once he seeks recognition and/or enforcement of a judgement domestically or abroad. The defendant is primarily interested in comprehensive information about the action initiated against him in a foreign court. Again, these interests are common to all parties involved in national or international litigation.[24]

However, the perception is different when it comes to the issue of interests of states participating in the service of process. Do states have interests in the area of service of process at all?

---

[22] Ibid, N. 31.

[23] *Hausmann*, "Auslegungsprobleme der Europäischen Zustellungsverordnung," *The European Legal Forum*, 2007, II–1.

[24] *Hausmann*, ibid.

III. 1. "Notice" as an Essential Part of United States Civil Procedure

In United States Civil Procedure, as derived from the Federal Constitutions' Due Process Clause, service fulfills the primary function to put the other side on notice of the law suit ("notice pleading"). Service is not an exercise of sovereign administrative authority. It is a matter between the parties and cannot be qualified as an authority's act since service does not trigger any sanctions.[25] It is not necessary to state the amount in dispute specifically. The United States Supreme Court requires the mode of service best suited to ensure actual notice to the defendant. If actual notice cannot be given, service by mail or by publication suffices.[26]

Domestic laws authorizing service abroad are those concerning court procedure, both federal and state. The requirements for summons and service are established by Federal Rule of Civil Procedure 4.[27] Section (d) provides for waiver of service; section (f) concerns service on an individual abroad; section (h) concerns service on a corporation, and section (j) service on a foreign State. Under Rule 4 (f) service is to be made by internationally agreed means where applicable, and, if not subject to an international agreement, additional methods are permitted that are "reasonably calculated to give notice." Rule 4 (f) (3) is worded as a catch-all provision and "allows any other means not prohibited by international agreement, as the court orders." These methods may also include service of process by electronic means on foreign defendants outside the scope of the Hague Service Convention. In general, United States courts seem to be inclined to authorize email service in cross-border situations when the foreign defendant has successfully prevented receipt of service by traditional methods and utilizing email is either the preferred or the sole method of communication.[28]

---

[25] *Bischof*, Die Zustellung im internationalen Rechtsverkehr in Zivil- oder Handelssachen, 1997, 172.

[26] *Mullane v. Central Hanover Bank and Trust Company*, 339 U.S. 306; Hay, US-amerikanisches Recht, 4 ed. 2008, N. 156.

[27] http://www.law.cornell.edu/rules/frcp/Rule4.htm. The majority of U.S. States has adopted court rules and procedures that follow Fed. R. Civ. P 4 (f).

[28] See Part Three, II.B. of the US-responses to the questionnaire of July 2008 relating to the practical operation of the Convention (http://www.hcch.net/index_en.php?act =publications.details&pid=4598&dtid=33); with reference to f. ex. *Philip Morris USA Inc. v. Veles Ltd.*, 2007 WL 725412; *Williams v. Advertising Sex LLC.*, 231 F.R.D. 483 2005); *Rio Properties, Inc. v. Rio Int'l Interlink*, 284 F.3d 1007 (9th Cir. 2002). Generally, see *Stewart and Conley*, E-mail Service on Foreign Defendants: Time for an International Approach?, 38 Georgetown Journal of International Law 755 (2007).

Given this view, the United States had no problems outsourcing the service of process of U.S. inbound complaints pursuant to the Hague Service Convention to the private company "Process Forwarding International."[29]

III. 2. The Formal German Insistence Upon Sovereignty vis à vis the Increasing Relevance of Practicality

III. 2. a) International Service as an Exercise of Sovereign Administrative Authority

The traditional German understanding of the law of international service has long been dominated by the characterization as an exercise of sovereign administrative authority ("*Hoheitsakt*")[30] so that violation of the sovereignty of the receiving state must be avoided. The first function of service is to give the receiving state control about the involvement of its companies and residents in foreign actions. It allows the Federal Ministry of Justice and the Central Authorities under the Hague Convention to look at the big picture, to circulate information among themselves about the status of the judicial cooperation and to initiate diplomatic interventions if needed.[31] The second function, according to *Stürner*, is to use sovereignty as a "shield" for its resident companies and residents by prohibiting private direct service.[32] In reverse, German Service authorities are not authorized to act within another state's territory unless international treaties expressly allow it.[33] § 183 of the Code of Civil Procedure in both, old and new version, in force since November 13, 2008,[34] is reminiscent of this understanding. It represents an exception to the general rule, which requires involvement of (foreign) authorities, as the following interpretation of the rule will show.

---

[29] Current Address: 633 Yesler Way, Seattle WA 98104—2725 (http://hagueservice.net). The service of process contract is currently resolicited by the Department of Justice; http://hcch.e-vision.nl/upload/wop/2008usa14.pdf.

[30] BVerfG, NJW 1995, 649: "Die Zustellung ist ein staatlicher Hoheitsakt, mit dem ein ausländisches Gerichtsverfahren gefördert wird"; *Geimer, G.*, Neuordnung des internationalen Zustellungsrechts, 1999, p. 130; *Siegrist*, Hoheitsakte auf fremdem Staatsgebiet, 1987, 169 et seq.; disputed by *Schack*, Internationales Zivilverfahrensrecht, 4. ed. 2006, No. 589 et seq.

[31] *Stürner* (supra Fn. 4), 65.

[32] *Stürner*, "Europäische Urteilsvollstreckung nach Zustellungsmängeln," Festschrift für Heinrich Nagel (1987), 446, 453.

[33] *Zöller/Geimer*, ZPO, 27th ed. 2009, § 183 N. 4.

[34] Art. 8 (2) of "Gesetz zur Verbesserung der grenzüberschreitenden Forderungsdurchsetzung und Zustellung vom 30.10.2008"; Federal Law Gazette 2008 I, p. 2122.

III. 2. b) The Tendency towards Direct Postal Service

§ 183 of the Code of Civil Procedure in its revised version reads—in the author's translation—as follows:

(1) Service abroad may be effected according to existing international treaties. If pursuant to international treaties, documents may be served directly by postal service, such service shall be effected by registered mail, return receipt required, otherwise, upon request by the trial court's chief judge, service shall be effected directly by the authorities of the foreign state.

(2) If service pursuant to paragraph 1 is impossible, service shall be effected by the competent diplomatic or consular mission of Germany or the otherwise competent authorities. In particular, service pursuant to sentence 1 shall be used if international agreements do not exist, the competent authorities of the respective state are unwilling to render judicial assistance or specific reasons justify such a service.

(3) A German citizen enjoying the right of immunity and belonging to a foreign representation of Germany shall be served upon request by the trial court's chief judge through the foreign mission.

(4) Adequate evidence of service is the acknowledgment of receipt in cases of paragraph 1, sentence 2, clause 1. Service pursuant to paragraph 1, sentence 2, clause 2 and paragraphs 2 and 3 shall be evidenced by the certificate of the requested authority.

(5) The provisions of Regulation (EC) No. 1393/2007 of the European Parliament and of the Council of 13 November 2007 on the Service in the Member States of Judicial and Extrajudicial Documents in Civil and Commercial matters and the provisions repealing Regulation (EC) No. 1348/2000 (OJ L 324 p. 79) remain unaffected.

According to the introductory remarks of the official explanatory statement to § 183 ZPO, the underlying rationale of the rule is to clarify the priority of international treaties over national law as to service of process.[35] It must be noted, however, that the express statement to this effect in § 183 (1) is merely declaratory, and that the competence of the German legislature ends there. It is bound by international treaties, and cannot provide for more extensive national rules; doing so would jeopardize the recognition and enforcement of German court decisions

---

[35] Official Record of the German Bundestag (*BT-Drucksache*) 16/8839 p. 19 et seq.; also emphasized by *Zöller/Geimer*, ZPO, 27th ed. 2009, § 183 No. 1 et seq. who already comments briefly upon the new provisions.

abroad.[36] Therefore, the priority of service pursuant to international treaties is not the most important feature of the new law nor has it been, albeit not so clearly worded, under its predecessor version. In that context, the official explanatory statement points out that § 183 (1) intentionally does not extend the possibility to serve process by registered mail beyond the scope of international treaties with respect to those states not bound by treaties that may accept such service. This is to guard against the risk that such states might nonetheless deny recognition and consequently enforcement of a judgment rendered on the basis of such service later on.[37]

As provided in § 183 (1) ZPO, the primary method of service is service through registered mail with return receipt. This method is cost effective and time saving. For example, German representations abroad are released from tasks of service. Furthermore, it will presumably expedite the proceedings if methods provided for in international treaties are used instead of the way via German consular and diplomatic missions. However, due to reservations by some German central authorities, it was apparently agreed that the instrument of direct postal service allowed by § 183 (1) No. 1 ZPO in its old version was to be used only in relation to the United States.[38]

The fact that service by consular or diplomatic authorities is treated in a separate paragraph in § 183 (2) ZPO highlights the principle of subsidiarity of this method of service. It is limited to cases outside the scope of international treaties or available only if easier forms of service are not available for legal or practical reasons.[39] In conformity with past

[36] Official Record of the German Bundestag (*BT-Drucksache*) 16/8839 at p. 20.

[37] Official Record of the German Bundestag (*BT-Drucksache*) 16/8839 at p. 20; *Zöller/Geimer*, ZPO, 27th ed. 2009, § 183 No. 6: The ratio legis would also call for direct service if the respective state tolerates it without being bound by international law.

[38] Direct postal service has already been possible under Article 6 of the German-British Convention on the Conduct of Legal Proceedings of 20 March 1928, brought into force again with effect from 1 January 1953 (Federal Law Gazette 1953, II, p. 116), http://www.rechtshilfe-international. This database contains the administrative rules for legal aid in civil law issues (“*Rechtshilfeordnung für Zivilsachen*”), applicable laws in relation to foreign countries (*“Länderteil”*) with the methods permitted for outbound and inbound service requests with regard to each country listed.

[39] Official Record of the German Bundestag (*BT-Drucksache*) 16/8839 at p. 20; Practical experience shows that the return of the receipt and/or a proper documentation that service has been completed is not always guaranteed. In the event that service by registered mail fails or be foreseen to fail, § 183 (1) 2nd sentence ZPO opens the usual and most

practice, § 183 (1) ZPO allows German courts to serve process by registered mail where allowed by international treaties regardless of the fact that Germany has objected to Art. 10 lit. a) of the Hague Service Convention. It states that "the Convention will not interfere with the freedom to send judicial documents, by postal channels, directly to persons abroad" unless the state of destination objects to this. The logic of this one-sidedness had already been discussed under the old law. If one characterizes § 6 sentence 2 ("service pursuant to Article 10 of the Convention shall not be effected") as a rule of general application (*"allseitige Verbotsnorm"*), postal service to the United States must involve the designated Central Authorities. Germany cannot ask for a facilitated outbound service it would not grant for actions serviced in Germany.[40] However, this qualification would overlook that the United States have not made a reservation to Art. 10 of the Convention and accept inbound service by regular postal services. The consequence is impartiality. Even though outbound service may be facilitated by use of registered mail with return receipt, inbound service of process in Germany is still denied such privilege. This may give rise to the objection of lack of reciprocity. In that respect, the German Government observed in its official statement to the draft of the new § 183 ZPO that this imbalance would not incur "automatically" but would be problematic only if the other state being a member to the Hague Service Convention invoked the principle of reciprocity.[41] So far, there are no such known cases.

The amended version of § 183 (2) reflects the fact that service of process through federal diplomatic and/or consular missions is the most complex and time-consuming method of service abroad and is therefore justified only in exceptional cases. It is relevant for instance, with respect to the few states that adhere both to the Hague Convention on Civil Procedure of 1954 and the Hague Convention on Civil Procedure of 1905. The German legislature expects that the guidelines outlined in the 2nd sentence of § 183 (2) will not only facilitate the application of the rule, but, in light of the third guideline ("specific reasons"), allow for flexible handling on a case-by-case basis. Specific reasons always justifying diplomatic service are service on foreign diplomats or on states themselves, provided that German courts have juris-

widespread way provided for by international treaties to serve process through the authorities directly without having to get the diplomatic services involved.

[40] In favor of general application *Heidrich*, "Amts- und Parteizustellungen im internationalen Rahmen: Status quo und Reformbedarf," EuZW 2005, 743, 746.

[41] Official Record of the German Bundestag (*BT-Drucksache*) 16/8839 at p. 38.

diction in the first place. Diplomatic channels of service are mandatory in those cases as they generally involve federal foreign policy interests.[42]

III. 3. Summary: Practicality over Sovereignty?

If the function of service is to inform the addressee reliably about the proceedings commenced against him, official state assistance is not required to ensure such actual notice. § 183 (1) and (2) of the Code of Civil Procedure, requiring involvement of (foreign) authorities, show that direct postal service is still an exception to the general rule, although direct postal service is promoted. Such means of service is encouraged among the Member States of the European Union, as clearly stated in Art. 14 of Regulation (EC) 1393/2007: "Each Member State shall be free to effect service of judicial documents directly by postal services on persons residing in another Member State by registered letter with acknowledgement of receipt or equivalent." It becomes clear that practicality is reconcilable with sovereignty in the EU and that notions of sovereignty become less important in the relation to third countries, such as the United States.

Article 34 of Council Regulation 44/2001[43] is another modern European example and shows that interests of national sovereignty have less importance in international service today. Pursuant to Art. 34 (2), a judgment shall not be recognised when it was given in default of appearance, if the defendant was not served with the document instituting the proceedings or with an equivalent document in sufficient time and in such a way as to enable him to arrange for his defence, unless the defendant failed to commence proceedings to challenge the judgment when it was possible for him to do so.[44] Thus, the emphasis is on reliable and fast information of the parties to the litigation.

Although Regulation 44/2001 is designed to facilitate the judicial cooperation among the EU states pursuant to Art. 61, 65 of the EC-treaty,

---

[42] Official Record of the German Bundestag (*BT-Drucksache*) 16/8839 at p. 20; diplomatic service f. ex. in BVerfG, 2 BvR 1476/03, order of February 15, 2006, http://www.bverfg.de/entscheidungen/rk20060215_2bvr147603.html ("Distomo").

[43] Council Regulation (EC) No. 44/2001 of December 2002 on jurisdiction and the recognition and enforcement of judgments in civil and commercial matters ("Brussels I"), OJ 2001 L 012, as amended by Commission Regulation 1490/2002, [2002] OJ C. 225.

[44] Art. 34 (2) is a harsh rule as shown by *Hay*, "The Development of the Public Policy Barrier to Judgment Recognition Within the European Community," The European Legal Forum, 2007, I-289, I-292.

the following remarks will show that the Hague Service Convention must be interpreted in the same way.

IV. The Influence of the Hague Service Convention

The preamble of the Hague Service Convention emphasizes its purpose to create appropriate means to ensure that judicial and extrajudicial documents to be served abroad shall be brought to the notice of the addressee in sufficient time. Its text, today in force in 59 Contracting States[45] with different declarations and reservations, is rather self-explanatory. The purpose is to improve the organization of mutual judicial assistance by simplifying and expediting the technical handling and acceleration of service of documents.[46] In line with Regulations (EC) 1393/2007 and 44/2001, the purpose of the Hague Service Convention is therefore to give notice. International Service shall be facilitated, barriers to be abolished and not erected.

IV. 1. Not Mandatory but Exclusive Character of the Service Convention?

The seemingly contradictory phrase that the Hague Service Convention is not mandatory but exclusive means the following: Contracting states want to obtain additional and simplified means to serve process. They do not want to waive possibilities for domestic service existing under applicable national law. The decision by the United States Supreme Court in *Volkswagenwerk Aktiengesellschaft v. Schlunk* (1988) serves to illustrate. The Court held that the Hague Service Convention does not apply in the case of service on the domestic subsidiary of a foreign parent when the former is the latter's involuntary agent. Thus, when service is to be made in a Convention country, litigants in federal or state court must make use of the Convention as the exclusive means of service. But signatory nations are not obliged to use foreign service if the lex fori allows for domestic service of documents, e.g., as in *Schlunk*, on the United States alter ego subsidiary of the defendant German manufacturer. This differentiation has

---

[45] http://www.hcch.net/index_en.php?act=conventions.text&cid=17. The latest Contracting State is the former Yugoslav Republic of Macedonia (since December 23, 2008). Among the Member States are Bosnia and Herzegovina (since June 16, 2008), Croatia, Hungary, Netherlands and Slovenia. No information is available whether negotiations with Serbia are ongoing.

[46] Model forms of Request, Certificate and Summary can be found at http://www.hcch.net/act/form14e.pdf.

not led to any difficulties in the United States or in Germany. *Schack* argues that it would have helped to clarify the intention of the Hague Service Convention if the Contracting States had specified when foreign service must be used.[47] As it stands, the parties can avoid the application of the Convention if national procedural law is structured accordingly. The Convention then is therefore an option. If the *lex fori* allows for domestic service of documents, the Convention need not be followed; if the documents must be sent abroad, the Hague Convention is the exclusive means.[48] Every Contracting state decides whether to use the Convention's method of central authorities or alternatively, to provide for any other national means of service.[49]

This optional character of the Hague Convention also became obvious in the *Bertelsmann* case. The American court simply did not care whether service was blocked in Germany, because the plaintiffs had been able to serve a member of the Bertelsmann management board in the United States pursuant to Rule 4 (h) (1), (e) (1) of Federal Rules of Civil Procedure. Also, any attempts by Bertelsmann to shield itself against service in Germany would have been futile after six months anyway as also noted by the First Senate in its 1994 order.[50] Art. 15(2) of the Hague Service Convention allows each Contracting State to declare—and the United States have made this declaration—that the Court may give judgment even without a receipt of a certificate of service or delivery, if every reasonable effort to effect service has been made and no less than six months have elapsed without certificate of any kind. Nationally blocking service is therefore an ill-suited means to protect a German defendant as pointed by the First Senate and most commentators.[51]

---

[47] *Schack* (supra Fn. 8), 827; *Hausmann* (supra Fn. 23), II-2.; *Schlosser*, EU-Zivilprozeßrecht, 2. ed. 2003, 504 et seq.

[48] *Scoles/Hay*, Conflict of Laws, 4th ed. 2004, § 12.7, p. 529. *Hay*'s view that the Hague Service Convention has eliminated the "notification au parquet" (domestic fictitious service of French law) is not shared by *Schack* (supra Fn. 8) with recourse to the facultative character of the Convention. The official German position is that the notification au parquet has not effectively been abolished but that the means of Art. 15 Service Convention are a compromise protecting both parties, Official Record of the German Bundestag (*BT-Drucksache*) 7/4892 at p. 40.

[49] See for example *Schlunk v. Volkswagenwerk Aktiengesellschaft*, 108 S. Ct. 2104. The U.S. Supreme Court has not rendered any major decision in this area since then.

[50] BVerfG, NJW 1995, 650.

[51] *Rasmussen-Bonne* (supra Fn. 8), 334 with emphasis upon Art. 15 (2); *Schack* (supra Fn. 8), 827; *Von Hein* (supra Fn. 9), 115; *Stürner* (supra Fn. 4), 65 with emphasis upon the option of domestic service.

IV. 2. The Interpretation of the Phrase "Civil and Commercial Matters"

The interpretation of "civil and commercial matters" to which the Hague Service Convention applies (Art. 1) is not in the focus of these remarks. Suffice it to say that both terms are not defined and should be construed autonomously due to their multilateral context. The Koblenz court had followed this method but concluded that, at least in antitrust cases, class actions for treble damages served the goal of maintaining free competition and superseded private interests in receiving compensatory damages.[52] This characterization of treble damages as being in the realm of public law, is shared by no one.[53] The 2003 Special Commission urged a broad and liberal interpretation of the phrase "civil and commercial matters."[54] With exception of the Koblenz court, all German Courts have adopted a wide interpretation of Article 1 of the Service Convention.[55] The United States, in its responses to the questionnaire of July 2008, stated that they will consider any non-criminal service request that emanates from a tribunal or other authority with proper jurisdiction in the matter as "civil and commercial" for purposes of service under the Convention.[56] The German Ministry of Justice basically shares this understanding. Both governments consider the following subjects to definitely be civil or commercial matters: Bankruptcy or insolvency in general, Reorganisation under bankruptcy laws, Insurance, Employment, Anti-trust and competition, Consumer protection. Their views differ on the following subjects: Social security, Taxation, Regulation and oversight of financial markets and stock exchange (e.g. in matters possibly involving insider trading) and proceeds of crime. These are considered as "civil" in the United States understanding and of a public nature from a German point of view.

---

[52] IPRax 2006, 25, 31.

[53] The traditional German characterization is that "Civil and Commercial matters are those in which private parties dispute about their private law rights against each other and not about their rights as citizens vis-à-vis the government, The fact that public interest considerations shape the content of the applicable law is inherent in all positive law. It becomes even more visible in the concept of regulation through (private) litigation. The mere fact that the public interest—as specified by the legislator or the common law judge—is relevant in the law of damages does not turn every American tort process into a criminal or administrative proceedings," *Halfmeier*, Book Review of *Hopt/Kulms/von Hein* (supra Fn. 7), http://www.germanlawjournal.com/article.php?id=784, 1164.

[54] Conclusions and Recommendations Nos 69 to 72, http://www.hcch.net/upload/wop/lse_concl_e.pdf.

[55] See the decisions cited supra Fn. 14.

[56] Part. II., A (supra Fn. 28).

IV. 3. The German Objection under Article 10 of the Hague Service Convention

At the time of ratification of the Hague Service Convention, Germany opposed Art. 10 (a) ("the freedom to send judicial documents, by postal channels, directly to persons abroad"). It admitted direct service in Germany only via the German Central authorities.[57] Germany objected because it wanted to be certain that the recipient of the documents in Germany really receives the documents to be served in the prescribed language version. Despite the facilitated and encouraged use of postal direct service under § 183 ZPO, as discussed above, Germany probably will not withdraw its reservation. However, Germany is not the only state that has deposited reservations against the alternative channels of transmission under Art. 10 (a), (b) and (c). Rather, in total 24 Contracting states have made reservations.[58]

Given its view that service is a private act, the United States has not filed such a reservation.

V. Interpretation of Article 13 (1) of the Hague Service Convention

The last orders of the Second Senate dealt extensively with the limits of judicial assistance imposed by Art. 13 of the Convention. Under this provision, the "State addressed may refuse to comply therewith only if it deems that compliance would infringe its sovereignty or security." While Art. 13 is the object of much comment by German scholars and business lawyers, it is not noted in the United States. As of October 2008, the United States have indicated that the only requests for service to have been refused by a requested State were cases involving service on a Foreign State under the Foreign Sovereign Immunities Act.[59]

[57] Publication about enactment of the Hague Service Convention of June 21, 1979, Federal Law Gazette II, 779.

[58] Table reflecting Applicability of Articles (8), 10(a), (b) and (c), 15(2) and 16(3) downloadable under http://www.hcch.net/upload/applicability14e.pdf.

[59] Part II, V. (supra Fn. 28).

V. 1. The *Ordre Public* Concept underlying Art. 13

In its most recent orders, the Second Senate departs from its position taken in the 2003 Bertelsmann decision and returns to the liberal attitude of the First Senate's 1994 decision. In this earlier ruling, the Senate had emphasized in an *obiter dictum* that the protection of Art. 13 (1) of the Hague Service Convention must not be equated with domestic public policy in general. It left open the possibility of refusing service of process if this would violate human rights. In its *Bertelsmann* decision, the Second Senate interpreted this reservation clause broadly. It argued that allowing service of process when the underlying claims were manifestly frivolous might be contrary to the rule of law guaranteed by the German constitution. This characterization allowed a considerably stricter control than the First Senate had in mind. Fortunately, now the pendulum swings back to cooperation. The Second Senate accepts that the conventional terminology is deliberately narrower than the general *ordre public* reservation, contained for example in Art. 6 and Art. 40 (3) of the German Conflict of Laws Act or in § 328 (1) No. 4 of the Code of Civil Procedure. The *ordre public* concept of Art. 13 must not be used to give effect to all manner of private law concerns. It must rather have a restricted, convention-specific meaning and not be burdened by other public policy notions that are extraneous for Convention purposes.

These boundaries are not exceeded and the *ordre public* of Art. 13 is not violated if the foreign statement of claims contains one or even all features that are characteristic of American civil litigation but are unknown to the German legal system. Enormous punitive and treble damages, attention drawing class action suits, the high costs of pre-trial discovery and the American rule on costs (which conflicts with the German principle that the losing party must reimburse the winner for the costs related to the litigation) are elements of foreign law which "must be respected in principle, even when they do not conform with the German view in an individual case, if foreign actions were generally measured according to the standards of the German legal system, and as a result, relief could not be granted where the action was based on a legal institution unknown to German law."[60]

This interpretation reaffirms the scope of review of Art. 13. It only asks whether compliance with the service request would jeopardize sovereignty or security of the requested state. How the foreign action will even-

[60] See BVerfGE 108, 238 (247-248).

tually develop once service has been effected is irrelevant for the decision whether to comply with the service request. Art. 13 (2) supports this interpretation by stating that the requested state may not refuse to comply with the request solely on the ground that its internal law would not permit the action upon which the application is based.

If the purpose of the Service Convention and the literal interpretation of Art. 13 require such a limited and narrow scope of review, what is left for infringement of "judicial" sovereignty and security? The authors of the expert opinion suggest that an example would be an action for damages against a judge of the country in which service is requested based upon on the judge's judicial activities. Another example, which has in fact been decided by the OLG Düsseldorf, is an antisuit injunction directed against proceedings in the country in which service is requested.[61]

This interpretation of Art. 13 does not have any implications for the enforcement of any later judgment. The *ordre public* concept of Art. 13 sets a much narrower standard than the general *ordre public*. Neither the refusal nor the grant of service has any impact whatsoever on the ordre public analysis when it comes to the issues of recognition and enforcement of a foreign judgment.[62]

V. 2. The Escape Device: Obvious Abuse of the Legal Action from the Outset

The BVerfG left itself an out: Service may be refused if the objective and the specific circumstances of the legal action indicate that there has been an obvious abuse of law from the outset.[63] It is doubtful whether in light of these narrowly circumscribed statements, circumstances under which such an obvious abuse of a legal action can arise at all.

The OLG Celle[64] is the only German Court that has prohibited service in reliance on the Bertelsmann-Napster case. The facts of the case were as follows: The plaintiff had filed an action in New York federal court against the German defendant claiming damages in the amount of approx.

---

[61] See *Hopt/Kulms/von Hein* (supra Fn. 7), 115; for the infringement by an antisuit injunction, see OLG Düsseldorf of January 10, 1996, 3 VA 11/95, ZZP 109 (1996), 221 with critical comment by *Stürner*, 224.

[62] *Hopt/Kulms/von Hein* (supra Fn. 7), 126 et seq.

[63] Supra II.2., in particular text to Fn. 20 to 22.

[64] Order of June 1, 2007, 16 VA 1/07, JURIS = NdsRpfl 2007, 331 = OLGR Celle 2008, 88 making no reference to OLG Koblenz (supra Fn. 11) which had also focused on abuse of action in its *obiter dictum*.

$ 25 Million. The plaintiff had temporarily lived in Göttingen at his business partner's address. The business partner had designated the plaintiff as his heir and later died. Subsequently, all apartments in the house, the plaintiff has inherited, were destroyed by a fire. The defendant has been the property manager of the house. Apart from that, his relation to the plaintiff's damage remained unclear.

The Court held that service of process would violate Art. 13 of the Convention and therefore suspended the order for service. It started out by saying that the reservation clause must be interpreted restrictively in a convention-specific meaning. However, the particular circumstances of the case would justify an exception to this rule since the statement of claim violated fundamental constitutional principles. Here, the amount of damages was obviously frivolous and only claimed to jeopardize the existence of the complainant. Furthermore, the amount of damages and the actual damage were evidently unrelated. A violation of the law was not at all evident. The court further noted that the plaintiff has randomly sued numerous other parties, such as police department, the City and the Local Court of Göttingen. Lastly, the Court found it to be important that the previously filed six actions against other defendants in United States courts in this matter had all been dismissed as abusive by United States Courts.[65]

The OLG Celle suspended the service order by the Central Authority in obvious deference to and out of concern for the plight of the complainant who had also argued vigorously that to defend against the action in a United States Court would cost him a fortune and that he would not be reimbursed because of the American rule on costs. The judgment indeed shows that the statement of claim had been somewhat bizarre and chaotic.

The ruling probably complies with the latest orders of the Second Senate of the BVerfG. There was obviously no basis for the amount of the claim lodged and the complainant had evidently no relationship with the conduct of the complaint. But the reasoning of the Court leaves some more serious issues open: Should the issue when a claim is evidently egregious not be decided by the forum court of the requesting state, perhaps after a hearing of the complainant/defendant? Or asked from another perspective: Are German central authorities authorized or even obligated to decide whether a plaintiff who is requesting service has filed a frivolous claim in his forum court?

---

[65] Ibid, JURIS N. 15.

The OLG Frankfurt has ruled that it is the forums court responsibility to decide whether a party commits an abuse of law. In the context of service, notions of due process would require a prior hearing of the American plaintiff. It further ruled that the detailed examination of the plaintiff's intention must be reserved for the judge in the forum state.[66] The OLG Celle apparently had not granted the American plaintiff this hearing before rendering its decision. However, it had the opportunity to see from the available records of the New York proceedings that the plaintiff's intentions have been qualified as frivolous by all US-courts.

In service matters, in principle, the requested state is neither permitted nor obligated to evaluate whether the action is abusive. The BVerfG correctly states in its order of January 24, 2007: "Pursuant to the Hague Service Convention, German authorities are not responsible to review a foreign statement of claims on the basis of the pertinent procedural law of the requested state upon its admissibility. Rather, the formalization of the service process wants to exclude that such a review is made."[67] This thought is also true with respect to the question whether the statement of claim is substantiated (*Schlüssigkeitsprüfung*) respectively founded. This is not only true by an *a fortiori* conclusion that *révision au fond* is prohibited at the recognition and enforcement stage. But it is rather impossible to decide as early as on the service stage whether the action seems founded with respect to the merits and the terms of amount.[68] The German Code of Civil Procedure also does not know such an ex officio evaluation before service. A statement of claim is served upon the defendant without any checks on the merits.[69] Furthermore, such a review and evaluation process would delay the proceedings. *Schütze* has suggested this problem could be

---

[66] OLG Frankfurt, order of February 13, 2001, 20 VA 7/00, NJW-RR 2002, 357. The Koblenz Court (supra Fn. 11) took another position. It interpreted the plaintiffs' statement that their conduct was "de facto legal" (quoted at least three times, 34, 36, 38) as a confession that they were aware that their conduct violated U.S. antitrust law, a view that the Court shared. The Court therefore not only found the action abusive from a German but also from the United States legal perspective. *Von Hein* (supra Fn. 7), 120, calls this approach the "germanocentric reinterpretation" of Articles 1 and 13.

[67] RIW 2007, 213 (in the author's translation).

[68] *Oberhammer*, "Deutsche Grundrechte und die Zustellung US-amerikanischer Klagen im Rechtshilfeweg," IPRax 2004, 40, 44; *Stadler* (supra Fn. 18), 1049; *Stürner* (supra Fn. 4), 64; *Schack* (supra Fn. 8), 830.

[69] Referring to national standards concerning international service the orders (supra Fn. 14) of OLG Celle, JURIS, N. 29; OLG München, JURIS, N. 13;OLG Düsseldorf, JURIS, N. 16; OLG Naumburg, 9 and OLG Karlsruhe, 6 et. seq; and OLG Düsseldorf, February 19, 1992, 3 VA 1/91, NJW 1992, 3110, 3111.

overcome in the case of class actions by establishing a rebuttable assumption that such actions constitute an abuse of law per se.[70] This presumption would reverse the exception to the principle of article 13 Hague Service Convention. As such, it will never be accepted internationally. For reasons for due process, the plaintiffs would have to be granted the time to rebut this presumption in the service proceedings and the entire process of service would be slowed down. This, in turn, would conflict with the urgency of the preliminary proceeding requesting that service be blocked.[71]

One word with respect to the function of Central Authorities: According to Art. 2 of the Service Convention, the Central Authority undertakes to receive requests for services, to arrange for service by one of the means of Art. 5 and to complete and return the certificate of service.[72] This is an administrative and not a judicial function. Central Authorities shall not be put in the position of having to judge and to accept the extra work load for which they are not responsible. Fruitless and useless litigation in the forefront of the substantive litigation itself would be the consequence.[73] The Central Authority of the German State of Lower Saxony therefore rightfully complied with the request for service when it served the documents upon the later complainant.

VI. Conclusion

The latest orders of the Federal Constitutional Court and Higher Regional Courts of Appeal show that the *Bertelsmann* decision has been a regrettable anomaly. Fortunately, the pendulum has swung back to the rather liberal attitude in favor of cooperation the First Senate took as early as 1994. But the Hague Service Convention can only serve its purpose to facilitate and to enhance intergovernmental judicial assistance if it is not used as battlefield for fights about legal institutions unknown to the other Contracting states' law. It codifies the legitimate interest of the requested state

[70] Zur Zustellung US-amerikanischer Klagen in Deutschland, in: Festschrift für Boguslavskij (2004), 325.

[71] *Hopt/Kulms/von Hein* (supra Fn. 7), 144.

[72] The Central Authority of Berlin must only serve pursuant to Art. 5 (1) (a), if the documents are written in or translated into the German language, Art. 5 (3) in connection with § 3 of the German Implementing Statute of the Hague Service Convention. A certified translation is not required, Order of May 15, 2007, 1 VA 6/07, JURIS, N. 9, 10.

[73] This delay is a fact as the analysis of the cases after the *Bertelsmann* order collected and reviewed by *Rasmussen-Bonne* (supra Fn. 8) illustrates.

that international service is effected in an orderly way in order to ensure the defendant due process. The methods of direct postal service in § 183 of the German Code of Civil Procedure support the use of the Convention. German Courts have clarified that the Convention does not require a "*pre-trial on the merits*"- check of the action. Art. 13 of the Hague Service Convention must not be used to give effect to all manner of private law concerns. The backdoor left open by the Federal Constitutional Court for declining service requests should only be opened cautiously in cases when the action itself is at its face evidently abusive from the outset. This facts have probably been present in the order of the OLG Celle but it should have granted the American plaintiff a hearing pursuant to § 29a FGG before deciding whether to block service. Overall, only compliance with International Law limits ensures that the Hague Service Convention is adhered to by other Contracting States in the interests of service recipients. Thus, states should avoid "resort to other means of domestic service which would make the legal position of defendants in foreign jurisdictions considerably more burdensome."[74]

[74] BVerfG, order of June 14, 2007 (supra Fn. 17 in its English version), N. 31, with reference to *Hopt/Kulms/von Hein* (supra Fn. 7), 155 et seq.

Internationale Schiedsgerichtsbarkeit über Kulturgut-Streitigkeiten

KURT SIEHR

I. Probleme

Schiedsklauseln werden normalerweise in Verträge aufgenommen, die für den Fall von Streitigkeiten die Zuständigkeit eines Schiedsgerichts vorsehen. Das ist in aller Regel anders bei Streitigkeiten über Kulturgut. Die Parteien kennen sich nicht, sie sind durch keinen Vertrag miteinander verbunden und stehen sich als Fremde gegenüber.[1] Meistens macht eine Partei geltend, sie sei Eigentümer eines Objekts, und die Gegenpartei bestreitet dies und nimmt das Objekt für sich in Anspruch. Wenn es zu keiner gütlichen Einigung kommt und die fordernde Partei die Kosten eines Rechtsstreites nicht scheut, treffen sich die Kontrahenten vor Gericht. Vergleichen sich die Parteien nicht, muss das Gericht entscheiden, eventuell eine Berufungsinstanz angerufen werden und schließlich hat das letztinstanzliche Gericht das endgültige Urteil zu sprechen. Das kann lange dauern und sehr teuer sein.[2] Deshalb hat man schon früh daran gedacht, internationale Schiedsgerichte mit der Entscheidung über Kulturgut-Streitigkeiten zu betrauen.[3] Diese Bemühungen haben nur sehr beschränkt

---

[1] Das ist z. B. anders, wenn Parteien einer Versteigerung (Kommission) eine Schiedsvereinbarung für den Fall einer Streitigkeit aus dem Kommissionsverhältnis vereinbaren.

[2] Im Fall *City of Gotha v. Sotheby's* beliefen sich die gerichtlichen und aussergerichtlichen Kosten (zwei solicitors und zwei barristers, nämlich ein Queen's Counsel und ein Junior Counsel) auf £ 1 Millionen. Vgl. *Michael H. Carl/Herbert Güttler/Kurt Siehr:* Kunstdiebstahl vor Gericht, Berlin 2001, 223 (Kostenentscheidung vom 21.4.1999). Deshalb die Forderung nach einem internationalen Fonds zur Deckung solcher Kosten, vgl. *Folarin Shyllon:* The Recovery of Cultural Objects by African States through the UNESCO and Unidroit Conventions and the Role of Arbitration: Uniform Law Review 5(2000) 219-241 (231-234).

[3] Vgl. *Kurt Siehr:* Resolution of Disputes in International Art Trade. Third Annual Conference of the Foundation „The Venice Court of National and International Arbitration", Venice, 29-30. September, 2000: International Law FORUM du droit international 3(2001) 64-68.

Erfolg gehabt. Frage ist also, was für diesen Misserfolg verantwortlich ist und wie diese Rechtslage verbessert werden könnte.

II. Bisherige Erfahrungen

II. 1. Multilaterale Konventionen

Gewisse internationale multilaterale Übereinkommen sehen vor, dass die Parteien ihren Streit einem Schiedsgericht zur Entscheidung übertragen können. Dies sieht z.B. der Artikel 8 II des Unidroit Übereinkommens vom 24.6.1995 über gestohlene oder rechtswidrig ausgeführte Kulturgüter vor.[4] Notwendig ist eine gesonderte Schiedsvereinbarung der Parteien eines Rückgabe- oder Rückführungsbegehrens. Bis jetzt ist für ein Begehren, das unter das Unidroit-Übereinkommen fällt, keine solche Vereinbarung bekannt geworden.

Die UNESCO-Konvention vom 2.November 2001 über den Schutz von Kulturgut unter Wasser[5], die kürzlich in Kraft getreten ist,[6] enthält in Artikel 25 eine dreistufige Regelung für Streitigkeiten zwischen Staaten. (1) Zuerst sollen die Staaten versuchen, den Streit durch Verhandlungen nach Treu und Glauben oder durch andere friedliche Mittel der Verständigung zu lösen. (2) Wenn dies misslingt, können die Parteien der UNESCO ihren Streit zur Schlichtung (mediation) unterbreiten. (3) Sofern diese Schlichtung unterbleibt oder misslingt, haben die Parteien nach Teil XV (Settlement of Disputes: Artikel 279 – 303) des Seerechtsübereinkommens der Vereinten Nationen vom 10.12.1982[7] zu verfahren, es sei denn sie haben ein Schiedsgericht nach Annex VII (Arbitration) oder VIII

---

[4] Abgedruckt in: Uniform Law Review N.S. 1(1996) 110 und 6(2001) 566.; International Journal of Cultural Property 5(1996) 155.; International Legal Materials 34(1995) 1330. Cp. also *Emily Sidorsky:* The 1995 UNIDROIT Convention on Stolen or Illegally Exported Cultural Objects—The Role of International Arbitration: International Journal of Cultural Property 5(1996) 19-72.; *dies.*, Cultural Property Disputes and the Draft Unidroit Convention—Possible Applications of International Arbitration: American Review of International Arbitration 4(1993) 475-518.; *Folarin Shyllon:* The Recovery, oben N. 2.; *ders.*, The Nigerian and African Experience on Looting and Trafficking in Cultural Objects, in: *Barbara T. Hoffman* (Hrsg.): Art and Cultural Heritage. Law, Policy and Practice, Cambridge 2006, 137-144. (141-142).

[5] International Journal of Cultural Property 11(2001) 107.

[6] Das Übereinkommen ist am 2.1.2009 für die ersten 20 Vertragsstaaten in Kraft getreten.

[7] BGBl. 1994 II 1799; auch in: International Tribunal for the Law of the Sea (ed.), Basic Texts (2005), Leiden 2005, 97.

(Special Arbitration) zum Seerechtsübereinkommen gewählt. Wenn eine Partei keine Vertragspartei des UNESCO-Übereinkommens ist, verweist dessen Artikel 25 V auf Annex V (Conciliation) und Annex VII (Arbitration) zum Seerechtsübereinkommen.[8]

Der Unterschied zwischen dem Unidroit-Übereinkommen und dem UNESCO-Übereinkommen besteht darin, dass der Artikel 8 II des Unidroit-Übereinkommens mehr oder weniger deklaratorischer Natur ist; denn Privatparteien dürften auch ohne diese Norm ihren Streitigkeit einem Schiedsgericht zur Entscheidung unterbreiten. Das ist anders bei dem UNESCO-Übereinkommen. Hier sind Staaten Parteien eines Rechtsstreits und für sie kann vorgeschrieben werden, welche Streitbeilegungsinstanzen sie anzurufen haben und welche Abweichungen (z.B. Wahl eines Schiedsinstanz) hiervon zulässig sind.

II. 2. Bilaterale Staatsverträge

Am 26.2.2006 haben das italienische Ministero per i Beni e le Attività Culturali durch Minister Rocco Buttiglione und das Metropolitan Museum of Art in New York durch seinen damaligen Direktor Philippe de Montebello eine Vertrag unterzeichnet, durch den illegal aus Italien verschwundene Kulturgüter (u.a. der Krater des Euphronios) an Italien zurückgegeben werden und mittlerweile auch zurückgegeben sind, soweit sie nicht mit dem Vermerk „lent by the Republic of Italy" im Museum bleiben.[9] Dieser Vertrag sieht unter Ziffer 9 vor, dass die Parteien irgendwelche Kontroversen über die Auslegung des Vertrages freundschaftlich beilegen werden und, falls dies nicht gelingt, die Streitfragen einem Schiedsgericht, zusammengesetzt aus drei Schiedsrichtern, nach den Schiedsregeln der Internationalen Handelskammer unterbreiten wollen. Bis jetzt scheint es noch zu keiner Kontroverse zwischen den Parteien gekommen zu sein.

II. 3. Vermittlung bestimmter Kommissionen

Washington Conference Principles on Nazi-confiscated Art vom 3. Dezember 1998 ermutigen unter ihrer Nr. XI alle Staaten, "to develop national processes to implement these principles, particularly as they relate

---

[8] Vgl. hierzu *Brooks W. Daly:* Arbitration of International Cultural Property Disputes: The Experience and Initiatives of the Permanent Court of Arbitration, in: *Hoffman* (Hrsg.): oben N. 4, 465-474. (468-470).

[9] The Metropolitan Museum of Art – Republic of Italy Agreement of February 21, 2006, International Journal of Cultural Property 13(2006) 427.

to alternative dispute resolution mechanisms for resolving ownership issues".[10]

II. 3. a) Bundesrepublik Deutschland

Die Bundesrepublik Deutschland hat die "Beratende Kommission im Zusammenhang mit der Rückgabe NS-verfolgungsbedingt entzogener Kulturgüter, insbesondere aus jüdischem Besitz" eingesetzt, die – besetzt mit anerkannten Persönlichkeiten des öffentlichen und wissenschaftlichen Lebens – am 14.7.2003 zum ersten Mal zusammentrat und sich konstituierte.[11] Die Kommission spricht Empfehlungen aus, wenn beide Parteien mit der Befassung ihres Falles durch die Kommission einverstanden sind.[12] Bis zum Juni 2008, also binnen fünf Jahren seit ihrer Konstituierung, hat die Kommission drei Empfehlungen abgegeben. Im ersten Fall empfahl sie Rückgabe dreier Gemälde an die Erben der ehemaligen Eigentümer.[13] Im zweiten Fall empfahl sie, die Rückgabe einer Plakatsammlung an den ehemaligen Eigentümer abzulehnen, weil die Sammlung in der DDR war und der Eigentümer für sie im Jahre 1961 mit DM 225.000 als Wiedergutmachung von der Bundesrepublik entschädigt worden war.[14] Im dritten Fall schließlich wurde empfohlen, die Erben des enteigneten Eigentümers zu entschädigen, weil nicht klar war, ob der Verkauf des Gemäldes im Jahre 1941 in Not oder unter Zwang erfolgte oder nicht.[15]

Dieses magere Ergebnis ist wohl darauf zurückzuführen, dass einerseits deutsche Museen die NS-verfolgungsbedingt entzogenen Kulturgüter normalerweise freiwillig herausgeben, also keiner Empfehlung durch die Kommission bedürfen, und dass andererseits in umstrittenen Fällen wie z.B. bei Ernst-Ludwig Kirchners „Berliner Straßenszene" eine Partei nicht

---

[10] International Journal of Cultural Property 8(1999) 142 mit Einleitung *Andrea G. Raschèr:* ibid. 338-342.

[11] Vgl. die Mitteilung unter http://www.lostart.de/nn_50658/Web/DE/Kommission/Index.html?_nnn=true

[12] Vgl. letzten Satz der Mitteilung in voriger Note.

[13] Pressemitteilung des Presse- und Informationsamts der Bundesregierung vom 12.1.2005: „Rückgabe NS-verfolgungsbedingt entzogener Kulturgüter – Erste Empfehlung der Beratenden Kommission".

[14] Pressemitteilung des Presse- und Informationsamts der Bundesregierung vom 25.1.2007: „Zweite Empfehlung der Beratenden Kommission für die Rückgabe NS-verfolgungsbedingt entzogener Kulturgüter".

[15] Pressemitteilung des Presse- und Informationsamts der Bundesregierung vom 12.6.2008: „Empfehlung der Beratenden Kommission für die Rückgabe NS-verfolgungsbedingt entzogener Kulturgüter".

bereit war oder es unterließ, die Kommission um eine Empfehlung zu bitten.[16]

II. 3. b) Frankreich

In Frankreich wurde erst im Jahre 1999 die „Commission d'indemnisation des victimes de spoliations" (CIVS) gebildet, die einzelne Schicksale jüdischer Bürger und ihrer Entschädigung oder Wiedergutmachung zu beurteilen und entsprechende Empfehlungen abzugeben hat.[17] Schiedsrichterliche Funktionen nimmt die CIVS nicht wahr.

II. 3. c) Niederlande

In den Niederlanden wirkt die „Adviescommissie Restitutieverzoeken Cultuurgoederen en Tweede Wereldoorlog" (Advisory Committee on the Assessment of Restitution Applications for Items of Cultural Value and the Second World War; sog. Ekkart Committee, genannt nach dem ersten Vorsitzenden des Komitees Prof. R.E.O. Ekkart). Sie wird auf Bitten beider Parteien tätig[18] und verfährt dabei seit kurzem auf Grund des Art. 7:900 BW (vaststellingsovereenkomst).[19] Dieses Komitee hat sehr viel mehr als die deutsche Beratende Kommission zu tun gehabt.[20] So hat sie im Jahr 2005 die Rückgabe von 267 Kunstwerken der Sammlung des Kunsthändlers Jacques Goudstikker (1897-1940) empfohlen,[21] und dem ist die niederländische Regierung auch gefolgt.[22]

II. 3. d) Österreich

In Österreich ist beim Bundesministerium für Unterricht und kulturelle Angelegenheiten ein Beirat gebildet worden, der den Bundesminister bei der Feststellung jener Personen zu beraten hat, denen Kunstgegenstände

---

[16] *Matthias Weller:* The Return of Ernst Ludwig Kirchner's *Berliner Straßenszene* – A Case Study: Art Antiquity and Law 12(2007) 65-74.

[17] Vgl. *Isabelle le Masne de Chermont/Laurence Sigal-Klagsbald:* À qui appartenaient ces tableaux? Looking for Owners, Paris 2008, 53.

[18] Art. 2 Abs. 3 des Dekrets des niederländischen Kultusministers vom 16.11.2001 über die Einsetzung des Advisory Committee, in: Advisory Committee (Hrsg.), Report 2007, Den Haag 2008, 73.

[19] Art. 2 Abs. 2 der Regulations on binding recommendations procedure vom 3.12.2007, in: Advisory Committee (Hrsg.), oben vorige Note, 81.

[20] Vgl. die jährlichen Berichte des Komitees.

[21] Advisory Committee (Hrsg.), Annual Report 2005, Den Haag 2006, 7 ff.

[22] Vgl. *Pieter den Hollander:* Roofkunst. De zaak-Goudstikker, Amsterdam 2007, 300 ff; *Peter Sutton* (Hrsg.): Reclaimed. Painting from the Collection of Jacques Goudstikker, Bruce Museum and The Jewish Museum New York 2008.

zu übereignen sind. Dies sieht § 3 des Bundesgesetzes von 1998 über Rückgabe von Kunstgegenständen aus den Österreichischen Bundesmuseen und Sammlungen vor.[23] Auch hier also fungiert der Beirat nicht als Schiedsgericht.

II. 3. e) Vereinigtes Königreich

Seit April 2000 berät das „Spoliation Advisory Panel“ (SAP), zusammengesetzt aus historisch und juristisch vorgebildeten Fachleuten, Antragsteller, öffentliche Museen und den Secretary of State darüber, ob Kunstwerke, die während der Nazi-Zeit von 1933 -1945 verloren gegangen sind und die sich heute im Besitz eines britischen Museums befinden, an die ursprünglichen Eigentümer zurückzugeben sind.[24] Auch dieses Panel ist häufig mit Ersuchen befasst worden und hat seine Stellungsnahmen abgegeben.[25]

Es ist vorgeschlagen worden, in Großbritannien ein „Human Remains Advisory Panel“ zu berufen, das für menschliche Überreste (human remains) ein Forum für Rückgabeforderungen sein könnte.[26]

II. 3. f) Vereinigte Staaten von Amerika

Die Vereinigten Staaten haben schon seit Erlass des Convention on Cultural Property Implementation Act von 1983 ein „Cultural Property Advisory Committee“, das den Präsidenten der USA in Sachen des UNESCO Übereinkommens von 1970 über Maßnamen zum Verbot und zur Verhütung der rechtswidrigen Einfuhr, Ausfuhr und Übereignung von Kulturgut[27] berät.[28] Speziell für „Holocaust Assets“ hat das Parlament den „U.S. Holocaust Assets Commission Act of 1998“ erlassen.[29] Diese Kommission hat die Vermögenswerte, die sich im Besitz der Bundesregierung einschließlich des „Board of Governors of the Federal Reserve System“ und

---

[23] Österr. BGBl. 1998 I Nr. 181.

[24] Vgl. die Dokumente des SAP bei: http://www.culture.gov.uk/what_we_do/cultural_property/3296.aspx

[25] Vgl. z.B. Report of the Spoliation Advisory Panel in Respect of Three Rubens Paintings now in the Possession of the Courtauld Institute of Art, London, November 2007.

[26] Vgl. *Norman Palmer:* Litigation: The Best Remedy?, in: International Bureau of the Permanent Court of Arbitration (Hrsg.), Resolution of Cultural Property Disputes, Den Haag/Zürich 2004, 265-290. (286 f.).

[27] 823 UNTS 231; dt.BGBl. 2007 II 627; SR 0.444.1.

[28] 19 U.S.C.SA. § 2605 (1999 und Cumulative Annual pocket Part 2008).

[29] 22 U.S.C.A. § 1621 Note (2004 und Cumulative Annual Pocket Part 2008).

jeder „Federal Reserve Bank" befinden, zu erforschen und darüber zu berichten. Diese Kommission wird also kaum über Kunstwerke in amerikanischen Museen zu entscheiden haben. Diese Kommission hat jedoch die Museen ermuntert, selbst Provenienzforschung zu betreiben.[30]

II. 3. g) Zwischenergebnis

All die Kommissionen, Komitees und Panels sind keine Schiedsgerichte, die unter Wahrung prozessualer Garantien endgültig entscheiden. Es sind nur Gremien, die entweder eine gütliche Einigung anstreben und der entscheidenden Instanz eine bestimmte Entscheidung nahe legen.

II. 4. Individuelle Schiedsklauseln

Natürlich bleibt es den Parteien unbenommen, im Einzelfall ihren Streit um Kulturgüter einem Schiedsgericht zu unterbreiten. Dies haben Maria Altmann und die Republik Österreich in ihrem Rechtstreit um Rückgabe von Gemälden von Gustav Klimt getan. In der am 15.1.2006 entschiedenen Schiedssache über fünf Klimt-Gemälde (darunter das Gemälde „Adele Bloch-Bauer I")[31] wurde die Rückübereignung auf Grund des Bundesgesetzes vom 4.12.1998 über die Rückgabe von Kunstgegenständen aus den Österreichischen Bundesmuseen und Sammlungen (KunstrückgabeG) verfügt,[32] jedoch die Anwendbarkeit des KunstrückgabeG im zweiten Schiedsspruch vom 7.5.2006, betreffend die Rückübereignung von Klimts Gemälde „Amalie Zuckerkandl", verneint.[33] Diesen Schiedsspruch haben die Kläger erfolglos angefochten und dessen Aufhebung wegen Verstoßes gegen Grundwertungen des österreichischen Rechtsordnung (ordre public) nach § 611 Abs. 2 Ziff. 8 österr. ZPO Vergeblich verlangt. Damit ist eine schnelle Lösung des Streites hinfällig geworden.

---

[30] Report of the AAMD [Association of American Museum Directors] Task Force on the Spoliation of Art during the Nazi/World War II Era, http://www.aamd.org/papers/guideln.php

[31] Arbitration Award vom 15. 1. 2006, abrufbar unter: http://www.adele.at/Schiedspruch/award.pdf; hierzu *Martha G. B. Lufkin:* A Sea-Smoke at the Austrian National Gallery. Republic of Austria et al. v. Altmann, Decision of Austrian Arbitral Court, 15th January 2006: Art Antiquity and Law 11(2006) 351-369.

[32] Österr. BGBl. 1998 Nr. 181.

[33] Schiedsspruch von 7.5.2006, bei: http://www.bslaw.com/altmann/Zuckerkandl/Decisions/decisions.pdf hierzu *Georg Graf:* Arme Amalie! – Kritische Anmerkungen zum Schiedsspruch in Sachen Amalie Zuckerkandl: Österr. NotZ 2007, 65-79.; *Nikolaus Pitkowitz:* Ordre public – widriger Klimt-Schiedsspruch: ecolex 2007, 663-666. Bestätigt durch OGH 1.4.2008: ecolex 2008, 433.

II. 5. Zwischenergebnis

Bis jetzt gibt es nur sehr wenige Schiedssprüche über Kulturgut-Streitigkeiten.[34] Wieso diese Art der Streiterledigung so selten benutzt wird, soll nun untersucht werden.

III. Probleme im Einzelnen

III. 1. Schiedsfähigkeit

Die Schiedsfähigkeit (arbitrability) eines Anspruchs ist nach dem „UNCITRAL Model Law on International Arbitration" (Model Law)[35] keine besondere Vorsaussetzung für ein internationales Schiedsverfahren. Die Schiedsfähigkeit wird nur durch bestimmte Gesetze des Forumstaates eingeschränkt, wonach bestimmte Rechtsstreitigkeiten keinem Schiedsgericht zu unterbreiten sind (Art. 1 Abs. 5 Model Law). Auch die „Permanent Court of Arbitration Optional Rules for Arbitrating Disputes between Two Parties of Which Only One Is a State" (Optional Rules) von 1991[36] sagen nichts über die Schiedsfähigkeit als einer besonderen Voraussetzung eines Schiedsverfahrens. Übereinstimmung besteht allerdings darüber, dass vermögensrechtliche Ansprüche einem Schiedsverfahren unterworfen werden können, wie es u.a. die § 1030 Abs. 1 Satz 1 dt. ZPO, § 582 Abs. 1 Satz 1 österr. ZPO und Art. 177 Abs. 1 schweiz. IPRG vorsehen, also Gesetze, die sich eng an das Model Law anlehnen.

Im Fall der Schiedsklausel, die dem Schiedsgericht im Falle Altmann zugrunde lag,[37] hätte also das Schiedsgericht das österreichische Recht fragen müssen, ob dieses eine Klage auf Herausgabe von Kulturgut ausschließlich den staatlichen Gerichten vorbehält und damit ein Schiedsverfahren untersagt. Die §§ 577 ff. österr. ZPO sind kürzlich neu gefasst worden und am 1.7.2006, also nach der Fällung beider Schiedssprüche im

---

[34] Dies war auch das Ergebnis der Genfer Tagung vom 17.10.1997, vgl. die Vorträge in: *Quentin Byrne-Sutton/Fabienne Geisinger-Mariéthoz* (Hrsg.): Resolution Methods for Art-Related Disputes, Zürich 1999, und der Bericht von *Quentin Byrne-Sutton:* Resolution Methods for Art-Related Disputes, Art-Law Centre, Geneva (October 17, 1997): International Journal of Cultural Property 7(1998) 249-257.

[35] UNCITRAL Model Law on International Arbitration 1985 with amendments as adopted in 2006, Vienna 2008, 1 ff.

[36] Abgedruckt in: Permanent Court of Arbitration Basic Documents, Den Haag 1998, 73.

[37] Vgl. oben N. 31 und 33.

Fall Altmann in Kraft getreten.[38] Auf die Schiedssprüche ist daher das bisher geltende Recht anzuwenden (Art. VII Abs. 2 SchiedsRÄG 2006). In §§ 577 ff. österr. ZPO a.F. konnten die Parteien insoweit einen Schiedsvertrag vereinbaren, als sie über den Gegenstand des Verfahrens einen Vergleich abzuschließen fähig waren (§ 577 Abs. 1 österr. ZPO a.F.). Diese Vorschriften trennten noch nicht zwischen interner und internationaler Schiedsgerichtsbarkeit und machten deshalb die objektive Schiedsfähigkeit von der Befugnis zu einem Vergleich abhängig. Wie immer dem sei, im Fall Altmann konnte die Republik Österreich über den Rückforderungsanspruch verfügen, denn das KunstrückgabeG von 1998 mit seinem Beirat räumt dem Bundesministerium für Unterricht und kulturelle Angelegenheiten ein weites Ermessen bei der Rückgabe von Kunstgegenständen ein. Für einen solchen Rechtsstreit gilt im Übrigen das, was Art. 177 Abs. 2 schweiz. IPRG sagt: „Ist eine Partei ein Staat, ein staatlich beherrschtes Unternehmen oder eine staatlich kontrollierte Organisation, so kann sie nicht unter Berufung auf ihr eigenes Recht ihre Parteifähigkeit m Schiedsverfahren oder die Schiedsfähigkeit einer Streitsache in Frage stellen, die Gegenstand der Schiedsvereinbarung ist." Deshalb wohl hat das Schiedsgericht in Sachen Altmann seine Zuständigkeit ganz kurz bejaht, und auch die Republik Österreich hat den Schiedsspruch vom 15.1.2006 anerkannt und die der Klägerin zugesprochenen Gemälde sofort herausgegeben.

Heute dürfte im Recht der internationalen Schiedsgerichtsbarkeit allgemein anerkannt sein, dass vermögensrechtliche Ansprüche selbst dann schiedsfähig sind, wenn sie öffentlich-rechtlicher Natur sind und die Parteien über den Streitgegenstand einen öffentlich-rechtlichen Vertrag schließen können.[39] § 582 österr. ZPO n.F. ist dagegen zurückhaltender und verlangt, dass der vermögensrechtliche Anspruch, der Gegenstand eines Schiedsverfahrens ist, von den ordentlichen Gerichten zu entscheiden wäre. Doch auch hier stören öffentlich-rechtliche Normen nicht, soweit sie nur beiläufig im Zivilverfahren anzuwenden sind. Das war wohl im Altmann-Fall gegeben; denn die Klägerin berief sich auf ihr Eigentum und auch das Schiedsgericht ging der Eigentumsfrage eingehend nach.

---

[38] Schiedsrechts-Änderungsgesetz 2006 – SchiedsRÄG 2006, österr. BGBl. 2006 I Nr. 7. Vgl. hierzu ausführlich *Christian Hausmaninger* in: *Fasching/Konecny:* Kommentar zu den Zivilprozeßgesetzen, 4. Band/2. Teilband, 2. Aufl. Wien 2007, §§ 577 ff. ZPO.

[39] Begründung des Entwurfs eines Gesetzes zur Neuregelung des Schiedsverfahrensrechts: BT-Drucksache 13/5274, S. 35.

III. 2. Schiedsvereinbarung

Für Schiedsverfahren über Kulturgüter gelten keine besonderen Vorschriften über die Form einer Schiedsvereinbarung. Sie sollte der Vorschrift des Art. II des New Yorker Übereinkommens von 1958[40] entsprechen, damit sie überall anerkannt wird. Die einzige Schwierigkeit besteht darin, die Parteien zu einer Schiedsvereinbarung über ihren Disput zu bringen. Das ist bisher verhältnismässig selten gelungen. Verbreitet ist dagegen ein gerichtlicher oder außergerichtlicher Vergleich der Parteien, in dem der bisherige Besitzer des Kunstwerkes dieses behält und der Anspruchsteller vom Besitzer entschädigt wird.[41]

III. 3. Schiedsgericht

Für einen Rechtsstreit wählt man entweder ein institutionelles Schiedsgericht oder ein ad hoc-Schiedsgericht. Im Fall Altmann einigte man sich auf ein Schiedsgericht, besetzt allein mit österreichischen Schiedsrichtern. Das ist erstaunlich, aber wohl aus zwei Gründen zu erklären. Zum einen wollte Österreich in dieser verfahrenen Situation wohl eigene Schiedsrichter haben, da nach österreichischer Auffassung allein österreichische Gerichte zuständig sind, über den Rechtstreit gegen die Republik Österreich zu entscheiden.[42] Zum andern ging es um ein Sprachenproblem. Alle Unterlagen und Gutachten in der Sache waren in deutscher Sprache geschrieben und einem nicht der deutschen Sprache mächtigen Schiedsrichter hätten all diese Dokumente übersetzt werden müssen.[43] Das wäre sehr

---

[40] Übereinkommen über die Anerkennung und Vollstreckung ausländischer Schiedssprüche vom 10.6.1958, dt. BGBl. 1961 II 122; österr. BGBl. 1961 Nr. 200; SR 0.277.12.

[41] So geschehen etwa im Streit der Galerie Beyeler in Riehen bei Basel um Wassily Kandinsky's „Improvisation X" (2002), im Streit des Art Institute in Chicago um Edgar Degas's „Landscape with Smokestacks" (1998) und bei der Rückgabe und dem Rückkauf von Lucas Cranachs „Madonna and Child in a Landscape" durch das North Carolina Art Museum in Raleigh, N.C.

[42] Vgl. Altmann v. Republic of Austria, 142 F.Supp.2d 1187 (C.D. Cal. 2001), 317 F.3d 954 (9th Cir. 2002), 327 F.3d 1246 (9th Cir, 2003); 541 U.S 677 (2004). Hierzu vgl. *John J. Gibbons/Terry Myers/Rudolf Dolzer:* Zur Reichweite der US-Gerichte in Internationalen Angelegenheiten. Die Entscheidung des US Supreme Court vom Juni 2004: RIW 2004, 899-903., *Burkhard Hess:* ein transatlantischer Rechtstreit um ein weltberühmtes Gemälde Gustav Klimts im Wiener Belvedere, in: Grenzüberschreitungen. FS Peter Schlosser, Tübingen 2005, 257-273.; *Christoph H. Schreuer:* Staatenimmunität in den USA: ecolex 2004, 781-784.

[43] Vgl. etwa *Rudolf Welser/Christian Rabl:* Der Fall Klimt. Die rechtliche Problematik der Klimt-Bilder im Belvedere, Wien 2005, als Gutachter für Frau Altmann; dagegen *Heinz*

teuer geworden. Man sieht: es kommt sehr auf den Einzelfall an, welche Schiedsrichter man für das Schiedsgericht wählt.

III. 4. Schiedsverfahren

Das Schiedsverfahren dürfte normalerweise keine großen Schwierigkeiten bereiten. Zu fragen ist allerdings, ob die Parteien sich darauf einigen wollen, dass das Gericht *ex aequo et bono* entscheidet. Das haben die Parteien im Altmann-Fall nicht getan. Die Parteien wollten ihr Recht und nach diesem Recht (hier: österreichisches Recht) sollte entschieden werden.

Sofern sich die Parteien auf eine Mediation einigen, liegt die Einigung bei den Parteien und diese können schließlich eine Vereinbarung treffen, die auch außerrechtliche Gesichtspunkte berücksichtigt.[44]

III. 5. Schiedsspruch und dessen Endgültigkeit

Wer sich auf ein Schiedsverfahren einlässt, muss wissen, dass ein Schiedsspruch zwischen den Parteien den Rechtstreit endgültig erledigt. Der Schiedsspruch kann noch vor den staatlichen Gerichten angefochten werden, aber dies dürfe nur in Ausnahmefällen möglich sein. Zum Beispiel im Altmann-Fall ist der zweite Schiedsspruch vom 7.5.2006 angefochten worden, aber offenbar immer noch nicht entschieden.[45]

III. 6. Vollstreckung des Schiedsspruchs

Die meisten Schiedssprüche werden wie im ersten Altmann-Fall freiwillig erfüllt. Wenn es jedoch zu einer zwangsweisen Durchführung kommt, wird der Schiedsspruch auf Grund des New Yorker Übereinkommens von 1958 im Ausland anerkannt und vollstreckt.[46]

IV. Zusammenfassung

Die nationale und internationale Schiedsgerichtsbarkeit spielt bei Kulturgut-Streitigkeiten eine verhältnismässig geringe Rolle. Das liegt nicht so sehr an der Materie, sondern an der Tatsache, dass Parteien erst dann vor

---

Krejci: Der Klimt-Streit, Wien 2005, und eine Auseinadersetzung zwischen diesen Autoren in der Österreichischen Juristen-Zeitung 2005, 689 ff., 733 ff., 817 ff., und der Österreichischen Notariats-Zeitung 2005, 257 ff. und 321 ff.

[44] Vgl.in anderem Zusammenhang *J. Christian Wichard/Wend B. Wendland:* Mediation as an Option for Resolving Disputes between Indigenous/Traditional Communities and Industry Concerning Traditional Knowledge, in: *Hoffman* (Hrsg.): oben N. 4, 475-482.

[45] S. oben N. 33.

[46] S. oben N. 40.

die Möglichkeit einer Schiedsvereinbarung gestellt sind, wenn eine Streit zwischen ihnen bereits entstanden ist und nicht – wie üblicherweise – wenn eine späterer Streit nur möglich ist. Wenn jedoch die Fronten einmal verhärtet sind, werden die staatlichen Gerichte angerufen und vielleicht später ein Vergleich abgeschlossen.

Die Schiedsurteile im Fall Altmann sind insofern außergewöhnlich, als dem Schiedsverfahren eine Klage in Kalifornien als einen exorbitanten Gerichtsstand („long arm-statute" des „doing business" in Kalifornien) vorausgegangen war und auch die Immunität der Republik Österreich verneint wurde. Das Schiedsurteil war also alles andere als normal und geheim. Trotzdem sollte man die Anstrengungen nicht aufgeben, für Streitigkeiten über Kulturgüter eine Schiedsinstanz bereitzustellen, der die Parteien ihr Anliegen zur Entscheidung anvertrauen können. Illusionen darf man sich jedoch nicht hingeben.[47] Das liegt an mehreren Umständen. Es gibt keinen typischen Kulturgüterstreit, sondern Streitigkeiten über „Holocaust-Art", über „human remains", über Kulturgüter, die schon vor Jahrzehnten oder Jahrhunderten ins Ausland gebracht wurden, und über normale Diebstähle und Schmuggelware. Jeder Fall oder jede Fallgruppe liegt anders und hat ihre eigenen Probleme. Das fängt bereits mit der Sprache an. Wo jüdische Bürger in Deutschland, Frankreich oder Ungarn enteignet wurden und alle Dokumente in deutscher, französischer oder ungarischer Sprache vorliegen, hat es wenig Sinn, Schiedsrichter zu benennen, welche diese Sprachen im Original nicht lesen können. Wo heute kein gerichtlich durchsetzbarer Anspruch besteht, werden sich die Parteien kaum einem Schiedsgericht anvertrauen. Schließlich sind Schiedsgerichte dort überflüssig, wo Gegenstände, seien sie gestohlen oder nicht, seien sie menschliche Überreste (human remains) oder Kultgegenstände, freiwillig zurückerstattet werden. Gleichwohl gilt auch hier: Die einvernehmlich gewählte Schiedsinstanz ist im Zweifel besser geeignet, eine Kulturgut-Streitigkeit zu entscheiden, als ein einseitig bestimmtes staatliches Gericht.

---

[47] Ebenso *Hannes Hartung:* The Holocaust and World War II Looted Art. Arbitration between Great Dreams and Reality, in: International Bureau (Hrsg), Resolution, oben N. 26, 327-337.

About the Rome II Regulation: The European Unification of the Conflict Rules to Torts

LAJOS VÉKÁS

Professor Várady's interest and worldwide acknowledged scientific work fall principally to international arbitration and to the private international law.[1] I'd like to celebrate him, an old friend of mine, on his birthday by a paper about a milestone in the harmonization of the European private international law: the Rome II Regulation on the law applicable to non-contractual relations.

I. General survey

I. 1.

The Rome II Regulation[2] applies from 11 January 2009 in situations involving a conflict of laws to non-contractual obligations.[3] It is the first time in history that 26 states in Europe have a *unified conflict of laws sys-*

---

[1] *Commercial Arbitration – A Transnational Perspective* (with John Barcelo and Arthur von Mehren), 4th ed., Thomson–Reuters–West, 2009; *Language and Translation in International Commercial Arbitration*, T.M.C. Asser Press, 2006. *Medjunarodno privatno pravo* (with Bernadett Bordás, Gašo Knežević and Vladimir Pavić), 9th ed., Belgrade, 2007.

[2] Regulation (EC) No 864/2007 of the European Parliament and the Council of 11 July 2007 on the law applicable to non-contractual relations (Rome II), OJ L 199/40 of 31 July 2007. See *S. Leible/M. Lehmann*: Die neue EG-Verordnung über das auf außervertragliche Schuldverhältnisse anzuwendende Recht ('Rom II'), RIW 2007, p. 721 et seq.; *A. Junker*: Die Rom II-Verordnung: Neues Internationales Deliktsrecht auf europäischer Grundlage, NJW 2007, p. 3675 et seq.; *S. Corneloup/N. Joubert*: Le règlement communautaire "Rome II" sur la loi applicable aux obligations non contractuelles. Paris 2008; *G. Wagner*: Die neue Rom II-Verordnung, IPRax 2008, p. 1 et seq.

[3] According Article 31, the Regulation applies to events giving rise to damage which occur after the entry into force of the Regulation, i.e., of 20 August 2007 [Art. 254(1) EC]. See *E. Jayme/Ch. Kohler*, IPRax 2007, p. 49, note 17.

tem for an important part of Private International Law.[4] Hungary as a member of the European Union belongs to these countries. The uniform conflicts rules on non-contractual obligations have a long legislative history started with the EC-Draft Convention of 1973,[5] and have been the subject of heavy discussion in legal literature.[6] Especially in the field of international torts, the regulation will have a high practical importance.

The common European rules in most cases practically abolish national conflicts rules. Article 3 of the Regulation sets forth universal application: any law specified by Rome II shall be applied whether or not there is the law of a Member State. It means that the Regulation sets forth application to third countries too *(loi uniforme).*

I. 2.

The Regulation shall apply, in situation involving the conflict of laws, to non-contractual obligations both in civil and commercial matters. Non-contractual obligations for the purposes of the Regulation are obligations

---

[4] To the history of the Rome II Regulation see *Hamburg Group* for Private and International Law: Comment of 23 September 2002 on the European Commission's Draft Proposal for a Council regulation on the Law Applicable to Non-Contractual Obligations. RabelsZ 2003, p. 1 et seq.; *C. Nourissat/E. Treppoz*: Quelques observations sur l'avant-projet de proposition de règlement du Conseil sur la loi applicable aux obligations non contractuelles 'Roma II'. Clunet 2003, 7 et seq.; *P. Huber/I. Bach*: Die Rom II-VO (Kommissionsentwurf und aktuelle Entwicklungen), IPRax 2005, p. 73 et seq.; *R. Weintraub*: Rome II and the Tension between Predictability and Flexibility. Riv. dir. int. priv. proc. 2005, 561 et seq.; *P. Mankowski*: Entwicklungen im Internationalen Privat- und Prozessrecht 2004/2005 (Teil 1), RIW 2005, p. 481 et seq.; *A. Malatesta* (ed.): The Unification of Choice of Law Rules on Torts and Other Non Contractual Obligations in Europe, 'The Rome II' Proposal, Padova 2006; *M. Sonnentag*: Zur Europäisierung des Internationalen außervertraglichen Schuldrechts durch die geplante Rom II-Verordnung, ZVglRWiss 2006, p. 256 et seq.; *F. Guerchoun/S. Piedelièvre*: Le règlement sur la loi applicable aux obligations non contractuelles ('Roma II'). Gaz. Pal. 2007, Doctrine 3186 et seq.; *H. Koziol/Th. Thiede*: Kritische Bemerkungen zum derzeitigen Stand des Entwurf einer Rom II-Verordnung, ZVglRWiss 2007, p. 235 et seq.; *R. Wagner*: Das Vermittlungsverfahren zur Rom II-Verordnung, in: *D. Baetge/J. von Hein/M. von Hinden*: Die richtige Ordnung: FS Kropholler. Tübingen 2008, p. 715 et seq.

[5] See *A. E. von Overbeck/P. Volken*: Das internationale Deliktsrecht im Vorentwurf der EWG. RabelsZ 1974, p. 211 et seq.; *O. Lando*: The EC-Draft Convention on the Law Applicable to Contractual and Non-Contractual Obligations, RebelsZ 1974, p. 6 et seq.

[6] See under note 4; further *J. von Hein*: Die Kodifikation des europäischen Internationalen Deliktsrechts, ZVglRWiss 2003, p. 528 et seq. and the Volume 9(2007) of the Yearbook of Private International Law, p. 1 et seq.

arising out of tort/delict, unjust enrichment, *negotiorum gestio* or *culpa in contrahendo*. The Rome II shall apply also to non-contractual obligations that are likely to arise. *Culpa in contrahendo* is an autonomous concept in the Regulation; it should not necessarily be interpreted within the meaning of national law.

The rules regarding the scope of application are followed by the individual areas of the non-contractual obligations (torts etc.) and by general provisions dealing with the scope of the law applicable, overriding mandatory provisions, exclusion renvoi, with public policy[7] of the forum.

I. 3.

The *national conflicts rules* will play a role in the future only in the fields excluded from the scope of the Regulation. According to Article 1(2), the following non-contractual obligations are excluded from the scope of the Regulation:

(a) non-contractual obligations arising out of family relationships and relationships deemed by the law applicable to such relationships to have comparable effects including maintenance obligations;
(b) non- contractual obligations arising out of matrimonial property regimes, property regimes of relationships deemed by the law applicable to such relationships to have comparable effects to marriage, and wills and succession;
(c) non-contractual obligations arising under bills of exchange, cheques and promissory notes and other negotiable instruments to the extent that the obligations under such other negotiable instruments arise out of their negotiable character;
(d) non-contractual obligations arising out of the law of companies and other bodies corporate or unincorporated regarding matters such as the creation, by registration or otherwise, legal capacity, internal organisation or winding-up of companies and other bodies corporate or unincorporated, the personal liability of officers and members as such for the obligations of the company or body and personal liability of auditors to a company or to its members in the statutory audits of accounting documents;

---

[7] *J. Mörsdorf-Schulte*: Spezielle Vorbehaltsklausel im Europäischen Internationalen Deliktsrecht, ZVglRWiss 2005, p. 192 et seq.

(e) non-contractual obligations arising out of the relations between the settlors, trustees and beneficiaries of a trust created voluntarily;
(f) non-contractual obligations arising out of nuclear damage;[8]
(g) non-contractual obligations arising out of violations of privacy and rights relating to personality, including defamation.

The majority of these exceptions belongs to a specific area of private law other than tort law: matrimonial, family and inheritance law or to claims arising from negotiable instruments and from internal disputes regarding trusts and corporations. These areas have their own conflict of law rules. Contrary to these exceptions the violations of privacy and rights relating personality including defamation are genuine tort law cases. The lack of applicability in this area is simply due to the fact the drafters could not find a commonly acceptable solution.[9]

I. 4.

It is important to mention that *Denmark* does not take part in the adoption of Rome II, and is not bound by it or subject to its application. The Regulation is however, applicable in all other Member States, even when the place of injury lies is Denmark.

I. 5.

Unfortunately, the Rome II Regulation has not reached the expected complete unification of the European conflict rules concerning *traffic accidents*.[10] According to Article 28(1), the Regulation does not prejudice the application of the Hague Convention on law applicable to traffic accidents

[8] See *U. Magnus*: Probleme des internationalen Atomhaftungsrecht, in: *D. Baetge/J. von Hein/M. von Hinden*: Die richtige Ordnung: FS Kropholler, Tübingen 2008, p. 595 et seq.

[9] See *K. Siehr*: European Private International Law of Torts. Violation of Privacy and Rights Relating to Personality, Riv. dir. int. priv. proc. 2004, p.1201 et seq.; *M. von Hinden*: Ein europäisches Kollisionsrecht für die Medien. Gedanken zur Fortentwicklung der Rom II-Verordnung, in: *D. Baetge/J. von Hein/M. von Hinden*: Die richtige Ordnung: FS Kropholler, Tübingen 2008, p. 573 et seq.

[10] *A. Staudinger*: Das Konkurrenzverhältnis zwischen dem Haager Straßenverkehrsübereinkommen und der Rom II-VO, in: *D. Baetge/J. von Hein/M. von Hinden*: Die richtige Ordnung: FS Kropholler, Tübingen 2008, p. 691 et seq.; *K. Siehr*: Kollisionen des Kollisionsrechts, in: *D. Baetge/J. von Hein/M. von Hinden*: Die richtige Ordnung: FS Kropholler, Tübingen 2008, p. 211 et seq. (225).

of 4 May 1971.[11] (It is the case concerning other international conventions as well.) It means that the Hague Convention applies in the 12 Member States which belong to this Convention[12] and the Rome II Regulation applies only in the other 14 countries. Thus, in this very important field, *forum shopping* remains in the European Union despite the efforts to unify the conflict-of-law rules on the law applicable to torts.[13]

II. Torts/Delicts

II. 1. Freedom of Choice

In the logic of the system of Rome II, the first step in determination of the law governing torts/delicts (as every other non-contractual obligation) is *the choice-of-law agreement*. Party autonomy is acknowledged in the Regulation.[14] Article 14 allows the parties to choose any law they want, not only the *lex fori* or the law with which the case is connected. Unless parties are not pursuing a commercial activity, they can choose the law only by an agreement entered into after the event giving rise to the damage occurred. These restrictions meant to protect the interests of the weaker party. The parties' freedom to chose the applicable law is a subject to further restrictions:

- the choice must be expressed, or demonstrated with reasonable certainty by the circumstances of the case;
- the choice of a foreign law can not displace overriding mandatory rules of the forum;
- in domestic cases, a choice of foreign law can not displace the mandatory rules of the law that would apply without the choice;

---

[11] An amended proposal of the Commission of 21 February 2006 [COM (2006) 83 final] wanted to give precedence to the Rome II Regulation over two international conventions (the Hague Convention on the law applicable to traffic accidents of 4 May 1971 and the Hague Convention on the law applicable to products liability of 2 October 1973) in case where all the material aspects of the particular case were located in one or more Member States. This proposal has been defeated, mainly because of difficulty faced in distinguishing the intra-community from the extra-community situations.

[12] Austria, Belgium, Czech Republic, France, Latvia, Lithuania, Luxembourg, the Netherlands, Poland, Slovenia, Slovakia and Spain.

[13] Concerning the similar problem in the field of product liability see below under II. 3. b).

[14] Compare *S. Leible*: Rechtswahl im IPR der außervertraglichen Schuldverhältnisse nach der Rom II-Verordnung, RIW 2008, p. 257 et seq.; *G. Rühl*: Rechtswahlfreiheit im europäischen Kollisionsrecht, in: *D. Baetge/J. von Hein/M. von Hinden*: Die richtige Ordnung: FS Kropholler, Tübingen 2008, p. 187 et seq.

- in intra-community cases, the choice of the law of a non-member state can not displace mandatory provisions of Community law; and
- the choice may not affect the rights of third parties.[15]

The party autonomy extends also to product liability cases (Article 5), environmental damages (Article 7) and damages caused by an industrial action (Article 9). However, a choice-of-law-agreement does not affect the law applicable to torts arising from unfair competition and restrictive trade practices, as covered by Article 6, and from an infringement of intellectual property rights, as designated by Article 8. The first restriction meant to protect collective interests, the latter however can hardly be regarded as a convincing solution.[16]

The practical importance of the party autonomy in the area of torts/delicts is limited. The parties have little cause to agree on a law if they are not bound by a pre-existing (mainly contractual) relationship, because the chosen law could put one of them at a disadvantage.[17]

II. 2. *Lex loci damni*

In relation to obligations arising out of a tort/delict, Article 4(1) states that the applicable law shall be the law of the country in which the damage occurs.[18] Rome II designates the place of *direct damage* as connecting factor for torts, irrespective of the country in which the event giving rise to the damage occurred and irrespective of the country (or countries) in which the indirect consequences of that event occurred. It means that consequential costs, immaterial damage, indirect damage to third persons ("secondary or consequential damage") are not regarded as separate connecting factors in Rome II, similarly to former conflicts law of Hungary and other Member States. This was the opinion of the European Court of Justice in the *Marinari* case: "The place where the damage occurred under Article 5(3) of the Brussels Convention does not include the place where the victim suffered financial damage arising from the initial damage and suffered by him in another Contracting State."[19]

---

[15] These restrictions can also be found in the Rome I Regulation.

[16] Similar opinion by *Th. M. de Boer*: Party Autonomy and its Limitations in the Rome II Regulation, in: Yearbook of Private International Law, 9 (2007), p. 29.

[17] Similarly *Th. M. de Boer*: Party Autonomy and its Limitations in the Rome II Regulation, in: Yearbook of Private International Law, 9 (2007), p. 29.

[18] Similar terminology is used in Art. 5 Nr. 3 of the Brussels I Regulation of 2001.

[19] ECJ, C-364/93, Marinari v. Lloyds Bank [1995] ECR I-2719.

The country in which the direct damage occurs is in fact the country where the legally protected interest is injured: the place of injury. Recital 16 of the Regulation preamble states that *lex loci damni* strikes a fair balance between the interests of the person claimed to be liable and the person sustaining the damage, and also reflects the modern approach to civil law liability especially the development of system of strict liability.

In France and in the majority of Member States the place of injury as connecting factor is not a new phenomenon. These countries acknowledged it also before the Regulation. Hungary does not belong to these countries because its PIL preferred the place of conduct-rule [§ 32 (1) PIL Act of 1979],[20] and the place of direct damage is only alternatively applicable, based on a comparative better-law approach of § 32 (2) PIL Act of 1979. Therefore Article 4 (1) of Rome II represents for Hungary a new basic conflicts rule of international tort law.

The material scope of the application of the basic rule has been limited by special rules in Rome II. Important tort situations are not covered by Article 4 (1). Consequently the material scope of application of this provision is practically reduced to torts which are predominantly committed as "point" or "location" delicts. The most typical examples for such delicts are traffic accidents with tortuous consequences, for which the place of direct damage is the place of the accident, i.e. the location, where the entire delict was consummated. In the case of strict liability the place of the risk (preparatory act, omission, for example) is irrelevant for the occurring of the damage. Accordingly, the place of direct damage as connecting factor will be applied.

II. 3. Exceptions to the Basic Rule

According the Recital 19, specific rules should be laid down for special torts/delicts where the general rule does not allow a reasonable balance between the interests at stake. Therefore the *lex loci damni* does not have significance for torts related to product liability, and it affects only partly competition law and environmental damage. These exceptions are covered by special rules in Article 5-7. Similarly, infringements related to intellectual property[21] and industrial actions fall under special rules in Article 8-9. These torts are typical distance delicts which involve a crossing of a legal border at some point between the conduct and the result. Article 5-9 of

[20] Similarly in § 48 (1) Austrian PIL Act of 1978.

[21] See *H. Schack*: Das auf (formlose) Immaterialgüterrechte anwendbare Recht nach Rom II, in: *D. Baetge/J. von Hein/M. von Hinden*: Die richtige Ordnung: FS Kropholler, Tübingen 2008, p. 651 et seq.

Rome II set forth independent conflict of laws rules; a return to Article 4 is only required in as far as these special rules expressively mandate it.

II. 3. a)

The rules in Article 5[22] cover all forms of liability arising from damage caused by a product, whether the liability is strict or fault-based.[23] The term of "product" is not defined in the Regulation; however, the Commission refers[24] to the definition of product in Article 2 of the Council Directive 85/374 EEC of 25 July 1985 on the harmonisation of *product liability* in the Member States.[25] This solution seems to be generally accepted.[26] Concerning the concept of the person claimed to be liable the Commission refers to the various persons who are potentially liable under Article 3(2) of the Product Liability Directive.[27] But the rule is not limited to those persons. For Article 5 of Rome II the person claimed to be liable can be any person. The rule in Article 5 is not restricted to consumers; it applies to any person sustaining any damage caused by a product.

The special connecting factors for product liability cases in Article 5 are, in successive order, the following:

- the habitual residence of the person sustaining damage if the product marketed in that country and if this marketing was reasonably foreseeable for the producer or, failing that,
- the place of acquisition of the product if the product was marketed in that country and if this marketing was reasonably foreseeable for the producer or, failing that,
- the place of occurrence of damage if that product was marketed in that country and if this marketing was reasonably foreseeable for the producer.[28]

---

[22] In the first reading opinion of the European Parliament, this article had been deleted. The reason given by the reporteur Diana Wallis was that the flexibility of a general rule would be preferable to rigid special rules: P6_TA(2005) 0284, 6 July 2005, *OJ* C 157 E, 6.7.2006, p. 371; Legal affairs (JURI), PE 349.977, p. 38 et seq.

[23] COM (2003) 427 final, p. 15.

[24] COM (2003) 427 final, p. 13.

[25] OJ L210, 7.8. 1998, p. 29 as amended by Directive 1999/34 EC of the European Parliament and of the Council of 10 May 1999: OJ L 141, 4.6. 1999, p. 20.

[26] See *P. Huber /M. Illmer*: International Product Liability. A Commentary on Article 5 of the Rome Regulation, in: Yearbook of Private International Law, 9 (2007) p. 30 et seq.

[27] COM (2003) 427 final, p. 15.

[28] See more detailed *P. Huber/M. Illmer*: International Product Liability. A Commentary on Article 5 of the Rome Regulation, in: Yearbook of Private International Law, 9

It's a pity that these rules have not been synchronised with those of the Hague Convention on the Law Applicable to Products Liability of 2 October 1973.[29] This Convention provides for a more complex system of cumulative connecting factors than the Regulation. The connecting factors of the Convention are the following:

- the place of injury,
- the place of the habitual residence of the person directly suffering damage,
- the principal place of business of the person claimed to be liable, and
- the place where the product was acquired by the person directly suffering damage.

The applicable law is determined along a ladder of these connecting factors, and two of them must be present in the same state for applying that state's law. If, however, the person claimed to be liable could not have foreseen the marketing of the product causing the damage in the relevant state, the determined law does not apply.

According to Article 28 of the Rome II Regulation, the Regulation does not prejudice the application of international conventions to which one or more Member States are parties at the time, when this Regulation is adopted and which lay down conflict-of-law rules relating to non-contractual obligations.[30] It means that the Regulation does not prevail over the Hague Convention and therefore (similarly to the conflict rules on traffic accidents) there are two different regimes of conflict rules on product liability in the European Union. The Hague Convention determines the applicable law for product liability cases in Finland, France,

(2007) p. 30 et seq.; *A. Spickhoff*: Die Produkthaftung im Europäischen Kollisions- und Zivilverfahrensrecht, in: *D. Baetge/J. von Hein/M. von Hinden*: Die richtige Ordnung: FS Kropholler, Tübingen 2008, p. 671 et seq.

[29] See the critique of the non-synchronization in: "Stellungnahme der 2. Kommission des Deutschen Rates für internationales Privatrecht".
http://ec.europa.eu/justice_home/news/consulting_public/rome_ii/deutscher_rat_internat_privatrecht_de.pdf p. 20 et seq.

[30] An amended proposal of the Commission of 21 February 2006 [COM (2006) 83 final] wanted to give precedence to the Rome II Regulation over two international conventions (the Hague Convention on the law applicable to traffic accidents of 4 May 1971 and the Hague Convention on the law applicable to products liability of 2 October 1973) in case where all the material aspects of the particular case were located in one or more Member States. This proposal has been defeated, mainly because of difficulty faced in distinguishing the intra-community from the extra-community situations.

Luxembourg, the Netherlands, Slovenia and Spain, whereas Article 5 of the Rome II Regulation applies in the remaining 20 Member States.[31]

II. 3. b)

Article 6 of the Rome II Regulation concerns the law applicable to *unfair competition* and acts restricting free competition (*antitrust*).[32] In matters of unfair competition, the conflict-of-law rule protects competitors, consumers and the general public and ensures that the market economy functions properly. The connection to the law of the country where competitive relations or the collective interests of consumers are, or are likely to be, affected generally satisfies these objectives.

The law applicable to a non-contractual obligation arising out of an act of unfair competition shall be the law of the country where competitive relations or the collective interests of consumers are, or are likely to be, affected. Where an act of unfair competition affects exclusively the interests of a specific competitor, Article 4 shall apply. This special rule in Article 6 is not an exception to the general rule in Article 4(1) but rather a clarification of it.

When the market is, or is likely to be, affected in more than one country, the person seeking compensation for damage who sues in the court of the domicile of the defendant, may instead choose to base his or her claim on the law of the court seized, provided that the market in that Member State is amongst those directly and substantially affected by the restriction of competition out of which the non-contractual obligation on which the claim is based arises; where the claimant sues, in accordance with the applicable rules on jurisdiction, more than one defendant in that court, he or she can only choose to base his or her claim on the law of that court if the restriction of competition on which the claim against each of these defendants relies directly and substantially affects also the market in the Member State of that court. The non-contractual obligations arising out of

[31] For the future, the adoption of the Rome II Regulation has precluded the Member States to enter into international conventions regarding subject matters covered by the Regulation.

[32] In the Commission's original proposal this article dealt only with unfair competition: COM (2003) 427 final, Brussels 22.7.2003. In the first reading opinion of the European Parliament, this article had been deleted. The reason given by the reporteur Diana Wallis was that the flexibility of a general rule would be preferable to rigid special rules: P6_TA(2005)0284, 6 July 2005, *OJ* C 157 E, 6.7.2006, p. 371; Legal affairs (JURI), PE 349.977, p. 38 et seq.

restrictions of competition cover infringements of both national and Community competition law.

For the purposes of the Regulation, the concept of restriction of competition covers prohibitions on agreements between undertakings, decisions by associations of undertakings and concerted practices which have as their object or effect the prevention, restriction or distortion of competition within a Member State or within the internal market, as well as prohibitions on the abuse of a dominant position within a Member State or within the internal market, where such agreements, decisions, concerted practices or abuses are prohibited by Articles 81 and 82 of the EC Treaty or by the law of a Member State.[33]

II. 3. c)

The large delicts type of *cross-border environmental (emissions) damage* cases[34] is handled in Article 7.[35] In the Regulation, environmental damage should be understood as meaning adverse change in a natural resource, such as a water, land or air, impairment of a function performed by that resource for the benefit of another natural resource or the public, or impairment of the variability among living organisms. For this type of tort the determination of place of perpetration is often difficult.[36] Under many domestic liability systems, cases of environmental liability are governed by strict liability. Recital 11 of the Rome II Regulation expressly states that the conflict-law-rules set out in this Regulation should also cover torts arising out of strict liability.

---

[33] See more detailed *M. Hellner*: Unfair Competition and Acts Restricting Free Competition, in: Yearbook of Private International Law, Volume 9 (2007), p. 49 et seq.; *W.-H. Roth*: Internationales Kartelldeliktsrecht in der Rom II-Verordnung, in: *D. Baetge/J. von Hein/M. von Hinden*: Die richtige Ordnung: FS Kropholler, Tübingen 2008, p. 623 et seq.; *P. Mankowski*: Das neue Internationale Kartellrecht des Art. 6 Abs. 3 der Rom II-Verordnung, RIW 2008, p. 177 et seq.; *U. Scholz/G. Rixen*: Die neue europäische Kollisionsnorm für außervertragliche Schuldverhältnisse aus wettbewerbsbeschränkendem Verhalten, EuZW 2008, p. 327 et seq.

[34] See the famous precedent in cross-border environmental case law in Europe: Bier v. Mines de Potasse d'Alsace: Rechtbank Rotterdam 8.1.1979, Nederlandse Jurisprudentie 1979, No. 113, 15.

[35] In the first reading opinion of the European Parliament, this article had been deleted. The reason given by the reporteur Diana Wallis was that the flexibility of a general rule would be preferable to rigid special rules: P6_TA(2005)0284, 6 July 2005, *OJ* C 157 E, 6.7.2006, p. 371; Legal affairs (JURI), PE 349.977, p. 38 et seq.

[36] See *Th. Kadner Graziano*: La responsibilité délictuelle en droit international privé européen, Bâle 2004, p. 50 et seq.

If the parties do not reach an agreement on the applicable law, the general rule for torts in Article 4(1) apply. It means that a claim arising out of environmental damage or damage sustained by persons or property as a result of such damage is governed by the law of the country in which the damage occurs, irrespective of the country in which the event giving rise to the damage occurred and irrespective of the country (or countries) in which the indirect consequences of the event occur. *Lex loci damni* can generally be expected as the first objective connecting factor for cross-border environmental damage cases, because victims normally except to be compensated according to the standards of the law of the place where their interests are damaged. Under this solution equal treatment can be guaranteed for all victims who suffer damage in the same country and also for persons who cause damage in the same country, for the latter regardless of the place from which they are acting.

According Article 7, the person seeking compensation can base his or her claim on the law of the country in which the event giving rise to the damage occurred. This is a rule of *ubiquity* for cross-border environmental damage. It means that the person seeking compensation can opt for the application of the law of the place of acting of the tort-feasor. The rule of ubiquity as it is used to the determine the applicable law for torts is familiar to Hungarian lawyers: § 32 (1) and (2) of the law-decree on PIL guarantees a similar option for the victim.[37] In the recent decades, however, the international literature argued in favour of the rule of ubiquity for environmental damage only, and rejected such rules for other complex torts.[38]

In Recital 25 of the Regulation, the European legislator provides arguments for the rule of ubiquity of the EC Treaty, the precautionary principle, the preventive function of liability laws and the "polluter pays" principle. The legislator states that these reasons fully justified the use of

[37] Similarly: Germany [partly only since 1 January 1999: Art. 40. (1) EGBGB], Italy [Art. 62. (1)] and some other Member States. The Swiss PIL Act (Art. 138) adopts the rule of ubiquity for environmental torts only.

[38] See, e.g., *G. Betlem /Ch. Bernasconi*: European Private International Law, The Environment and Obstacles for Public Authorities. Law Quarterly Review 2006, p. 138 et seq.; *Ch. von Bar*: Internationales Privatrecht, Vol. II. München 1991, 668 et seq.; *J. Kropholler*: Intarnationales Privatrecht, Tübingen 2006, § 53 IV 2. a); *J. von Hein*: Das Günstigkeitsprinzip im Internationalen Deliktsrecht. Tübingen 1999, p. 121 et seq. Other opinion: *Th. Kadner Graziano*: Gemeineuropäisches Internationales Privatrecht, Tübingen 2002, p. 252 et seq. In favour of the application of the law of the country in which the damage occurred: *S. Leible/A. Engel*: Der Vorschlag der EG-Kommission für eine Rom II-Verordnung, EuZW 2004, p. 10.

the principle of discriminating cross-border polluters in favour of the person sustaining the damage. The Regulation leaves to the national courts the question when the choice can be made between the law of the country in which the damage occurred and the law of the country in which the event giving rise to the damage occurred. According to Recital 25, this question should be determined in accordance with the law of the Member State in which the court seized: the *lex fori* should decide on the deadline by which a choice must be maid when using the option under Article 7.[39]

The author of this paper shares the opinion that Article 7 of Rome II does not make a distinction between claims for damages and claims prohibitory or mandatory injunctions and, in principle, it should not be possible to opt for different laws to apply for damages and injunctions.[40]

II.4. Common Habitual Residence

Article 4(2) takes un exception to *lex loci damni*, creating as special connection where the parties have their habitual residence in the same country at the time when the damage occurs. In such cases the law of the country of the common habitual residence of the person claimed to be liable and the victim shall apply.[41] This rule applies also for product liability cases, damages caused by unfair competition and acts restricting free competition and by industrial action. It does not apply, however, for environmental damages and for non-contractual obligations arising from an infringement of an intellectual property right.

Common habitual residence means that the parties had the centre of gravity of their lives in the same country.[42] Article 23 of Rome II provides only a non-comprehensive definition of "habitual residence." It governs the situations of companies and other bodies as well as natural persons acting in the course of their business activity; however it does not give a

---

[39] A new Art. 46a of the German EGBGB wants to regulate this problem for cases falling into the jurisdiction of German courts, as it was before in Art. 40 (1) of EGBGB: IPRax 2008/4, p. 364.

[40] See Th. Kadner Graziano, "The Law Applicable to Cross-Border Damage to Environment," in *Yearbook of Private International Law*, Volume 9 (2007), p. 76.

[41] Indirectly, also the 1971 Hague Convention on the law applicable to traffic accidents makes use of this connecting factor.

[42] To the concept of habitual residence see *D. Cavers:* Habitual Residence: A Useful Concept?, Am. Univ. L. R. 21(1972), p. 475; *Dicey/Morris/Collins:* The Conflict of Laws. London 2006, 6–125 et seq.; *P. Rogerson:* Habitual Residence: The New Domicile? I. C.L.Q. 49 (2000), p. 86; *D. Baetge:* Der gewöhnliche Aufenthalt im Internationalen Privatrecht, Tübingen 1994.

definition for natural persons who are not acting in the course of their business occupation. Till the European Court of Justice will provide guidelines on the relevant criteria, application of a comparative approach could help achieving a uniform solution in the Member State. The concept of habitual residence emerges in several national systems of private international law and in many Hague Conventions.

II. 5. The Escape Clause

The Regulation counts on practical tort cases which bear a strong relationship to a contract or cases presenting other more significant connection, and therefore the general rules in Article 4(1) and (2) are not appropriate. For such cases, Article 4(3) formulates an escape clause: "Where it is clear from all the circumstances of the case that the tort/delict is manifestly more closely connected with a country other than that indicated in paragraphs 1 or 2, the law of that other country shall apply. A manifestly closer connection with another country might be based in particular on a pre-existing relationship between the parties, such as a contract, that is closely connected with the tort/delict in question."[43] Article 4(3) demands a "manifestly" closer connection. Such situation can occur where a tort/delict is closely linked to a contractual relationship and where the applicable law should be that of the contract. This case is explicitly mentioned in Article 4(3) as an example of a manifestly closer connection. In such a case it is reasonable to provide for the same law to govern liability in both contract and tort.[44] Evidently, the escape clause can not be used as a constant possibility for correction.[45] The court should analyse first the general rules in Article 4(1) and (2), and it can turn to paragraph (3) only when the general rules definitely do not fit.

Article 5(2) incorporates the escape rule of Article 4(3) by repetition for product liability cases.[46] By way of reference in Article 6(2), the es-

---

[43] See *J. von Hein*: Die Ausweichklausel im europäischen Internationalen Deliktsrecht, in: *D. Baetge/J. von Hein/M. von Hinden*: Die richtige Ordnung: FS Kropholler, Tübingen 2008, p. 553 et seq.

[44] To the same conclusion the *Hamburg Group* for Private and International Law: Comment of 23 September 2002 on the European Commission's Draft Proposal for a Council regulation on the Law Applicable to Non-Contractual Obligations. RabelsZ 2003, p. 18.

[45] Same opinion by *G. Hohloch*: Basic Principles of Rome II (Place of the injury, habitual residence, closer connection and substantive scope), in: Yearbook of Private International Law, Volume 9(2007), p. 12 et seq.

[46] See the example of the liability of "bystanders" for the application of the escape clause in the field of product liability by *P. Huber /M. Illmer*: International Product Liability. A

cape clause is applicable also for cases where an act of unfair competition affects exclusively the interests of a specific competitor.

III. Conclusion

The Rome II Regulation is an important step forwards in the unification process of the conflict rules within the European Union. Although the final version has corrected many weak points and mistakes of the Commission's preliminary draft, Rome II could have been better if it had taken some advantages of the GEDIP proposal[47] and other amendments. One may not forget, on the other hand, that a European regulation is always a result of compromises. In this particular case, Rome II is the result of compromises between flexibility and legal certainty, between traditional solution and innovations etc.

According to the review clause in Article 30, not later that 20 August 2011, the Commission shall submit to the European Parliament, the Council and the European Economic and Social Committee a report on the application of this Regulation. Two rules are certain candidates for the revision:

- the exclusion of non-contractual obligations arising out of violations of privacy and rights relating to personality, including defamation, in Article 1(2) g) and
- the prejudice rule concerning international conventions, especially the Hague Convention on the law applicable to traffic accidents of 4 May 1971, in Article 28(1).

Commentary on Article 5 of the Rome Regulation, in: Yearbook of Private International Law, 9(2007), p. 46.

[47] Proposal for a European Convention on the Law Applicable to Non-contractual Obligations adopted at the Luxembourg meeting of 25-28 September 1998. http://www.drt.ucl.ac.be/gedip/gedip-documents-8pe.html. Compare *S. C. Symeonides*: Rome II: A Centrist Critique, in: Yearbook of Private International Law, 9(2007), p. 149 et seq. (172).

The United States and the Jurisprudence of International Tribunals

JOHAN D. VAN DER VYVER

On March 31, 2004, the International Court of Justice (ICJ) handed down its judgment in the case of *Avena and Other Mexican Nationals* (*Mexico v. The United States of America*),[1] condemning the United States for non-compliance with Article 36 of the *Vienna Convention on Consular Relations* of April 24, 1963 (VCCR),[2] ratified by the United States on November 24, 1969. Article 36 applies when a national of State A is arrested or has been committed to prison or custody pending trial, or is detained in any other way, in State B. It places an obligation on States B (a) upon the request of the detainee to inform the consular post of State A, without delay, of the arrest or detention of a national of the sending State (State A); (b) to forward, without delay, any correspondence addressed by the person arrested, in prison, custody or detention to the consular post of State A; and most importantly, (c) to inform the person arrested, in prison, custody or detention, without delay, of his or her rights under this provision. The United States as a matter of course—it would seem—does not comply with these obligations, notably by not informing foreigners arrested, or in prison, custody or detention of their rights under Article 36.

Jurisdiction of the ICJ to adjudicate disputes arising out of the interpretation or application of the VCCR derives from an *Optional Protocol to the Vienna Convention on Consular Relations concerning the Compulsory Settlement of Disputes* of April 24, 1963,[3] ratified by the United States on November 24, 1969.

---

[1] *Avena and Other Mexican Nationals* (*Mexico v. the United States of America*), 2004 I.C.J. 12 (31 March 2004).

[2] *Vienna Convention on Consular Relations*, 596 U.N.T.S. 261 (entered into force on 18 March 1967).

[3] *Optional Protocol to the Vienna Convention on Consular Relations concerning the Compulsory Settlement of Disputes*, 596 U.N.T.S. 487 (entered into force on19 March 1967).

When the judgment in *Avena* was handed down, President George W. Bush, on 28 February 2005, issued a *Memorandum for the Attorney-General*, proclaiming:

> I have determined, pursuant to the authority vested in me as President by the Constitution and the laws of the United States of America, that the United States will discharge its international obligations under the decision of the International Court of Justice in the *Case Concerning Avena and Other Mexican Nationals (Mexico v. United States of America) (Avena)*, 2004 ICJ 128 (Mar. 31), by having State courts give effect to the decision in accordance with the general principles of comity in cases filed by the 51 Mexican nationals addressed in that decision.[4]

However, shortly thereafter, President Bush announced that he will be cancelling ratification by the United States of the Optional Protocol. On March 7, 2005, Secretary of State Condoleezza Rice notified the Secretary-General of the United Nations of the United States' withdrawal from the Optional Protocol.

The matter subsequently came before the U.S. Supreme Court in the case of *Sanchez-Llamas v. Oregon*; *Bustillo v. Johnson*.[5] The judgment in that case turned in part on the binding effect of the ICJ's interpretation of the obligations of the United States as a State Party to the VCCR; the question whether or not the United States is *obliged* to comply with the VCCR *as interpreted by the ICJ*. The majority opinion answered the question in the negative and held instead that the ICJ's interpretation of those obligations merely deserves "respectful consideration" by American courts.[6] The fact that the exercise of jurisdiction of the ICJ is based on consent, and that the United States actually *agreed* that its dispute with Mexico over the meaning of Article 36 and the consequences of non-compliance with its provisions be adjudicated by the ICJ, seemingly did not count for anything in the majority's reasoning in *Sanchez-Llamas*. Nor did Article 94 of the Charter of the United Nations, which provides:

> Each Member State of the United Nations undertakes to comply with the decision of the International Court of Justice in any case to which it is a party.[7]

A subsequent case, *Medellin v. Texas*, dealt more specifically with the power of the President to instruct state courts to comply with a treaty ob-

---

[4] *Memorandum for the Attorney General, reprinted in* 44 I.L.M. 964 (Febr. 28, 2005).

[5] *Sanchez-Llamas v. Oregon; Bustillo v. Johnson*, 548 U.S. 331 (June 28, 2006).

[6] *Id.*, at 353; and *see also Breard v. Greene*, 523 U.S. 371, at 375 (April 14, 1998).

[7] *Charter of the United Nations, art. 94*, 1976 Y.B.U.N. 1043; 59 Stat. 1031; T.S. No. 993; reprinted in 3 BEVANS 1153.

ligation of the United States.[8] Medellin was one of the Mexicans whose death sentence was in issue in *Avena*. He unsuccessfully sought review of his conviction on the ground of not having been informed of his right to consular access, and following refusal of the Federal District Courts to grant him relief, he applied to the U.S. Court of Appeal for the Fifth Circuit, which, based on the procedural default rule, also denied his application.[9] Medellin also applied for, and was granted, *certiorari* in the U.S. Supreme Court.[10] While his case was pending in the U.S. Supreme Court, President Bush issued the *Memorandum to the Attorney-General* referred to above. Medellin thereupon filed a new petition for *habeas corpus* in a Texas court, based on the *Memorandum*.[11] The U.S. Supreme Court dismissed Medellin's case, stating that the writ of *certiorari* was improvidently granted and noting that there was the possibility that "Texas courts will provide Medellin with the review he seeks pursuant to the *Avena* judgment and the President's memorandum."[12]

The Texas Court of Criminal Appeals finally decided on basis of the Supreme Court's decision in *Sanchez-Llamas* that the decision of the ICJ was not binding on the Court,[13] that the President "has exceeded his constitutional authority by intruding into the independent powers of the judiciary,"[14] and that the *Memorandum* ordering the Court to give effect to the *Avena* judgment "cannot be sustained under the express or implied powers of the President."[15]

The U.S. Supreme Court again granted a writ of *certiorari*,[16] and in *Medellin v. Texas* in essence upheld the decision of the Texas Court of Criminal Appeals, holding that the treaty provisions in issue were not self-executing in the United States,[17] that the Texas courts need not apply them, and that President Bush had no authority to ask them to do so.[18]

This, in a nutshell, summarizes the attitude of the United States in respect of its obligations under the norms of international law as officially

---

[8] *Medellin v. Texas*, 128 S. Ct. 1346 (March 25, 2008).
[9] *Medellin v. Dretke*, 371 F.3d 270 (5th Cir. 2005).
[10] *Medellin v. Dretke*, 543 US 1032 (Dec. 10, 2004).
[11] See *Ex parte Medellin*, 206 S.W.3d 584, 586 (Tex. Crim. App. June 22, 2005).
[12] *Medellin v. Dretke*, 544 US 660 (May 23, 2005).
[13] *Ex parte Medellin*, 223 S.W.3d 315, 332 (Tex. Crim. App. Nov. 15, 2006).
[14] *Id.*, at 335.
[15] *Id.*, at 348.
[16] *Medellin v. Texas*, 127 S.Ct. 2129 (April 30, 2007).
[17] *Medellin v. Texas*, *supra* note 8, at 1356–67.
[18] *Id.*, at 1367–1372.

defined by an international tribunal. This essay is dedicated to our dear friend and colleague, Tibor Várady. Várady was appointed legal advisor at the Federal Ministry of Foreign Affairs of the Federal Republic of Yugoslavia (as it then was) and is a member of the Hague Permanent Court of Arbitration. He acted as agent and counsel in eleven cases before the ICJ, and played a critical role as counsel for the Defendant in the ruling of the ICJ in the *Case Concerning Application of the Convention on the Prevention and Punishment of the Crime of Genocide (Bosnia and Herzegovina v. Yugoslavia)* (the Bosnia genocide case). His dedication to, and participation in implementation of, the (international) rule of law stands in stark contrast to the defiance by the United States of reminders of its obligations under the norms of international law as authoritatively proclaimed by international tribunals.

I. The Nicaragua Case

The American distrust of international tribunals was sparked by, or at least gained impetus from, the 1984 judgment of the ICJ in the *Case Concerning Military and Paramilitary Activities in and Against Nicaragua (Nicaragua v. United States of America)*,[19] in which the Court rejected American objections *in limine* to the exercise of jurisdiction by the ICJ to resolve a dispute between Nicaragua and the United States based on military and logistical support afforded by the United States to the Contras—a rebel group that sought to overthrow the Government of Nicaragua.

On August 14, 1946, the United States submitted itself to the compulsory *ipso facto* jurisdiction of the ICJ in terms of Article 36(2) of the Statute of the ICJ,[20] which meant in effect that international disputes between the United States and any other State that was also subject to the compulsory *ipso facto* jurisdiction of the ICJ could be brought before that Court by either party without any further agreement. In objecting to the jurisdiction of the Court in the *Nicaragua Case*, the United States argued that Nicaragua had not done the same and therefore had no standing to bring the case before the ICJ.

---

[19] *Case Concerning Military and Paramilitary Activities In and Against Nicaragua (Nicaragua v. United States of America): Jurisdiction and Admissibility*, 1984 I.C.J. 391 (26 Nov. 1984).

[20] *Statute of the International Court of Justice*, art. 36(2), 59 Stat. 1055 (26 June 1945) (hereafter "ICJ Statute").

Nicaragua had been a Member State of the League of Nations established after World War I, and on September 24, 1929 made a Declaration accepting the compulsory *ipso facto* jurisdiction of the Permanent Court of International Justice (PCIJ) that was established by the League of Nations and which can be seen as the predecessor of the ICJ. In terms of Article 36(5) of the Statute of the ICJ, declarations accepting the compulsory *ipso facto* jurisdiction of the PCIJ "and which are still in force" are recognized, without further ado, as acceptance of the compulsory jurisdiction of the ICJ. Evidence showed that on December 4, 1934, the executive authorities of Nicaragua actually approved the Statute of the PCIJ and the Protocol of Signature of December 16, 1920 to which the Statute was attached, and that the Nicaraguan Senate on February 14, 1935 decided to ratify those instruments. The problem was, though, that no records could be found in the files of the League of Nations showing that Nicaragua had actually submitted its instruments of ratification of the Statute and the Protocol to the League of Nations. This, the United States submitted, showed that Nicaragua never became a Party to the PCIJ, that Article 36(5) was therefore not applicable, and that Nicaragua could not without special agreement bring an action against the United States in the ICJ.

In its 1984 decision on jurisdiction and admissibility, the ICJ rejected the arguments advanced by the United States, holding that the Nicaraguan Declaration of 24 September 1929 was still a declaration "in force" and that ratification of the ICJ Statute by Nicaragua "provided it with the institutional foundation which it thus far lacked."[21] The Court noted that Nicaragua has always considered itself bound by the compulsory jurisdiction provisions of the ICJ,[22] and that other States have never challenged its submission to those provisions.[23] Nicaragua furthermore appeared on the "List of States which have recognized the compulsory jurisdiction of the International Court of Justice, or which are still bound by their acceptance of the Optional Clause in the Statute of the Permanent Court of International Justice" published in the ICJ Yearbook, 1946–47.[24]

The United States also advanced several other objections to the jurisdiction of the ICJ in the case, and the admissibility of the case, brought

---

[21] *Case Concerning Military and Paramilitary Activities In and Against Nicaragua (Nicaragua v. United States of America): Jurisdiction and Admissibility*, *supra* note 19, at pars. 37, 109.

[22] *Id.*, at par. 39.

[23] *Id.*, at par. 40.

[24] *Id.*, at par. 37.

against it by Nicaragua. For example, insofar as the Plaintiff State's case was based on the unlawful use of armed force, or on a breach of the peace or acts of aggression, the matter is one exclusively within the jurisdiction of the Security Council of the United Nations.[25] The Court again rejected this submission, noting that Article 24 of the Charter of the United Nations entrusted the Security Council with "primary responsibility," and not exclusive responsibility, for the maintenance of international peace and security.[26]

The Reagan administration responded to the jurisdiction/admissibility decision of the Court by declining to participate in the further proceedings of that case,[27] and on October 7, 1985, President Ronald Reagan terminated the compulsory jurisdiction of the ICJ over the United States with effect six months from that date.[28] The United States remained bound by existing treaties that afforded jurisdiction to the ICJ to adjudicate disputes arising from such treaties (such as the Protocol to the VCCR), and could furthermore on an *ad hoc* basis agree to the exercise of jurisdiction by the ICJ in any international dispute to which it is a party.

The ICJ eventually condemned the United States for its military operations in Nicaragua in support of militia attempting to overthrow the Government of that country.[29] It decided in part (by 12 votes to 3) that the United States, "by training, arming, equipping, financing and supplying the *contra* forces or otherwise encouraging, supporting and aiding military and paramilitary activities in and against Nicaragua, had acted, against the Republic of Nicaragua, in breach of its obligation under customary international law not to intervene in the affairs of another State";[30] and further (by the same margin), that by conducting certain military attacks in 1983-84 and resorting to the use of force on Nicaraguan territory, the United States "has acted, against the Republic of Nicaragua, in breach of its obli-

---

[25] *Id.*, at par. 89.

[26] *Id.*, at par. 95.

[27] *See Case Concerning Military and Paramilitary Activities In and Against Nicaragua (Nicaragua v. United States)*, 1985 I.C.J. 1 (22 January 1985).

[28] *Department of State Letter and Statement Concerning Termination of Acceptance of ICJ Compulsory Jurisdiction*, 24 I.L.M. 1742 (1985); *and see* Michael P. Van Alstine, *The Death of Good Faith in Treaty Jurisprudence and a Call for Resurrection*, in 93 Georgetown L.J., 1885, at 1938 (2005).

[29] Dominic McGoldrick, *Political and Legal Responses to the ICC*, in THE PERMANENT INTERNATIONAL CRIMINAL COURT: LEGAL AND POLITICAL ISSUES 389, at 413 (eds. Dominic McGoldrick, Peter Rowe & Eric Donnelly, 2004).

[30] *Case Concerning Military and Paramilitary Activities In and Against Nicaragua (Nicaragua v. United States of America): Merits*, 1986 I.C.J. 13, at 146 (27 June 1986).

gation under customary international law not to use force against another State."[31]

II. The International Criminal Court

There are strong indications that a resolve of the Bush administration to damage as much as it can the image of the International Criminal Court (ICC) is a remnant of Washington's indignation over the Nicaragua judgments of the 1980's. John Bolton, for a while U.S. Ambassador to the United Nations, almost invariably included in his attempts at ridiculing the ICC and what it stands for, attacks on the ICJ, referring, for example, to "the highly politicized nature of its decisions."[32]

The United States from the outset approached the establishment of an international criminal court with preconceived notions that can perhaps best be described as "cautious and indifferent."[33] This, perhaps, was in conformity with the historical assessment of one analyst that led him to conclude:

> The US has tended to support international criminal courts where the US government has (or is perceived by US officials to have) a significant degree of control over the court, or where the possibility of prosecuting US nationals is either expressly precluded or otherwise remote.[34]

The United States over time seemingly did become supportive of an international criminal tribunal.[35] The *Foreign Relations Authorization Act, Fiscal Year 1994 and 1995*, recorded as follows the "Sense of the Senate on the Establishment of an International Criminal Court":

> (1) the establishment of an international criminal court with jurisdiction over crimes of an international character would greatly strengthen the international rule of law;

---

[31] *Id.*, at 146-47.

[32] John Bolton, *Courting Danger: What's Wrong with the International Criminal Court*, in 54 THE NATIONAL INTEREST 60, at 66 (Winter 1998/99).

[33] Timothy C. Evered, *An International Criminal Court: Recent Proposals and American Concerns*, in 6 PACE INT'L L. REV. 121, at 157 (1994).

[34] John P. Cerone, *Dynamic Equilibrium: The Evolution of US Attitudes toward International Criminal Courts and Tribunals*, in 18 EUR. J. INT'L L.277, at 315 (2007).

[35] *See* Benjamin B. Ferencz, *International Criminal Courts: The Legacy of Nuremberg*, 10 PACE INT'L L. REV. 203, at 226-27 (1998) (referring to statements of President Bill Clinton and U.S. Ambassador to the United Nations Bill Richardson in support of the ICC); David Stoelting, *Status Report on the International Criminal Court*, in 3 HOFSTRA L. & POL'Y SYMP. 223, at 276-82 (1999).

> (2) such a court would thereby serve the interests of the United States and the world community; and
> (3) the United States delegation should make every effort to advance this proposal at the United Nations.[36]

The Senate did add that it would not ratify a treaty establishing the court "which permits representatives of any terrorist organization, including but not limited to the Palestine Liberation Organization, or citizens, national or residents of any country listed by the Secretary of State ... as having repeatedly provided support for acts of international terrorism, to sit in judgment on American citizens,"[37] or one that would not guarantee that the court would take no action infringing upon or diminishing the rights of American citizens under the First and Fourth Amendments to the Constitution of the United States, as interpreted by the United States.[38]

The support of the United States for the establishment of a permanent international criminal tribunal was conditional upon one overriding premise: The U.S. Government must be afforded the power to veto the prosecution of American nationals before such a tribunal. The United States thus participated in the Conference of Diplomatic Plenipotentiaries that was held in Rome on June 15 through July 17, 1998 for the establishment of an international criminal court[39] with the primary resolve to secure that American nationals will not be subject to the jurisdiction of the court without the consent of the American Government. In an interview with the *Washington Post*, Ambassador at Large for War Crimes Issues and leader of the American delegation in Rome, David Scheffer, said it quite bluntly: "Any arrangement by which a UN-sponsored tribunal could assert jurisdiction to prosecute Americans would be political poison in Congress,"[40] Earlier, Senator Jesse Helms, at the time Chairman of the Senate Special Committee on Foreign Relations, in a letter addresses to Secretary of State Madeleine Albright (dated March 26, 1998) stated that he was "unalterably opposed to the creation of a permanent U.N. criminal court," adding

---

[36] *Foreign Relations Authorization Act, Fiscal Year 1994 and 1995*, § 517(b), H.R. 2333, 103rd Cong., 108 Stat. 382, at 469 (1994).

[37] *Id.*, at § 518.

[38] *Id.*, at § 519.

[39] The ICC Statute was adopted by the Rome Conference on 17 July 1998 and entered into force on 1 June 2002 following its ratification by 60 states. To date, 108 States have ratified the Statute.

[40] Lippman *"Ambassador to the Darkest Areas of Human Conflict,"* WASHINGTON POST, at A19 (18 Nov 1997).

that "[a] treaty establishing such a court without a clear U.S. veto will be dead-on-arrival at the Senate Foreign Relations Committee."[41]

The major argument advanced in support of what came to be known as "American exceptionalism" within the ICC context was founded on the only-super-power syndrome. It has been argued that, being the only remaining super power in the world, the United States has also become the primary peace-keeping force of our times; and American troops engaged in peace-keeping operations abroad do not want to run the risk of prosecutions in an international criminal tribunal for acts committed in the interest of peace and security on earth. In an address at the University of Oklahoma College of Law delivered on February 24, 1998, Ambassador Scheffer explained:

> [N]o other country shoulders the burden of international security as does the United States. In the post-Cold War world, the U.S. military is called upon to defend our national security from a wide range of threats; to carry out mandates from the Security Council; to fulfill our commitments to NATO; to help defend our allies and friends; to achieve humanitarian objectives, including the protection of human rights; to combat international terrorism; to rescue Americans and others in danger; and to prevent the proliferation or use of weapons of mass destruction. ... It is in our collective interests that the personnel of our militaries and civilian commands be able to fulfill their many legitimate responsibilities without unjustified exposure to criminal legal proceedings. The permanent court must not be manipulated for political purposes to handcuff governments taking risks to promote international peace and security and to save human lives. Otherwise, the permanent court would undermine the efforts to confront genocide, crimes against humanity, and war crimes.[42]

Justice Richard Goldstone, former Prosecutor in the International Criminal Tribunals for the former Yugoslavia and the International Tribunal for Rwanda, in a press interview at the Rome Conference gave short shrift to this reasoning: "I really have difficulty understanding that policy," he said: "What the US is saying is, 'In order to be peacekeepers ... we have to commit war crimes.'"[43] To this one might add that the United States does not have a mandate to engage in peace-keeping; that is a primary function of the United Nations Organization.

---

[41] Letter from Jesse Helms, Senator for North Carolina, to Madeline Albright, Secretary of State, dated March 26, 1998 (on file with the author).

[42] On file with author; *see also* Scheffer *"US Policy on International Criminal Tribunals"* 13 AM. UNIV. INT'L L. REV. 1389, at 1399 (1998); Scheffer *"The United States and the International Criminal Court"* 93 AM. J. INT'L L. 12, at 18-9 (1999).

[43] *Goldstone: US Stance Contradictory*, in 3 TERRA VIVA (17 June 1998).

Attempts of the United States to secure the exemption of American nationals from prosecution in the ICC were solidly rejected by the Rome Conference, essentially because a large majority of delegations were committed to the principle of equality before the law and equal protection of the laws. For that reason, the United States ranked among the seven States that voted against adoption of the ICC Statute. The Clinton administration nevertheless, on December 31, 2000, signed the ICC Statute.

Following the Rome Conference and even before President Bush took office, an influential lobby in Washington D.C. proposed a strategy of actually opposing the establishment of the ICC.[44] The response of Senator Jesse Helms (R-NC) to the outcome of the Rome Conference included the following assessment:

> Well, the International Criminal Court declares that the American people are under its jurisdiction—no matter what the US government says. The delegates in Rome included a form of "universal jurisdiction" in the court statute, which means that, even if the US never signs the treaty, or if the Senate refuses to ratify it, the countries participating in this court will still contend that American soldiers and citizens are within the jurisdiction of the court.
>
> That is an outrage—and will have grave consequences for our relations with every country that signs and ratifies this treaty....
>
> Because this court has such wide-ranging implications for the US, even if we are never a party to the treaty, I intend to seek assurances from the Clinton administration that:
>
> The US will never vote in the Security Council to refer a case to the court.
>
> The US will provide no assistance whatsoever to the court, either in funding, in-kind contributions, or other legal assistance.
>
> The US will not extradite [*sic*!] any individual to the court or, directly or indirectly, refer a case to the court.
>
> The US will include in all of its bilateral extradition treaties a provision prohibiting the treaty partner from extraditing [*sic*!] US citizens to this court.
>
> The US will renegotiate every one of its status-of-forces agreements to include a provision that prohibits a treaty partner from extraditing [*sic*!] US soldiers to this court, and not station forces in any country that refuses to accept such prohibition.
>
> The US will not permit a US soldier to participate in any Nato, UN or other international peacekeeping mission, until it has reached agreement with all Nato allies and the UN that no US soldier will be subject to the jurisdiction of this court.

---

[44] *See* Kai Ambos, *Der neue Internationale Strafgerichtshof: Strafverfolgung und Realpolitik*, in 39 ENTWICKLUNG UND ZUSAMMENARBEIT 224, at 225 col. 3 (1998).

The International Court is a threat to US national interests … and it is our responsibility to slay it before it grows to devour us.[45]

John Bolton, at the time Under Secretary of State for Arms Control and International Security in the Bush administration and who was to become United States Ambassador to the United Nations for a brief spell, was equally vicious in his condemnation of the ICC and particularly cunning in the promise to destroy it. Writing in *The National Interest*, he proclaimed:

[W]hether the ICC survives and flourishes depends in a large measure on the United States. We should therefore ignore it in our official posture, and attempt to isolate it through our diplomacy, in order to prevent it from acquiring any further legitimacy or resources.[46]

Following the election of George W. Bush as President, the United States embarked on a malicious campaign to undermine the ICC.[47] Displeasure of the United States Government with an international criminal justice system with jurisdiction over American nationals manifested itself in anti-ICC action on four fronts:[48] avoiding its liability as a signatory State of the ICC Statute;[49] enacting hostile legislation;[50] entering into bilateral inter-

---

45 Jesse Helms, *We Must Slay This Monster: Voting Against the International Criminal Court is Not Enough. The US Should Try to Bring It Down*, in FIN. TIMES, at 18 (July 31, 1998). As to the strong opposition of Jesse Helms to the ICC and his influence in devising and formulating U.S. policy in regard to the ICC, *see* LLOYD AXWORTHY, NAVIGATING A *NEW* WORLD: CANADA'S GLOBAL FUTURE, 203 (2003); Henry T. King & Theodore C. Theofrastous, *From Nuremberg to Rome: A Step Backward for U.S. Foreign Policy*, in 31 CASE WESTERN J. INT'L L. 47, at 79-81 (1999); Lawrence Weschler, *Exceptional Cases in Rome: The United States and the Struggle for an ICC*, in THE UNITED STATES AND THE INTERNATIONAL CRIMINAL COURT 85, at 90 (eds. Sarah B. Sewell and Carl Kaysen, 2000).

46 Bolton, *supra* note 32, at 71.

47 *See* William A. Schabas, *The International Criminal Court: The Secret of Its Success*, in 12 CR. L. FORUM: AN INT'L J. 415, at 424 (2001); Johan D. Van der Vyver, *American Exceptionalism: Human Rights, International Criminal Justice, and National Self-Righteousness*, in 50 EMORY L.J. 775, at 795–25 (2001).

48 For an overview of these responses, *see* McGoldrick, *supra* note 29, at 413–37.

49 President Clinton signed the ICC Statute on December 31, 2000; On May 6, 2002, John Bolton submitted a note to the Secretary-General of the United Nations informing him that "the United States does not intend to become a party to the … [ICC Statute]," and accordingly "has no legal obligations arising from its signature of December 31, 2000."

50 American Servicemembers' Protection Act of 2002, P.L. 107–206, 116 Stat. 899, 22 USC 7401 (hereafter "ASPA"); *and see* BRUCE BROOMHALL, INTERNATIONAL JUSTICE AND THE INTERNATIONAL CRIMINAL COURT: BETWEEN SOVEREIGNTY AND THE RULE OF LAW, 181 (2003); McGoldrick, *supra* note 29, at 435–37; Cerone, *supra* note 34, at 296–97.

national agreements to exempt American service members and officials from ICC jurisdiction;[51] and using its privileged status in the Security Council to blackmail the United Nations into giving in to its demands.[52]

I shall not elaborate any further on these American strategies of discontent. It will suffice for purposes of this survey to record only two further general observations.

The ICC Statute does afford to every State in the world (non-Party Sates to the ICC Statute included) the power to preclude the exercise of jurisdiction by the ICC over nationals of the State concerned. A case is not admissible to be investigated by, and/or prosecuted in, the ICC if a State with a special interest in the matter conducts its own *bona fide* investigation into the allegation of wrongdoing. If an investigation has been conducted by the State concerned, the ICC can only proceed with its own investigation and/or prosecution if the investigation and/or prosecution in the national State is found to be a sham; that is, if the investigation and/or prosecution was not conducted by the national authorities with a view to bringing the suspect to justice, but instead with the intent of protecting the suspect from prosecution in the ICC.[53] In that sense, the United States (and all other States) has been granted a veto over the prosecution of its own nationals in the ICC: It must simply conduct its own genuine investigation into the matter, and if probable cause has been established proceed with its own prosecution of the suspect. However, the United States simply would not take yes for an answer.

The second and final observation worth recording is that the United States has more recently backed down somewhat from its initial hard-line approach toward the ICC. In terms of the so-called Nethercutt Amend-

---

[51] The United States abused and misapplied Article 98(2) of the ICC Statute, which makes surrendering of a suspect for trial in the ICC subordinate to "obligations under international agreements" and which was intended to uphold status-of-forces agreements in place at the time a request for surrendering of a suspect to the ICC is sought.

[52] In terms of the American Servicemembers' Protection Act, the President of the United States "should use" its voice and vote in the Security Council to make participation of members of the American Armed Forces in peacekeeping and enforcement operations of the United Nations conditional upon a Security Council guarantee rendering them "permanently exempt" from prosecution in the ICC for acts of genocide, crimes against humanity, and war crimes committed in connection with such operations. ASPA, *supra* note 50, at § 2005(a). Applying this provision, the U.S. on June 20, 2002 vetoed the Security Council resolution that would have extended the U.N. peacekeeping mission in Bosnia-Herzegovina (UNMIBH). *See* McGoldrick, *supra* note 29, at 416–22.

[53] *Statute of the International Criminal Court*, art. 17, U.N. Doc. A/CONF.183/9 (17 July 1998), *reprinted in* 37 I.L.M. 1002 (1998).

ment, economic support funds may not be used to provide support to States Parties to the ICC Statute which have not entered into an Article 98(2) agreement with the United States designed to forestall the surrender of any American national to stand trial in the ICC.[54] The President may waive this prohibition. In March 2006, Secretary of State Condoleezza Rice, in response to a question regarding the "barring [of] military aid to countries that are members of the International Criminal Court" (with reference to Chile) warned that the United States, by sanctioning countries upon which it relies in its counter-terrorism and counter-drug efforts, might be shooting itself in the foot,[55] and it has also been noted that other countries, notably China, has come forward to provide military aid to those States.[56] The United States has consequently back-tracked and annually waived the sanctions it could impose under the Nethercutt Amendment in respect of a large number of States.

When in September 2005, the Security Council decided to refer the situation in Darfur for investigation to the ICC,[57] the United States abstained in the final vote but did not veto the resolution. Antonio Cassese, who headed the United Nations inquiry into the situation in Darfur, described this as "a turning point" for both the ICC and the United States.[58] Mr. John Bellinger, chief lawyer in the State Department, admitted that much when he stated that although the Bush administration will not permit

---

[54] *Foreign Operations, Export Financing and Related Programs Appropriation Act* of 2006, P.L. 109–102, § 574(a), 119 Stat. 2172 (2006).

[55] Condoleezza Rice, *Trip Briefing* (March 10, 2006), available at www.state.gov/secretary/rm/2006/63001.htm

[56] *See Posture Statement of General Bantz J. Craddock, United States Army Commander, United States Southern Command Before the 109th Congress Senate Armed Service Committee*, at 26 (14 March 2006) (noting that 11 countries within the Southern Command Area of Responsibility (AOR) remained sanctioned under the *American Servicemembers' Protection Act*, that one third of the countries within in the AOR were therefore unable to participate in U.S. sponsored military education, and that "[d]ecreasing engagement opens the door for competing nations and outside political actors who may not share our democratic principles to increase interaction and influence within the region," mentioning China by name. In the Q & A session of September 27, General Craddock, under the sub-heading "American Service-Members' Protection Act), noted that "there are negative unintended consequences that impact one half of the 92 countries in Europe and Africa through lost opportunities to provide professional military training with military officers and noncommissioned officers," and that he is in favor of "'delinking' the Military Education and Training (IMET) funding from ASPA sanction."

[57] S.C. Res. 1593 of 31 March 2005, U.N. Doc. S/RES/1593 (31 March 2005).

[58] Jess Bravin, *U.S. Warms to Hague Tribunal—New Stance Reflects Desire to Use Court to Prosecute Darfur Crimes*, in THE WALL STREET JOURNAL, at A4 (June 14, 2006).

American nationals to be prosecuted in the ICC, "we do acknowledge that it [the ICC] has a role to play in the overall system of international justice."[59]

III. The Inter-American Commission on Human Rights

The United States has ratified several human rights treaties that include adversarial proceedings to address non-compliance by a State Party with any provision of those treaties. Those include the *International Covenant on Civil and Political Rights* (1966),[60] ratified by the United States in 1992;[61] and the *Convention on the Elimination of All Forms of Racial Discrimination* (1965),[62] ratified by the United States in 1994.[63] In both instances the United States is subject to an inter-State adversarial proceeding,[64] but has declined to endorse the right of individual (American) victims of non-compliance with a provision of the Covenant or Convention to bring a complaint before the concerned governing body of the *Covenant on Civil and Political Rights* (the Human Rights Committee),[65] or the one overseeing implementation of the *Convention on the Elimination of All Forms of Racial Discrimination* (the Committee on the Elimination of Racial Discrimination).[66]

---

[59] *Ibid.*

[60] *Covenant on Civil and Political Rights*, G.A. Res. 2200A (XXI) of 16 Dec. 1966, 21 U.N. GAOR Supp. (No. 16) at 52, U.N. Doc. A/6316 (1966), 999 U.N.T.S. 171 (entered into force on 23 March 1976) (hereafter "ICCPR").

[61] 138 CONG. REC. S4781-01 (daily ed., April 2, 1992).

[62] *Convention on the Elimination of All Forms of Racial Discrimination*, G.A. Res. 2106 (A) (XX) of 21 Dec. 1965, 660 U.N.T.S. 195 (entered into force on 4 Jan. 1969) (hereafter "CERD").

[63] 140 CONG. REC. S.7634-02 (daily ed., June 24, 1994).

[64] Ratification of the CERD automatically subjects the ratifying State to the inter-State adversarial proceeding. CERD, *supra* note 62, art. 11. The competence of the Human Rights Committee to receive and consider communications in which a State Party claims that another State Party is not fulfilling its obligations under the Covenant is facultative (ICCPR, *supra* note 60, art. 41) but was accepted by the United States in its instrument of ratification (138 CONG. REC. S.4781, 4784 (daily ed. Apr. 2, 1992) (Declaration III(3)).

[65] Provision for an individual complaint procedure under the ICCPR is made in *Optional Protocol to the International Covenant on Civil and Political Rights*, G.A. Res. 2200 A (XXI) of 16 Dec. 1966, 21 U.N. GAOR Supp. (No. 16) at 59, U.N. Doc. A/6316 (1966), 999 U.N.T.S. 302 (entered into force on 23 March 1976). The United States has not ratified the Protocol.

[66] Facultative provision is made under the CERD for an individual complaint procedure. CERD, *supra* note 62, art. 14. The United States has not accepted that procedure.

A Member State of any of those two international instruments can therefore lodge a complaint with the Human Rights Committee or the Committee on the Elimination of Racial Discrimination if the United States were to violate any of its obligations under the Covenant or Convention (respectively). That, however, is of academic interest only, since the United States subjected its ratification of those international instruments to a package of reservations, understanding and declarations (RUD's) that excluded the binding force of any of their provisions which are not in conformity with existing American laws and practices;[67] that is to say, on account of the RUD's, the United States is not bound by the provisions which it does violate.

The Organization of American States (OAS) in 1969 adopted the *American Convention on Human Rights* under which the Inter-American Court on Human Rights was established.[68] The United States signed, but never ratified, the Convention and it is therefore not subject to the provisions of the Convention or the jurisdiction of the Court. However, as a Members State of the OAS, the United States is subject to investigations conducted by the Inter-American Commission on Human Rights (I-AmComHR), based on the *American Declaration of the Rights and Duties of Man*, adopted by the Ninth International Conference of American States held a Bogota in 1948.[69] Such investigations can be triggered by individual petitions but are confined to particular provisions of the *American Declaration of the Rights and Duties of Man*, namely alleged violations of the right to life, liberty and personal security (Article I), equality before the law (Article II), freedom of religion (Article III), freedom of expression (Article XVIII), freedom from arbitrary arrest (Article XXV), and due process of law (Article XXVI).[70]

---

[67] Van der Vyver, *supra* note 47, at 779–80.

[68] *American Convention on Human Rights*, arts. 33, 52–71, O.A.S Treaty Ser. No. 36 (1969), 144 U.N.T.S. 123 (entered into force on July 18,1978).

[69] *American Declaration of the Rights and Duties of Man*, O.A.S. Res. XXX (1948), O.A.S. Off. Rec. OES/Ser. L/V/I.4 Rev. (1965). In 1959, the Fifth Meeting of Consultation of Ministers of Foreign Affairs of the OAS adopted a resolution for the creation of an Inter-American Commission on Human Rights (hereafter "I-AmComHR"). Res. VII, Fifth Meeting of Consultation of Ministers of Foreign Affairs, Santiago, Chile, August 12–18, 1959, Final Act. OEA/Ser. C/II.5 (English), at 10–11 (1959). The Statute of the I-AmComHR was adopted in 1960 "to promote respect for human rights." *Statute of the Inter-American Commission of Human Rights*, *reprinted in* BASIC DOCUMENTS PERTAINING TO HUMAN RIGHTS IN THE INTER-AMERICAN SYSTEM, O.A.S. Doc. OEA/Ser. L.V/II. 82, doc. 6, rev. 1, at 93 (1992). The I-AmComHR began functioning in 1960.

[70] Thomas Buergenthal & Dinah Shelton, PROTECTING HUMAN RIGHTS IN THE AMERICAS: CASES AND MATERIALS 50 (1995).

The United States has been under investigation by the I-AmComHR on many occasions.

In 1990, Willie L. Celestine, who had been sentenced to death in the United States on charges of first-degree murder, brought an application before the I-AmComHR, claiming among other things that the death penalty was applied in the United States on a racially discriminatory basis.[71] In support of that submission, council for the complainant relied almost exclusively on statistical data showing that blacks are more likely to receive the death penalty than whites. The I-AmComHR gave judgment in favor of the United States, holding that statistical studies are in themselves insufficient to show racial discrimination in a particular case before the Commission; and furthermore, that Celestine was convicted of a serious offence (brutally raping and murdering an elderly lady).[72] Willie Celestine was executed while his case was pending before the I-AmComHR.

Earlier, in 1987, the juvenile justice system of the United States came under scrutiny in the I-AmComHR.[73] James Terry Roach and Jay Pinkerton were sentenced to death in separate trials for crimes committed while they were 17 years of age. The Commission decided that in Member States of the OAS a norm of customary international law with the force of *ius cogens* prohibits juvenile executions.[74] However, the Commission was convinced by the U.S. Government's submission that there did not at that point in time exist a norm of customary international law establishing 18 as the minimum age for the imposition of the death penalty, though, in the opinion of the Commission, such a norm "is emerging."[75] The Commission went on to find that the diversity in state practice within the United States in regard to the death penalty, making capital offences dependent not on the nature of the crime but on the place where the crime was committed,[76] amounted to a

---

[71] I-AmComHR, Res. No. 23/89, Case No 10/031 (United States) *Annual Report of the Inter-American Commission on Human Rights, 1989-1990* OEA/Ser L/V/II.77, doc. 7 rev. 1, 63–73 (17 May 1990).

[72] *Id.*, at par. 45.

[73] I-AmComHR, Res. No. 3/87, Case No. 9647 (United States) *Annual Report of the Inter-American Commission on Human Rights, 1985–1987* OEA/Ser L/V/II.71, doc. 9 rev. 1, original Spanish at 148 (22 Sept. 1987).

[74] *Id.*, at par. 56.

[75] *Id.*, at par. 60.

[76] A 16 year old child committing a capital offence in Virginia may receive the death penalty, but if the same individual committed the same crime on the other side of Memorial Bridge in Washington D.C. he cannot be sentenced to death. *See id.*, at par. 62.

denial of equal protection of the laws within the United States. The Commission stated in this regard:

> For the federal Government of the United States to leave the issue of the application of the death penalty to juveniles to the discretion of state officials results in a patchwork scheme of legislation which makes the severity of the punishment dependent, not, primarily, on the nature of the crime committed, but on the location where it was committed. Ceding to state legislatures the determination of whether a juvenile may be executed is not of the same category as granting states the discretion to determine the age of majority for the purpose of purchasing alcoholic beverages or consenting to matrimony. The failure of the federal government to preempt the states as regards the most fundamental right—the right to life—results in a pattern of legislative arbitrariness throughout the United States which results in the arbitrary deprivation of life and inequality before the law, contrary to Articles I and II of the American Declaration of the Rights and Duties of Man, respectively.[77]

Roach and Pinkerton were executed before the decision of the Commission was handed down.[78] The Commission decided (by 5 votes to 1) that in executing Terry Roach and Jay Pinkerton, the United States violated Article I of the *American Declaration of the Rights and Duties of Man* (the right to life).[79]

The I-AComHR entertained several applications concerning juvenile executions in the United States. In the 2002 *Case of Michael Domingues*, the Commission decided that an international norm had emerged, as a matter of *ius cogens*, establishing 18 years as the minimum age at which individuals are liable to face the death penalty.[80] The Commission noted that "by persisting in the practice of executing offenders under the age of 18, the U.S. stands alone amongst the traditional developed world nations and those of the inter-American system, and has also become increasingly isolated within the entire global community."[81] It decided that "the United States will be responsible for a further grave and irreparable violation of Mr. Domingues' right to life under Article I of the *American Declaration of the Rights and Duties of Man* if he is executed for crimes committed when he was 16 years of age."[82]

---

[77] *Id.*, at par. 62.

[78] In *Roach v. Aiken*, 474 U.S. 1039 (Jan. 9, 1986), the U.S. Supreme Court refused to order a stay of execution of Terry Roach. He was executed the following day.

[79] I-AmComHR, Res. No. 3/87, Case No. 9647, *supra* note 73, at par. 64

[80] I-AmComHR, Report No. 62/02 (Merits), Case No. 12.285, United States, par. 85 (Oct. 22, 2002).

[81] *Id.*, at par. 84.

[82] *Id.*, at par. 87.

There are numerous cases in which the United States proceeded with the execution of juveniles in spite of precautionary measures recommended by the I-AmComHR not to do so while the matter remained in dispute.[83] The Commission held that the executions amounted to violation of the juveniles' right to life and recommended that compensation be paid to their next of kin. In the latest case, the juvenile had already been executed before the matter was brought before the I-AmComHR. The Commission nevertheless ruled that the case was admissible for adjudication by the I-AmComHR.[84]

On March 1, 2005, the US Supreme Court in *Roper v. Simmons* proclaimed juvenile executions to be unconstitutional.[85] Although six of the judges (including one who concurred in the dissent) took international standards into account, no one of the judges referred to any of the cases that condemned the practice of juvenile executions in the United States. *Roper v. Simmons* did not entirely resolve the absence of equal protection of the laws in the United States, since, for example, the rules applying to prosecution of juveniles as though they were adults and punishments that can be inflicted for serious crimes remained different in different states.[86] The predicament that confronted the United States derived from the fact that, in international law, the United States constitutes a single entity; and secondly, that its federal Constitution only promises protection for a limited number of rights and freedoms (civil and political rights, to the exclu-

---

[83] *Case of Napoleon Beazley*, I-AmComHR, Report No. 101/03, Case No. 12.412, United States (Dec. 29, 2003); *Case of Douglas Christopher Thomas*, I-AmComHR, Report No. 100/03, Case No. 12.240, United States (Dec. 29, 2003); *Case of Gary T. Graham, now known as Shaka Sankefa*, I-AmComHR, Report No. 97/03, Case No. 11.193, United States (Dec. 29, 2003); *see also Case of Cesar Fierro*, I-AmComHR, Report No. 99/03, Case No. 11.331, United States (Dec. 29, 2003) (the Commission holding that should the applicant be executed, it would constitute an arbitrary deprivation of life).

[84] *Case of Tracy Lee Housel*, I-AmComHR, Report No. 16/04, Petition No. 129/2002, United States (Feb. 27, 2004).

[85] *Roper v. Simmons*, 543 US 551 (2005). In *Stanford v. Kentucky* 492 US 361 (1989), the U.S. Supreme Court had set the minimum age at which a juvenile may be sentenced to death at 16 years. On the same day, the U.S. Supreme Court decided that mentally retarded persons were not exempt from capital punishment (*Penry v. Lynaugh* 492 US 302 (1989)). The Court subsequently reversed this decision, holding that executions of the mentally retarded constituted cruel and unusual punishment and was therefore unconstitutional (*Atkins v. Virginia*, 536 US 304 (2002)).

[86] *See* Johan D. van der Vyver, *Municipal Legal Obligations of States Parties to the Convention on the Rights of the Child: The South African Model*, in 20 EMORY INT'L L. REV. 9, at 29–31 (2006).

sion of natural rights of the individual, economic, social and cultural rights, and solidarity rights), leaving important human values, such as the right to life and to human dignity, in the hands of state authorities.

The United States was also on several occasions condemned by the I-AmComHR for non-compliance with Article 36 of the VCCR. The Commission noted that "a hightened level of scrutiny" is called for in all capital cases, that non-compliance with the VCCR constituted a violation of the rules and principles of the due process of law, and that failure to comply with the VCCR amounted to arbitrary deprivation of the right to life of the convicted person.[87]

Which brings us back to where we started.

IV. The Vienna Convention on Consular Relations

The United States was condemned no less than three times by the ICJ for failure to comply with Article 36 of the VCCR, once in regard to a national of Paraguay (*Angel Francisco Breard*),[88] once in regard to two German nationals (*the LaGrand brothers*), [89] and in the most recent case involving 52 Mexicans (*Avena and 51 other Mexicans*).[90] In the first two cases, the United States, with the support of the U.S. Supreme Court,[91] declined to support provisional measures ordered by the ICJ not to proceed with executions of the convicted persons pending a final decision of the Court.[92] The Paraguayan citizen and one of the German nationals were executed while their respective cases were pending before the ICJ, and the other German national was executed on June 28, 2001, the day after

[87] *Case of Ramón Martinez Villareal*, I-AmComHR, Report No. 52/42, Case No. 11.753, United States, pars. 51, 52, 70 (Oct. 10, 2002); *see also Case of Cesar Fierro*, I-AmComHR, Report No. 99/03, Case No. 11.331, United States (Dec. 29, 2003) (noting that should the convicted person be executed, it would constitute an arbitrary deprivation of his right to life).

[88] *Case Concerning the Vienna Convention on Consular Relations (Paraguay v. United States)*, 1998 I.C.J. 247 (9 April 1998).

[89] *LaGrand Case (Germany v. United States of America) (Judgment)*, 2001 I.C.J. 465 (27 June 2001).

[90] *Avena & Other Mexican Nationals (Mexico v United States iof America)*, *supra* note 1.

[91] *Breard v. Green*, *supra* note 6; and *see also Federal Republic of Germany v. United States*, 526 U.S. 111 (1999).

[92] *Case Concerning the Vienna Convention on Consular Relations (Paraguay v United States)*, *supra* note 88; *LaGrand Case (Germany v United States of America) (Request for the Indication of Provisional Measures)*, 1999 I.C.J. 9 (3 March 1999).

judgment was given against the United States for non-compliance with Article 36 of the VCCR.[93]

In the *Paraguayan Case*, the ICJ in preliminary proceedings called on the United States to "take all measures at its disposal to ensure that Angel Francisco Breard is not executed pending the final decision in these proceedings."[94] The convicted person thereupon filed a petition for an original writ of *habeas corpus* and a stay application to "enforce" the ICJ ruling. In *Breard v. Green*, the U.S. Supreme Court decided, by 6 votes to 3, that the Applicant was not entitled to the relief sought, because he procedurally defaulted his claim under the VCCR, "if any,"[95] by failing to raise non-compliance by the United States with the Convention in the state courts.[96] Though judgments of the ICJ, according to the judgment, deserve "respectful consideration," the U.S. Supreme Court upheld the procedural default rule of the state of Virginia, because, in its view, "absent a clear and express statement to the contrary, the procedural rules of the forum State govern the implementation of the treaty in that State."[97] The fact that the convicted person was unaware of his rights under the VCCR and, in direct violation of the Convention, was not informed of those rights, was seemingly for purposes of the case neither here nor there. As noted by one analyst of the judgment:

> It was not that the Supreme Court found international law to be irrelevant; rather, it found its own view of international law to be more relevant than that of the International Court [of Justice]—so much that it was not even willing to await a final judgment.[98]

The Governor of the state of Virginia Jim Gilmore declined a request of Secretary of State Madeleine Albright for a stay of execution,[99] and Breard was executed before the ICJ could decide the case on its merits.

---

[93] *LaGrand Case (Germany v United States of America)*, *supra* note 89, at par. 127(4) (the ICJ deciding, by 14 votes to 1, that by not permitting the review and reconsideration of the conviction and sentence of the LaGrand brothers after having failed to comply with the provisions of Article 36(1) of the CVCR, the United States breached its obligations to the Federal Republic of Germany and the LaGrand brothers).

[94] *Paraguay v. United States*, *supra* note 88, at par. 41.

[95] *Breard v. Green*, *supra* note 6, at 375; and *see also id.*, at 376 (stating that the VCCR "arguably"confers on an individual the right to consular assistance following arrest).

[96] *Id.*, at 375.

[97] *Ibid.*

[98] Alex Glashausser, *Difference and Deference in Treaty Interpretation*, in 50 VILL. L. REV. 25, at 68–69 (2005).

[99] *See* Jonathan I. Charney & W. Michael Reisman, *Agora: Breard*, in 92 AM. J. INT'L L. 666, at 674–75 (1998); Carlos Manuel Vasquez, Breard *and the Federal Power to Re-*

Walter LaGrand and Karl LaGrand were convicted of an attempted bank robbery in Arizona in which a bank employee was killed and another seriously injured. They were sentenced to death, again without having been informed of their rights under the VCCR. The execution of Walter LaGrand was scheduled for March 3, 1999.[100] Germany consequently brought suit against the United States in the ICJ on that day. The ICJ, acting pursuant to Article 41 of its Statute, issued a provisional measure, as a matter of great urgency, stating:

> The United States of America should take all measures at its disposal to ensure that Walter LaGrand is not executed pending a final decision in these proceedings...[101]

The German Government on the same day (March 3), and only two hours before Walter LaGrand's scheduled execution, sought a preliminary injunction in the U.S. Supreme Court against the Government of the United States and the Governor of Arizona, but the Supreme Court refused to exercise jurisdiction in the case, based on "tardiness of the pleas and the jurisdictional barriers."[102] Walter LaGrand was executed on that very same day. The ICJ subsequently found that provisional orders issued under Article 41 of the Statute of the ICJ do have binding effect,[103] that the United States had not complied with its order of March 3, 1999,[104] and (by 13 votes to 2) that by failing to take all measures at its disposal to ensure that Walter LaGrand not be executed, the United States breached the obligation incumbent on it under the provisional order of March 3, 1999.[105]

Prominent American scholars agreed that provisional measures issued by the ICJ under Article 41 are binding, referring mostly to Article 94(2)

---

quire Compliance with ICJ Orders of Provisional Measures, in 92 AM. J. INT'L L. 683, at 684 (1998); Joshua J. Newcomer, *Messing with Texas? Why President Bush's Memorandum Order Trumps State Court Procedure*, in 79 TEMPLE L. REV. 1029, at 1035 (2006).

[100] Karl LaGrand was not to be executed on that day, because he was indisposed and had to be cured of his illness before he could be killed.

[101] *LaGrand Case (Germany v. United States of America) (Request for the Indication of Provisional Measures)*, 1999 I.C.J. 9, at par. 26 (March 3, 1999).

[102] *Federal Republic of Germany v. United States*, *supra* note 91. The Government of the United States enjoyed sovereign immunity and a foreign Government lacked standing to assert a claim against a state.

[103] *LaGrand Case (Germany v United States of America) (Judgment)*, *supra* note 89, at pars. 102-09.

[104] *Id.*, at par. 115

[105] *Id.*, at par. 128(5).

of the U.N. Charter that speaks of "the obligations incumbent upon ... [any party to a case] under a judgment rendered by the Court...."[106] One analyst stated the norm that applied to the provisional measure proclaimed by the ICJ in regard to the pending execution of Angel Breard in cautious diplomatic terms:

> An executive order postponing the execution of Angel Breard would have fallen, in my view, well within a fair, even modest, understanding of the President's authority to execute treaties, combined with his foreign affairs power.[107]

The ICJ also addressed the relevance of the procedural default rule which had been applied in the *Case of Breard*. It decided in essence that the rule did not as such violate Article 36 of the VCCR, but that its application in cases where the national authorities failed to inform the accused "without delay" of his rights under the Convention—thereby preventing him from seeking consular assistance and precluding Germany, on a timely basis, from retaining private counsel for the accused and otherwise assisting him in his defense—did constitute a violation of the Convention.[108]

Following the judgment on the merits, the U.S. federal Government requested the Governor of Virginia to grant a stay of execution. The Governor refused and Karl LaGrand was executed the following day (June 28, 2001).

In the *LaGrand Case*, Germany sought assurances that the United States will not in future repeat its unlawful acts of not informing a German national accused of a serious crime of his or her rights under the VCCR. The United States tendered its intention of complying with the Convention, and this was accepted by the ICJ as satisfying the German request.[109] Efforts of the United States included the publication of a brochure in January 1998 entitled: *Consular Notification and Access: Instruc-*

---

[106] U.N. Charter, *supra* note 7, art. 94(2); *and see* Louis Henkin, *Provisional Measures, U.S. Treaty Obligations, and the States*, in 92 AM. J. INT'L L. 679, at 680 (1998); Vasquez, *supra* note 99, at 685; Malvina Halberstam, LaGrand *and* Avena *Establish a Rights, But is There a Remedy? Brief Comments on the Legal Effect of* LaGrand *and* Avena *in the U.S.*, in 11 ILSA J. INT'L & COMP. L. 415, at 416 (2005).

[107] Vasquez, *supra* note 99, at 689.

[108] *LaGrand Case (Germany v United States of America) (Judgment)*, *supra* note 89, at pars. 90-91; and *see also id.* at par. 125 (the ICJ deciding that violations of Article 36 of the VCCR were caused "by the circumstances in which the procedural default rule was applied, and not by the rule as such").

[109] *Id.*, at par.124.

tions for Federal, State and Local Law Enforcement and Other Officials Regarding Foreign Nationals in the United States and the Rights of Consular Officials to Assist Them. The United States also produced a small reference card designed to be carried by individual arresting officers. It testified in the *LaGrand Case* that 60 000 copies of the brochure and 400 000 copies of the pocket card had been distributed. The ICJ decided in this regard and in response to that assurance:

> that should nationals of the Federal Republic of Germany nonetheless be sentenced to severe penalties, without their rights under Article 36, paragraph 1 (*b*) of the Convention having been respected, the United States of America, by means of its own choosing, shall allow the review and reconsideration of the conviction and sentence by taking account of the violation of the rights set forth in that Convention.[110]

This undertaking—it would seem—prompted the *Memorandum for the Attorney-General* issued by President George W. Bush on February 28, 2005. The Oklahoma Court of Criminal Appeals did actually respond positively to the *Memorandum*,[111] but the Texas Court of Criminal Appeals, with the subsequent approval of the U.S. Supreme Court, treated it with contempt in the case of *Meddelin v. Texas*; that is, after the U.S. Supreme Court was confronted *in Sanchez-Llamas v. Oregon; Bustillo v. Johnson* with the question whether or not American courts were bound by the ICJ's interpretation in *Avena and Other Mexicans* of the United States' treaty obligations under the VCCR.

Moises Sanchez-Llamas was one of the Mexicans whose conviction and sentence (in Oregon) was in issue in *Avena*; Mario Bustillo, convicted in Virginia, was a national of Honduras and not one of those Mexicans. Having procedurally defaulted, he argued that in his instance, too, American courts were bound, as a matter of federal law, to follow the ICJ's treaty interpretation in respect of the procedural default rule.

The binding effect of the ICJ's judgment in *LaGrand* took center stage in the U.S. Supreme Court's decision in *Sanchez-Llamas*. The judgment turned in part on the binding effect of the ICJ's interpretation of the obligations of the United States as a State Party to the VCCR; the question whether or not the United States is *obliged* to comply with the VCCR *as*

---

[110] *Id.*, at par. 128(7).

[111] *Torres v. Oklahoma*, 120 P.3d 1184 (Oklahoma C.C.A. 2005). Earlier, Osbaldo Torres, a Mexican national, in a petition for *certiorari* had raised the same issue as in *Breard*, but the U.S. Supreme Court refused to hear the case. *Torres v. Mullin*, 540 U.S. 1035 (2003).

interpreted by the ICJ. The majority opinion answered the question in the negative and held instead that the ICJ's interpretation of those obligations merely deserves "respectful consideration" by American courts.[112] The court proceeded on the assumption that for treaties to be given effect under American law, determining their meaning as a matter of federal law "is emphatically the province and duty of the judicial department."[113]

Following the Presidential *Memorandum for the Attorney-General* of February 28, 2005 and the subsequent procedural complexities outlined in the introductory paragraphs of this essay, the question as to the binding effect of the judgment of the ICJ in *Avena* and of the President's instruction to Attorneys-General to comply with that judgment, culminated in the decisions of the U.S. Supreme Court in the case of *Medellin v. Texas*.[114] The judgment of the Texas Court of Criminal Appeals and of the U.S. Supreme Court in that matter afforded a new twist to the issues at hand: Whether or not judgments of the ICJ are self-executing in the United States, and whether or not it was within the power of the President of the United States to instruct federal courts to uphold such judgments.

The U.S. Supreme Court first of all considered whether or not the United States was bound to comply with the decision of the ICJ, which in effect required that in the event of non-compliance with Article 36 of the VCCR the U.S. Government must "by means of its own choosing" remedy the consequences of non-compliance; that is—one may assume—by reviewing the conviction and sentence, and reconsidering the same in view of the consequences of non-compliance with Article 36 of the VCCR in the particular case. The Court noted that the exercise of jurisdiction by the ICJ is based on consensus, but decided that "submission to jurisdiction and agreeing to be bound are two different things."[115] In terms of Article 94 of the U.N. Charter, each Member State of the United Nations "undertakes to comply with the decision of the International Court of Justice in any case to which it is a party," but this does not mean that judgments of the ICJ will have "immediate legal effect in domestic courts."[116] The phrase "undertake to comply" (instead of "'shall' or 'must' comply with

---

[112] *Sanchez-Llamas v. Oregon; Bustillo v. Johnson, supra* note 5, at 353; and *see also Breard v. Greene*, 523 U.S. 371, at 375 (April 14, 1998).

[113] *Sanchez-Llamas v. Oregon; Bustillo v. Johnson, supra* note 5, at par. 353-54, with reference to *Marbury v. Madison*, 1 Cranch 137, at 177 (1803).

[114] *Medellin v. Texas, supra* note 8.

[115] *Id.*, at 1358.

[116] *Supra*, the text accompanying note 7.

an ICJ judgement"), according to the majority judgment, entails a commitment for future action to comply.[117]

In deciding, in effect, that in virtue of the "future action exception" Article 94 is not self-executing in the United States, the Court also referred to other provisions of international instruments with a bearing on ICJ judgments: Article 94(2) of the U.N. Charter, leaving it up to the Security Council in cases of non-compliance with an ICJ judgment to "make recommendations or decide upon measures to be taken to give effect to the judgment";[118] Article 35(1) of the ICJ Statute, which confines the jurisdiction of the ICJ to disputes between States;[119] Article 59 of the ICJ Statute, which proclaims that decisions of the ICJ "has no binding force except between the parties and in respect of that particular case."[120]

The judgment of the U.S. Supreme Court in *Medellin v. Texas* (and in *Sanchez-Llamas*) will not go down in history as the acme of judicial excellence. The logic of differentiating between submitting oneself to the jurisdiction of a court of law and agreeing to be bound by its decision is beyond reasonable comprehension. One analyst (sympathetic to the Court's reasoning) sought to explain the American schizophrenic dualism in relation to international/municipal obligations as follows: By consenting to have the ICJ resolve the nation's international obligations, the United States did not cede control of the domestic application of treaties:

> If the International Court, in a proper exercise of its jurisdiction, renders a judgment against the United States, failure to abide by it is a violation of international law. That does not mean, however, that U.S. courts are bound to obey judgments of the International Court.[121]

There are compelling reasons for believing that the U.S. Supreme Court's position is not constitutionally kosher. Consider the following:

In virtue of the Supremacy Clause in the American Constitution, treaties entered into under the authority of the United States are (part of) "the

---

[117] *Medellin v. Texas*, *supra* note 8, at 1358.

[118] *Id.*, at 1359–60, with reference to U.N. Charter, *supra* note 7, art. 94(2).

[119] *Medellin v. Texas*, *supra* note 8, at 1360, with reference to ICJ Statute, *supra* note 20, art. 35(1); and *see also Sanchez-Llamas v. Oregon; Bustillo v. Johnson*, *supra* note 5, at 355.

[120] *Medellin v. Texas*, *supra* note 8, at 1360–61, with reference to ICJ Statute, *supra* note 20, art. 59; and *see also Sanchez-Llamas v. Oregon; Bustillo v. Johnson*, *supra* note 5, at 354–55.

[121] Glashausser, *supra* note 98, at 75; and *see also id.*, at 74 (stating that the United States has never decided to have its federal courts bow to other courts "as to all matters of international law").

supreme Law of the Land"[122] and therefore self-executing in the United States. There are admittedly several exceptions to the rule, including one that applies to treaties which clearly do not create an immediate binding obligation but contemplates future action. To hold that the undertaking of Member States stipulated in Article 94 of the U.N. Charter to comply with judgments of the ICJ denotes future action of the kind that would render a treaty obligation that was in issue in the judgment non-self-executing, simply boggles the mind. As noted by Breyer, J. (dissenting), an undertaking to comply clearly means placing oneself under an obligation to execute the judgment.[123] Affording to the Security Council the power to take a State Party to task for not complying with a judgment of the ICJ in a matter that involved that State Party as a litigant before the Court (as per Article 94(2) of the U.N. Charter), and confining the jurisdiction of the ICJ to inter-State disputes (as per Article 35(1) of the ICJ Statute), have absolutely nothing to do with the American constitutional decree rendering treaties self-executing in the United States.

Perhaps the most blatant lack of understanding of the law regulating self-executing treaties displayed by the Plurality in *Medellin* was its reliance on Article 59 of the ICJ Statute. That Article was inserted in the ICJ Statute (upon insistence of civil law countries) to exclude application of the *stare decisis* rule to judgments of the ICJ.[124] It has nothing to do with the application as part of "the supreme Law of the Land" of "Treaties made, or which shall be made, under the Authority of the United States" as proclaimed in the Supremacy Clause.

Nor, in virtue of the Supremacy Clause, ought one to confine the pertinence of ICJ judgments interpreting the treaty obligations of the United States to "respectful consideration."[125] Justice Stevens was quite right in asserting that the U.S. Supreme Court is unfaithful to the Supremacy Clause "when it permits state courts to disregard the Nation's treaty obli-

---

122 *Constitution of the United States*, art. VI, § 2.

123 *Medellin v. Texas*, *supra* note 8, at 1384 (Breyer, J., joined by Souter and Ginsberg, JJ., dissenting); *and see* WEBSTER'S THIRD NEW WORLD DICTIONARY OF THE ENGLISH LANGUAGE (including in its circumscription of "undertake," "to take upon oneself solemnly or expressly: put oneself under obligation to perform" (1966).

124 *See* 1 RESTATEMENT OF THE FOREIGN RELATIONS LAW OF THE UNITED STATES, par. 103, comment b (at 36–37).

125 *See Sanchez-Llamas v. Oregon; Bustillo v. Johnson*, *supra* note 5, at 353; and *see also id.*, at 382–83 (Breyer, J., joined by Stevens, Souter and Ginsburg, JJ., dissenting). *See further Cummings Inc. v. U.S.*, 454 F.3d 1361, at 1366 (Fed. Cir. 2006) (stating that the opinion of an international court "can be consulted for its persuasive value, if any").

gations."[126] It has been said that in their relationship with international tribunals, municipal courts must act as "agents of the international order."[127] Publicist Louis Henkin has observed that "international agreements, whether concluded by treaty or by executive agreement, are binding on the states;"[128] and it should be equally apparent that an "ICJ ruling is binding on the U.S. courts, state and federal."[129] The American *Restatement of the Law* stipulates that decisions of international tribunals adjudicating questions of international law "are persuasive evidence of what the law is."[130]

Interpretations of treaty provisions by the courts of other States Parties should also be afforded persuasive force. One analyst has noted a general trend in U.S. jurisprudence to afford prominence to foreign and international precedents interpreting treaty provisions that had been ratified by the United States.[131] It has thus been decided that "the opinions of our sister signatories" are "entitled to considerable weight."[132] In a subsequent case, even Justice Scalia agreed:

> We can, and should, look to discussions of other signatories when we interpret treaty provisions. Foreign constructions are evidence of the original shared understanding of the contracting parties. Moreover, it is reasonable to impute to the parties an intent that their respective courts strive to interpret the treaty consistently.[133]

Equally impugnable was the Plurality's finding in *Medellin* that the President lacked the competence to issue a directive to state courts to execute an international obligation of the United States.[134] The Constitution provides that the President "shall take Care that the Laws be faithfully

---

[126] *Torres v. Mullin*, *supra* note 111, at 1036-37 (separate opinion of Stevens, J.).

[127] RICHARD A. FALK, THE ROLE OF DOMESTIC COURTS IN THE INTERNATIONAL LEGAL ORDER 72 (1964).

[128] Henkin, *supra* note 106, at 681.

[129] Halberstam, *supra* note 106, at 416; *and see Torres v. Mullin*, *supra* note 111, at 1036 (Stevens, J. referring to the "authoritative interpretation" of Article 36 of the VCCR in the *LaGrand Case*).

[130] 1 RESTATEMENT OF THE FOREIGN RELATIONS LAW OF THE UNITED STATES, par. 103, comment b (at 37).

[131] Van Alstine, *supra* note 28, at 1936-37.

[132] *Benjamins v. British European Airways*, 572 F.2d 913, at 919 (CA 2, 1978), cited with approval in *Air France v. Saks*, 470 U.S. 392, at 404 (1985); and *see also European Airlines, Inc. v. Floyd*, 449 U.S. 530, 550 (1991) (stating: "We must also consult the opinions of our sister signatories").

[133] *Olympic Airways v. Husain*, 540 U.S. 644, at 660 (Scalia, J. dissenting).

[134] *See Medellin v. Texas*, *supra* note 8, at 1372.

executed";[135] and the laws to be faithfully executed includes treaties entered into by the United States as part of the supreme law of the land.[136] One analyst has noted that the President's "authority to manage foreign affairs to the exclusion of state policy has been recognized in a long list of judgements,"[137] and concluded that, under current Supreme Court jurisprudence, President Bush did have the power to issue the *Memorandum for the Attorney-General* "as a stopgap measure to compel action by state courts pursuant to his foreign affairs power."[138] It has been decided long ago that the power of the United States "is superior to that of the States to provide for the welfare or necessities of their inhabitants."[139]

---

[135] *Constitution of the United States*, art. II, Sec. 3; *and see* Newcomer, *supra* note 99, at 1044.

[136] Louis Henkin, *International Law as Law in the United States*, in 82 MICH. L. REV. 1555, at 1567 (1984) ("There can be little doubt that the President has the duty, as well as the authority, to take care that international law, as part of the law of the United States, is faithfully executed"); Jules Lobel, *The Limits of Constitutional Power: Conflicts Between Foreign Policy and International Law*, 71 VA. L. REV. 1071, at 1119 (1985) ("The President has a constitutional obligation to execute international law because it is the law of the land"); Arthur S. Miller, *The President and Faithful Execution of the Laws*, 40 VAND. L. REV. 389, at 405 (1987) (referring to the President's duty "to faithfully execute the laws—in this instance, international law"); Jordan J. Paust, Medellin, Avena, *the Supremacy of Treaties, and Relevant Executive Authority*, in SUFFOLK TRANSNAT'L L. REV. 209, at 218 (2008) (referring to the constitutionally-based mandate under which "the President must faithfully execute ... treaties of the United States"); Newcomer, *supra* note 99, at 1045 (noting that the "faith execution" Clause empowered the President to enforce the treaty).

[137] Newcomer, *supra* note 99, at 1042 (with reference, for example, to *American Ins. Assn. v. Garamendi*, 539 U.S. 396, at 425 (2003) ("The express federal policy and the clear conflict raised by the state statute are alone enough to require state law to yield"); *United States v. Lara*, 541 U.S. 193, at 201 (2004)(confirming that the President is the legislative agent or rule-making authority in respect of treaties).

[138] Newcomer, *supra* note 99, at 1054; and *see also id.*, at 1073 (noting that "President Bush's Avena Order was justified as a necessary stopgap in a larger foreign policy program and dealt with the executive unique ability to deal with foreign affairs"); Paust, *supra* note 136, at 217 ("The directive operates as part of treaty processes over which the President has relevant constitutional powers and, in a sense, operates as a treaty-executive directive"); *id.*, at 220–21 ("[T]he President had a duty to assure that there would be compliance with the judgment of the ICJ in the *Avena* case, ... and the President chose to faithfully execute that treaty-based obligation by issuing a presidential determination and directive to various states ..."); *id.*, at 231 ("[T]he President's determination and directive have primacy in view of his primary power to assure settlement of international disputes in accordance with treaty obligations, his power to execute treaty obligations, and his more general foreign affairs power").

[139] *Sanitary District v. United States*, 266 U.S. 405, at 426 (1925).

As to concerns expressed in *Medellin* in regard to a Presidential directive issued to state courts "that reaches deep into the heart of the State's police powers and compels state courts to reopen final judgments and set aside neutrally applicable state laws," and which, in the opinion of the Court, infringes the states' "primary authority for defining and enforcing the criminal law,"[140] it is perhaps important to note that the judgment in *Avena* and the President's *Memorandum* only applied to those foreign national on death row to whom the *Avena* judgment applied.[141] The Bush *Memorandum* furthermore did not require courts to set aside the convictions or sentence simply because of the failure of law enforcement agencies to comply with Article 36 of the VCCR. Al that was required was reconsideration of the convictions and sentences imposed in light of the rights of the convicted persons under the VCCR.[142]

Consider, for example, the response of the Oklahoma Court of Criminal Appeals in the case of *Torres v. Oklahoma.*[143] The Court in that case noted that consular assistance at the instance of the Government of Mexico is as a matter of course centered upon two issues: competent legal representation and avoidance of the death penalty. In the circumstances that attended the conviction of Torres, legal representation was not the issue. However, the Mexican Government is known to have gone to great lengths in the past in capital cases to avoid the death sentence of its nationals. Since the Governor granted clemency in that case, there was no prejudice shown that resulted from non-compliance with the VCCR.[144] The Court therefore decided that the convicted person was not entitled to the relief sought.

Even if one were to assume that the Presidential *Memorandum* was not binding on state courts, one may well ask what Texas courts had to lose by complying with the directive. As noted by Stevens, J. (concurring): "The cost to Texas to complying with *Avena* would be minimal, ... On the other hand, the costs of refusing to respect the ICJ's judgment are significant."[145]

Perhaps the main flaw in the Supreme Court's reasoning was making the President's power to enforce the law of the United States dependent on self-execution of the international treaty concerned —and to add injury to insult, discarding applicability of the Supremacy Clause on flimsy grounds (hold-

[140] *Medellin v. Texas*, *supra* note 8, at 1372.

[141] Newcomer, *supra* note 99, at 1054–56, 1073.

[142] Frederic L. Kirgis, *Introductory Note to Bush Memorandum on Avena and U.S. Supreme Court Decision in Medellin*, 44 I.L.M. 961, at 962 (2005).

[143] *Torres v. Oklahoma*, *supra* note 111; *and see* Glashausser, *supra* note 98, at 67–69.

[144] *Torres v. Oklahoma*, *supra* note 111, at 1118.

[145] *Medellin v. Texas*, *supra* note 8, at 1377 (Stevens, J., concurring).

ing that undertaking to comply with a decision of the ICJ merely signifies a commitment for future action). Self-execution of a treaty provision affords to an individual citizen the right to base an action or found a defense on the treaty provision *per se* (in the absence of implementation legislation) and has nothing to do with the function and competence of the President to implement a treaty provision against the state.

The question whether or not the judgment of the U.S. Supreme Court is right or wrong, defensible or indefensible, or legally and morally appropriate, is for purposes of this survey beside the point. Its decision has become law, and this is all that matters for purposes of establishing the prevailing disposition of the United States in regard to jurisprudence of international tribunals. So, what is the prevalent precedent established by the Plurality in *Meddelin*?

The United States violates its obligations under an international treaty involving the rights of foreign nationals. The United States agrees to submit its dispute with the national State of the victims over the consequences of its unlawful act to be decided by an international court of law. The United States undertakes beforehand to comply with the decision of the international court of law. According to the U.S. Supreme Court, this does not establish a legal obligation on the part of the United States to abide by its international obligation or to comply with the decision of the international court of law. Nor did it accept the power of the President of the United States under the prevailing foreign relations regime of American law to direct state courts to review convictions and sentences imposed that may have been influenced by violation of the rights of the persons convicted and sentenced. Nor does it matter that the very lives of the persons whose rights have been violated were at stake. And to add injury to insult, the President has now decided that violations by the United States of its international obligations will in future not as a matter of course be submitted for adjudication to an international court of law.

I have deliberately avoided detailed excursions into the reasoning of the Court, exactly because the final outcome of the case is what really matters within the context of the present survey. However, there is at least one bit of detail that is particularly instructive. The provisions of Article 94(2) of the U.N. Charter, according to the majority judgment in *Medellin*, "confirms that the U.N. Charter does not contemplate automatic enforceability of ICJ decisions in domestic courts."[146] In case of non-compliance with a judgment of the ICJ, Article 94(2) leaves it up to the Security

[146] *Medellin v. Texas*, *supra* note 8, at 1359.

Council to make recommendations or decide upon measures to be taken to give effect to the judgment.[147] The President and the Senate "were undoubtedly aware" of this "diplomatic—that is, nonjudicial remedy" when it ratified the Optional Protocol to the VCCR, which affords to the United States "the unqualified right to exercise its veto of any Security Council resolution."[148] Applying "the probative impact of Senate ratification debates and understandings in creating a 'legislative history' for international agreements" was in itself, according to David Bederman, "the most astonishing interpretative move in Medellin."[149] What is even more astonishing is that which the U.S. Supreme Court derived from this norm of hermeneutics: Telling us that submission of the United States to the compulsory jurisdiction of the ICJ was decided upon by the President and the Senate with the knowledge, and upon the understanding, that the United States can disregard judgments of the Court at will and without any adverse consequences. From a rule-of-law perspective, that is just quite disgusting!

V. Germany's Assessment of Avena

Shortly after the U.S. Supreme Court's decision in *Sanchez-Llamas* was handed down, the German Federal Constitutional Court (*Bundesverfassungsgericht*) considered the binding effect of interpretations of the ICJ regarding international treaty obligations under the VCCR.[150] It might be noted in passing that jurisdiction of the Federal Constitutional Court in the case (protesting the conviction of a Turkish national and an accomplice arrested and charged with murder without having been informed of their rights under the VCCR) was clouded in complicated issues deriving from the fact that the German Constitutional Court only has jurisdiction to decide constitutional matters. The Constitutional Court based its jurisdiction on the assumption that failure to inform a foreign national of his or her right to consular assistance implicates the right to a fair trial; and although

---

[147] *U.N. Charter*, *supra* note 7, art. 94(2).

[148] *Medellin v. Texas*, *supra* note 8, at 1359.

[149] David J. Bederman, Medellin*'s New Paradigm for Treaty Interpretation*, in 102 AM. J. INT'L L. 529, at 534 (2008).

[150] *Case of F. & T.*, 2 BvR 2115/01 vom 19.9.2006; and for an analysis of the judgment, *see* Jana Gogolin, Avena *and* Sanchez-Llamas *Come to Germany—The German Constitutional Court Upholds Rights under the Vienna Convention on Consular Relations*, in 8 GERMAN L.J. 261 (2007); Klaus Ferdinand Gärditz, *Article 36, Vienna Convention on Consular Relations—Treaty Interpretation and Enforcement—International Court of Justice—Fair Trial—Suppression of Evidence*, in 101 AM. J. INT'L L. 627 (2007).

the Basic Law of Germany does not expressly mention the right to a fair trial, the Court had developed a fair trial doctrine, applicable especially in criminal trials.[151]

As far as the binding effect of interpretation of the VCCR by the ICJ is concerned, the Constitutional Court decided in essence that:

- Under the German Constitutional system, ratified treaties have the status of federal law (GG. Art. 59(2)) and German courts must apply them in the same way as they would federal law as required by GG. art. 20(3).[152]
- The provisions of Article 36 of the VCCR are specific enough (*hinreichend bestimmt*) to be self-executing;[153]
- If Germany is a Party to an actual dispute before the ICJ involving the VCCR, German courts are bound to give effect to the judgment of the ICJ;[154]
- If Germany is not a Party to the actual dispute before the ICJ, it is not bound under international law to the decision of the ICJ; but German courts must nevertheless consider the decision as a guide, because the ICJ has been entrusted with authority to interpret the VCCR.[155]

The Federal Constitutional Court therefore actually applied the *Avena* judgment of the ICJ as municipal law of Germany, even though Germany was not a Party in that case. The Court decided that for States that are not Parties to a case, ICJ decisions have an "orientation significance" (*Orientierungswirkung*):

> The special meaning of the decision flows further from the institutional position of the International Court of Justice as the "supreme judicial organ of the United Nations." (UN Charter Article 92), which under Article 1 of the Optional Protocol of the Consular Convention applies to judicial settlement of lawsuits concerning the interpretation or application of the Convention. Practically, the States Parties, which must already avoid future disputes over violations of the Convention, must also conduct themselves in accordance with decisions rendered against other States.[156]

---

[151] *See* Gogolin *supra* note 150, at 266-67.

[152] 2 BvR 2115/01, *supra* note 150, at par. 52.

[153] *Id.*, at. par. 53.

[154] *Id.*, at. par. 60.

[155] *Id.*, at. par. 61, 62.

[156] 2 BvR 2115/01, *supra* note 150, at par. 61: "Die besondere Bedeutung der Entscheidungen ergibt sich ferner aus der institutionellen Stellung des Internationalen Gerichtshofs als 'Hauptrechtsprechungsorgan der Vereinten Nationen' (Art. 92 UN-Charta), das

The Federal Constitutional Court based its commitment to uphold interpretations of international law by the ICJ upon the favorable disposition toward international law (*Völkerrechtsfreundlichkeit*) of the German Basic Law,[157] defined by one analyst as "an overarching commitment of the German Basic Law towards international law."[158] Equally decisive in this regard is the fact that Germany ratified the Protocol to the VCCR, thereby subjecting itself to interpretations of the VCCR by the ICJ.[159]

Conclusion

There are indeed compelling practical reasons why States Parties to the VCCR should abide by interpretations of provisions of the Convention by the ICJ:

- Because the ICJ is "the principal judicial organ of the United Nations,"[160] deference to its authoritative interpretations of treaty provisions is "particularly compelling."[161]
- Uniformity in treaty interpretations is an important consideration, and "the ICJ's position as an international court specifically charged with the duty to interpret numerous international treaties (including the Convention) provides a natural point of reference for national courts seeking that uniformity."[162]

---

nach Art. 1 des Fakultativprotokolls zum Konsularrechtsübereinkommen zur gerichtlichen Beilegung von Streitigkeiten über die Auslegung oder Anwendung des Übereinkommens berufen ist. Faktisch müssen sich die Vertragsstaaten, schon um die künstige Feststellung von Konventionsverletzungen gegen sich zu vermeiden, daher auch nach Urteilen richten, die gegen andere Staaten ergangen sind."

157 *Id.*, at par. 43; *and see* Art. 25 GG (providing that general rules of international law constitute part of the federal law, are superior to federal statutory law, and are self-executing in Germany).

158 Gogolin *supra* note 150, at 268.

159 *See* 2 BvR 2115/01, *supra* note 150, at par. 61.

160 U.N. Charter, *supra* note 7, art. 92; *and see* Alex Glashausser, *What We Must Never Forget When It is a Treaty We are Expounding*, in 73 CIN. L. REV. 1243, at 1263 (2005); Steven Arrigg Koh, *"Respectful Consideration" After Sanchez-Llamas v. Oregon: Why the Supreme Court Owes More to the International Court of Justice*, in 93 CORNELL L. REV. 243, at 249 (2007).

161 Van Alstine, *supra* note 28, at 1938; and *see also* Koh, *supra* note 160, at 268 (stating that judgments of the ICJ are (compellingly authoritative").

162 *Sanchez-Llamas v. Oregon; Bustillo v. Johnson*, *supra* note 5, at 382-83 (Breyer, J., joined by Stevens, Souter and Ginsberg, JJ., dissenting); 2 BvR 2115/01, *supra* note 150, at par. 62; and *see also* Van Alstine, *supra* note 28, at 1937; Koh, *supra* note 160,

- International courts "have the ability and expertise to take principles negotiated and developed by states and increase their precision and applicability to contemporary circumstances,"[163] and ICJ judges "have a greater awareness of the subtleties of international treaties than a US Supreme Court Justice."[164]
- The United States, by failing to accord true "respectful consideration" to ICJ interpretations of its obligations under the VCCR, runs the risk of losing the reciprocal protection of its own nationals abroad,[165] and without consular assistance, Americans detained in a foreign country might be left without U.S. constitutional guarantees such as the right to counsel and Miranda warnings.[166]
- By not upholding ICJ interpretations of international treaty obligations, the United States discredits its reputation as a leader in the world in promoting and upholding human rights values.[167]

In the United States there have been occasional (official) voices calling in the wilderness to afford prominence to ICJ decisions. In 1990, Congress recorded its sense concerning an enhanced role of the ICJ in resolving international disputes, stating:

> The Congress commends and strongly supports efforts by the United States to broaden, where appropriate, the compulsory jurisdiction and enhance the effectiveness of the International Court of Justice.[168]

U.S. Supreme Court Justice Sandra Day O'Conner wrote in similar vein:

> Just as state courts are expected to follow the dictates of the Constitution and federal statutes, I think domestic courts should faithfully recognize the obligations imposed by international law. The Supremacy Clause of the United States Constitution gives legal force to foreign treaties, and our status as a free nation demands faithful compliance with the law of free nations.[169]

---

at 268. *See further id.*, at 246 (Prof. Koh emphasizing the ICJ's interest in uniform treaty interpretations).

[163] Allison Marston Danner, *When Courts Make Law: How the International Criminal Tribunals Recast the Laws of War*, in 59 VAND. L. REV. 1, at 51 (2006).

[164] Koh, *supra* note 160, at 269.

[165] *Id.*, at 270.

[166] *Id.*, at 268.

[167] *Id.*, at 270.

[168] *Sense of Congress Concerning an Enhanced Role of the International Court of Justice in Resolution of International Disputes*, par. (b), Public Law 101-246, § 411, 104 Stat. 69 (Febr. 16, 1990).

[169] Sandra Day O'Conner, *Federalism of Free Nations*, in INTERNATIONAL LAW DECISIONS IN NATIONAL COURTS 13, at 18 (eds. Thomas M. Frank & Gregory H. Fox, 1996).

Directives in regard to international law reflected in the original intent of the Founding Fathers bear evidence of the fact that they, too, designed a political dispensation founded on *Völkerrechtfreundlichkeit*. One need not be a seasoned historian to recapture the mind-set of leaders of the New Nation who had the audacity to embark on a unilateral declaration of independence from Great Britain, the political Goliath of the time. A great priority for them was to secure that the New Nation be accepted within the caring fold on the international community of States;[170] and the primary pre-condition for that to happen was for them to endorse a solemn commitment to honor and to uphold respect for and observance of international law. They did that by proclaiming that "all Treaties made, or which shall be made, under the Authority of the United States, shall be the Supreme Law of the Land,"[171] and to entrust Congress with a competence "To define and punish Piracies and Felonies committed on the high Seas, and Offences against the Law of Nations.[172]

Establishing a reputation as a trustworthy treaty partner was regarded as an important precondition for securing the safety of the nation.[173] There is ample evidence to show that the Founding Fathers regarded the power to enter into treaties important, "especially as it relates to war, peace, and commerce ..."[174] John Jay, for one, noted that violation of treaties is for the most part one of the "*just* causes of war."[175] He also argued that treaties entered into by the United States could not be amended by legislation: "[L]et us not forget, said he, "that treaties are made not by only one of the contracting parties, but by both, and consequently that as the consent of both was essential to their formation at first, so must it ever afterwards be to alter or cancel them."[176]

Subsequent judgments of the U.S. Supreme Court, culminating in *Medellin v. Texas*, have blatantly belied such directives in deference to

---

[170] Glashausser, *supra* note 160, at 1251 (noting that "especially in its fledgling state, the country greatly depended on the good graces of others in the international community).

[171] *U.S. Constitution*, art. VI, Clause 2.

[172] *Id.*, art. I, Section 8, Clause 10; *and see* Johan D. van der Vyver, *Prosecuting Offences Against the Law of Nations in the United States*, in 20 EMORY INT'L L. REV. 473 (2006).

[173] Glashausser, *supra* note 98, at 39.

[174] THE FEDERALIST No. 64, at 432 (John Jay) (Jacob E. Cooke ed., 1961).

[175] THE FEDERALIST No. 3, at 14 (John Jay) (Jacob E. Cooke ed., 1961); *and see* Detlev F. Vagts, *The United States and Its Treaties: Observance and Breach*, in 95 AM. J. INT'L L. 313, at 327–28; Glashaussen, *supra* note 160, at 1251.

[176] THE FEDERALIST No. 64 at 437 (John Jay) (Jacob E. Cooke ed., 1961); *and see* Steward Jay, *The Status of the Law of Nations in Early American Law*, in 42 VAND. L. REV. 819, at 828 (1989).

international law. Their treatment of ICJ decisions "stemmed from a highly U.S.-centric conception of the Court's obligations."[177] "Respectful consideration" of ICJ decisions seemingly meant no more than a duty to take note of those decisions, while maintaining an unfettered discretion to reject them.[178] One analyst stated, with reference to the "respectful consideration" bit in *Breard*, that the Court "grudgingly acknowledged the International Court's order," and noted "its casual dismissal of the International Court's authority."[179] The same author found, more generally, that compared to the courts of other countries, "U.S. courts have given perhaps the least deference to the decisions of international tribunals such as the International Court [of Justice],"[180] and that treating the ICJ's judgments as binding "is relatively rare" in the United States.[181]

Perhaps the German model might provoke a pristine re-assessment in the United States of the binding force of ICJ judgments.

177 Koh, *supra* note 160, at 259.

178 *See* Carsten Hoppe, *Implementation of* LaGrand *and* Avena *in Germany and the United States: Exploring a Transatlantic Divide in Search of a Uniform Interpretation of Consular Rights*, in 18 EUR. J. INT'L L. 317, at 330 (2007).

179 Glashausser, *supra* note 98, at 68.

180 *Id.*, at 66.

181 *Id.*, at 67.

Bibliography of Tibor Várady

(S/C = in Serbo-Croatian; H = in Hungarian)

A/ Books, Theses, Course Materials

A.1 Theses

1. "On the Application of Substantive Law in International Commercial Arbitration" (S/C). Master's Thesis, Belgrade University, 1967.
2. "Jurisdiction to Adjudicate and Jurisdiction as a Recognition Standard in Divorce Cases, with regard to Custody and Alimony Cases in Yugoslav and American Law Respectively, and the Possible Ways of Cooperation between the Two Legal Systems relating to these Issues." Master's Thesis, Harvard University, 1968.
3. "On the Development of an Autonomous Law of International Trade through International Commercial Arbitration - with Special Reference to European Socialist Countries." Doctoral Thesis (SJD), Harvard University, 1970.

A.2 Books

4. "Implementation and Protection of Rights Containing Foreign Elements" (S/C). The section on Private International Law in the *Great Legal Handbook*. Belgrade, 1972.
5. *Great Legal Handbook*. 2nd amended edition. Belgrade, 1977.
6. with S. Triva, B. Poznić and N. Vorgić. *Settlement of Disputes by Arbitration* (S/C). Novi Sad, 1973.
7. *International and Internal Conflict Rules* (S/C). Belgrade, 1975.
8. *Encyclopedia of the Law pertaining to Property Relations and of the Law of Associated Labour,* Volume II, author of the texts concerning the "General Part of Private International Law and on International Property Law" (S/C). Belgrade, 1978.
9. *Concluding Contracts with Foreign Partners*, Volume I, editor and author of 4 contributions (S/C). Novi Sad, 1979.

10. *Concluding Contracts with Foreign Partners*, Volume II, editor and author of 3 contributions (S/C). Novi Sad, 1979.
11. *Fundamentals of Private International Law* (S/C). Novi Sad, 1977.
12. *Private International Law II* (S/C). Novi Sad, 1980.
13. *Die Grundmerkmale des neuen Gesetzes über langfristige Produktionskooperation, geschäftlich-technische Zusammenarbeit sowie den Erwerb und überlassen materiellen Rechts auf Technologie* (Brochure). Belgrade, 1979.
14. with N. Balog. *Joint Ventures, Long-Term Economic Cooperation with Foreign Firms*. Belgrade, 1979.
15. *International Technology Transfer under Yugoslav Law* (S/C). Belgrade, 1980.
16. *Private International Law* (S/C). Novi Sad, 1983.
17. *Private International Law*. 2nd ed. (S/C). Novi Sad, 1987.
18. *Private International Law*. 3rd ed. (S/C). Novi Sad, 1990.
19. *Private International Law*. Reprint of 3rd ed. (S/C). Novi Sad, 1996.
20. with Arthur Von Mehren and John Barceló. *International Commercial Arbitration—A Transnational Perspective*. West Group, 1999.
21. with Arthur Von Mehren and John Barceló. *International Commercial Arbitration—A Transnational Perspective, Documents Supplement*. West Group, 1999.
22. co-edited with M. Kontra, R. Phillipson, T. Skutnabb-Kangas. *Language: A Right and a Resource*. Budapest–New York: CEU Press, 1999.
23. co-edited with Arthur Von Mehren and John Barceló. *International Commercial Arbitration—Teacher's Manual*. West Group, 2001.
24. with Bernadett Bordás and Gašo Knežević. *Private International Law* (S/C). Novi Sad, 2001.
25. with Arthur Von Mehren and John Barceló. *International Commercial Arbitration—A Transnational Perspective*. 2nd ed. Thomson & West, 2003
26. with Arthur Von Mehren and John Barceló. *International Commercial Arbitration—A Transnational Perspective, Documents Supplement*. 2nd ed. Thomson & West, 2003.
27. with Bernadett Bordás and Gašo Knežević. *Private International Law* (S/C). 6th ed. Novi Sad, 2003.
28. with Arthur Von Mehren and John Barceló. *International Commercial Arbitration – Teacher's Manual*. 2nd ed. Thomson & West, 2003.

29. with Arthur Von Mehren and John Barceló. *International Commercial Arbitration—A Transnational Perspective*. 3rd Edition. Thomson & West, 2006.
30. with Arthur Von Mehren and John Barceló. *International Commercial Arbitration—A Transnational Perspective, Documents Supplement*. 3rd edition. Thomson & West, 2006.
31. with Arthur Von Mehren and John Barceló. *International Commercial Arbitration—Teacher's Manual*. 3rd ed. Thomson & West, 2006.
32. *Language and Translation in International Commercial Arbitration,* T.M.C. Asser Press, 2006.
33. with Bernadett Bordás, Gašo Knežević, and Vladimir Pavić. *Private International Law* (S/C). 8th ed. Belgrade, 2007.
34. with Bernadett Bordás, Gašo Knežević, and Vladimir Pavić. *Private International Law* (S/C). 9th (unchanged) ed. Belgrade, 2007.
35. "Speeches before the International Court of Justice" (S/C), in *Srbija pred Međunarodnim sudom pravde*, Vol. I. Belgrade, 2007. 57–68; 76–89; 109–112; 729–745; 762–778; 814–821.
36. with John Barceló. *International Commercial Arbitration—A Transnational Perspective*. 4th ed. Thomson/Reuters & West, 2009.
37. with John Barceló. *International Commercial Arbitration—A Transnational Perspective, Documents Supplement*. 4th ed. Thomson/Reuters & West 2009.
38. with John Barceló. *International Commercial Arbitration—Teacher's Manual*. 4th ed. Thomson/Reuters & West, 2009.

A.3 Course Materials, Readers

39. International Business Law - Selected Topics (cyclostyle) Gainesville Florida 1981.
40. Socialist Law in a Period of Change, (cyclostyle) Berkeley, 1991.
41. Legal Problems in East-West Trade (cyclostyle), Emory, Atlanta, 1992.
42. Legal Problems in Doing Business in Eastern Europe (cyclostyle), Central European University, Budapest 1993.
43. International Commercial Arbitration (cyclostyle) Central European University, Budapest 1993.
44. Contracts—A Comparative Introduction (cyclostyle) Central European University, Budapest 1993.

45. Advanced International Dispute Settlement (cyclostyle) Central European University, Budapest 1997.
46. Law and Ethnicity Vol. I and Vol. II - Reader (cyclostyle) Central European University, Budapest 1998.
47. Law and Ethnicity - Attempts to Chart Interethnic Justice, Reader, Budapest 2000.
48. World Law - reader, co-author Harold Berman (cyclostyle), Emory University, Atlanta, 2001.
49. European Private International Law (cyclostyle) Central European University, Budapest 2002.
50. Law and Ethnicity, Reader, Budapest, Central European University, 2002.
51. International Business Transactions, Reader, Central European University, 2003.
52. Language and Culture in International Dispute Resolution, Reader, Central European University Budapest – Inter-University Center Dubrovnik, 2004.
53. International Business Transactions, Reader, Budapest, Central European University, 2006.
54. Law and Ethnicity, Reader, Vol. I and II, Central European University 2007.
55. Law and Ethnicity, reader, Vol. I and II, Central European University, 2008.

B/ Articles in English, French and German

56. Resolving the Merits of the Disputes in the Practice of the Arbitration Tribunal at the Federal Economic Chamber, *Jugoslovenska revija za međunarodno pravo*, 2–3/1970, 349–363.
57. Internal Conflict of Laws in Yugoslavia, *Netherlands International Law Review*, 2/1976, 137–150.
58. Technical Checking and Expertise within the Process of Institutionalization of International Trade Arbitration, *Collection of the International Congress on Arbitration Materials*, Moscow 1972, 373–383.
59. Application of Foreign Law by Non-Judicial Authorities, *Essays on the Law of International Trade*, The Hague 1976, 204–216.
60. Der rechtliche Rahmen für ausländische Investitionen in Jugoslawien, *Zehn Jahre nach dem Anfang, Jahrbuch für Ostrecht*, I/1978, 111–141.

61. Immunity of State Property from Execution in the Yugoslav Legal System, *Netherlands Yearbook of International Law*, 1979, 85–95.
62. Neue Entwicklungen bei Investitions-und Kooperationsverträgen mit ausländische Partner, in *Die jugoslawische Investitions-und Kooperationsgesetzgebung*, Cologne 1979, 30–41.
63. Foreign Law Before Domestic Authorities, *Realities and Gestures, Festschrift Zajtay*, Tübingen 1982, 489–508.
64. Transfert de téchnologie dans les contrats Yougoslaves de coopération industrielle à long terme avec un partenaire étranger, Revue internationale de droit comparé, *Journées de la Société de législation comparé*, Paris 1982, 337–352.
65. Les développements nouveaux concernant la reconnaissance et l' exécution des sentences arbitrales en Yougoslavie, *Revue de l'arbitrage* 2/1983, 163–176.
66. Some Observations on the New Yugoslav Private International Law Code, *Rivista di diritto internazionale privato e processuale*, 1/1983, 69–86.
67. Notes sur le nouveau Reglement de la Cour d'Arbitrage auprès de la Chambre économique de Yougoslavie, *Revue de l'Arbitrage*, 1/1984, 171–177.
68. New Developments with respect to the Recognition and Enforcement of Foreign Court Decisions in Yugoslavia, in *Current Trends of Conflicts of Laws in Central-Eastern Europe*, Trieste 1984, 137–148.
69. On the First Yugoslav Private International Law Code, *Yugoslav Law*, 3/1984, 203–222.
70. Zur Anerkennung deutscher Scheidungsurteile in Jugoslawien, *IPRax* 3/1984, 249–253.
71. 6 short reports submitted at ILA conferences:

    a/ Notes on the Participation of Governments and (foreign owned) Enterprises in International Trade Arbitration, *Report of the 57th Conference*, Madrid 1976, 25–26.

    b/ Jurisdiction in International Traffic Accidents, *Report of the 57th Conference*, Madrid 1976, 455–457.

    c/ Arbitration between Parties from Industrialized and Less Developed Countries, *Report of the 60th Conference*, Montreal 1982, 297–298.

    d/ State Immunity, *Report of the 60th Conference*, Montreal 1982, 340–342.

    e/ State Immunity, *Report of the 63d Conference*, Warsaw 1988, 985.

f/ International Commercial Arbitration, Multiparty Arbitration, *Report of the 63d Conference*, Warsaw 1988, 505–506.

72. On the Management Structure of Enterprises with Foreign Participation in Socialist Countries - with Special Reference to Yugoslavia, in *The Legal Structure of the Enterprise*, Budapest 1985, 473–486.
73. Selbstverwaltung in jugoslawischen Arbeitsorganisationen und ihre rechtliche Grundlagen - mit besonderer Rücksichtigung der aussenwirtschaftlichen Organisationen, *Theoretische Fragen des Wirtschaftsrechts*, Budapest 1986, 261–276.
74. Chronique de jurisprudence yougoslave, *Journal du droit international*, 3/1986, 745–770.
75. Die Eigenarten der internen Gesetzkollisionen in Jugoslawien, *Zeitschrift für Rechtsvergleichung*, 1/1987. 38–52.
76. Conflits de lois - Yougoslavie, Juris classeurs, *Législation comparé* 2/1989.
77. L`obligation alimentaire en Droit international privé - Yougoslavie, in *L'obligation alimentaire en Droit international privé*, Vol. 2, Paris 1987, 129–180.
78. Anerkennung und Vollstreckung ausländischer Entscheidungen in Jugoslawien, *Das neue Recht und die Rechtsprechung, Rabels Zeitschrift*, 4/1987, 632–680.
79. On Appointing Authorities in International Commercial Arbitration, *Emory Journal of International Dispute Resolution*, 2/1988, 311–357.
80. Assumptions of Compatibility and Correspondence in Post-War Yugoslav Private International Law, *Liber Memorialis Francois Laurent*, Brussels 1989, 1151–1166.
81. Yugoslavia - National Report, in *Der Schadenersatz in Ost-West-Außenwirtschaftsverhältnissen*, Bonn 1990, 141–151.
82. Civil Codes and Administrative Regulations in International Trade Relations, *Questions of Civil Law Codification*, Budapest 1990, 175–183.
83. Provisional Measures in International Commercial Arbitration -with Special Reference to Yugoslav Standpoints, in 8 *Hague-Zagreb-Ghent Essays on the Law of International Trade*, 1991, 147–162.
84. On the Foreign Investment Legislation in Yugoslavia, *Revue de Droit des Affaires Internationales* 1990 No. 4–5, 621–630.
85. Arbitration Despite the Parties?, in *Law and Reality, Essays on National and International Procedural Law*, M. Nijhoff Publishers 1992, 351–376.

86. Collective Minority Rights and Problems in Their Legal Protection; The Example of Yugoslavia, 6 *East European Politics and Societies*, 260–282 (1992).
87. Transformation of Social Property - Serbia, Financial Times, *East European Business Law*, April 1992, 26–27.
88. On the Position of International Law in the Process of Transformation in Europe - An Essay in Realism and Idealism, *Jugoslovenska revija za međunarodno pravo* 3/1993, 236–242 and 35 *Acta Juridica Hungarica* 1993 No. 3–4, 121–128.
89. Survey of Presidential Powers in Eastern Europe - ex-Yugoslavia, *East European Constitutional Review*, Fall 1993/Winter 1994, 75–81 (co-author Nenad Dimitrijevic).
90. One Life in Many Countries, 29 *War Report Oct./Nov*. 1994, 20–21.
91. Remarks on Cultural Pluralism and Multiethnicity in Ethnic Societies, in *Interculturality in Multiethnic Societies*, ed. B. Jakšić, Belgrade 1995, 39–46.
92. The Emergence of Competition Law in (Former) Socialist Countries, 47 *American Journal of Comparative Law*, (1999) 229–275.
93. Minorities, Majorities, Law, and Ethnicity - Reflections of the Yugoslav Case, 19 *Human Rights Quarterly* 9–54 (1997).
94. Collective Rights of Minorities and Majorities within the Context of International Law, in *Dual Images - Multiculturalism on Two Sides of the Atlantic*, published by The Royal Society of Canada and the Hungarian Academy of Sciences, Budapest 1996, 113–125.
95. The Predicament of Peacekeeping in Bosnia, 28 *Cornell International Law Review*, (1995) 701–707.
96. A Note on Peace with Difference - Introductory paper in *Report on the Situation of National and Other Minorities on the Territory of Bosnia-Herzegovina, Croatia, and Serbia-Montenegro*, Brussels 1996, 1–4.
97. *Nation States, Ethnic Societies, and Minorities* - paper submitted to the II. Conference organized by the Hungarian Academy of Sciences and the Royal Society of Canada, in Quebec, October 25–30, 1996.
98. *A Note on Integration, Stability, and Diversity* - paper submitted at the International ECSA Conference "On the State of the EU Integration - Enlargement and Institutional Reforms" - Budapest, November 6–10, 1996.
99. The Courtesy Trap - Arbitration "if no amicable settlement can be reached," 14 *Journal of International Arbitration*, 5–12 (1997).

100. On the Chances of Ethnocultural Justice in Central-Eastern Europe - with Comments on the Dayton Agreement, in *Can Liberal Pluralism be Exported?* edited by W. Kymlicka and M. Opalski, Oxford 2002, 135–149.
101. International Commercial Arbitration in Hungary, 1 *Review of Arbitration in Central and Eastern Europe*, Zagreb 2000, 11–35.
102. Citizens, Minorities, Majorities, The Constitutive, Nation-Building, Others, in *Constitutional Position of Citizen and People in Bosnia and Herzegovina*, Sarajevo, 1998, 166–168.
103. *Lapine v. Kyocera - Three Questions, Richmond Journal of Global Law and Business*, April 1999 Symposium, on website http://law.richmond.edu/general/student.htm.
104. Remuneration of Arbitrators as a Threshold Issue - Economic Sense and Procedural Realities, in *Corporations, Capital Markets and Business in the Law* (Liber Amicorum Richard M. Buxbaum) Ed. Baums, Hopt and Horn, Kluwer 2000, 585–599.
105. *On the Precepts of the Legal Framework of Stability in Majority-Minority Relations* (Remarks in a South East European Context), www.sigov.si/mzz/ang/index.htm.
106. Chances for Ideas in a Post-Dissident Intellectual Environment, 14 *NEW MOMENT* 2000, 142–151.
107. Notes on Ideological Precepts as Formants of Private Law in Central-East European Countries, 2 *Global Jurist Frontiers*, Issue 2, Article 1, 2002 http://www.bepress.com/gj/frontiers/vol2/iss2/art1; also in Opening Up European Law, Stämpfli Publ., Sellier Publ. And Carolina Academic Press, 2007, 127–139.
108. The Language Issue in International Commercial Arbitration – Notions and Questions, *Prawo Priwatne Czasu Przemian* (Festchrift Soltysinski), Poznan 2005, 923–954.
109. Challenge of Arbitral Awards in Recognition Proceedings on Grounds of Shortcomings Pertaining to Language, in *Balancing of Interests – Liber Amicorum Peter Hay*, Frankfurt 2005, 435–450.
110. Language-Related Strategies in Preparing Arbitration, 7 *Across Languages and Cultures* 2006, 209–223.
111. On the Option of a Contractual Extension of Judicial Review of Arbitral Awards or: What is Actually Pro-Arbitration, 56 *Zbornik Pravnog fakulteta u Zagrebu* (2006), 2–3, 253–276.
112. Breaking Developments in International Law: A Conversation on the ICJ's Opinion in Bosnia and Herzegovina v. Serbia and Montenegro (Panel discussion, other participants: Th. Meron, B. Stern, L. Sadat),

published in *ASIL*, Proceedings of the 101st Annual Meeting 2007, 215–228.

113. Harold Berman – An Empathy for Difference that Made All the Difference, 57 *Emory Law Journal* 2008, 1455–1458.

114. On Tying Ideals To Some Meaning, 22 *Emory International Law Review*, 2008, 133–138.

C/ Articles in Serbo-Croatian and in Hungarian

C.1. On Private International Law

115. Da li naše norme o sukobu jurisdikcija kod sporova o čuvanju i vaspitanju dece pružaju dovoljno zaštite jugoslovenskom građaninu? *Glasnik*, 2/1970, 15–22.

116. Direktna i indirektna nadležnost u brakorazvodnim sporovima sa stranim elementom, *Zbornik-Novi Sad*, V/1971, 105–125.

117. Mogućnosti za poboljšanje međunarodne saradnje u oblasti egzekvature sudskih odluka, *Glasnik*, 11/1972, 18–25.

118. Sukob zakona u odlučivanju spoljnotrgovinskih arbitraža, *Zbornik-Novi Sad*, VI/1972, 245–256.

119. *Uporedni pregled pravnih problema koji se pojavljuju prilikom bilateralnog sporazumevanja o multinacionalnim vodenim tokovima (deo projekta "Organizacija i finansiranje vodoprivrede u SAPV")*, Novi Sad, 1972, 1–36.

120. Odnos međunarodnog i interlokalnog sukoba zakona i jurisdikcija, *Zbornik-Novi Sad*, VII/1973, 223–237.

121. Kolizione norme pred nejedinstvenim pravnim poretkom, *Jugoslovenska revija za međunarodno pravo*, 1–3/1974, 108–129.

122. Strani elemenat kao pretpostavka za primenu kolizionih normi, *Zbornik-Novi Sad*, 1974, 65–81.

123. Problem kvalifikacije kod unutardržavnog sukoba zakona, *Pravni život*, 6–7/1975, 13–26.

124. Zastarelost i autonomija volje u međunarodnom privatnom pravu, *Prinosi za poredbeno proučavanje prava i međunarodno privatno pravo*, 8/1975, 3–18.

125. Sukob i saradnja zakona socijalističkih republika i pokrajina, *Zbornik za društvene nauke Matice srpske*, 1976, 217–231.

126. Primena stranog prava od strane matičara, *Zbornik-Novi Sad*, X/1976, 371–382.

127. Rešavanje sukoba zakona i sukoba nadležnosti između republike i pokrajina i između samih pokrajina u SR Srbiji, *Institut za uporedno pravo Beograd*, 1974, 1–27.
128. "Conflit mobile" u međunarodnom privatnom pravu, *Godišnjak Pravnog fakulteta u Sarajevu*, 1977, 359–377.
129. *Međunarodna pravna pomoć*, Pokrajinski sekretarijat za pravosuđe i opštu upravu, Novi Sad, 1978, 1–11.
130. Uz Uredbu sa zakonskom snagom o međunarodnom privatnom pravu NR Mađarske, *Strani pravni život* 107/1980, 3–7.
131. Merodavno pravo za obavezu izdržavanja u našem međunarodnom privatnom pravu i unutrašnjem kolizionom pravu, *Zbornik-Novi Sad*, 3/1981, 53–73.
132. O mogućnosti dosledne primene kolizionih normi koje ukazuju na strano pravo, *Jugoslovenska revija za međunarodno pravo*, 1–3/1981, 69–89.
133. Pravna sredstva protiv odluka spoljnotrgovinskih arbitraža, *Savremeni problemi spoljnotrgovinske arbitraže*, Belgrade 1982, 57–76.
134. Određivanje merodavnog prava za drumske saobraćajne delikte, *Drumski saobraćajni delikti sa elementom inostranosti*, Novi Sad 1983, 11–20.
135. *Pravna sredstva protiv odluka međunarodnih trgovinskih arbitraža - Model pravila UNCITRAL*, Institut za uporedno pravo, Belgrade 1983, 1–23.
136. *Rešavanje sukoba zakona u SR Srbiji- deo Projekta "Ostvarivanje odnosa između SAPV i SR Srbije u oblasti zakonodavstva*," Novi Sad 1984, 1–18.
137. Domicil naših radnika na privremenom radu u inostranstvu i međunarodna pravna saradnja, Pravo - *Teorija i praksa*, maj 1985, 23–32.
138. Razvoj međunarodnog privatnog prava, *Arhiv za pravne i društvene nauke*, 1–2/1986, 307–324.
139. Podloge za kompatibilnost i podudarnost u međunarodnom privatnom pravu, *JRMP* 2–3/1986, 189–203
140. Reciprocitet kod priznanja stranih sudskih odluka u našem novom međunarodnom privatnom pravu, Pravo, *Teorija i praksa*, 1/1988, 10–18.
141. A belső jogszabályösszeütközések jellegzetességei Jugoszláviában, *Jogtudományi Közlöny*, 9/1986, 424–432.

C.2. On International Commercial Law and the Law of East-West Trade

142. Spoljnotrgovinska arbitraža i internacionalizacija ordre public, *Zbornik-Novi Sad*, III/1969, 103–115.
143. Spoljnotrgovinska arbitraža i internacionalističko koncipiranje autonomije volje, *Zbornik-Novi Sad* IV/1970, 143–153.
144. Od srednjevekovnog do savremenog lex mercatoria, *Anali Pravnog fakulteta u Beogradu*, 1–2/1971, 109–119.
145. A választottbíràskodás mai dilemmái, *Létünk* 5/1972, 123–126.
146. Ustavni amandman XXII i novi propisi o zajedničkim ulaganjima domaćeg i stranog kapitala, *Glasnik*, 3/1972, 21–25.
147. Ugovor o ulaganju sredstava stranih lica u domaće OUR i samoupravljanje u udruženom radu, *Zbornik-Novi Sad* XI/1977, 59–73.
148. Ugovor o prenosu materijalnog prava na tehnologiju, *Zbornik-Novi Sad*, 1979, 1–33.
149. Pravne mogućnosti za osnivanje predstavništva jusgoslovenskih privrednih organizacija u stranim zemljama, *Izvršno Veće Skupštine SAPV*, 1979, 1–33.
150. Transfer tehnologije u ugovorima o dugoročnoj industrijskoj saradnji sa stranim partnerom, *Pravni život* 11/1982, 1175–1188.
151. Pravni okviri viših oblika privredne saradnje sa zemljama Afrike i Bliskog Istoka, *Privreda i pravo*, 3–4/1983, 36–46.
152. Savremene tendencije razvoja imuniteta države, *Anali Pravnog fakulteta u Beogradu*, 1–4/1983, 133–149.
153. Strategija našeg tehnološkog razvoja i pravni okviri međunarodnog transfera tehnologije, *Pravo-Teorija i praksa*, 1/1984, 33–45.
154. Napomene o pravnim instrumentima za zaštitu slabije strane u ugovorima međunarodnog privrednog prava, *Anali Pravnog fakulteta u Beogradu*, 3–4/1985, 337–345.
155. Određivanje merodavnog prava pred spoljnotrgovinskim arbitražama, *Ugovori u međunarodnoj trgovini* I, Belgrade 1987, 300–319.
156. O zaštiti interesa domaćih sticalaca kod ugovora o međunarodnom transferu tehnologije, *Inovacije, transfer tehnologije, tehnološki razvoj*, Rijeka 1983, 97–116.
157. Pravne mogućnosti i okviri stranih investicija u Nigeriji, *Zbornik-Novi Sad*, XVII/1985, 87–105.
158. Ugovori o prenosu know-how u industrijski razvijenim zemljama, *Pravo-Teorija i praksa*, 11/1985, 112–114.
159. Pravni okviri upravljanja privrednim preduzećima u koje je uložen strani kapital, s posebnim osvrtom na socijalističke zemlje, Ekonom-

ski fakultet Subotica, *Teorija i praksa organizovanja upravljanja* 1985, 1–25.

160. *O nekim karakteristikama međunarodnih trgovinskih arbitraža kojima se obraćaju jugoslovenske OUR*, Umnoženi referat za učesnike Savetovanja u organizaciji Udruženja pravnika Jugoslavije, Neum 20-22 mart 1986 1–27.
161. O zaštiti interesa domaćih sticalaca u zemljama u razvoju kod ugovora o međunarodnom transferu tehnologije, *Transfer tehnologije u zemlje u razvoju* I, Novi Sad 1986, 1–21.
162. Pitanje garantija prenosioca prilikom transfera tehnologije u zemlje u razvoju, *Transfer tehnologije u zemlje u razvoju* I, Novi Sad 1986, 56–73.
163. Pitanje restriktivnih klauzula u pravima SAD i SR Nemačke, *Transfer tehnologije u zemlje u razvoju* I, Novi Sad 1986, 121–145.
164. Međunarodnopravni aspekti ulaganja stranog kapitala u domaće organizacije, Pravo, *Teorija i praksa*, 4–5/1986, 80–89.
165. Zajednička ulaganja u socijalističkim zemljama - Uporednopravna skica – Pravo, *Teorija i praksa*, 4–5/1989, 161–168.
166. O Zakonu o trgovačkim društvima Mađarske, *Evropa danas*, 1–2/1989, 79–82.
167. O konceptu vlasništva i vlasničkih garantija kod stranih ulaganja, *Prinosi* No. 23 1989, 16–36.
168. Volja stranaka i granice ovlašćenja arbitara, *JRMP* 1–2/1991 20–32.
169. Izvršenje arbitražnog ugovora u pogledu imenovanja arbitara, *Pravni zivot* 11–12/1993, 1841–1849.
170. Intervencija suda u pogledu konstituisanja arbitraže, *Pravni život* 9–10/1994, 1351–1360.
171. Választottbíráskodás a felek ellenében? *Magyar Jog* 1995, 51–64.
172. Zamka naglašenih dobrih namera, *Pravni život* No. 12/IV 1997, 247–256.
173. Foreword to the Serbian edition of Folsom-Gordon-Spanogle, International Business Transactions in a Nutshell (Međunarodni trgovački poslovi, Novi Sad 1997, Predgovor).
174. O jeziku arbitraže, *Arbitraža* 2003, 11–27.
175. Međunarodna trgovinska arbitraža na evropskom prostoru, in *Evropski sodni prostor - European Judicial Area*, Maribor 2005, 1–9.
176. O prevodu i o skrivenom polaznom jeziku u međunarodnoj trgovinskoj arbitraži, in *Liber Amicorum Dobrosav Mitrović*, Belgrade 2007, 603–618.

C.3. On Minority Rights

177. Ostvarivanje ravnopravnosti jezika naroda i narodnosti SAPV u nastavi na višim i visokim školama, *Bilten Pokrajinskog zavoda za javnu upravu*, 1/1980, 97–106.
178. Vajdaság SZAT nemzetei és nemzetiségei nyelvi egyenrangúságának érvényesítése az egyetemi színtű oktatásban, *Létünk* 1/1980, 135–143.
179. Nemzetiségek Jugoszláviában és a nemzetközi szabályzás esélyei, *Létünk*, 6/1990, 597–602.
180. Narodnosti u Jugoslaviji i mogućnosti međunarodne regulative prava narodnosti (manjina) Pravo-Teorija i praksa 1991, *Poseban broj* (Special issue) 80–84.
181. Kollektív kisebbségi jogok, és azok jogi védelmének problémái; a jugoszláv példa, *Létünk* 4–5/1992, 272–291.
182. Tézisek a (volt) Jugoszlávia kisebbségeinek minimális jogairól, *Magyar Szemle*, 2/1993, 174–185.
183. Bevezető megjegyzések a Jugoszláviák magyarságáról, *Létünk* 1-2/1994, 9–12.
184. Egyenlőségkeresés etnikai társadalmakban, *Beszélő* 1996 aug.-szept. 44–58.
185. Osvrt na kolektivna većinska i manjinska prava, in *Položaj manjina u Saveznoj republici Jugoslaviji*, published by the Serbian Academy of Sciences and Arts, Belgrade 1996, 77–85.
186. A kollektív jogok kérdéséről, *Magyar Kisebbség* 1996 3. (5.) 39–51.
187. Kisebbségi érdekérvényesítés lehetőségei Európában - Jogi aspektusok, in *Kisebbségi érdekérvényesítés, önkormányzatiság, autonómiaformák*, Budapest 1997, 30–36.
188. Csoportsemlegesség és csoportérzékenység, in *Magyarország 2000*, Budapest 1997, 304–307.
189. Građani, manjine, većine, konstitutivni, državnotvorni, ostali, in *Ustavni položaj građanina i naroda o Bosni i Hercegovini*, Sarajevo 1998, 46–48.
190. A magyar jogfejlődés határon túlról nézve, in *Negyedik Magyar Jogászgyűlés*, Budapest 1998, 403–416.
191. O šansama za etnokulturnu pravdu u Centralno-istočnoj Evropi -sa osvrtom na Dejtonski sporazum, *Habitus* 1999/Special Issue, 69–82.
192. Széljegyzetek nemzetiségről, állampolgárságról, identitásról és multikulturalizmusról, *Európai Szemmel* 4/1999, 36–39.
193. Beleške o toleranciji, koka koli i Kučima in *Tolerance/Tolerancija*, ed. by B. Jakšić, Belgrade 1999, 133–138.

194. Kisebbségi jogok a volt Jugoszlávia területén a világháborúk után és a közelmúlti délszláv háború küszöbén, in *Kisebbségjog a Vajdaságban*, Novi Sad 2000, 46–55.
195. Manjinska prava na područjima bivše Jugoslavije nakon svetskih ratova i na pragu nedavnog trećeg rata, in *Manjinska prava i njihova primena u Vojvodini*, Novi Sad 2000, 40–48.
196. Etnikai egyensúly és demokrácia esélyei Közép-Kelet Európában - széljegyzetekkel a Daytoni Egyezményől, in *Konfliktusok és kezelésük Közép-Európában*, Budapest 2000, 37–49.
197. Komolyan venni az autonómiakoncepciókat, in *Sorskérdéseink*, Novi Sad 2003, 107–113.
198. Kolektivna prava manjina u Madjarskoj, in *Društvene nauke o Srbima u Madjarskoj*, published by the Serbian Academy of Sciences and Arts, Budapest 2003, 183–190.
199. Dileme oko jednakosti i identiteta – s osvrtom na položaj srpske nacionalne manjine u Hrvatskoj i Mađarskoj, in *Položaj i identitet srpske manjine u Jugoistočnoj i Centralnoj Evropi*, Published by Srpska Akademija Nauka i Umetnosti, Belgrade 2005, 21–30.

C.4. On Public International Law

200. Borba za oslobođenje Zimbabve i međunarodno pravo, *Antikolonijalna revolucija, socijalna, politička i ekonomska emancipacija u svetu*, Belgrade-Zagreb-Skopje, 1985, 197–203.
201. *Opšta deklaracija o pravima čoveka*, Novi Sad 1985.
202. Egyenrangúság a nemzetközi kapcsolatokban, *Magyar Szó*, 27.I.1980.
203. O nepristrasnosti u resavanju međunarodnih sporova, *Zbornik Novi Sad* XIII/4, 1989, 163–179.
204. Pártatlanság és részrehajlás nemzetközi viták rendezésében, *Létünk* 3/1991, 197.

C.5. On Jurisprudence

205. Erkölcs és igazságosság mint korrektiv a szocialista polgári jogban, *Új Symposion*, 1/1965, 17–27.
206. Jog és ponyva, *Létünk* 6/1972, 89–104.
207. Pravičnost u međunarodnom privatnom pravu, *Zbornik za društvene nauke Matice srpske*, 58/1973, 30–44.
208. Peschka: A modern jogfilozófia alapproblémái, *Zbornik za društvene nauke Matice srpske*, 39/1974, 133–145.
209. Pravo i šund, *Dometi* 7/1976, 17–36.

210. O uslovima uključivanja na području imovinskih odnosa, *Pravo i društvo* I, JAZU, Zagreb 1982, 25–27.
211. Jegyzetek a mai marxista jogi gondolkodásról, *Létünk* 2/1983, 329–340.
212. Američko pravosuđe i kulturna revolucija šezdesetih godina, *Radio Zagreb*, III Program 21.I.1984, 1–16.
213. Jogszemlélet Lukács kapcsán, *Létünk* 6/1985, 961–964.
214. Az amerikai igazságszolgáltatás és a hatvanas évek kultúrforradalma, *Létünk*, 1/1987, 79–88.
215. Upotreba i zloupotreba prostora prava, *Anali Ogranka SANU u Novom Sadu* 2004, 2005, No. 1 (2006) 65–71.
216. Upotreba i zloupotreba prostora prava (ili: kratak esej o naslovima zakona), *Glas CDII SANU*, Belgrade 2005, 117–135.

C.6. On Civil Law

217. Neka pitanja u vezi sa uslovom i rokom u građanskom pravu, *Zbornik-Novi Sad*, I/1966, 109–128.
218. Pojam stvari u građanskom pravu, *Pravni život* 2/1965, 3–16.

C.7. On other Subjects

219. Posztmodern társadalombírálat, *Létünk* 3–4/1989, 529–538.
220. Nyilatkozat (Jugoszláviai katonaszökevények helyzetéről), *Létünk* 1–2/1994, 102–108.
221. Magyarok Vajdaságban, *Szivárvány* 1994/3, 147–150.
222. Granice - Razlozi za i protiv u koje jednako verujem, in *Granice - izazov interkulturalnosti*, Belgrade 1997, 77–82.
223. Građani, manjine, većine, konstitutivni, državotvrni, ostali, in *Ustavni položaj građana i naroda u Bosni i Hercegovini,* Sarajevo, 1998, 46–48.
224. A magyar jogfejlődés határon túlról nézve (edited version), *Magyar Szemle* 11–12/1998, 19–31.
225. "A jog vállaljon több szerepet mint ami szokásos," interview, *Fundamentum* 3/1999, 53–63.
226. Beleške o toleranciji, koka koli i Kučima, in *Tolerance/Tolerancija,* ed. by Božidar Jakšić, Belgrade, 1999, 133–138.
227. Srbi i Mađari - lične beleške o srpsko-mađarskim odnosima, in *Jugoslavija i svet 2000,* Belgrade 2000, Published by "Evropski pokret u Srbiji," 175–181.

228. O iskušenjima intelektualaca u post-disidentsko doba, *Republika* 286/2001, 49–52.
229. Zapis o pokretnim stepenicama, in *The International and the National – Essays in Honour of V. Dimitrijević*, Belgrade, 2003, 253–256.
230. A kommunista piacgondolkodásról, in *Beszélő*, 2007/7–8, 21–30.
231. Koszovó: szerb (és nem csak szerb) hitek és tévhitek, in *Földrész – Nemzetközi és Európai Jogi Szemle*, 2008/1, 27–35.
232. A másik nyelv, *Létünk* 2008/4, 9–15.

D/ in Romanian (translation from English)

233. Minoritati, majoritati, lege si etnicitate: reflecti asupra cazului iugoslav, in *Polis* 2/2000, 101–128.

E/ Book Reviews

Over 30 book reviews

F/ Literary Works

Books:

- *Vagy nem maga az élet a legjobb időtöltés* - Úti esszék, Novi Sad, 1971.
- *Történelemközelben*, Novi Sad, 1995.
- *Mit i moda*, Novi Sad, 1978.
- *Az egérszürke szoba titka*, Novi Sad, 1976.
- "The Secret of the Mouse-Grey Room,"- in 18 New Writing and Writers, John Calder, London and Riverrun Press New York, 1981—translation of the "Egérszürke szoba titka."

Essays, short stories, reviews of literary books

Between 50 and 60 essays, short stories and book reviews in various /mostly Yugoslav/ literary magazines.

List of Authors

John J. Barceló III – William Nelson Cromwell Professor of International and Comparative Law and Reich Director, Berger International Legal Studies Program, Cornell University School of Law (USA)

David J. Bederman – K.H. Gyr Professor of Private International Law, Emory University (USA)

Peter Behrens – Dr. iur. (Hamburg), MCJ New York University (USA), Professor Emeritus of Law, University of Hamburg Germany, Managing Director of the Institute for European Integration at the Europa-Kolleg Hamburg (Germany), Recurring Visiting Professor at the Central European University, Budapest (Hungary)

László Burián – Professor of Law, Pázmány Péter Catholic University, and ELTE University, Budapest (Hungary)

Richard M. Buxbaum – Jackson H. Ralston Professor of International Law University of California Berkeley (USA)

Nenad Dimitrijevic – Professor of Politics, Central European University, Budapest (Hungary)

Yehuda Elkana – President and Rector, Central European University, Budapest (Hungary)

Richard D. Freer – Robert Howell Hall Professor of Law, Emory University (USA)

Guy Haarscher – Professor of Law, Free University of Brussels (Belgium), Recurring Visiting Professor of Law, Central European University, Budapest (Hungary)

Attila Harmathy – Professor Emeritus of Civil Law, ELTE University, Budapest (Hungary)

Peter Hay – L.Q.C. Lamar Professor of Law, Emory University (USA); Honorary Professor, Universität Freiburg (Germany); Professor Emeritus at the University of Illinois (USA) and at the Technische Universität Dresden (Germany); Recurring Visiting Professor of Law at the Central European University, Budapest (Hungary)

László Kecskés – Professor of Law, University of Pécs (Hungary)

János Kis – Professor of Philosophy, Central European University, Budapest (Hungary)

Ferenc Mádl – Professor Emeritus of Law, ELTE University, Budapest (Hungary); President of Hungary (2000–2005).

Vladimir Pavić – Assistant Professor, Faculty of Law, University of Belgrade (Serbia)

Hans-Eric Rasmussen-Bonne – Dr. iur. (Dresden), LL.M. (Illinois), Honorary Professor at the Technische Universität Dresden (Germany), Senior Partner in the law firm of WEITNAUER, Attorney in Berlin (Germany), Attorney-at-Law in New York (USA)

Kurt Siehr – Dr. iur. (Hamburg), M.C.L. (Michigan), Professor Emeritus of Law, University of Zürich (Switzerland)

Lajos Vékás – Professor of Law, ELTE University, Budapest (Hungary)

Johan D. van der Vyver – I.T. Cohen Professor of International Law and Human Rights, Emory University School of Law (USA)